CRASH COURSE IN JEWISH HISTORY

בס״ד
10/12

To Rachel + Jim
[illegible]
Mazal Tov on your wedding!!
Our past is our future!
All the Best
[illegible]

The miracle and meaning of Jewish history

CRASH COURSE *in* JEWISH HISTORY

From Abraham to Modern Israel

KEN SPIRO

First published 2010
Revised edition 2011

ISBN 978-1-56871-532-2

Published and distributed by:
TARGUM PRESS, INC.
22700 W. Eleven Mile Rd.
Southfield, MI 48034
E-mail: targum@targum.com
Fax: 888-298-9992
www.targum.com

In conjunction with:
AISH.COM
1 Western Wall Plaza
P.O.B. 14149
Jerusalem, Israel
www.aish.com

Distributed by:
TAGUM PRESS US
250 44th St
Brooklyn NY 11232
718-232-0856

Printed in Israel

To Tzvi, Daniel, Chava, Sarah, and Adina

Remember days long gone by. Study the years of each generation. Ask your father and let him tell you, and your grandfather, who will explain it (Deuteronomy 32:7).

Dedicated to the blessed memory of

Roya Geiderman
Rivka Leah bat Sarah

Roya was the "Ruth" of the community,
due to her compassion, chesed, and dedication
to the Jewish people and its History.

The light of her soul inspired all of us and will
always radiate.

With love
The Julis Family

In loving memory of our parents

Helene (Geego) and Melvin J. Berman, *z"l*

Barbara Naomi and Mark J. Sands, *z"l*

who exemplified determination, humility,
integrity, and selflessness and who lived by the
Torah value *Kol Yisrael areivim zeh la zeh* –
each Jew is not only responsible for himself,
but for every other Jew.

Dennis and Debra Berman

This book is dedicated
In honor of our children

Ryan, Ginger, and Lily

By Richard and Phylise Sands

In memory of

Constance and Leo Feinstein

By the Chesed Foundation

In memory of

Rabbi Jacob and Debbie Rubenstein, *z"l*

For whom learning and teaching
was life's passion.

With love,

Diana and Michael David Epstein

In honor of Ken and Ruth Spiro
and their children, Tzvi, Daniel, Chava, Sarah, and Adina
By Dr. Ronald and Nina Spiro

Yasher koach to Ken Spiro for your inspirational leadership in the community, Israel, and the entire Jewish people. Keep up the great work!

Love the Kuflik family

We want to express our tremendous appreciation for your tireless efforts and dedication.
Yasher Koach

The Avericks, Gottliebs, Holtzs, Krachtmans, and Wachs families

Contents

PART V: THE LONG ROAD HOME

Foreword

Zechor yemos olam, binu shenos dor vador. She'al aveicha v'yagedcha, zekeinecha v'yomru lach. *(Devarim 32:7)*

Of the many ways to obtain an understanding of what our Creator is all about, the Torah recommends a study of Divine Providence as revealed in Jewish history. We Jews very much live in the present, with an eye to the future. An awareness of our past is not a matter of sentiment, nor is it to serve as a convenient means by which to escape the difficulties of life today. Our heritage builds for us an understanding of our unique role within the family of nations and clearly defines our destiny.

Sadly, so many Jews are totally unaware of the fascinating history of our people.

Ken Spiro's *Crash Course in Jewish History* provides a comprehensive overview of our past with an emphasis on its relevance to Jewish life today. His live presentation has already provided many with an accurate understanding of our history and a true sense of Jewish pride. In book form, the message of Jewish destiny is now being made available in an informative, pleasant manner to the masses. I look forward to its widespread distribution and a greater awareness of the special role the Creator has reserved for our people.

Rabbi Yitzchak Berkovitz
Dean of the Jerusalem Kollel

TIMELINE OF JEWISH HISTORY

YEAR	EVENT	CHAPTER #
3761 B.C.E.	Creation of Adam; beginning of civilization	#1
1812 B.C.E.	Time of Abraham begins	#3 #4, #5
MESOPOTAMIAN AND EGYPTIAN CIVILIZATIONS REIGN		
1712 B.C.E.	Time of Isaac begins	#6
1652 B.C.E.	Time of Jacob begins	#6
1544 B.C.E.	Joseph sold into slavery	#7
1522 B.C.E.	Joseph welcomes his family to Egypt	#8
1428 B.C.E.	Israelites enslaved in Egypt	#9
EGYPTIAN CITIES OF PITHOM AND RAMSES ARE BUILT		
1392 B.C.E.	Time of Moses begins	#9
1312 B.C.E.	Exodus	#10
1312 B.C.E.	Torah is given at Mount Sinai	#11, #12
CANAANITE TRIBES OCCUPY PROMISED LAND		
1272 B.C.E.	Conquest of Promised Land. Time of Judges begins	#13, #14, #15
PHILISTINES OCCUPY COASTAL AREA OF ISRAEL		
879 B.C.E.	Saul anointed king	#16
877 B.C.E.	Time of King David begins	#17, #18
836 B.C.E.	Time of King Solomon begins	#19
825 B.C.E.	First Temple completed	#19
ASSYRIAN EMPIRE RISING IN THE NORTH		
796 B.C.E.	Israel split into two kingdoms	#20
555 B.C.E.	Assyrians overrun northern Israel; Ten Tribes are lost	#21
547 B.C.E.	Sennacherib attacks Jerusalem	#22
BABYLONIANS TAKE OVER ASSYRIAN EMPIRE		
422 B.C.E.	Babylonians conquer Israel and destroy the Temple	#23
PERSIANS TAKE OVER BABYLONIAN EMPIRE		
370 B.C.E.	Jews return to Israel from Babylonian exile	#24
355 B.C.E.	Miracle of Purim	#24
352 B.C.E.	Construction of Second Temple begins	#25
347 B.C.E.	Time of the Great Assembly begins	#26
GREEKS TAKE OVER PERSIAN EMPIRE		
331 B.C.E.	Greeks enter Jerusalem	#27
245 B.C.E.	Torah is translated into Greek; Greeks persecute Jews	#28
138 B.C.E.	Revolt of the Maccabees	#29
135 B.C.E.	Miracle of Hanukah	#29
ROMANS TAKE OVER GREEK EMPIRE		
63 B.C.E.	Romans invade Israel	#30
37 B.C.E.	Herod the Great begins his rule	#31
32 B.C.E.	Time of Hillel and Shammai	#32
34 C.E.	Death of Jesus; beginnings of Christianity	#39
66 C.E.	The Great Revolt of Jews against Rome begins	#33
70 C.E.	Jerusalem conquered by the Romans, 17th of Tammuz	#34
70 C.E.	Temple destroyed by the Romans, 9th of Av	#35
132 C.E.	Rebellion of Bar Kohba	#36
136 C.E.	Rabbi Akiva martyred	#37
190 C.E.	Mishna compiled by Rabbi Judah HaNasi	#38

TIMELINE OF JEWISH HISTORY (CONTINUED)

YEAR	EVENT	CHAPTER #
325 C.E.	Constantine: Roman Empire becomes Christian	#40
FALL OF ROME & RISE OF BYZANTINE EMPIRE / RISE OF ISLAM		
638 C.E.	Islamic Conquest of Jerusalem	#41, #42
1040	Time of Rashi begins	#43
1096	Time of Crusades begins	#44
1131	Time of Maimonides begins	#43
1144	First blood libel	#45
1263	Time of Nachamanides; the Great Disputation	#46
1348	The Black Plague	#46
1478	The Inquisition begins	#47
1492	Jews epelled from Spain. Columbus discovers America	#47
OTTOMAN EMPIRE TAKES OVER THE MIDDLE EAST		
1517	Protestant Reformation; time of Martin Luther	#49
1567	Jews invited into Poland	#48
1570	Time of the Ari and the Kabbalists	#50
1648	Chmielnicki Massacres in Eastern Europe	#48
1676	Death of Shabbetai Tzvi, false messiah	#50
TIME OF THE ENLIGHTENMENT		
1654	First Jews arrive in America	#54
1700	Time of the Ba'al Shem Tov, founder of the Hassidic Movement, begins	#51
1772	Time of the Mitnagdim and Vilna Gaon	#51
AMERICAN REVOLUTION AND FRENCH REVOLUTION		
1791	Emancipation of the Jews begins in Europe	#52
1791	Jews herded into Pale of Settlement in Russia	#55
1810	Reform Movement begins in Germany	#53
1881	Jews made scapegoats for murder of the Czar	#56
1882	First aliyah (large migration) to Israel	#61
1887	Conservative Movement founded in America	#57
1894	Dreyfus Affair in France	#58
1897	First Zionist Congress	#62
WORLD WAR I / FALL OF OTTOMAN EMPIRE		
1917	Balfour Declaration	#63
1920	British Mandate for Palestine begins	#63
1933	Hitler comes to power in Germany	#59
WORLD WAR II		
1942	Final Solution formulated by the Nazis	#60
1947	Partition of Palestine by the UN	#64
1948	State of Israel declared	#64
1948	War of Independence	#65
1964	PLO founded	#65
1967	Six Day War and Reunification of Jerusalem	#65
1973	Yom Kippur War	#66
1982	First Lebonon War	#66
2006	Second Lebanon War	#66
2008 ISRAEL CELEBRATES ITS 60TH BIRTHDAY		

AUTHOR'S NOTE

A word about conventions:

The Bible

All references to the Bible apply to the Hebrew Bible which in the Jewish tradition is called the *Tanach*. The word *Tanach* is an acronym for its three essential parts — *Torah*, *Nevi'im* (Prophets), and *Ketuvim* (Writings). The Torah includes the Five Books of Moses — Genesis, Exodus, Leviticus, Numbers, and Deuteronomy. *Nevi'im* include the works of the prophets such as Samuel, Isaiah, Jeremiah, Ezekiel, etc. *Ketuvim* include other writings such as Psalms, Proverbs, the Book of Esther, the Book of Ruth, etc.

God

Within the Bible, God is referred to by several different names. The holiest of these is the Tetragrammaton, which is the four-letter name of God that Jews are forbidden to pronounce. Whenever this name of God appears in prayer, Jews substitute the word *Adonai* (meaning "Lord"). When this name is cited in other contexts, the Hebrew word HaShem (meaning "the Name") is used. Throughout this book, I have opted to use the more familiar God or Lord.

Jews

Throughout this book, I use the term "Jews" to refer to the people known by that name today, although this was not always so. The earliest biblical references use the term "Hebrews," meaning "those from the other side," and later, "Israelites" or "Children of Israel." (The patriarch Jacob was renamed "Israel" and thereafter his descendants bore his name.) When the Kingdom of Israel split after the death of King Solomon, ten tribes — later to be known as the Ten Lost Tribes — were situated in the north and their kingdom was still called Israel, while the remainder, living in the south, were called by the name of the royal tribe, Judah. From it comes the name "Jew," which first appears in the Book of Esther and which has stuck to this day. It is interesting to note that the Hebrew root of Judah means "thanks," and so the Jews could be called "the grateful people."

Dates

This book relies on the traditional Jewish dating system for ancient history — that is, for the dates "before the common era," or B.C.E. The Jewish dating system and the Christian dating system vary by as much as 164 years for the Assyrian, Babylonian, and Persian periods, but by the time we get to the Roman period (i.e., the Christian year 1) the discrepancy disappears.[1] Why?

While it is beyond the scope of this book to present a detailed explanation of the various chronologies of the ancient world, I will explain briefly the dominant dating systems used by modern historians.

The Jewish dating system is taken primarily from a book called *Seder Olam Rabbah*, dating back to the second century C.E. and attributed to Rabbi Yosef ben Halafta. The sources for the dates in this book come from rabbinic traditions recorded in the Talmud, as well as from numerous chronologies recorded in the Bible.

It is also essential to remember that traditional Jewish chronologies (since the beginning of the Jewish calendar almost 6,000 years ago), have always been based on absolute and highly accurate astronomical phenomena: the movement of the moon around the Earth (months) and that of the Earth around the sun (years). A combination of an unbroken tradition of the Bible and an accurate, astronomical, time-based system gives traditional Jewish chronology a high degree of accuracy, especially when it comes to the major events of Jewish history.

Contrary to what one might think, the chronology used by modern historians is far from exact. It was not until the twentieth century that the entire world recognized a universal calendar system — the Christian calendar (also known as the Gregorian calendar). If we go back in time, however, the calendar situation was far more chaotic. Accurate historical records were almost unheard of, and every empire used its own calendar system which was often based on totally different criteria. With no unbroken historical traditional and no universally accepted standard for how to calculate time, there is no non-Jewish equivalent to *Seder Olam Rabbah*, nor to the Jewish calendrical calculation system passed down from antiquity.

So how do we get the chronology that historians use today?

Historians in the late nineteenth and early twentieth centuries worked backwards and pieced it together. Data from records of ancient Rome, Greece, Mesopotamia, and Egypt (including chronicles of major events such as battles between empires) were combined with archaeological finds and major astronomical phenomena such as solar eclipses, and dates were then calculated by applying various scientific dating methods.

Because there are margins of error in virtually all of these dating systems and much is open to interpretation, significant debates erupted among various scholars that continue to this day. Therefore, the chronologies used by modern historians are by no means 100 percent accurate, and we often find disagreements as to the exact dates of major ancient events and dynasties.

Because this book is written from the traditional Jewish perspective, and because Jewish chronology makes a stronger case for historical accuracy, I have chosen to use modern equivalents of the traditional Jewish dates.[2]

Rabbi Ken Spiro
kspiro@aish.com

1.
OVERVIEW

This book is designed as a basic overview of Jewish history — all 4,000 years of it.

Usually, when someone mentions the word "history," people break out in a cold sweat. They remember their days in high school, and they associate history with the memorization of names, dates, places, and events necessary only for exams and then promptly forgotten. This is probably why Mark Twain said, "I never let my schooling interfere with my education."

So, before we actually begin talking about Jewish history, let's talk a little bit about why we need to learn history in the first place. What is history? What purpose does learning history serve?

History is, first of all, the testing ground of ideas. In the words of the eighteenth century English statesman, Lord Henry Bolingbroke: "History is philosophy with examples." We can talk in theory about ideas, but the passage of time clearly shows us which ideas are right or wrong — what works and what doesn't. So, for instance, a hundred years ago a communist and a capitalist could debate which system would dominate the world, but recent history has shown us that communism has failed and capitalism — although it has taken some lumps — continues unabated (even in communist China).

There are many great lessons that can be learned from history. As the Spanish-American philosopher, George Santayana said, "Those who cannot remember the past are destined to repeat it."

So the basic reason to learn history, in general, is that people tend to remain the same. Empires rise and fall, technology changes, geopolitical realities of the world alter, but people seem to do the same stupid things over and over. And unless we learn the lessons of the past and apply them to the future, we're destined to get stuck in the same rut and repeat the same mistakes time and again.

This we also learn from the Bible:

> Remember days long gone by. Study the years of each generation. Ask your father and let him tell you, and your grandfather, who will explain it.[3]

But there is more. Since its earliest beginnings, Judaism has looked at history with a different eye. In fact, it has introduced to the world a number of highly revolutionary concepts — for one, the idea of God who acts in history, and for another, the idea of history as a process leading to a destination.

This means that not only do we want to learn history to avoid the mistakes made in the past, but also because we have a place to get to. That's an incredibly empowering idea — that we're going somewhere, we have a goal, there's a finish line. And this gives us another reason not to make the same mistakes — we want to get to that destination as quickly and as painlessly as possible.

So, therefore, in this book we are not going to focus as much on names, dates, places — although these are very important to know, and there are plenty of them here — but the emphasis will be on the patterns and lessons.

The history we learned in school is the history of power. The big battles, the big empires, the people who made the big noise. But Jewish history is not the history of power. It's the history of ideas. It's subtle history, below the surface, behind the scenes.

When we look at history from the viewpoint of ideas, we see things in a totally different way. This perspective doesn't change the facts, it only changes how we understand them. It's very important to keep this in mind throughout this book as we examine the causes and effects underlying the events.

Cycles in History

Another profound Jewish contribution to the understanding of history is the idea of cycles in time. For thousands of years, the ancient Greek view of time held sway: time has neither beginning nor end, it has always existed and it goes on forever. The ancient Greeks (and other pagan cultures) also believed that various gods needed humans to serve them. Humans were putty in their hands with no control over their destiny. In ancient Greek literature, the underlying theme of all tragedies is the futility of fighting against your fate.

If you combine these two concepts (the infinity of time and fatalism), you come up with a very negative and un-empowering view of history and destiny; you're on a treadmill going nowhere, and nothing you do really matters.

The Jewish take on history and destiny is radically different. If we were to draw it, it would look like a giant Slinky, an image that suggests the idea of repetition that is not static. This is how historical cycles work, according to the Jewish world view.

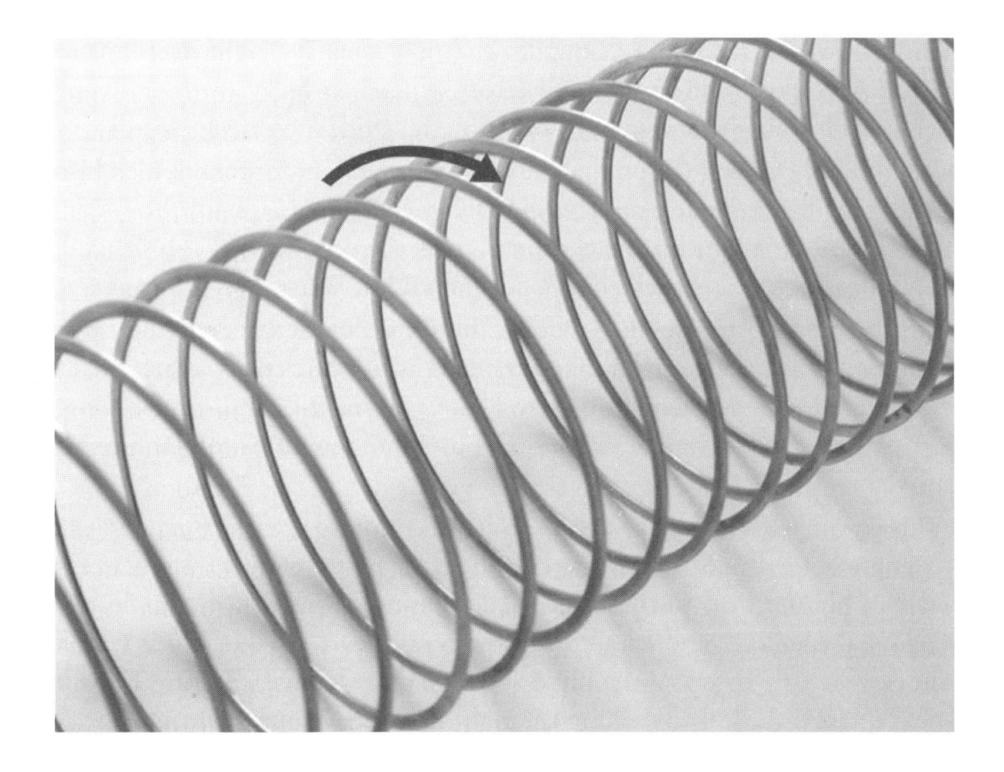

This model also applies to Jewish holidays. While other peoples' holidays are purely commemorative of past historical events, Jewish holidays, while commemorating the past, are also opportunities for the future. Each holiday in the yearly cycle has a unique spiritual power associated with it. For example, Pesach is the holiday of freedom, and it focuses on free will; Sukkot is the holiday of joy, and it demonstrates how to properly relate to the physical world. As we travel through this yearly cycle and encounter the holidays, we are supposed to grow in our understanding of the concepts they communicate. It's a bit like getting a yearly software upgrade. But if we miss the opportunity, we have to wait until it comes around again next year.

This is also how the cycle of history works. Unlike the fatalistic Greeks, Judaism believes that we have free will, our decisions matter, and we control our destiny. Because our destiny is in our hands, we have to earn our forward progress — whether individually during our lifetime, or collectively during the course of human history — it is up to us to make the right decisions and move forward. Because we have to earn our forward progress through our own efforts, we are constantly cycled through challenges that enable us to use our free will to make the correct decisions and move forward. If we don't decide, or make the wrong decisions, we will be re-cycled through the same challenge again until we get it right. So how do we know what the right decisions are? There are two possibilities: trial and error (which can be a very long, painful process), or learning from the past, by using the guidebook that is history.

It is precisely for this reason that we must learn and understand Jewish history. The great thirteenth century Jewish scholar, Nachmanides said, "The actions of the fathers are a sign for the children." This is a very famous Jewish saying, and Nachmanides was not the only one who said it. What does it mean?

On the microcosmic level — within the stories of Genesis relating earliest Jewish history — we see that what happened to the ancients was repeated by their children. On a macrocosmic level, the personalities and interactions of the patriarchs and matriarchs are a model for all of Jewish history and human history as well.

This is why we have to pay extra special attention to what's going on at this early phase of the Bible, because here is where the patterns are set. In these early narratives lies the map to the future. The destiny of the Jewish people, their strengths, weaknesses, and relationships with non-Jews — all of this is revealed in the early Jewish history of the Bible. Jewish history is Jewish destiny. Learning from the past is the key to making the right decisions about the future.

Additionally, we must remember that the Jewish people are one of the oldest surviving people on planet Earth. And because they have been spread out all over the world, we have to pay attention to all of human history. In fact, to learn Jewish history means to build a great deal of general knowledge of the history of the world at large, as we shall see.

Part I

A MAN, A FAMILY, A NATION

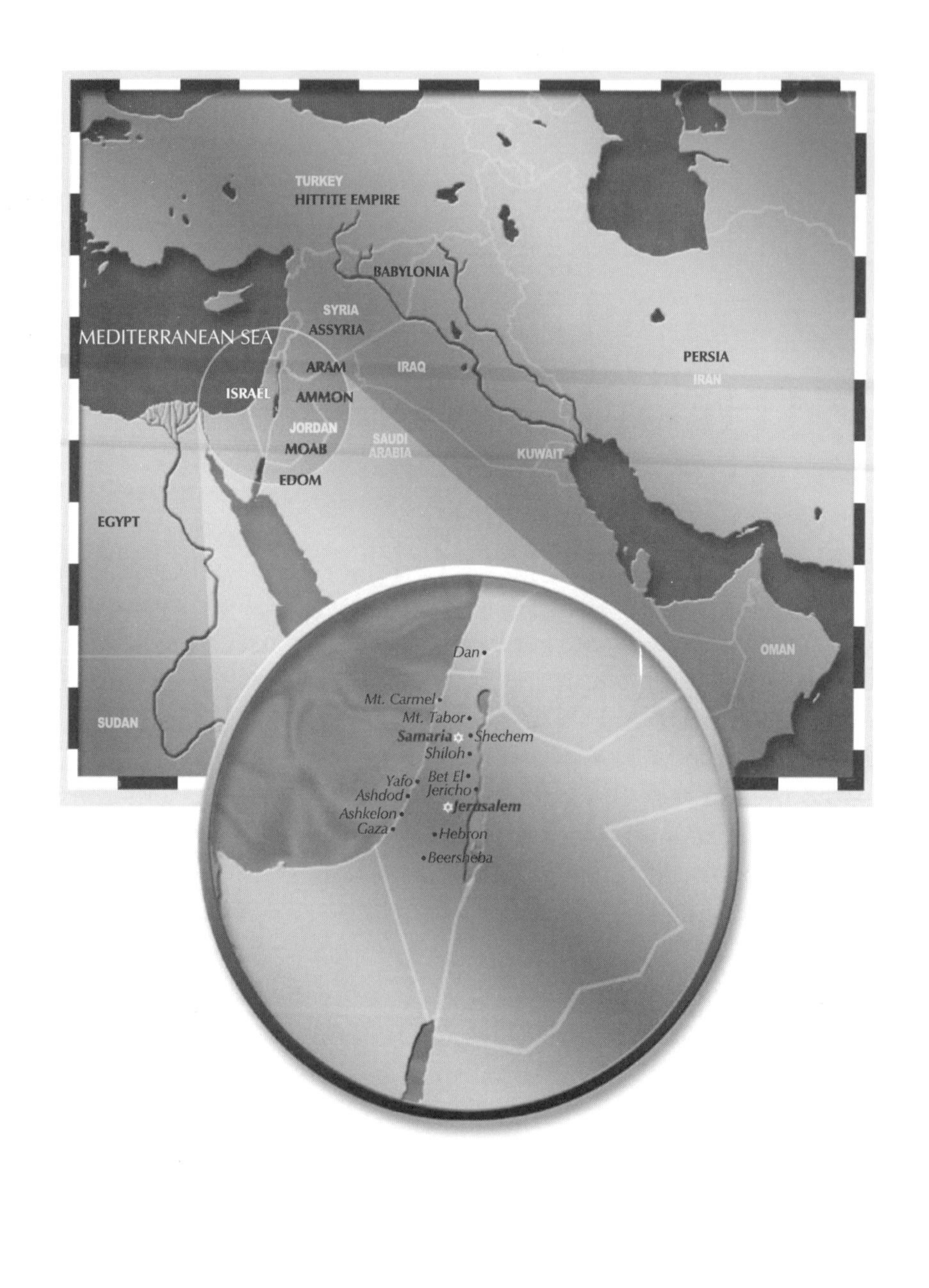
TURKEY
HITTITE EMPIRE
BABYLONIA
SYRIA
ASSYRIA
MEDITERRANEAN SEA
ARAM
IRAQ
PERSIA
IRAN
ISRAEL
AMMON
JORDAN
MOAB
SAUDI ARABIA
KUWAIT
EDOM
EGYPT
OMAN
SUDAN
Dan
Mt. Carmel
Mt. Tabor
Samaria
Shechem
Shiloh
Yafo
Bet El
Ashdod
Jericho
Jerusalem
Ashkelon
Gaza
Hebron
Beersheba

2.
THE BIBLE AS HISTORY

It's generally assumed that people have always recorded and studied history, but that's not true. As a matter of fact, if you go back more than a couple of thousand years, you'll find people had no interest in history. The first historian in the Western world is usually considered to be Herodotus, a Greek who lived in the fifth century B.C.E., who has been given the title, "Father of History." Columbia University historian, Joseph Yerushalmi, author of a highly praised book called *Zakhor: Jewish History and Jewish Memory*, says that "If Herodotus was the father of history, the fathers of meaning in history were the Jews."[4]

This is a profound idea.

The first of the stories that we will examine in this book predates Herodotus by about 1,300 years. It is the story of Abraham, and it takes place some 3,700 years ago.

In reality, Jews were recording history long before Herodotus, but while Herodotus might have recorded events, the Jews looked at the deeper meaning behind the events. That deeper meaning can be found most importantly and most significantly within the stories of the Bible itself.

Now, don't make the mistake of thinking the Bible is a history book, even though it does contain history within it. For example, when Abraham first appears in the Book of Genesis, he is already seventy-five years old. He's one of the most significant figures in Jewish history, and yet the Bible doesn't tell us anything about him as a child or as a young adult — we pick up his story when he is already an old man.[5]

This is because the Bible is not concerned with giving us all the details of Abraham's life. It is interested only in history as a means of teaching us the important lessons of life — it's a book of theology, and it sets forth the Jewish worldview first and foremost. Therefore, it focuses on the basic information that we need to know to understand reality.

How Accurate Is the Bible?

For thousands of years, humanity accepted the traditional Jewish view as to the authorship of the Bible. According to this view, the Five Books of Moses (Genesis, Exodus, Leviticus, Numbers, and Deuteronomy) were dictated by God to Moses during the forty years the Jews wandered in the desert after their flight from Egyptian bondage. However, during the nineteenth century, a philosophical movement known as the Enlightenment attacked this traditional view. Enlightenment scholars created what they claimed was a more "rational" approach to the issue of authorship of the Bible. The basic theme of this modern theory (called Higher Biblical Criticism) was that the Five Books of Moses were primarily a collection of myths and folklore, passed down orally for generations and eventually written down at a later point in history. According to this view, the great figures of the Bible (Abraham, Isaac, Jacob, and Moses) were folk heroes who probably never existed, and the events described in the text were at best folklore and at worst complete fantasy.

While the Enlightenment's theories of authorship were largely based on debatable textual analysis and speculation, the one source of possible hard evidence could come from comparing the biblical text to the archaeological remains of the period. If the traditional view is correct, then it should be supported by archaeological finds. Of course, in the nineteenth century archaeology was in its infancy. It took a while to unearth any evidence, and the archaeological quest continues.[6] Although the topic of authorship of the Bible is beyond the scope of this book, it is definitely worth a little time to discuss the historical accuracy of the text. So what does archaeology have to say about the accuracy of the Bible?

The definition of archaeology is "the discovery and interpretation of the physical remains of previous civilizations and peoples." Note that within the very definition of archaeology is the word "interpretation." How one archaeologist interprets the meaning of a particular find can be very different from another archaeologist's assessment of the same find.

Archaeology is not a hard science. It is not like math where one plus one clearly equals two. In archaeology, the subjectivity of the archaeologist can play a huge role in the conclusion he or she draws.

When archaeologists find a chiseled stone, a shard of a vessel, or a chunk of a building, they try to decide what it means — often they disagree. The find has no label on it, unless it's a written document, and even written documents are open to interpretation. So when people make definitive statements about what archaeology does or doesn't say, you have to be very careful, because the archaeologists' bias affects how they interpret the information.

As far as the early books of the Bible are concerned, there is little direct archaeological evidence for the characters described there.[7] There is, however, a huge amount of indirect or circumstantial evidence — names, places, business contracts, marriage contracts, migratory patterns. That is as far as the early books of the Bible are concerned. But once we get to later books — for example, the Book of Kings from 2,800 years ago — there is excellent direct evidence, including the written records of other empires. Unfortunately, the early events exist, more or less, in a historical vacuum and also in an archaeological vacuum.

Keep in mind that the same thing that applies in a court of law applies to archaeology: lack of evidence is no evidence of lack. The fact that we haven't found Abraham's camel saddle doesn't mean Abraham didn't have a camel or a saddle.[8]

Another point to consider is how little has actually been excavated to date. If archaeologists had excavated the entire Land of Israel, from south to north, and found no evidence to support the Bible, then we could make a more definitive statement about what the archaeological record supports. But this is not the case. Until today, dozens and dozens of sites remain totally unexplored, and even the sites which have been excavated (for example, Hazor, Megiddo, Gezer, Lachish, and even Jerusalem) have only been partially excavated. It is probably safe to say that at least 90 percent remains to be unearthed.

Archaeology doesn't definitively prove the Bible, but it certainly doesn't discredit it. In fact, the more we find, the more we see that there's a tremendous amount of historicity in the text.[9]

In summary, the Bible is not a book of history, yet it contains quite a bit of information about ancient history and culture, and this information is more or less borne out by archaeology. The Bible is, first and foremost, a book of teachings, and it is the ideal way to learn the patterns of history. And if we understand that we're learning history to discover these patterns so that we won't repeat them, then we have to pay extra special attention to what is going on in the Bible.

Professor Adam Zartal, chairman of the department of archaeology at the University of Haifa, put it up thus:

> After years of research, I believe it is impossible to explore Israel's origins without the Bible. At the same time, the research should be as objective as possible. The Bible should be used cautiously and critically. But, again and again, we have seen the historical value of the Bible. Again and again, we have seen that an accurate memory has been preserved in its transmuted narratives, waiting to be unearthed and exposed by archaeological fieldwork and critical mind work.[10]

3.
DAWN OF CIVILIZATION

Using the Bible as a guide, we begin counting the Jewish Year One from the creation of Adam, who is seen as the physical and spiritual pinnacle in terms of the creation of the world.

As the Book of Genesis relates it, God created man at the very end of the creation process — after He created darkness, light, water, sky, earth, oceans, continents, sun, moon, fish, birds, insects, and animals. And man was unique among the other creatures inhabiting the earth, not just because he gave rise to an amazingly innovative group of descendants (i.e. us), but because he was created *b'tzelem Elokim*, "in the image of God."[11] This means he had a soul — a higher, spiritual, intellectual essence — a divine spark we human beings all have.

There is a profound lesson rooted in the idea of starting the Jewish calendar from the creation of Adam. Just as the movie director starts the cameras rolling when the big actors show up on the set (even though years of preparation may have gone into the project before the actual filming starts), so, too, does God start His Earth clock when Adam — the first human being — appears on the scene.

Once Adam was completed, God took off His cosmic watch, so to speak, handed it to Adam, and said, "Now we switch to Earth time." A day became a revolution of the Earth on its axis, a year the Earth's trip around the sun, etc. According to Jewish chronology, God took off His watch about 5,770 years ago.[12] In the way the Western world counts time, this coincides with the dawn of civilization. The earliest civilizations in the world, according to most opinions, began in the Middle East, in an area called the Fertile Crescent.

The Fertile Crescent

The Fertile Crescent encompasses the area that starts in the south at the Nile Delta in Egypt, and extends through the Levant (the middle section where Israel is located), up to the Euphrates and Tigris Rivers in today's Iraq.

These three great rivers contribute mightily to the fertility, and consequent desirability, of this area. The Nile is an incredible river, the largest in the world. Without the Nile, Egypt would be a desert. In ancient times, 3% of Egypt was arable land and 97% was desert. Also the Euphrates and the Tigris Rivers are mighty rivers that run from Turkey into Iraq. Historians have dubbed the area between them "Mesopotamia," which is Greek for "in the middle of two rivers."

There is some debate among scholars whether the first civilization sprang up in Egypt or in Mesopotamia (specifically in the section of Mesopotamia called Sumer), but we can be fairly sure that the first hallmark of civilization — writing — originated in the Fertile Crescent.

Though we take it for granted today, writing was a tremendous invention. It began with pictographs. You drew a stick figure and that stood for "man"; you drew a square and that stood for "house"; you drew an oval and that stood for "eye." Later those pictures evolved into more abstract symbols which stood for phonetic sounds, until eventually there came about a system of three "letters," each representing a sound and combining together to make a word that conveyed an idea. (To this day, Hebrew is based on a three-consonant root system.)

Writing, the single greatest human invention, is the hallmark of civilization. All the technology and knowledge of today depends on the collective accumulation of accurately transmitted information, which now comes so fast we can't keep up with it.

From the Jewish perspective, the ability to express oneself — whether through writing or speech — personifies what human beings are all about. The Book of Genesis states that when God created the first human being, Adam, He "breathed into his nostrils the breath of life and man became a living soul." The Hebrew phrase *l'nefesh chayah*, "living soul," can also be translated as "a speaking soul."[13]

The Hebrew

Of the two earliest civilizations that developed in the Middle East, Egypt is unusual because it is surrounded by desert and so it is virtually unapproachable. Egyptian civilization lasted almost 3,000 years. This is an incredibly long period of time for a civilization to survive. Why did Egypt survive for so long? Because of its isolation, it was very difficult to invade.[14] It took the Greeks — specifically, Alexander the Great — to finish Egypt off, and then it became a Greek colony.

Mesopotamia had no such natural defenses — no mountains, no deserts — and it was a very desirable, fertile land. Basically, it was a giant flood plain sitting in the middle of the great migration route of many ancient peoples. Any conqueror who came out of Asia or out of Europe usually set foot there. Not surprisingly, this land changed hands many times as it was conquered by each new rising civilization — the Assyrians, Babylonians, Persians, Greeks, Romans, and then, of course, the Muslims.

This tumultuous place is where our story begins — at the bottom of the Tigris and Euphrates Rivers, in the cradle of civilization. This was the logical place for civilization to begin in terms of the development of agriculture and culture. And it was also a logical place for Abraham to appear. Since Abraham's destiny was to change the world, he had to be at the center of civilization. If he were born an Eskimo or a Native American, all of human history would have been different.

Abraham appears when civilization is already well under way, at a period of time commonly known as the middle period of the Bronze Age, around the eighteenth century B.C.E. Early civilizations are characterized by the metals they predominantly used and the middle period of the Bronze Age in the Middle East extends from 2200 B.C.E. until 1550 B.C.E. (from about 4200 to 3550 years ago).

The history of the world up to this time had been one long tale of woe, as the Bible tells us. First Adam severed his relationship with God by eating from the Tree of Knowledge of Good and Evil, thus bringing mortality into the world. Murder, violence, and idolatry followed, with society organized along the principle of "might makes right." Humanity forgot about God who had created them, worshipping nature — the sun, the moon, the trees, etc. and a whole legion of gods they invented. When it seemed like things couldn't get any worse, God decided to "clean up" the world via the great Flood, sparing only the family of Noah, who was the one decent guy at that time.

But the second time around proved no better, and humanity continued to decline spiritually and morally until the Tower of Babel. At that time people united for the wrong reason — to rebel against God.[15] It seemed as if another "clean up" was imminent. But, when all seemed lost, along came one man who changed the course of history. That one man would be known as the man who stood alone on the "other side" — the meaning of the word *Ivri* (i.e., "Hebrew") that describes him. He stood on the other side, alone against the entire world.

So this is how our story begins — a man against the world. The place is the Middle East, specifically ancient Mesopotamia. And the man is named Abram, soon to become Abraham.

4.
ABRAHAM

More than one hundred years ago author Mark Twain pondered the enigma of the Jews and posed a fascinating question:

> If the statistics are right, the Jews constitute but one percent of the human race. It suggests a nebulous dim puff of star dust lost in the blaze of the Milky Way. Properly the Jew ought hardly to be heard of; but he is heard of, has always been heard of. He is as prominent on the planet as any other people, and his commercial importance is extravagantly out of proportion to the smallness of his bulk. His contributions to the world's list of great names in literature, science, art, music, finance, medicine and abstruse learning, are also way out of proportion to the weakness of his numbers. He has made a marvelous fight in this world, in all ages: and has done it with his hands tied behind him. The Egyptian, the Babylonian, and the Persian rose, filled the planet with sound and splendor, then faded to dream-stuff and passed away; the Greek and the Roman followed and made a vast noise, and they are gone; other peoples have sprung up and held their torch high for a time, but it burned out, and they sit in twilight now, or have vanished.... All things are mortal but the Jew; all other forces pass, but he remains. What is the secret of his immortality?[16]

The answer to his question can be found in the remote beginnings of the Jewish people — in the earliest stories in the Bible. Just as these early stories define the paradigm for future events, so too, the earliest personalities in Genesis define the model for the collective nature of the Jewish people throughout history.

If this is the case, then from the Jewish perspective, the most important biblical character to understand is Abraham — the first Jew, or perhaps more accurately, "the proto-Jew." Abraham personifies everything that could be characterized as the "Jewish personality." His kindness, sense of mission, and idealism — and most importantly his strength of character to stand alone against the world — are reflected in all the generations of the Jewish people that have come after him.[17]

In an almost entirely polytheistic world that had completely lost its way, using only the power of his intellect, Abraham chose to see the reality of one God. When we first meet Abraham in the Book of Genesis,[18] he is already seventy-five years old, and God tells him to leave everything familiar behind and go on a journey. As far as we know, this was the first time that God spoke to him, and until that point Abraham had lived his whole life without any kind of outside confirmation that his ideology of monotheism was correct. This says a lot about Abraham's dedication to truth.[19]

Abraham was the ultimate truth-seeker. Can you imagine being the only person in the world to believe in an idea that no one else can comprehend or accept? How many would have the courage to even whisper it to their best friend?

But Abraham didn't care what anyone else thought. He chose to lay his life on the line for the ultimate cause — bringing humanity back to God. This also helps explain the concept of "the chosen people." Abraham, in effect, said to God, "I choose to live with the reality of You and to bring all of humanity back to that reality." God then said to Abraham, "Then I choose you and your descendants."

The Chosen

What were the Jewish people, as descendants of Abraham, chosen for? They were given the responsibility to repair the world — what in Hebrew is known as *tikkun ha'olam* — to elevate the world to the highest moral and spiritual level possible. This is the national-historic mission of the Jewish people.

Because the Jews have undertaken this special responsibility, they will never be allowed to be like anyone else. Balaam, the evil prophet who sought to curse the Jews without success, said it best: "It is a nation that dwells alone and is not reckoned among the other nations."[20]

If we look at the values of the world at the time the Jewish people make themselves first known as a force for change, we see that it was a world riddled with cruelty. There was little regard for human life, a conquest mentality dominated, rights belonged to a privileged few, and there was no pity for the have-nots. The Jews brought into this world the heretofore unknown values of respect for life and family, social responsibility for the poor and downtrodden, the concept of justice, equality, peace, and free education[21] (values which, incidentally, have since become part and parcel of liberal democracy). They had nothing personally to do with inventing these groundbreaking concepts — and they would be the first to admit it. The Jews have always insisted that these values came from God and that they were merely the people chosen to disseminate them worldwide as part of their *tikkun ha'olam* mission begun by Abraham.

To take on such a mission, to dedicate yourself heart and soul to a cause greater than you, takes tremendous strength of character. And so, it is not surprising that the one attribute that stands out more than any other about Abraham is his uncompromising drive. This drive truly epitomized the essence of what Abraham was about, and it can be seen manifest in every generation of the Jewish people as an indelible mark of the collective Jewish character.

It is because of this drive that the Jews have historically been tremendous overachievers and have stood at the forefront of virtually every major advance, cause, or social movement in world history. (Jews have not only been awarded a disproportionate number of Nobel prizes for their intellectual contributions, but have led movements such as Communism, socialism, feminism, civil rights, labor unionization, etc.)[22]

Notes social philosopher Ernest Van den Haag:

> Asked to make a list of the men who have most dominated the thinking of the modern world, many educated people would name Freud, Einstein, Marx and Darwin. Of these four, only Darwin was not Jewish. In a world where Jews are only a tiny percentage of the population, what is the secret of the disproportionate importance the Jews have had in the history of Western culture?[23]
>
> The Jews have invented more ideas, have made the world more intelligible for a longer span and for more people than any other group. They have done this indirectly, always unintentionally and certainly not in concert, but nevertheless comprehensibly...Jews may call themselves humanists or atheists, socialists or communists...they may even dislike their Jewishness and deny it in scientific terms. But, rarely do they refuse to carry it.... They won't give up being Jewish even when they consciously try to — when they change their names, intermarry and do everything to deny Jewishness. Yet they remain aware of it, and though repudiating

> it, they cling to it; they may repress it, but do act it out symptomatically. Their awareness of their Judaism is shared by others simply because their denial is so ambivalent. Unconscious or not, at least some part of every Jew does not want to give up its Jewishness.[24]

Unconscious or not, at least part of every Jew does not want to give up the legacy of Abraham. As Van den Haag concludes:

> Jews continue to feel the yoke, the task, the moral mission of being Jews — of preserving themselves as such, and to the surprise, scorn, and at times hatred of the rest of the world, of refusing to become anything else.[25]

The moral mission of the Jews was called into action when God spoke to Abraham (then called Abram) and sent him on a journey of a lifetime — a journey which still continues for his descendants:

> God said to Abram, "Go forth from your land, from your birthplace, and from your father's house to the land that I will show you."[26]

Abraham's Journey

We know that the Bible isn't like the writings of Charles Dickens. Dickens got paid by the word, and he would be as verbose as possible. In the Bible, God did the exact opposite. Rather than fill the text of the Bible with pages of details, He limits the narrative to the bare minimum, giving us only relevant information that we need to know. So the question we have to ask is, Why does God, who uses words so sparingly throughout the whole Bible, state this command so emphatically and seemingly repetitively? "Go forth from your land" and "from your birthplace" and "from your father's house."

If you grew up in a specific house for a specific period of time, that would be home for you. Whenever you would think of home — no matter where you've lived after that and how comfortable you've been — that would be the place to come to mind. Connection to home is very deep and fundamental. So God is saying to Abraham: "Don't just leave your land and your hometown, separate yourself from it all on the most basic emotional level."

More importantly, from the macrocosmic, historical perspective, God is saying to Abraham, and therefore to the Jewish people, his descendants: "Separate yourself completely and go in a different direction."

The journey that God is directing Abraham to undertake is not just a physical journey, it's a journey through history that is going to be different from anyone else's. Abraham is going to become a father to a unique nation with a unique destiny: "A nation that dwells alone and is not reckoned among the rest of the nations."[27] This concept of the Jews as a unique nation manifests itself in the double standard constantly applied to modern Israel.

This is the first unique characteristic of Jewish history.

In this command to Abraham, we see God directing him not only to leave his homeland, but to go to a specific piece of real estate which will later be known as the Land of Israel. This is the initial promise of the land to Abraham and his descendants, which will be repeated by God several times thereafter. From this point on, we will see that there is a special relationship between the Land of Israel and the Jews.

This special relationship is the second unique aspect of Jewish history. (We will discuss this relationship in more detail in the next chapter.)

The third unique aspect of Jewish history we see in the next verse:

"I will make you into a great nation, I will bless you and make your name great, and you will be a blessing."[28]

This verse conveys God's promise that He will be actively involved in Jewish history: "I will make you...."

In the seventeenth century when Blaise Pascal, the great French philosopher of the Enlightenment, was asked by Louis XIV for proof of the supernatural, he answered, "The Jewish people, Your Majesty." Why? Because he realized that the survival of the Jewish people up to the seventeenth century violated all the laws of history. Can you imagine what he'd say if he knew that the Jews have made it to the twenty-first century?!

Jewish history is a supernatural phenomenon. The Jewish people should never have come into existence. Abraham's wife Sarah was barren, and that should have been the end of the story. Abraham would have died childless, and his mission would have died with him. But it didn't. A miracle happened.

Besides Pascal, many scholars and well-known personalities have taken note that Jewish history is in fact unique and that it violates all the laws of history. Writes the Russian philosopher Nikolai Berdyaev:

> [The Jews'] destiny is too imbued with the "metaphysical" to be explained either by material or positive historical terms.... Their survival is a mysterious and wonderful phenomenon, demonstrating that the life of this people is governed by special predetermination.... The sur-

> vival of the Jews, their resistance to destruction, their endurance under absolutely peculiar conditions and the fateful role played by them in history; all these point to the particular and mysterious foundations of their destiny....[29]

The Jewish people came into being miraculously and survived all of human history miraculously, outlasting even the greatest empires. Things have happened to the Jews that haven't happened to other peoples. This is so because the Jews are a nation with a unique mission, a nation with a unique history — a nation whose role is so essential that it cannot be allowed to disappear.

To live for 2,000 years as a nation without a national homeland is not normal. It's unique in human history. To reestablish a homeland in the place that was yours 2,000 years ago is not normal. It's unprecedented.

A Blessing

Other unique aspects of Jewish history are spelled out in God's communication to Abraham. The fourth is found in the latter half of the verse quoted earlier: "and you will be a blessing."

The tiny Jewish nation that should never have come into existence and should certainly never have survived will profoundly impact all of humanity.[30]

More than 3,700 years after the birth of Abraham, there is no doubt that the world has been profoundly blessed by the Jews. In the words of John Adams, second president of the United States:

> I will insist that the Hebrews have done more to civilize men than any other nation.... They have given religion to three-quarters of the globe and have influenced the affairs of mankind, more and more happily than any other nation, ancient or modern.[31]

You can see the incredibly positive impact the Jews have had on the world. The most basic of all is that the Jews have contributed the values that are now linked with democracy — the values that come from the Torah — such as respect for life, justice, equality, peace, love, education, social responsibility etc.

And finally, the fifth unique aspect of Jewish history:

"I will bless those who bless you, and curse those who curse you, and through you will be blessed all the families of the earth."[32]

God is saying here to Abraham that he and the Jewish people, his descendants, will be under God's protection. The empires, nations and peoples that are good to the Jews will do well. Empires, nations, and peoples that are bad to the Jews will do poorly. And He repeats that the whole world is going to be changed positively by the Jewish people.

You can literally chart the rise and fall of virtually all the nations of the Western world and the Middle East by how they treated the Jews. Consider, for example, Spain, Turkey, Germany, Poland, United States of America, etc. (Ironically, most nations have treated the Jews both benevolently and malevolently. It is an oft-repeated pattern that the Jews are first invited into a country and later persecuted and expelled from the same country. We will see this pattern time and time again as we go through the history of the Jews in Diaspora.)

Part of this phenomenon, by the way, is not so supernatural, because if you have a group of people living within your country — an educated, driven, dedicated, loyal, creative, well-connected people — and if you're nice to them and you allow them to participate and contribute in a meaningful way, your country is going to benefit. If you crush those people and expel them, you're going to suffer, because of the economic fallout. But, of course, there's much more going on than just that. In the words of Thomas Newton, the Bishop of Bristol, who lived in the late 1700s:

> The preservation of the Jews is really one of the most signal and illustrious acts of divine Providence...and what but a supernatural power could have preserved them in such a manner as none other nation upon earth has been preserved. Nor is the Providence of God less remarkable in the destruction of their enemies, than in their preservation.... We see that the great empires, which in their turn subdued and oppressed the people of God, are all come to ruin.... And if such has been the fatal end of the enemies and oppressors of the Jews, let it serve as a warning to all those, who at any time or upon any occasion are for raising a clamor and persecution against them.[33]

So we have a final pattern — the rise and fall of nations and empires is going to be based on how they treat the Jews, which is an amazing idea, and one you can clearly see demonstrated in human history.

From these three verses in Genesis we perceive the key patterns underlying all of Jewish history.

Abraham's journey is the paradigm. His personal life (and the life of his immediate descendants) is going to be a mini-version, a microcosm, of what Jewish history is all about.

5.
THE PROMISED LAND

The early history of the Jewish people begins in the twelfth chapter of the Book of Genesis, when God first speaks to Abraham, and continues through the next thirty-eight chapters, ending with the death of Jacob and Joseph. This segment can best be described as the development of the "family" of Israel, which in the Book of Exodus will become a "nation."

We have already learned that Abraham was born in Mesopotamia, specifically in Ur Kasdim (in today's Iraq) then moved with his father to Haran (in today's southern Turkey), and that is where God instructed him to go to "the land that I will show you" — which turned out to be the land then known as Canaan, later as the Land of Israel.

This particular piece of real estate came to be known as the Promised Land, because promises regarding it are repeated several times in the Book of Genesis. For example:

> On that day, God made a covenant with Abram, saying: "To your descendants I have given this land, from the river of Egypt as far as the great river, the Euphrates. The land of the Kenites, Kenizites, Kadmonites, the Hittites, Perizites, Refaim, the Emorites, Canaanites, Girgashites, and Yevusites.[34]
>
> "And I will give to you and to your descendants after you, the land of your temporary residence, all the land of Canaan as an eternal possession and I will be a God to them."[35]

We say that Judaism encompasses three core ideas: God, Torah, and the

Land of Israel. The Land of Israel is not a pay off. God did not say to Abraham: "Support me and if monotheism spreads throughout the world, I will give you a good piece of real estate for your own." God gave Abraham and his family the Land of Israel as a unique homeland where his descendants are supposed to create the model nation for the world.

The Land of Israel is a special place; it's the only place on the Planet Earth where the Jewish people can achieve their mission. The model nation cannot come to be anywhere else. So, it is very important to understand the Jewish relationship with the land.

A Sensitive Place

The Land of Israel is a special place, a spiritually sensitive place, a place of tremendous potential. And so, it's also a place where one has to behave in a special manner. As Moses told the Jews just before they were to cross its borders:

> For the land which you come to possess — it is not like the land of Egypt that you left...the eyes of the Lord, your God, are always upon it, from the beginning of the year to the year's end.[36]

The Jews were only given this land because of their mission. If they abandoned the mission, they would lose the land.

This is another very important lesson in Jewish history, which is repeated time and again, and it is also one of the most oft-repeated prophecies. The Jewish people will only live and prosper in their homeland if they maintain their relationship with God and carry on the mission of Abraham:

> It will be that if you listen to My commandments that I command you today...then I shall provide rains for your land in its proper time, the early rains and the late rains, so that you may gather your grain, your wine, and your oil. I will provide grass in your field for your cattle, and you will eat and be satisfied. But beware, lest your heart be seduced and you go astray and serve gods of others and bow to them. Then the anger of God will blaze against you. He will restrain the heavens so there will be no rain and the ground will not yield its produce. And you will be swiftly banished from the goodly land that God gives you.[37]

Throughout the early part of the Bible, God is constantly talking about giving the Jewish people the Land of Israel and reaffirming that commitment.

Indeed, Rashi, the great eleventh-century biblical commentator, asks a question of the very first sentence in the Bible: Why does God begin the Bible with the creation of the universe? If the Bible is a book of theology for the Jews, why not begin with the creation of the Jewish nation and go immediately to the story of Exodus? That's when the Jews become a nation, get the Torah, and go into the land. Rashi answers that, in the future the nations of the world will accuse the Jewish people of being thieves, saying, "You have stolen the land from the Canaanite nations." God begins the Bible here, at the creation of the universe to tell the world: "I am the Creator of the universe. Everything is mine. I choose to give the Land of Israel to the Jewish people."[38]

Virtually every nation in the world bases its claim to its land on conquest. A people came (for example, the English or the Spanish), conquered the indigenous people (for example, the Native Americans), took the land, settled it, and called it by a new name (for example, United States of America). "Might makes right" is the historical claim of almost all nations in history. "To the victor belongs the spoils" or, in this case, the land.

However, the Jewish people base their claim on God's promise. It is a moral claim because God is God, and God is, by definition, truth and morality. God gave the Jewish people the Land of Israel. Without that, the only claim the modern State of Israel can make is that it is stronger and was able to win all its wars with the Arabs.

This is an extremely important point that is often lost on modern Israeli politicians and those who seek to defend the State of Israel (which is not a religious state and often far removed from Jewish values). It is the Bible that gives the Jews their only moral claim to the land.

Indeed, the early founding fathers of the modern State of Israel, even if they were not religious, were deeply steeped in the realization of biblical heritage of the Jewish people and their connection to the land. Israel's first prime minister, David Ben Gurion, had an appreciation of the necessity of anchoring a modern, even secular, Israeli state in the Bible and Jewish tradition. (We'll discuss Zionism later in the book.)

Ishmael

After Abraham arrived in the Promised Land, he was faced with a dilemma. His wife Sarah was barren, and she wanted Abraham to have an offspring. She suggested that Abraham take a surrogate wife — Hagar, who joined Abraham's camp when he passed through Egypt. Hagar was the daughter of the Pharaoh, and she had elected to travel with Abraham as Sarah's maidservant. Great people have great servants. And so, Abraham took Hagar as his second wife and from that relationship was born a child by the name of Ishmael.

But Ishmael did not inherit Abraham's mission. He went off to establish his own lineage; this is all recorded in the Book of Genesis, chapter 16.

When we look back on history, we see that two great monotheistic faiths branched off from Judaism during the last 2,000 years: Christianity and Islam.

Islam is a religion that originated with the Arab peoples more than 1,300 years ago. The Arabs, according to their own tradition and according to the Jewish tradition, are the descendants of Ishmael. One of the great attributes of Arab culture is hospitality. And the Bible tells us that Abraham was famous for his hospitality, a trait which he clearly passed on to his son.

It seems, therefore, that even though Ishmael did not carry on Abraham's mission, he couldn't help but be great. Even though his descendants did not become the chosen people, he carried within himself some of the greatness of his father Abraham. He was blessed.

By the way, the Bible says specifically that Ishmael would be great and that he would be at odds with the rest of the civilized world:

> You shall call his name Ishmael.... And he will be a wild man; his hand will be against every man, and every man's hand against him.... Keep your hand strong on him, for I will make of him a great nation.[39]

When it was clear that Ishmael would not carry on the mission, God told Abraham (who was then ninety-nine) that Sarah (who was eighty-nine) was going to become pregnant. And this is how Isaac was born — supernaturally.

As we noted earlier, this is one of the unique aspects of Jewish history — from its very beginnings, it's supernatural. By all the laws of nature Abraham and Sarah should have died childless, and the Jewish nation never should have come into existence.

Before Sarah conceived, God told Abraham:

> Your wife Sarah will bear you a son, and you will name him Isaac. I will establish My covenant with him as an eternal covenant for his descendants after him. And as for Ishmael...I have blessed him and I will make him fruitful and will increase him exceedingly. He will become the father of twelve princes, and I will make him into a great nation. But I will establish My covenant with Isaac whom Sarah will bear to you at this time next year.[40]

So Isaac was the person selected by God to carry on the mission of Abraham, the mission of the Jews. A rivalry which existed between Sarah and Hagar would be carried on by their children, Isaac and Ishmael. Because of this rivalry Hagar and Ishmael were sent away from Abraham's household. [41]

The rivalry established here would carry on for generations, and it is viewed as the metaphysical root of the modern rivalry between the descendants of Isaac (the Jews) and Ishmael (the Arabs).[42]

6.
ISAAC AND HIS SONS

The most dramatic event of Isaac's life was being offered as a sacrifice by his father Abraham, at God's command. To offer up his beloved son was Abraham's most challenging test — indeed, the ultimate test of faith given to any human being. If Isaac died, so would the promise of a great nation from his lineage. Abraham demonstrated his supreme trust in God, and Isaac his supreme trust in his father.

As Abraham was poised to carry out the deed — atop Mount Moriah — God sent an angel to stay his hand, directing Abraham to sacrifice a ram instead. The Bible tells us that having done so, "Abraham called the name of this place 'God will see,' and it is so called to this day...."[43]

We must remember Mount Moriah, as it will have huge importance later on.

We won't take the time to examine the other details of Isaac's life, because we want to focus instead on the patterns that are set here for the rest of Jewish history. And one of the great patterns we see with Isaac is a rerun of a situation that Abraham also confronted. The Book of Genesis[44] relates that Abraham went to the land of the Philistines, and he lived among them for a while. But he had some problems — for example, they tried to take his wife, Sarah.

A few years later,[45] Isaac faced the same situation. He was living among the Philistines somewhere in the coastal area (of today's Israel), and they tried to take his wife, Rebecca. Also his servants started having problems with the servants of Abimelech, the king of the Philistines.

And what happened eventually? The Philistines became jealous of Isaac's success and threw him out, even though he had done nothing to deserve it as far as the Bible tells us. In addition, they plugged up all the wells that Isaac had dug[46] — an illogical act given the value of water in the arid climate of the Middle East and the difficulty of digging wells.

But then something interesting happened — Abimelech came after Isaac and said, "I see that we prospered because of you." Because once Isaac left, things went downhill for the Philistines. Their economy declined, nothing was going well, and the Philistines came to realize it was because of the Jews' departure. So the king asked Isaac to return.

This is the great pattern of Jewish interaction with non-Jews in history. The Jews are often invited in. The country does incredibly well because of their contribution.[47] Then for no reason — there is virtually no example in history of Jews ever doing anything that caused them to be hated the way they've been hated — the country decides to throw the Jews out, undermining its own economy in the process. So the Jews are thrown out, the country suffers, and sometimes they are invited back in. This is what's going to happen over and over again. It's so irrational yet such an oft-repeated pattern. It's probably the greatest love-hate relationship in history, the syndrome of "can't live with 'em and can't live without 'em."

The Twins

Isaac married Rebecca, who became pregnant with twins. While still in the womb, the twins — who would be named Esau and Jacob — were already fighting. (Suffice to say, it was a difficult pregnancy for Rebecca.) And almost as soon as they were born, the rivalry between them began.

Although they were twins, Jacob and Esau had totally different personalities, and they were also physically very different. The Bible describes Esau as hairy and Jacob as smooth-skinned. Esau was a hunter, a man of action. Jacob was a scholar, a man of thought.

It's also clear from the narrative that Isaac favored Esau, the firstborn of the twins. He was just a couple of minutes older, but that could be significant when it came time to decide who would inherit the family mantle. Isaac probably realized that, as a man of action, Esau was a doer and that changing the world requires such a personality.

But Rebecca clearly favored Jacob. She no doubt loved Esau, but with her feminine intuition[48] she sensed that there was something amiss in his personality. Though Esau had "the gift of gab" and could fool his father, his mother saw through him.[49]

As the Bible relates, one day, when Esau was hungry, he sold his birthright to Jacob for a pot of lentils:

Jacob was once simmering a stew, when Esau came home exhausted from the field. Esau said to Jacob, "Give me gulp of that red stuff! I'm famished!" He was therefore given the name Edom [Red]. "First sell me your birthright," replied Jacob.... He [Esau] made an oath and sold his birthright to Jacob. Jacob then gave Esau bread and stew. He ate it, drank, got up and left. He thus rejected the birthright.[50]

When he was old and blind, Isaac decided to give each of his sons a blessing, and, of course, he wanted to give an extra-special blessing to the firstborn, unaware that Esau had already rejected his birthright.

When a great, spiritually connected person like Isaac gives someone a blessing, that blessing has tremendous power of potentiality and it can have a huge impact not only on the recipient of the blessing but also on history itself.

Although Esau didn't really want the position of the firstborn, with all the responsibility it entailed to carry on his father's mission, he did want the blessing of wealth and power which went along with it. But Rebecca realized that the blessing had to go to Jacob, as he was the one who was willing and able to change the world in the manner of Abraham.

So, while Esau was off hunting to catch something for his father's dinner, Rebecca took charge. She covered Jacob's arms with a goat skin so they would feel hairy like Esau's to poor, blind Isaac. And then Jacob would receive the blessing of the firstborn instead.

The Symbols

It's a mistake to read the Bible stories only on a simplistic, first-grade, Sunday-school level. This is not simply the story of some old, blind man who's confused by his wife and son. There are very profound things going on here.

When Isaac encountered Jacob pretending to be Esau, he said, "The voice is Jacob's voice, but the hands are the hands of Esau."[51]

What does "the voice" symbolize? Speech is uniquely human. Animals may communicate, but they cannot speak or express abstract ideas. Speech is therefore representative of spirituality and intellect. Later in our story, Jacob will have his name changed to Israel[52] and his children will create the Jewish nation. The voice is, therefore, symbolic of the real power of the Jewish people — their spirituality and intellect.

Golda Meir once said that she was angry at God for making the Jews wander in the desert for forty years and then bringing them to the only place in the Middle East without oil. That is precisely the point — the Land of Israel is weak in natural resources. The people of Israel are its greatest natural resource. Their intellect, drive, and spirituality have given them an edge that has not only enabled them to outlast the greatest empires in history, but to impact the world far out of proportion to the smallness of their number. Jacob's voice represents the spiritual power of the Jewish people.

The hand symbolizes the power of action, of might — it is the hand that wields the sword and the pen.[53] Esau, who embodied the power of the sword, gave rise, through his descendants, to the Roman Empire (or "Edom," as the Bible calls it). The power of Rome clearly lay in its ability to conquer, build, and dominate. Even after its decline and fall, the spirit and power of Rome perpetuated itself in the new powers of the Western world. And, of course, it was the Romans (as in the Roman Catholic Church) who converted the world to Christianity, the other great monotheistic faith.

So in Esau, we see yet another example of an offshoot of the children of Abraham, who, like Ishmael, did not carry on the mission, yet became a great power, both physically and spiritually.

As intense as the rivalry was between Isaac and Ishmael (the Jews and the Arabs) they were only half-brothers. Jacob and Esau were twins with the same genetic material. Their rivalry (as expressed by the subsequent rivalry between Israel and Rome/Western world) is understood to be the ultimate rivalry in history. It embodies nothing less than a cosmic struggle.

These two — Jacob and Esau — started fighting in-utero, and they have been fighting throughout history. The battle continues until today and will not end until the final showdown during the Messianic Era.

It's never been an even battle. Esau's descendants have always been stronger in the physical sense, but the Jewish people have had spiritual strengths and inner resources. Furthermore, their destiny is ultimately to triumph and bring all humanity back to God.

Amalek

The descendants of Abraham can't help but be great. We see that those who do not come from the line of Isaac and Jacob but through Ishmael and Esau also have a huge impact on the world. Indeed, the greatest enemies of the Jews have come from within the family.

Who is the ultimate enemy of the Jewish people in history?

The nation of Amalek.

This is a people who epitomize evil and rebellion against God. There is a commandment in the Bible to wipe them off the face of the earth. With Amalek there is no compromise — it's a fight to the finish. This is a nation whose pathological hatred of the Jews is so great that they will show no mercy. Given half a chance, they will wipe the Jews off the face of the earth. (We will see the role they play many times in history, particularly in chapters 16, 24, and 59.)

The progenitor of the nation of Amalek was Esau's grandson by his son Eliphaz.[54] From this individual named Amalek would emerge the Amalekite nation — the nemesis of the Jewish people. Some 2,000 years ago, Rabbi Simon bar Yochai, who wrote the chief work of the Kabbalah, the *Zohar*, said that "It's a known law that Esau hates Jacob."[55] This is a spiritual law of reality, so to speak, that describes the interaction between the Jews and descendants of Esau.

This deep-seated hatred is embedded in the collective psyche of the descendants of Esau, but it is especially concentrated in the descendants of Amalek. To understand this rivalry is to understand the deeply rooted anti-Semitism of those nations that emerged from Rome. No matter what happens, the descendants of Esau are going to hate the Jews.[56]

It all began here, when Jacob received the blessing and then Esau discovered what happened. Isaac, too, realized that he had been deceived. He was not angry, however, because he saw for the first time that Jacob was capable of action and could carry on the mission.

But Esau was bent on murder. To save Jacob's life, Rebecca sent him away, telling him to go quickly to Haran (the former home of Abraham, located in today's southern Turkey). In Haran lived her ne'er-do-well brother Laban — Lavan in Hebrew, meaning "white," though Laban was anything but.

Mr. White

On his way to Haran, Jacob stopped for a night's rest and had a momentous vision.

He dreamed of a ladder extending up to heaven, with angels going up and down. In the dream, God repeated the promises He made earlier to Abraham and Isaac:

> I am the Lord, the God of Abraham, your father, and the God of Isaac. I will give to you and your descendants the land upon which you are lying. Your descendants will be like the dust of the earth. You shall spread out to the west, to the east, to the north, and to the south. All the families on earth will be blessed through you and your descendants.[57]

Awakening in awe, Jacob declared, "God is truly in this place.... It must be God's temple. It is the gate to heaven!"

Jewish tradition[58] holds that this place was Mount Moriah, where Abraham had brought Isaac for the sacrifice that never was, and which would become the site of the future Temple.

When Jacob finally arrived in Haran, the first member of his family he encountered was his cousin Rachel, and from their first meeting, he realized that she was his soul mate. As he had arrived penniless on his uncle's doorstep, he offered to work for free for seven years to win her hand.

Laban agreed. But at the end of the seven years, he pulled a switch on the wedding day, substituting Rachel's older sister Leah and then demanding that Jacob work another seven years for Rachel. (Many biblical commentators have drawn a parallel between this switch and the switch that Jacob pulled to get Esau's blessing.)

In the end, Jacob wound up with four wives — Leah, Rachel, and their handmaidens Zilpah and Bilhah. These four women gave birth to thirteen children — twelve sons and one daughter — named Reuben, Simon, Levi, Judah, Dan, Naftali, Gad, Asher, Issachar, Zebulun, Joseph, Benjamin, and Dinah.

Unlike previous generations, where a child went off in a different direction and did not follow in the footsteps of Abraham, all of Jacob's sons would be totally dedicated to the mission. They would be a core group, an extended family that would form the nation meant to change the world.

Despite Laban's attempts to keep him dependent and working for peanuts, Jacob managed to accumulate a big fortune. Reading the Bible, it is fascinating to watch Jacob metamorphose. As a young boy, he started out totally straight and pure (sort of like the worst kind of guy for a poker game), but forced to interact with his double-talking brother and his scheming uncle, he successfully developed the skills necessary to overcome the challenges they presented.

This is yet another great pattern in Jewish history. During the long exile, the Jews have constantly found themselves at a disadvantage, economically and politically marginalized, with their hands tied behind their back. In order to survive, they had to learn to be very resourceful and creative. History has proven that, despite having the odds constantly stacked against them, when given the slightest opportunity, the Jews have done remarkably well, even in a very hostile environment.

His character transformation completed, Jacob is told by God that he must return to the Land of Israel because he has a mission. Just as Abraham knew that Israel was the only place where Jewish potential could be actualized, so too, Jacob realized that this was the only place to be. Despite his lingering fear of Esau's revenge (even though twenty years has passed), he gathered up all his family and his belongings and headed for home.

On the way, he had another momentous vision — a spiritual encounter in which a mysterious stranger[59] appeared to him and wrestled with him until daybreak. When the stranger saw that he could not defeat Jacob, he dislocated the upper joint of Jacob's thigh, which would prove a permanent disability. Even so, Jacob demanded a blessing from him. To this the stranger responded: "Your name will no longer be Jacob, but Israel. You have become great before God and man. You have won."[60]

This is the first appearance in the Bible of the name "Israel," by which the descendants of Jacob would be called (Children of Israel, Bnei Israel, Israelites),[61] and by which the Promised Land would be also known.

The Great Embrace

Come morning, Jacob/Israel is more ready than ever for his encounter with Esau. And this brings us to another scene which foreshadows a powerful pattern in Jewish history: the reunion of the brothers.

As he was making his way home, Jacob heard that Esau was coming out to meet him with an army of 400 men. In response, he used his wits to come up with a multipronged strategy to protect himself against any eventuality.

First, he prepared for war by dividing his family into two parts; in case one was attacked, the other part would survive. Next, he pursued the diplomatic track by sending elaborate gifts to Esau. Finally, he prayed, realizing that ultimately the outcome of the coming encounter was in God's hands.

We know that the Jewish sages believed strongly in the concept that the actions of the fathers are a sign to the children. Later in history, when the rabbis would have to interact with Roman officials, they would first study the story of Jacob's meeting with Esau. They knew that Jacob's strategy toward Esau was the key to successful Jewish negotiations with Rome.

As it happened, Esau did not try to kill Jacob.[62] Instead, he embraced him warmly and invited Jacob to travel together with him, with an implied offer that they would eventually live together. It is interesting to speculate what would have been if the spiritual-intellectual power of Jacob united with the physical power of Esau. But that did not happen. Jacob was not interested in the offer, no doubt aware that Esau still harbored deep enmity toward him. He told his brother, in effect: "You go ahead of me. I'll catch up later."

Now we know from the narrative that Jacob never did catch up. So what is the deeper meaning behind his statement?

In effect, Jacob (representing the great intellectual, spiritual force in human history) said to Esau (the great physical force): "I give you permission to go on ahead and dominate human history physically. But at the end of days, we'll get together and the tables will be turned."[63]

This "end of days" refers to the Messianic Era when the whole world will follow the Jewish lead and come to recognize the one God and live according to one standard of morality, in peace and brotherhood. The Jewish mission will then be fulfilled. In the meantime, Esau is going to dominate.

The ultimate struggle in history will be between Jewish ideas and the ideas of Esau and the culture that Esau is going to create. Jewish sources depict this as nothing less than a cosmic battle, and, as we shall see it is a major theme in Jewish history.

FAMILY TREE OF EARLY JEWISH PEOPLE
Abraham through the twelve sons of Jacob

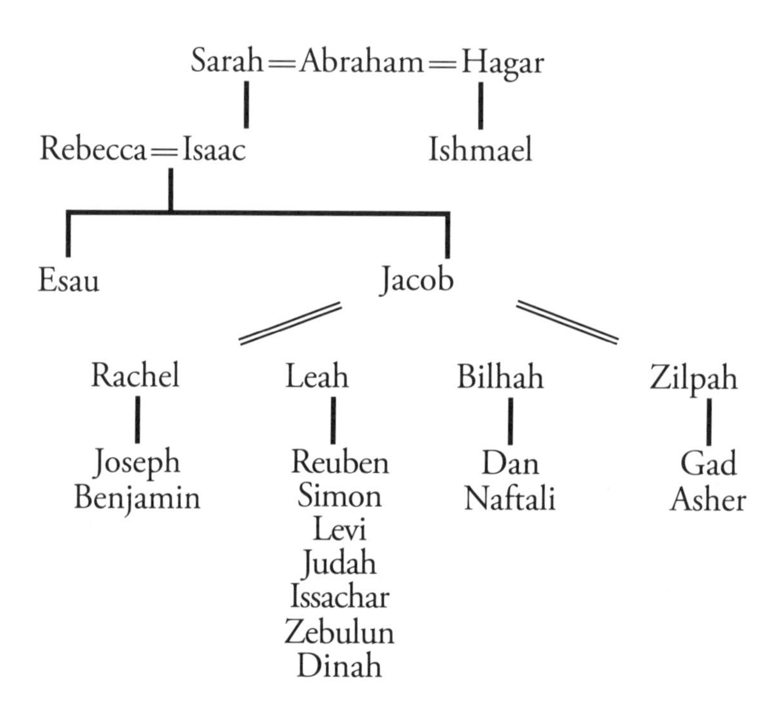

7.
JOSEPH

Had Jacob married Rachel as he had intended — instead of being tricked into marrying Leah — Joseph would have likely been his firstborn son. But, although he was Jacob's eleventh son, Joseph dominates the biblical narrative of the twelve brothers, and in his story, we see a great many historical patterns.

To begin with, the Bible tells us that Joseph had a key position in the family as a result of his being the long-awaited first child of Jacob's beloved wife. His father seemed to show him a considerable amount of favoritism — for one thing, he bought him a special coat — and this engendered jealousy from his brothers.

However, it would be a mistake to view their behavior simplistically, as typical of a dysfunctional family. While these people without a doubt made mistakes, spiritually they were on an incredibly high level. So we have to look carefully at what happened.

Joseph was having portentous dreams, and he interpreted those dreams. As we learn later in the Bible, he had a special gift for dream interpretation, and his dreams and interpretations were accurate and prophetic. He told his brothers, for example, that one day they would bow to him (which did indeed happen many years later). To his brothers, though, his dreams appeared to verge on megalomania. And since they knew that they were the family that was meant to build a nation to change the world, they probably thought that he was endangering the whole future of humanity. They knew the family history: that in each generation there was one "bad apple" — first Ishmael, then Esau. It is possible that they concluded that Joseph must be the bad one in this generation.[64]

They contemplated killing him, but instead they sold him into slavery. They took his fancy coat, smeared it with goat's blood and presented it to Jacob as if Joseph had been killed by a wild animal. Meanwhile, Joseph was taken by a caravan of the Ishmaelites to Egypt, where he became a slave in the household of a nobleman named Potiphar.

Ancient Egypt

At this juncture, we have to consider what Egypt was like at that time in history. Egypt was the second of the two great civilizations in existence (the first was the Mesopotamian civilization, described in chapter 3).

Geographically, Egypt was then mostly desert, except for the Nile River. The Nile is the greatest river in the world, and if it didn't flow through Egypt, the country would be just sand. In ancient times, only 3 percent of Egypt was inhabitable, arable land.

A huge desert is a great natural defensive barrier, making Egypt totally isolated and virtually impossible to invade. (The Hyksos invaded it once, the Assyrians, too, then finally Alexander the Great. But that's only three times in 3,000 years.) Egypt was the longest-surviving civilization in human history and it changed very little over the three millennia that it lasted. Consider how little Egypt changed in 3,000 years and how much the modern world has changed in a few hundred years; it's mindboggling how stable that society was, thanks largely to its unique geography.

Although we don't have exact dates for the beginning of the Egyptian civilization, it is believed to have started in the early period of the Bronze Age, over 5,500 years ago. It was a very sophisticated culture, considering the feats of engineering that the pyramids represent. The Great Pyramid of Khufu, known as "Cheops," is the largest, covering thirteen acres and reaching a height of 500 feet; it is composed of over two million blocks of stone all together weighing more than five million tons and was built by people who lacked iron tools. (It was also the tallest man-made structure in the world for more than 4,000 years!)

Even with all of our modern technology, we would have a hard time duplicating such a feat today. The Egyptians obviously had sophisticated stone- cutting techniques and engineering knowledge, enabling them to move large blocks of stone. They had pulleys, they had levers, and they had virtually unlimited muscle power. It is estimated that Cheops took 100,000 men and thirty years to build.

Why spend so much effort on building a tomb? Because the Egyptians were also spiritually sophisticated. It was a dark spirituality, but not to be lightly dismissed. They were preoccupied with death, which is why they perfected mummification, and their holy book was called the *Book of the Dead*. How's that for a lively read?

They believed that the Pharaoh was a living god, he had absolute power, and that the Pharaoh's position in the afterlife would affect the prosperity of Egypt. The future of Egypt was dependent on the Pharaoh's proper entry into the afterlife. So you had to make a really good tomb for him, and you had to give him the right gifts, and you had to make sure that he entered the afterlife correctly, otherwise it would be bad for everybody. And this is why it was a national project of the entire Egyptian people to create such extraordinary tombs for the Pharaohs.

Of course, this very sophisticated culture was as antithetical to Judaism as is humanly possible, because it practiced idolatry. They worshipped an estimated 2,000 different gods in ancient Egypt. Gods with hippo heads, and falcon heads, and crocodile heads. This was a civilization that was idolatrous to the extreme — very religious and spiritual in its own sense, and yet very idolatrous at the same time. They were not primitive or superstitious or stupid; they understood spiritual power and were a very sophisticated people who truly believed in the power of idolatry.[65]

This is a crucial point to understand about ancient civilizations. In our modern arrogance we often tend to look at the ancients as less sophisticated or even primitive. We have science and modern technology. What did they have thousands of years ago? The answer is: plenty. Ancient civilization's knowledge of engineering, math, astronomy, medicine, etc. was often very impressive. Spiritually, the contrast is even more extreme. Jewish tradition and archaeology both show that the ancients were much more spiritually connected than we are today. Thousands of years ago there was real spiritual power, both idolatrous and pure, that could be tapped into. Today, we have largely lost this connection. This explains why ancient civilizations put so much effort into religion and religious construction, and why the idolatry portrayed in the Bible had such a powerful allure.

Jewish tradition teaches that ancient Egypt, besides being a place of idolatry, was also a place of immorality — a very licentious place.[66] So to throw young Joseph into this environment was bad news. Very bad news.

Mrs. Potiphar

Separated from the monotheistic influence of his family at an early age (he was seventeen when sold as a slave), Joseph had another major disadvantage for a licentious society — he was very handsome, which explains why his master's wife, Mrs. Potiphar, found him very attractive.

Besides that, Joseph had a lot going for him — he was very smart and hard-working, and he rose from his position as a lowly teenage servant to head of Potiphar's household. This is the classic historic pattern of the Jews in the Diaspora, which will be repeated over and over again for thousands of years: they arrive impoverished in a foreign land, deal with a bad situation, work hard, and very rapidly rise to the top.

Now Potiphar's wife was not happy that Joseph refused her advances. Eventually, she picked a time when everyone was out of the house attending a national celebration, and she tried to entice him. He ran away. Outraged, she screamed rape.

Mr. Potiphar came home, and he clearly did not believe her, since if he did Joseph would have been executed on the spot. Nevertheless, to appease his wife, he had Joseph thrown into a dungeon.[67]

Instead of being the head servant, Joseph was now a helpless prisoner. This is a familiar scenario for the Jews in the Diaspora. They enter a country, they rise, they fall, and then have to start at the bottom somewhere else.

Once in prison, Joseph rose quickly to become the head prisoner. (Even as a prisoner you can't keep a Jew down.) And this is where he encountered the Pharaoh's wine steward and the Pharaoh's baker who had offended their master and been thrown into the same dungeon as Joseph. And it just so happened that both men had dreams.

Now, as we know, Joseph was a master dream interpreter, and not surprisingly, he interpreted their dreams. He told the wine steward that the Pharaoh would restore him to his position, and he told the baker that he was going to lose his head. And that's exactly what happened.

When the wine steward was leaving prison, Joseph asked him to put in a good word for him with the Pharaoh, hoping that maybe he would get released. But the wine steward forgot all about him, and Joseph had to sit in prison for another two years.

Even in this little detail there is a pattern for the future. Historically Jews have not been able to count on the non-Jewish world for help. It is the rare gentile who has come forward to help the Jews in their time of need.[68]

Pharaoh's Dreams

Then the Pharaoh himself had a couple of disturbing dreams. He dreamed of seven fat cows coming out of the Nile and being devoured by seven thin cows.

And then he dreamed of seven fat sheaves of wheat being devoured by seven thin sheaves of wheat. These dreams were real nightmares, and the Pharaoh was very disturbed. So, he assembled all his magicians, soothsayers, and astrologers and demanded an explanation, but none of them could figure out what the dreams were about. And then, suddenly, the wine steward piped up, "I remember, there was a Jewish kid in prison who interprets dreams...."

This proved to be the ultimate Jewish success story. Joseph was taken out of prison, given a shower and a shave, and brought before the Pharaoh. When he heard the dreams, Joseph told the Pharaoh: "There's going to be seven years of plenty followed by seven years of famine."

"What should I do?" asked the Pharaoh. And Joseph advised, "You'd better stockpile all the grain in Egypt so that when the famine comes you'll have what to eat." Joseph then outlined an entire plan to prepare for the famine. Impressed, the Pharaoh said, "You thought of it, you do it."

And this is how Joseph, at age thirty, became the viceroy of Egypt — for all practical purposes the most powerful man in the whole land in terms of infrastructure of Egypt, then the most powerful empire in existence. How's that for promotion — from prisoner to viceroy.

Here, too, we see important patterns for the future. Throughout history, when the Jewish people rise, this rise can be very dramatic. And the situation they find themselves in, for better or for worse, can change very rapidly.[69]

Joseph married Osnat, the daughter of Potiphar, and had two sons, Menashe and Ephraim. To this day, observant Jews use his sons' names when they bless their male children every Friday night. Girls receive a blessing that they should be like Sarah, Rebecca, Rachel, and Leah — the great matriarchs of the Bible. One would assume that boys would receive the blessing that they should be like Abraham, Isaac, and Jacob, the great patriarchs, but instead they are told they should be like Ephraim and Menashe. Why? First, unlike all the previous brothers in the Bible — Cain and Abel, Ishmael and Isaac, Jacob and Esau, and even Joseph and his brothers — they loved each other and there was no jealousy between them. As we travel through Jewish history, we will see that a significant weakness of the Jewish people is *sinat chinam* — the causeless hatred of one Jew for another. This hatred has been one of the driving forces behind the disunity in the Jewish world to this day; it is a flaw that has haunted the Jewish people throughout history. Its primary source is rooted in the rivalry and jealousy that constantly plagues the Jewish people. Ephraim and Menashe stand as a model for the unconditional love essential for Jewish unity and the success of the Jewish people.[70]

There is another extremely important lesson we have to learn from Joseph's sons. Throughout history Jews have been rich and poor, free and enslaved, tolerated and persecuted, and it seems clear that it is much easier for Jews to remain Jews when things are bad. It's not the poor, persecuted Jews who assimilate, but the comfortable, accepted ones. And more Jews have probably disappeared through assimilation than through persecution. This remains one of the great challenges of Jewish history — how to stay Jewish when things are good. Ephraim and Menashe had the inner spiritual strength essential for Jewish continuity. They grew up as sons of the viceroy, they could have become totally assimilated, spoiled, Egyptian brats, yet it's very clear that they grew up completely loyal to their family mission in an environment that was incredibly hostile to their Jewish identity.

Once Joseph became viceroy the stage was set for his early dreams to come true when he saw his brothers bowing before him. And this is indeed what happened next.

8.
REUNION

An interesting thing happens in the Bible right in the middle of the Joseph story. Suddenly, the story stops. We leave off Joseph and return to the land of Canaan to pick up the story of Judah, the fourth oldest of the twelve brothers and a natural leader in the family. It is not immediately clear why we need to be informed of this slice out of Judah's life at this point in the narrative, but what we learn is this:[71]

Judah had three sons, the oldest of whom married a woman named Tamar. He died. At the time, the custom was that if a man died childless, his brother was obligated to marry the widow so that she could have children and perpetuate the deceased's name.[72] Accordingly, the second son married Tamar. He also died. Tamar was thus in line to marry the third son, but Judah stalled, fearing the same fate for his youngest son.

Realizing Judah would not honor the custom, and seeing herself growing older and childless, Tamar decided to take matters into her own hands.

As the Bible tells it, she disguised herself as a prostitute and waited for Judah to pass by. He promised her a goat, and she kept his staff and seal as collateral. But when he arrived with the goat, the "prostitute" was nowhere to be found.

Shortly thereafter, it was discovered that Tamar was pregnant, and she was sentenced to death for her promiscuity. Despite her situation, she did not embarrass Judah by publicly revealing that he was the father of her unborn child. Instead, she sent his staff and seal with the request, "Please, recognize to whom this belongs."

These were the very words that Judah had spoken to his father Jacob, when

— after having sold Joseph into slavery — he and his brothers took Joseph's coat and smeared it with the blood of a goat. They had claimed at the time that Joseph must have been devoured by wild animals. Through this parallel language, Judah was given a hint by God that his leading role in the sale of his brother was a terrible mistake.

Judah exclaimed, "She is more righteous than I."

Through this admission of guilt, Judah became the first person in the Bible to accept responsibility willingly, thereby becoming the archetypal example of sincere and wholehearted repentance. In this, he is the model Jewish leader, and the mantle of kingship will forever after belong to the tribe of Judah. His descendants (from his relationship with Tamar) will be King David and King Solomon, as well as the prophesied Messiah at the end of days.[73]

As unusual as the Judah and Tamar story is, the fact that it is even mentioned illustrates another unique aspect of the Bible. In general, there is very little history recorded from this period of time, and what little we have found is very far from what we today would call "objective history." A good example would be the chronicles of the rulers of Mesopotamia. According to these records, the genealogy of these kings goes back to the gods, and the kings themselves are usually portrayed as flawless, ideal rulers. The Bible, on the other hand, is unique for its objective and even hypercritical treatment of both the Jewish people and their leaders. Since the purpose of the Bible is to educate, nothing is overlooked or whitewashed. There are no skeletons in the closet. Instead, they are all dragged out into the open for everyone to see. The Anglo-Jewish writer Israel Zangwill said it best: "The Bible is an anti-Semitic book. Israel is the villain, not the hero, of his own story. Alone among epics, it is out for truth, not high heroics."[74]

The Famine

The stage was thus set for the repentance of the brothers and their reunion with Joseph.

Meanwhile, the famine had hit, and it affected not only Egypt but the entire region. Egypt — thanks to Joseph's foresight — was the only place that had storehouses full of grain.

Jacob sent the brothers in search of provisions, keeping just the youngest, Benjamin, by his side. Unaware that Joseph was still alive, Jacob feared for the safety of Benjamin, Joseph's full brother and the only surviving child of his beloved wife, Rachel.

When the brothers arrived in Egypt, they paid the usual homage to the viceroy, not realizing that he was the long-lost brother whom they had sold into slavery. After all, when they last saw him, he was a boy of seventeen, and now he was almost forty and dressed in the finery befitting his station.

At this point in the narrative, Joseph could easily have revealed himself, but he didn't. Instead he kept his identity a secret and ran his brothers through one of the most interesting and emotional dramas in the entire Bible.

Joseph recognized that his brothers' hatred had posed a mortal danger to him in the past and, if left untreated, would continue to pose an eternal danger to the Jewish people in the future. Unless they recognized their mistake, felt true remorse, and changed, this hatred would resurface throughout history. He knew that he had to force his brothers into repentance.

The great medieval Jewish scholar Maimonides sets out the Jewish way of repentance: First, you recognize what you've done wrong. Next, you commit never to do it again. But the true test comes when you find yourself in the same situation, and you don't repeat your mistake. Only then have you proved that that you've really changed.

This is exactly what Joseph decided that his brothers must do, and he engineered events to recreate the same situation as years before to get them to take responsibility for their past mistakes and to root out the damage caused by their fraternal jealousy. First, he accused them of being spies. They insisted, of course, that they were not spies, they were just a family of brothers with a father and a brother back home. If that was true, said Joseph, then go back and bring the other brother.

They were starting to realize that this was all happening to them because of what they had done to Joseph. And now they had to bring Benjamin! They knew that if something happened to him, it would kill their father.

But Joseph insisted they go home and bring Benjamin to him. Then, when they did as he asked, he planted a silver cup in Benjamin's bag, and accused them all of stealing. In response to their protests, he offered to let them go free and punish only Benjamin by taking him into slavery. This was the test — would they turn their backs on their brother to save themselves?

But, over time, they had become different people, and they would not make the same mistake twice. Judah argued passionately with Joseph, offering himself into slavery in place of Benjamin.[75] Hearing that, Joseph broke down in tears and revealed his true identity, with the memorable statement: "I am Joseph, is my father still alive?"

This is one of the great moments in the Bible, describing the brothers' reunion with Joseph, now an Egyptian viceroy.

Divine Plan

As the shock wore off, the first thought that Joseph's brothers probably had was: *And now we're dead!* But Joseph had no thoughts of revenge, as he made clear. His statement is one of the most significant explanations of what is going on in terms of Jewish history:

> Now do not worry, and do not be angry with yourselves that you sold me here, for it was to preserve life that God sent me before you. For it is two years that there has been famine in the land; and for another five years there will be no plowing or harvest. God sent me here before you to insure your survival in the land to keep you alive for a great deliverance. It was not you that sent me here, but God, and He made me as a viceroy to the Pharaoh, master of all his house, ruler over all the land of Egypt.[76]

Joseph is setting forward here one of the great principles of Jewish history — the idea that "God prepares the cure before the disease."[77]

At the beginning, we discussed the concept of history as a controlled process leading to a destination. Our decisions make a difference, but we're promised that we'll reach our collective destiny. Therefore, regardless of what path we take, God will always make sure that His goals are met. He will put the pieces into place. As events are unfolding, we don't see where and how the pieces fit, but when it's all over, it's plain that everything had a reason.

Joseph, who was a very intelligent person with a tremendous faith in God, realized that everything he went through in the past twenty-two years — his enslavement, his imprisonment, his rise to power — was part of a divine plan. He had to go to Egypt, because this was all part of this cosmic historical process that only became clear at the end of the story.

Jewish history (and all human history) is like a giant jigsaw puzzle with six thousand pieces. When the pieces are first poured out on the table, they make no sense, but by the time the puzzle is put together, we see that they all fit together perfectly; nothing is missing and nothing is extra; every piece has a purpose and a place.

This is the Jewish take on history. Everything fits. There are no accidents. It all comes together. Every event has a purpose in God's infinite plan, and when it's done, we look back and see that it all makes sense. It all fits.

Joseph saw that. He sent word back to his father, and Jacob was overjoyed, because he thought his son has been dead for all these years. They had a dramatic reunion, and all of Egypt came out to see the viceroy's family, who were all bowing to Joseph in fulfillment of the prophecy he saw in his dream.

Then the Pharaoh invited them all to come live in Egypt. And they took him up on the invitation. The Bible says that seventy individuals entered Egypt, consisting of Jacob, his twelves sons, their wives and children. The proto-Jewish nation arrived in Egypt. They were welcomed in. They were given the best real estate in the Nile Delta — the land of Goshen. They settled there happily and prospered. Everything seemed to be going great — until the Egyptians saw they were doing a little too well for comfort.

But when the Book of Genesis ends — with the deaths of Jacob and Joseph — everything is still okay. The problems are waiting to come in the Book of Exodus.

CHRONOLOGY FROM ADAM TO MOSES

NAME	LENGTH OF LIFE	FOUND IN BOOK OF
Adam	930 years	Genesis ch. 1–4
Seth	912 years	Genesis 4:25–5:6
Enosh	905 years	Genesis 5:3–10
Kenan	910 years	Genesis 5:9–14
Mahalalel	895 years	Genesis 5:12–17
Jared	962 years	Geneiss 5:15–20
Enoch	365 years	Genesis 5:18–24
Methuselah	969 years	Genesis 5:21–27
Lamech	777 years	Genesis 5:25–31
Noah	950 years	Genesis 5:28–9:28
Shem	600 years	Genesis 6:9; 9:18–27; 11:10–11
Arpachshad	438 years	Genesis 10:21–24; 11:11–13
Shelah	433 years	Genesis 10:24; 11:12–15
Eber	464 years	Geneiss 10:24–25; 11:14–17
Peleg	239 years	Genesis 10:25; 11:16–19
Reu	230 years	Genesis 11:18–21
Serug	148 years	Genesis 11:20–23
Nahor	148 years	Genesis 11:22–25
Terah	205 years	Genesis 11:24–32
Abraham	175 years	Genesis 11:26–25:11
Isaac	180 years	Genesis 21:1–28:5
Jacob	147 years	Genesis 25:24–49:33
Levi	137 years	Genesis 29:34 thru 49:7; Exodus 1:1–2
Kohat	133 years	Exodus 6:16–18
Amram	137 years	Exodus 2:1 & 6:18–20
Moses	120 years	Exodus 2:1, Leviticus, Numbers, Deuteronomy

9.
MOSES

The Exodus story is the central event of Jewish history. It is also a model for what happens later throughout the history of the Diaspora. Again and again we see the roller-coaster ride from high points to low. Generally, the higher the Jews manage to rise, the lower they fall and then, despite the odds, they rise again.

The Book of Exodus recounts the Jews going from a good situation (as when they were welcomed into Egypt by the Pharaoh himself) to a very bad situation (when they were enslaved) to the highest heights, the pinnacles of spirituality (when they were freed from slavery by God Himself and given the Torah at Mount Sinai).

At the point in time when the Exodus story begins, the family of seventy individuals that arrived in Egypt at the time of Joseph has grown to a nation of about three million people.[78] The supernatural, rapid increase in the Jewish population has made the Egyptians nervous — "There are too many of them, what if they rise up against us" — and Pharaoh is trying various cruel measures to keep them down. (This is a classic anti-Semitic pattern — the Jew in the Diaspora is always loyal to his host country, yet can never escape unfounded suspicions of treachery.)

The baby Moses was born shortly after Pharaoh had issued the genocidal decree: "Every boy who is born must be cast into the Nile...." His parents, Amram and Yocheved, initially decided to hide him, but after a few months realized that very shortly they would be found out. His mother, in order to save him somehow, put him in a waterproof basket and hid it in the reeds of the Nile. As we all know, he is found by none other than the daughter of the

Pharaoh, and it was she who gave him the name Moses, meaning "from the water." (Interestingly, several pharaohs have had the same name, for example, Thutmose.) Irony of ironies? It's all part of the plan. As noted earlier, God puts the cure before the disease. This is another classic case.

It does give one pause, though — that the savior of the Jewish people would be raised in the house of the ultimate enemy of the Jews. The only modern equivalent would be of some fellow who is meant to overthrow Nazi Germany being raised as Adolf Hitler's adopted grandson. That's what we have here. You realize what a wild story this is if you imagine it in a modern context.

Egyptian History

By the way, who is the Pharaoh in the story here?

If we translate Jewish chronology into the Christian dating system the Western world uses today, the events of Exodus happened circa 1314–1312 B.C.E. But we cannot just look into Egyptian history 3,300 years back for the right name. For one thing, the Egyptians kept a very different calendar — or more accurately, many different calendars. For another, the Egyptian chronologies we use in modern world history have only been calculated in the last two centuries, and there's a huge amount of educated guesswork involved in their time estimates. If you open any books on ancient Egypt, you'll get lots of different opinions as to when different pharaohs reigned.

Generally, the pharaohs associated with the Exodus are Seti and Rameses, who reigned during a period called "The New Kingdom" (1550–1050 B.C.E.). Rameses II was certainly the great builder of this period of time. And it's interesting that the Bible says that the Jewish slaves built the cities of Pitom and Ramses.[79] Of course, it took them 116 years to build these cities, so that covers the reign of more than one pharaoh.[80] (A common misconception is that the Jews built the pyramids, but as mentioned previously, these were built a thousand years earlier.)

Now what's fascinating is that, after Rameses, there was a period of chaos in Egypt; this much we know from available records. This would fit if Egypt was, in fact, destroyed by ten supernatural plagues; they would be in a bad state for a number of years afterwards. So there we may have some evidence of it.

The pharaoh after Rameses was his son Mernephtah, who ruled in the late thirteenth century B.C.E. Now what's most interesting is that in Thebes (modern Luxor in Egypt), Mernephtah carved a victory inscription on a large slab of black granite. Known as the Mernephtah Stele, it contains a record of

Mernephtah's military campaigns that included the area of Canaan, the Sinai, and Israel. It is the first extra-biblical mention of "Israel" anywhere in human history. We're talking about something that is around 3,200 years old. And this would correspond in Jewish chronology to some time after the Exodus story.

What does the stele say? "Israel is a widow. Her seed is no more." (Translation: "We've wiped out the Jewish people, they're gone.") This means that the ancient Egyptians lied when they recorded things. Jews are here today 3,200 years later, they hardly wiped the Jews out; in fact, it is the ancient Egyptians who are gone.

This is not surprising, as the ancient people were notorious for lying in their official records. Objective history was nonexistent. Events that were recorded were usually grossly exaggerated and chronicled solely to glorify the accomplishments of the ruler of the country. Egyptian battle inscriptions show the Pharaoh as larger than life slaughtering his enemies. He is always victorious, and no dead Egyptians appear anywhere. Losses, failures, imperfections, and the like were never recorded by any ancient people.[81]

Compare this to the unique objectivity of the Bible, which records highly unfavorable events in the lives of the people whom it also portrays as great. (We cited the story of Judah and Tamar as an example in chapter 8.) But faults and failures must be mentioned; otherwise, how could the necessary lessons be learned?

Still, at this early time in history, the Mernephtah Stele provides a concrete reference to a people called Israel. This is a very significant piece of archaeology.

Prince of Egypt

Moses grew up as the grandson of the Pharaoh, whoever he was. The Pharaoh, as the ruler of the mightiest nation, was then the most powerful human being on earth.

Moses could easily have grown up totally assimilated. But the Pharaoh's daughter had hired his own mother as his nanny, which explains why he never lost the connection or the commitment to his people.[82] So much so, that when he was grown, he began to go out among his own people. On one such occasion he saw an Egyptian taskmaster beating a Jew and, unable to stand it, he killed the taskmaster. Then, of course, some Jews informed on him, which is another classic case we're going to see in Jewish history — Jews informing on other Jews. And Moses had to flee for his life.

Eventually he ended up in the land of Midian, which is across the Sinai Peninsula. There he met Jethro, an excommunicated priest who had several daughters, one of whom was named Tzipporah; Moses married her and they had two sons, Gershon and Eliezer (about whom we don't hear much), and he became a shepherd.

In this regard, he followed the example of the other great leaders of the Jewish people: Abraham, Isaac, Jacob, and Jacob's twelve sons were all shepherds. So, we have to ask why.

Now, if you've ever watched shepherds at work, you might have noticed that most of them sit around doing nothing except daydreaming. A shepherd has a lot of time to think, and this is an absolute prerequisite for being able to communicate with God. To elevate oneself to the highest level, where one transcends the physical reality and enters a higher dimension of speaking with the divine, requires a huge amount of work and a lot of time to think.[83]

Consider another reason why Jewish leaders were shepherds. The work of a shepherd involves managing large groups of living creatures. Leading the Jews is the hardest job on the planet. Jewish history clearly demonstrates how difficult and challenging it is to unify and lead the most individualistic nation on earth. Being a shepherd is good practice for this daunting task.

The Burning Bush

While Moses was tending the sheep, he had a vision of the burning bush — a most astounding experience.

The story of Moses' encounter with God at the burning bush is incredibly profound and laden with meaning, but for our purposes, we will consider the burning bush as synonymous with the Jewish people. The bush is burning, but it is never consumed by fire. So, too, the Jewish people seem to be a nation forever in danger of being destroyed, yet they are always miraculously preserved by divine intervention. On another level, we could say that the burning bush is also symbolic of the Jewish people who burn with the fire of Torah, with an ideology that is going to change the world.

When Moses encountered God at the burning bush, God identified Himself repeatedly — four times to be exact — as the God of his forefathers, Abraham, Isaac, and Jacob, with whom He had made an eternal covenant.[84]

This is an extremely important passage because later on in Jewish history many different people — the Christians, for example — are going to claim that God changed His mind, abandoned the Jews, and made a new covenant (new "testament" to use the Greek term) with them. But God made an "eternal" covenant with Abraham, Isaac, and Jacob, and He renewed it several times. We learn that God has a master plan for humanity and the Jews have an absolutely essential part in that plan.

At this juncture, God has decided to bring the Jews out of Egypt. And it's important to keep in mind that God put the Jews in Egypt in the first place.

It says in the Talmud that you have to bless the bad as well as the good.[85] Traditionally, whenever a Jew hears bad news (for example, that someone has passed away), the first response is "*Baruch Dayan Ha'emet* — Blessed is the True Judge." There is no concept in Judaism of a devil who does evil and competes with God. God is omniscient and omnipotent and nothing is outside His knowledge or control. While we finite human beings may perceive events as good or bad, from God's infinite perspective everything that happens is part of a master plan and ultimately for the good.

So, in effect, we come to understand that Egypt served as a womb where the Jews were formed as a nation in very difficult circumstances, so that when they were ready, God could bring them out and establish a special relationship with them. At the burning bush, God communicated this to Moses and then commanded, "Go back and tell the Pharaoh to let My people go."

"Let My People Go"

As commanded, Moses went back down to Egypt and confronted the Pharaoh with his brother Aharon: "The God of my forefathers told me to tell you: Let My people go."

The Pharaoh was incredulous. "What are you talking about? Who is this God? I don't know him."

The ancient Egyptians had around 2,000 gods. They took their spirituality and knowledge of the spiritual world very seriously. Since the Pharaoh didn't have a laptop to do a "god-search," you can imagine the Egyptian priests furiously flipping through their lists of the different gods, unable to find the deity that Moses was invoking.

The notion of one, infinite, all-powerful God was an idea that was incomprehensible to the ancient polytheistic people — it simply did not fit with their fragmented way of viewing the world.

Once he realized that the Pharaoh wouldn't listen to him, what did Moses do? Following instructions from God, he told Aharon to throw down his staff. It turned into a snake. If someone did something similar today it would make a huge impact, but the Pharaoh was not impressed. His magicians could do the same thing, even though Aharon's staff then swallowed the other staffs.[86]

It is very important to emphasize time and again that the ancient world understood spirituality in a way we cannot fathom. Today, we are spiritually on a much lower level. We talk about magic, but to us it is an illusion, not a actual manipulation of the forces of nature, as it was to them.

It is a fundamental idea of Judaism that there's a spiritual reality and a physical reality. You can transcend the physical into the spiritual; you can use the spiritual to manipulate the physical. And you can do this by accessing the dark, impure forces or the light forces. The Egyptians, who were very spiritually sophisticated, were able to access these dark/impure forces, and they knew how to turn a stick into a snake, so they were not impressed by what Moses did.

But Moses was just getting started.

10.
THE TEN PLAGUES

Once the plagues hit Egypt — blood, lice, frogs, etc. — the devastation continued for over a year.[87] Each plague was an open miracle, because each one represented a fantastic manipulation of nature. The laws of nature were turned upside down to help the Jews.

Open miracles are a very important part of early Jewish history. After the destruction of the First Temple they would cease, although arguably the Jews couldn't have survived this long without continual hidden miracles.

The obvious question we must ask when we examine the story of the Ten Plagues is: Why? Why did God choose to set the Jewish people free through this very long, drawn-out process that took an entire year? If He wanted, God, all-powerful Being that He is, could have made all the Egyptians drop dead on the first encounter with Moses, or He could have frozen them in place. Then, all the Jews could have packed up and left in five minutes.

To explain why the Ten Plagues had to be, we need to first explain the Jewish view of miracles in general.

The first point to focus on is that all existence — the entire process of the physical universe — is a miracle. We have become so used to it in our day-to-day lives that we simply don't notice it. As Sir Isaac Newton observed:

> For miracles are so called not because they are the works of God, but because they happen seldom and for that reason create wonder. If they should happen constantly according to certain laws impressed upon the nature of things, they would be no longer wonders or miracles but might

> be considered in philosophy as part of the phenomena of nature (notwithstanding their being the effects of the laws impressed upon nature by the powers of God) notwithstanding that the cause of their causes might be unknown to us.[88]

Judaism holds that nature does not act independently of God, but, at the same time, God does not like to interfere with it. God is certainly capable of doing whatever He likes, but He doesn't play around with the physical world and its workings. Therefore, most miracles are natural phenomena with awesomely good timing. The Ten Plagues are a notable exception to this rule.

The Ten Plagues were a clear example of God flipping the laws of nature on end. There was hail — which should have been frozen — that was on fire. There was darkness so dense that no one could see or move. And these supernatural things happened to Egyptians and not to the Jews next door. Why? Here is the reason:

The whole essence of idolatry is the belief that every force in nature has a god that controls it. In Egypt, they worshipped the Nile god, the sun god, the cat god, the sheep god, etc. The Ten Plagues demonstrated — not just for the Jewish people but for all of humanity, for all of history — that God alone controls all of nature, all of the physical world, and that there is nothing outside of His control.

If we examine the plagues carefully we can readily see that each one was designed to show God's control of all forces in nature: water and earth, fire and ice, insects, reptiles and mammals, light and darkness, and finally, life and death.

Archaeological Evidence

Do we have evidence for the Ten Plagues in archaeological records? Surely, the Egyptians would have recorded such amazing events!

First, we must understand that the events of the Exodus took place before there were historians, newspapers, or any other form of mass communication. As previously mentioned, any events that were recorded by ancient Egypt (or any other ancient civilization) were solely for the purpose of making them look good. Combine this idea with the knowledge that, thousands of years ago, people were far less impressed with the supernatural than we are today, and we have our answer.

The last thing that an Egyptian priest would inscribe on the wall of one of the temples 3,300 years ago would be the Exodus story, regardless of how amazing it seems to us today.

However, there is some circumstantial evidence that should be mentioned. As noted in chapter 9, there is recorded a ten-year period in Egyptian history when chaos reigned. There are other oblique references, the most famous being the Ipuwer Papyrus which describes various cataclysmic events in Egypt — blood everywhere, people dying, etc., right around this time.

Russian psychoanalyst, Immanuel Velikovsky, uses the Ipuwer Papyrus as the basis for his books *Ages in Chaos* and *Worlds in Collision*, in which he argues that the whole Exodus story is true, but that the plagues happened because a comet came close to the earth. He says the dust from the comet turned the water red, and the pull of the comet's gravitational field split the sea, etc.

However, if you read the Bible, you see that the plague of blood was not just water turning a "dusty red." The Midrash also tells us that Egyptians perished from this bloody water but not the Jews.

Despite that, there is an amazing amount of resistance on the part of the Egyptians — not just the Pharaoh, but the whole of Egypt — to let the Jews leave. It is classic anti-Semitism, "I don't care if I take my whole country down as long as I can take the Jews with me."

This is actually a very common historical pattern. You'll see this certainly when we get to Hitler — by 1944 the Germans needed the trains to send reinforcements to the Eastern Front in Russia, but they diverted them to ship Hungarian Jews to Auschwitz. They were losing the war, but their main focus was not to win, not even to save themselves, but to kill the Jews.

Finally, finally, after the death of the firstborn, the Pharaoh said, "Go!" The Jews left, the sea split, the Egyptians tried to follow them and drowned.

The Jews were free at last.

11.
MOUNT SINAI

Pesach is often described as the holiday of freedom. And in liberal democracies, freedom is often misunderstood as the ability to do whatever you like with no oppressive authority telling you what to do. But that is not how the Bible and Judaism define freedom.

The Jewish idea of freedom is best summarized by the famous expression: "Praise the servants of God who are not servants of Pharaoh."[89] That is, freedom is seen as a means to an end, not an end in and of itself; true freedom means to be free of outside influences and pressures so that we can be free to pursue ultimate meaning — a relationship with God.[90] In the specific context of the Exodus story, it means being free from an oppressive authority in order to commit to a chosen responsibility at Mount Sinai.

Which brings us to the question: What happened at Mount Sinai?

To answer quite simply, the Jewish people — every man, woman and child — had an encounter with God.

It was a totally unique event in all of human history. The Bible itself states[91] that this never happened any place else. You can check all history books, and you'll never find a similar story of God speaking to an entire people.

All other claims of revelation in human history are based on the experience of one individual or, at best, a small group of initiates. For example, Islam is founded on the teachings of Mohammed who said that an angel spoke to him in a cave and revealed to him the teachings contained in the Koran.

The notion of an entire people having an encounter with God Himself is unique to Judaism.

And it's the one claim that cannot be faked. So for example, I can claim that I had a vision last night and God spoke to me, and if I'm charismatic enough and you are gullible enough, you might believe that I am a prophet. But I can't convince *you* that you saw something that you know you didn't see. Maimonides summed it up perfectly when he wrote:

> The Jewish people did not believe in Moses our teacher because of the miracles he performed. If one believes in something because of miracles, he may suspect that they were performed through sleight of hand or sorcery.... We believe in Moses because of what happened at Mount Sinai. Our own eyes saw, not a stranger's, our own ears heard, and not another's.... The revelation at Sinai is the only real proof that Moses' prophecy was true and above suspicion....[92]

Jews say that they have kept the Torah for thousands of years, not because of miracles or any other supernatural phenomena of Jewish history, but because they all stood at Mount Sinai and heard God speak, and for generation after generation that very fact was passed down. And the story of the survival of the Jews as a people is, to a large extent, the story of the chain of transmission of Torah from one generation to the next.

A Nation Is Born

At Mount Sinai, the descendants of Jacob and his twelve sons — who had escaped from slavery in Egypt, and who had been known until then as Hebrews and/or Israelites — became the Nation of Israel. This is another unique event which says a lot about the Jewish people.

What's so unique about it? Well, consider how the French became "the French." Did they all wake up one morning to collectively decide they liked white wine and blue cheese, and they were going to speak French? No. It was a long process. As with every other nation, this process involved a people living in a specific geographic area for an extended period of time and evolving a common language and a common culture borne of a shared historical experience. Eventually, this people developed a political entity and government (with a king at its head) and they defined their boundaries, flew a flag, minted coins, and called the whole thing France.

For Jews, the process of becoming a nation started outside their national homeland — in fact, while they were in bondage and under the most adverse conditions that were designed to erase any cultural or historical identity. Jews did not become a nation by pledging allegiance to the State of Israel. A scraggly band of escaped slaves became a nation standing at the foot of Mount Sinai and saying to God, "We will do and we will listen" — that is, pledging to fulfill the commandments of the Torah and, in time, to understand the mission that came with it.

Just as Abraham many generations earlier made the choice and commitment to live, and if necessary to die, for the reality of the one God, these descendants of Abraham made the same commitment. That is what made them a nation. And that is why we say that Judaism is not just a religion — it's a national identity.

Being a Jew is not the same as being a Christian. Christianity is purely a religious belief. You can be British, American, French and still be a Christian.

Not so the Jews. The Jews can certainly become citizens of the countries in which they live; they can look and act like everyone else, but all the while, they and their neighbors know they are different. If they choose to deny this fact, the rest of the world will always remind them of it.

Being a Jew is being part of a distinct people and nation, which does have a land, language, and history. Most importantly, however, and what lies at the heart of Jewish identity, is a specific relationship with God — a commitment to carry out the mission of *tikkun ha'olam*. To maintain that relationship and fulfill that mission, the Jews subscribe to an all-encompassing worldview — another thing that makes them unique — that is spelled out in the Torah.

The Jewish national identity was forged by the experience at Mount Sinai where the Jews committed to a particular way of life to be lived in accordance with the commandments of the Torah, which is the guidebook for accomplishing their mission on a personal and national level.[93]

The Ultimate Scribe

After the original mass revelation, Moses spent forty days listening to God, who talked to him, dictating what came to be known as the basis of the Written Law, the 613 commandments of the Torah (which are encapsulated in Ten Statements, the so-called "Ten Commandments") and also the principles of how to apply these commandments (called the Oral Law).[94]

It is interesting that some 1,300 years after the Torah was given at Mount Sinai, when Christianity came on the scene, it adopted the Written Law — the Torah and other parts of the Hebrew Bible as part of its scriptures — but the Oral Law stayed uniquely Jewish. This is because it is the Oral Law that specifies how Jews must live every moment of their life.

It cannot be emphasized strongly enough how significant the Oral Law is. One can't live as a Jew without it. It's going to become a very important issue when we look at splinter sects in Judaism later in Jewish history.

The Written Law was written down over a period of forty years while the Jews wandered in the desert and God was dictating to Moses.[95] Although the Torah — Genesis, Exodus, Leviticus, Numbers, and Deuteronomy — are called the Five Books of Moses, Moses was not the author. God was the author. Moses was the scribe — the ultimate scribe. God dictated to Moses. However, it is also very clear — as the Bible says over and over — that Moses was unique among all prophets: "And there arose no prophet in Israel like Moses whom God knew face-to-face."[96]

Contrary to common misconception, prophecy is not the ability to predict the future, but a process whereby God communicates directly with someone, and He may reveal to him or her messages for humanity, profound spiritual truths, and sometimes what the future holds. Clearly, prophecy is not something that just happens to someone. To achieve prophecy means that a person is able to perfect him or herself and transcend to a higher level of spiritual reality; of course, what that level is depends on the prophet's direct experience of the Infinite. (For more details about the Jewish understanding of prophecy see chapter 25.)

Most prophets would be asleep or in a trance when God communicated with them via a vision and would later put that vision into words. Moses' prophecy was unique in that God spoke to him while awake and fully conscious, as the Bible testifies:

> And He said: Hear now My words. If there is a prophet among you, I, God, will make Myself known to him in a vision and will speak to him in a dream. Not so with My servant Moses, for he is the trusted one in all My house. With him, I speak mouth to mouth, openly, and not in dark speech; and he beholds the image of God.[97]

Moses heard God directly.[98] And the Five Books of Moses — that is, the Torah — are a direct dictation, which is why they have a unique position among all holy books of the Jewish people and a unique authority in the Jewish world.

12. THE GOLDEN CALF

After forty days on Mount Sinai, Moses came down with the Ten Commandments in hand. What he saw angered him to such an extent that he threw down the stone tablets, shattering them at the foot of the mountain. Below, where just a few weeks ago they'd stood in an encounter with God, the Jews were worshipping an idol, in direct violation of the law they had just been given.

The date of this infamous event is forever marked on the Hebrew calendar — the seventeenth of Tammuz. This would be the day later in history on which the walls of Jerusalem would be breached by the Babylonians and again by the Romans prior to the destruction of both the First and the Second Temples.

It is very important to analyze what happened with the Golden Calf and why the Bible criticizes this sin so harshly, for it gives us a better understanding of God's relationship with the Jews.

At face value, it seems like a totally idiotic thing to do. I mean, if I'd had an encounter with the Infinite Creator of the universe, and I heard Him say, "I am God, don't worship anything else," I don't think I would be stupid enough to be jumping around a golden cow a few days later. So what's going on in this story?

To answer that question, it is necessary to read the text of the Bible correctly — that is, ideally in its original Hebrew, but certainly with the commentators, because there's an oral tradition that must be studied along with the simple, very brief description in the text.

When Moses came down the mountain, were all three million Jews dancing around a Golden Calf? No. The Book of Exodus[99] says it was only about 3,000 people. That means that only about 1 percent of the Jews (one in a thousand) participated and 99.9 percent of the Jews did nothing wrong, although the majority should have stopped the minority.

Yet, the Bible makes it clear that God blamed the whole nation.

An Exacting Standard

We already mentioned that, among all ancient books, the Bible is unique in its objective criticism, and that the purpose of this criticism is to educate. But why the hypercriticism?

One of the great misconceptions of all time is "love is blind." Infatuation surely is, but true love is a magnifying glass for faults. While to love others means to focus on the beauty and the positive within them, it doesn't mean denying their faults. An excellent example of this is the relationship between parents and children. Parents typically love their children beyond measure, though they are well aware of their faults. Loving parents may be quite strict, for far worse than overly strict parents are parents who are neglectful.

If we transplant this parent analogy to God (a.k.a. our Father in Heaven) then the hypercritical nature of the Bible begins to make sense. While God is the God of all humanity, He has a special relationship with the Jewish people and constantly "has an eye" on them. He deliberately emphasizes their faults and mistakes in order to get their attention — to hammer home, in the strongest possible language, vital lessons that they must learn.

God holds the Jews to a very high standard because they have a unique responsibility in human history. The world won't reach perfection without the Jews, and if they fail at their mission, all of humanity will suffer. For this reason, the Bible uses hypercritical language to bring home some important principles:

According to your level of knowledge is your level of responsibility. Even the small mistakes of people in positions of power have huge consequences.

According to your level of responsibility is your level of accountability. The greater you are, the bigger the impact of your decisions; therefore, you must be held to an extremely high standard.

At Mount Sinai, the Jewish people were given the ultimate responsibility for the world, and these principles explain the criticism that God levels against them.

We also learn here another fundamental idea of the Torah — that every Jew is a guarantor for every other Jew. The nation of Israel is a "body" and the individual Jews are like "cells" in this body. If part of the body does something wrong, the whole body is held accountable.[100] (This theme of collective responsibility repeats itself over and over again in the Bible and throughout Jewish history, as we shall see.)

Judaism teaches you're either part of the problem or you're part of the solution, and that you have an obligation to be part of the solution. Being a bystander is not an option. Until today, the Bible is virtually the only moral/legal code in the world which demands that you actively do good.[101]

The Aftermath

As a sign of His displeasure over the Golden Calf, God distanced Himself from the Jewish people, and the Tent of Meeting (Moses' tent for communicating with God) was moved outside the camp, while Moses spent a lot of time dealing with the aftermath of the debacle. He smashed the idol, gathered loyal Levites around him, and executed those responsible.

(As you might have noticed, the Bible is not a liberal book. While it is full of the merciful acts of God, it also emphasizes that there are serious consequences for wrongdoing.)

Moses went back up the mountain on the first of Elul — Rosh Chodesh Elul. Elul is the month before Rosh HaShanah, the beginning of the Jewish year. He spent another forty days on the mountain and returned with the second set of tablets — a clear sign that God had forgiven the Jewish people.

What's the day Moses came back down? Yom Kippur.

As already mentioned, each Jewish holiday has a specific theme or focus. While the holidays are linked to specific historical events, on a deeper level they are connected to the different spiritual forces embedded within the yearly cycle. Each holiday in the cycle touches on a fundamental concept and serves as an opportunity for an improved relationship with God. From Yom Kippur comes the spiritual power of *teshuvah* — of repentance, of returning to closeness with God and repairing relationships with others.

AT MOUNT SINAI

DAY	HEBREW DATE	EVENT
1	15th of Nissan	Exodus from Egypt
50	6th of Sivan	Encounter with God at Mount Sinai
MOSES ON MOUNT SINAI FOR 40 DAYS RECEIVING THE TORAH		
90	17th of Tammuz	Moses comes down with Ten Commandments to see Golden Calf
MOSES ON MT. SINAI FOR 40 DAYS BEGGING GOD'S FORGIVENESS		
130	1st of Elul	Moses ascends to receive the second set of the Ten Commandments
MOSES ON MOUNT SINAI FOR 40 MORE DAYS		
170	10th of Tishrei (Yom Kippur)	God grants forgiveness and Moses descends with second set of tablets

As a sign of forgiveness God told Moses that He would again dwell among the Jewish people, and He instructed how His "home" was to be built:

"They shall make for Me a sanctuary, and I will dwell among them."[102]

Following this command, the Torah spends many chapters giving intricate instructions just exactly how this portable sanctuary (for subsequent travels) was to be built.

When finished, the sanctuary consisted of a large tent — called a "Tent of Meeting" — surrounded by a courtyard. Inside the courtyard was an altar where sacrifices were offered. In the tent were two rooms. The outer room held a seven-branched candelabra, a table with twelve loaves of bread on it, and an incense altar. The inner room — called the Holy of Holies — held the Ark of the Covenant. Inside the Ark were the two sets of the Ten Commandments — the broken set inscribed by God, and the second set inscribed by Moses.

Anyone who has seen *Indiana Jones and the Raiders of the Lost Ark* has seen a pretty good replica of what the Ark looked like. It was a wooden chest covered with gold, and it was decorated on top with two small statues of winged cherubs. The Talmud says that the two cherubs normally faced each other, but when the Jewish people were not getting along with God they would be turned away from each other.[103]

The whole structure — called the *Mishkan* in Hebrew — was not a portable synagogue or a museum. It was a tool to be used by the Jewish people individually and as a nation, to connect to God.

When it was completed, the Torah relates that the "clouds of glory" — a manifestation of divine Presence known as the Shechina — would literally rest on the sanctuary as a tangible sign that God was with the Jewish people.

When the sanctuary stood, people would feel holiness in the world in a way we can't begin to understand today. No amount of description can begin to give us a sense of what it would have been like to connect spiritually to God via the *Mishkan*. Today we are like people born blind — no description of the sense of sight can begin to replace the actual experience.

So central was the *Mishkan* to Judaism that following the account of the flight from Egypt and encounter with God at Mount Sinai, most of the rest of the Five Books of Moses are spent describing the construction of the *Mishkan*, its vessels and the priestly service that took place within it. So detailed is the description within the Written Law that further description within the Oral Law is not needed in order to construct it.

Because the *Mishkan* is now gone, only 369 of the 613 commandments are applicable, and most of those are negative commandments (of the "thou shall not" variety). Most of the positive commandments are focused on how to use the *Mishkan* to connect to God. The loss of that structure has had tremendous implications for the Jews' (and all of humanity's) ability to relate to God.

The service in both the *Mishkan* and later the Temple (which was its replacement) was carried out by the priests — in Hebrew, *kohanim*. The first *kohanim* were Moses' brother, Aharon; and Aharon's sons. This line has continued until today. Most interesting is the fact that recent genetic analysis of the Y-chromosomes of hundreds of *kohanim* from around the world proves that almost 80 percent are in fact descended from a common male ancestor who lived more than 3,000 years ago.[104]

Even though the Temple service has been discontinued since the destruction of the Temple by the Romans, the *kohanim* — who often have a last name like Cohen, Kahane, Kahn, Katz, or Cowen — are still awarded special honors in recognition of their unique status and responsibility.[105]

The *Mishkan* — which was readily dismantled and reassembled — accompanied the Jews in their wanderings in the desert for forty years. For 440 years, after they entered the Land of Israel but before they conquered Jerusalem, the Jews assembled it in several different locations. After David became king and made Jerusalem his capital, he planned to build a permanent structure just outside the city, atop Mount Moriah where Abraham had offered Isaac as a sacrifice to God and where Jacob had dreamt of a ladder to heaven. For reasons that we will explain later, he did not actualize his plan.

Finally, in 832 B.C.E., his son, King Solomon, built the First Temple there, and it became the permanent sanctuary until it was destroyed by the Babylonians in 422 B.C.E.[106] At this time, the Ark of the Covenant disappeared never to be seen again. (We will discuss the speculations where it might be hidden in chapter 22.)

Seventy years after the first destruction and exile, the Jews returned and rebuilt the Temple, which again was destroyed, this time by the Romans in 70 C.E., and not rebuilt again. The golden Dome of the Rock was built on the site by the Muslims in the year 691 C.E., and it has stood there ever since.

But we are getting ahead of the story. At this juncture in time, the Jewish people have experienced a national revelation. They've been given the Torah and built the sanctuary for God to dwell among them. Now they are ready to enter the Promised Land.

13.

THE TRAGEDY OF THE SPIES

After a year at Mount Sinai, the Jewish people packed up their portable sanctuary and came to the borders of the Land of Israel. They should have entered the land at this point, but instead, they selected twelve "scouts" or "spies" — one from each of the twelve tribes — and sent them in to do some reconnaissance work.

We have to spend a little time talking about the tragedy of the spies, because the implication of this event is going to reverberate throughout all of Jewish history. It happened on the ninth of Av — Tishah B'Av — which will become the most depressing date of the Jewish calendar. Virtually every major disaster in Jewish history is going to be connected to this date, including the destruction of both the First and Second Temples.

THE NINTH OF AV

YEAR	HEBREW DATE	EVENT
1312 B.C.E.	9th of Av, 2449	Israelites send out spies and hearing their report decide not to enter the Promised Land; as punishment for their lack of trust in God, they must wander the desert for 40 years
422 B.C.E.	9th of Av, 3338	First Temple destroyed by the Babylonians
70 C.E.	9th of Av, 3830	Second Temple destroyed by the Romans
135 C.E.	9th of Av, 3895	Bar Kohba revolt crushed by the Romans
1096 C.E.	9th of Av, 4856	First Crusade launched
1290 C.E.	9th of Av, 5050	Jews expelled from England
1492 C.E.	9th of Av, 5252	Jews expelled from Spain
1914 C.E.	9th of Av, 5674	World War I, prelude to the Holocaust, begins
1942 C.E.	9th of Av, 5701	Deportations from Warsaw Ghetto
1994 C.E.	9th of Av, 5754	Bombing of Jews in Buenos Aires

Again, actions of the Jews have huge consequences that reverberate through the ages. Jews have suffered throughout history because of that mistake they made "back then." So what was the terrible mistake of the spies?

These twelve spies spend forty days scouting out the land and they come back with a huge cluster of grapes and the following report: "We came to the land where you sent us, and it is indeed flowing with milk and honey, as you can see from its fruit. However, the people living in the land are aggressive, and the cities are large and well fortified...."

At this point, Caleb ben Yefuna, one of the spies, declared, "We must go forth and occupy the land," but the others shouted him down:

> They are too strong for us.... The land that we crossed to explore is a land that consumes its inhabitants. All the men we saw there were huge. While we were there, we saw giants.... We felt like tiny grasshoppers. That's all we were in their eyes.[107]

Besides Caleb, only Joshua ben Nun, who was Moses' chief student, dissented. But the Jewish people accepted the majority report of the spies, which went something like this: "We can't go into the Promised Land. It's a wonderful place all right, but if you are impressed by the size of the grapes, you should see the size of some of the people who eat them. No way we can beat them. We may as well go back to Egypt."

The people broke down in tears at this news and refused to budge, no matter what Caleb and Joshua said.[108]

Moses was absolutely horrified, and God was very angry. He issued two decrees of punishment: Because they displayed lack of faith after He had brought them so far, they would be doomed to wander in the desert for forty years — one year for every day they spied out the land — until the entire adult male population (except for the Levites who did not listen to the spies) had died off. The women, who always carried the standard of faith in Judaism, also didn't listen to the spies and would live to go into the land.

Because they cried on this day for no good reason, they would cry on this day in history for some very good reasons.

Death of Moses

So, they wandered for forty years.

It's interesting to note that virtually none of the text of the Bible deals with the details of their wandering. If you examine the Book of Numbers, you will notice that between chapter 18 and chapter 19 there is a gap of thirty-eight years. The only brief mention of the travels that took place during those thirty-eight years comes at the very end, in chapter 33.

Since the Bible was meant to be an instruction book and not a diary or chronicle, only events that communicate relevant lessons for future generations are recorded — other events are mentioned only briefly, or skipped altogether.

Near the end of the forty years of wandering, a traumatic event occurs which is related in detail.

The Bible states that the Jews found themselves (yet again) temporarily without water. As they did a number of times before, they complained about the situation, and God told Moses to speak to the rock, promising that water would flow.

For forty years Moses had had the hardest job on planet Earth, leading a stubborn group of people God Himself described as "stiff-necked." We've talked about the Jewish people's greatest strength and greatest weakness. What has been their greatest strength? Their stubborn dedication to an idea, which enabled them to exist for thousands of years as the only monotheists in the world and outlast the greatest empires in history. What has been their greatest weakness? Their stubborn dedication to an idea makes every Jew think he's right and every Jew think that he's going to change the world his way. This is a group that is incredibly difficult to unify and almost impossible to lead.[109]

(It is far easier to be the leader of a billion Chinese than the leader of a few million Jews. A humorous story illustrating this point is told about a meeting between former U.S. President Harry Truman and the future Prime Minister of Israel, Golda Meir. Truman was bemoaning the difficulties of leadership and remarked, "You have no idea what it is to be a president of a country of 200 million people." To which Meir responded, "You have no idea of what is to be a prime minister of a country of two million prime ministers.")

So after so many years of trying to lead this stubborn nation, Moses lost his temper for one moment. "You rebels!" he shouted. And instead of speaking to the rock as he was commanded to do, he struck it.

And then God said to Moses and to Aharon, "Because you did not believe in Me to sanctify Me in the eyes of the Children of Israel, you're not going to go into the Land of Israel with the Jewish people."[110]

The sages say that anger is a form of idolatry,[111] because if God runs the world, then everything that happens to you, whether for bad or for good, is the will of God. Losing your temper is a form of denial that God is running the world, a rejection of the idea that whatever happens is for your own good.

For Moses — the ultimate prophet to whom God spoke face-to-face — to get angry even for a few seconds, the consequences had to be awesome. And especially since it was done publicly, in front of the people.

This shows just how accountable people on such high levels are for any mistakes they make and the repercussions of those mistakes. We will see this over and over again throughout the Bible.

Moses, of course, saw his error right away and accepted God's judgment.

The Finale

Deuteronomy, the last of the Five Books of Moses, is his farewell address to the people, as he prepares them for entry into the Promised Land. He reviews the commandments and reiterates the Jewish national mission. The most common idea he repeats over and over again is: "Keep the Torah."

In a nutshell, Moses is saying here, "If you keep the laws between 'man and God' and between 'man and man,' everything will go fine for you. No other nation will touch you. You'll have material prosperity, and you will live to change the world. But if you don't keep the Torah, if you break your end of the bargain, then the land will vomit you out, your enemies will attack, and you will suffer."

The message is clear. The solution to all Jewish problems has nothing to do with external threats — external threats are merely symptoms of the deeper problem, which is always the Jews not keeping their side of the bargain. It always has to do with their relationship to each other and their relationship to God.

The late nineteenth and twentieth centuries were the first time in Jewish history when large numbers of Jews left God (by choice and not by force). And then they were left wondering, "Where is God?"

World War I broke out on the ninth of Av. The Germans swept into Eastern Europe beginning in 1914, uprooted Jewish communities and demolished centuries of tradition. It was the precursor of the horror to come — the Holocaust.

A Holocaust survivor writes:

> The quintessential element that distinguished this event [the Holocaust] was the search for God. Every Jew who remained in the ghettos and the camps remembers "the God Syndrome" that shrouded everything else. From morning till night we cried out for a sign that God was still with us.... We sought Him, but we did not find Him. We were always accompanied by the crushing and unsettling feeling that God had disappeared from our midst.[112]

Throughout the rest of history, Jews have viewed their worst problems — even such horrors as the mass slaugher of their people during the Crusades — as divine retribution for their mistakes. You would rarely find Jews before the twentieth century saying "Where is God?" They were almost always saying, "It's because of our wrongdoings that this has happened to us."

Prior to his death, Moses completed the writing of the Torah. He wrote out twelve scrolls, which were given out to each of the twelve tribes, and a thirteenth, which was placed in the Ark of the Covenant and eventually deposited in the Holy of Holies in the Temple. This last scroll served as the proof text for future scrolls to ensure the accuracy of transmission of the Torah.[113]

Having delivered his final message, Moses died and was buried on Mount Nebo somewhere in the mountains of Jordan. We are deliberately not told where it is, so nobody will worship at his grave over there.

Judaism is a meritocracy. Real leadership in Jewish history goes not to those who were born into the right families, but to those best suited for the job. So the job of the successor did not go to either of Moses' sons but to Joshua bin Nun, Moses' chief disciple who had proven his mettle in the incident with the spies.

He would be assisted (as was Moses) by a supreme legislative body of the seventy top Torah scholars known as the Elders (later known as the Sanhedrin, which means "council" in Greek). These, too, were chosen on the merit of their scholarship and integrity, thus creating history's first meritocracy.[114]

At this point in our story we have finished with the patterns of Jewish history seen in the Five Books of Moses and will now enter the next phase of Jewish history (and the next section of the Bible), which takes place in the Land of Israel.

Part II

IN THE LAND FLOWING WITH MILK AND HONEY

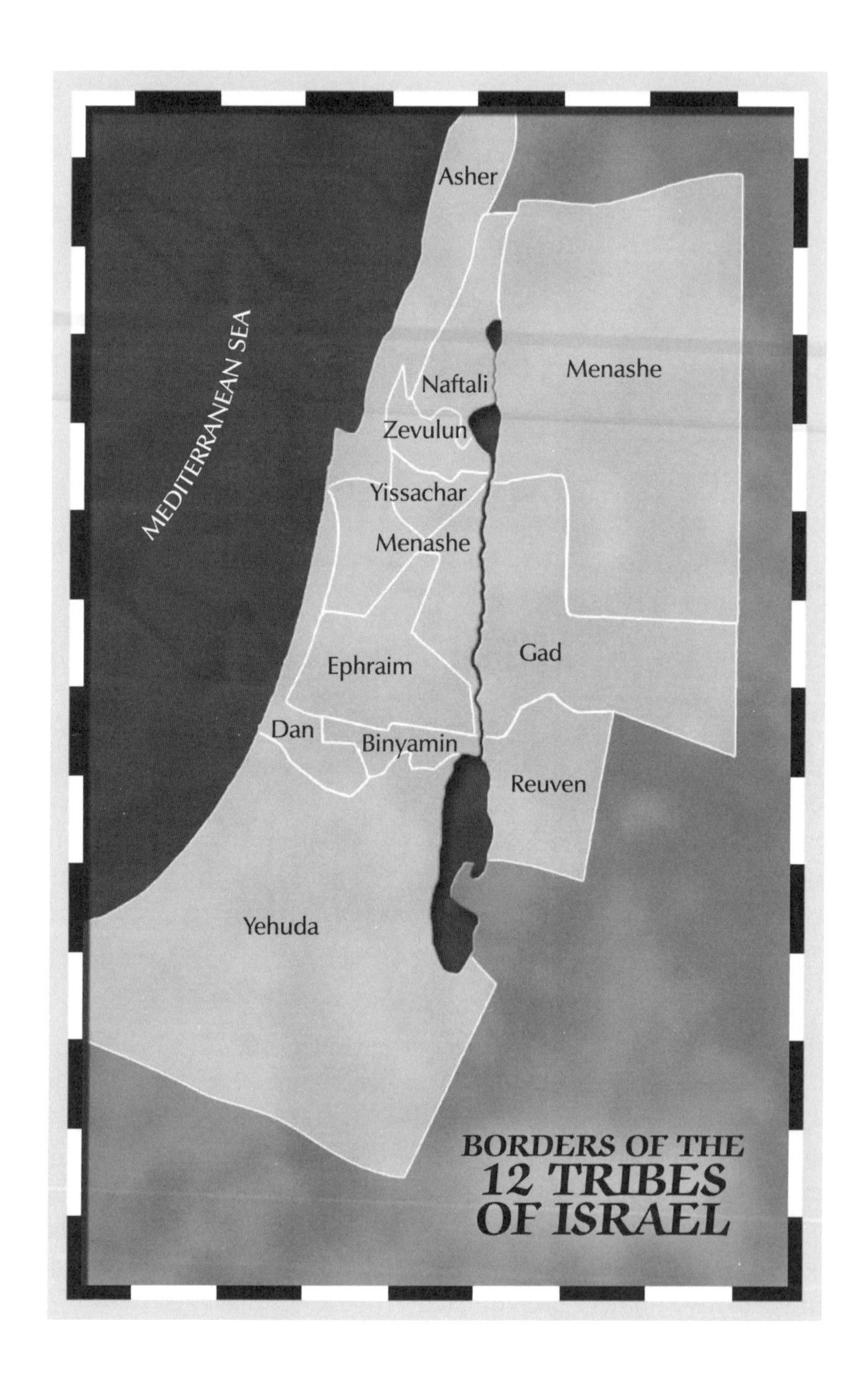
Asher
MEDITERRANEAN SEA
Naftali
Menashe
Zevulun
Yissachar
Menashe
Gad
Ephraim
Dan
Binyamin
Reuven
Yehuda
BORDERS OF THE
12 TRIBES
OF ISRAEL

14.
THE CONQUEST OF CANAAN

The Book of Joshua begins:

> And it was after the death of Moses, the servant of God, that God spoke to Joshua, the son of Nun, Moses' minister, saying: Moses My servant has died, so now arise and cross the River Jordan. You and all this nation go to the land which I give to the Children of Israel. Every place on which the soles of your feet will tread I have given to you, as I have spoken to Moses.... No man shall stand up to you all the days of your life. As I was with Moses, so shall I be with you. I will not weaken my grasp on you nor will I abandon you. Be strong and courageous for it is you who will cause this people to inherit the land that I have sworn to their fathers to give them.[115]

Joshua was one of the great leaders of Jewish history. The Talmud says of him: "The face of Moses was like the face of the sun, while the face of Joshua was like the face of the moon."[116] This is understood to mean that the greatness of Joshua was a reflection of his teacher, Moses, which is a tremendous compliment. But it also tells us that just as the sun is much greater than the moon, which only reflects sunlight, so too, there was a huge difference in the influence they wielded. Had Moses lived to enter the land, all of Jewish history and all of human history would have been different.

After the death of Moses, Joshua led the Jewish people for twenty-eight years,[117] the first fourteen of which are described in the Book of Joshua — seven years of conquest and seven years of settlement.

When Joshua first brought the Jews across the River Jordan into the Promised

Land, this tract of land known as Canaan had no single ruler. It was bounded by the Egyptian Empire in the south, and the Mesopotamian Empire in the north, but not claimed by either of them. Instead, it was occupied by seven Canaanite tribes whose members inhabited thirty-one fortified city states scattered all over the map, each ruled by its own "king." (Jericho was one of these city-states, as was Ai and also Jerusalem, where Canaanite tribesmen called Jebusites dwelled.)

Before they entered the land, the Jewish people sent an envoy to the Canaanites with the message, "God, the Creator of the Universe, has promised this land to our forefathers. We are now here to claim our inheritance, and we ask you to leave peacefully."

Needless to say most of the Canaanites laughed; only one tribe paid attention, packed up, and left.[118]

Meanwhile, Joshua had clear instructions from God that if the Canaanites don't leave, they should be wiped out, because they would corrupt the Jews with their idolatrous ways. God made it clear that the Canaanites were extremely immoral and could not be tolerated as neighbors.

It is well known today that living in a bad, gang-infested neighborhood destroys kids. You always have to be careful about outside influences. And this is exactly what happened here, as we shall see.

The Battle of Jericho

The Jews crossed the Jordan River, which stopped flowing to permit the crossing, entered the land, and fought a series of battles. The first was the battle of Jericho, located at the entrance to the heartland of Canaan. They circled the city walls blowing the ram's horn and the walls crumbled before their eyes.

Some archaeologists have suggested that the easy conquest of this heavily-fortified city was made possible by a well-timed earthquake. But isn't it remarkable that precisely when the Jewish people needed the city to fall, there was a natural disaster that demolished their enemies? No matter how you explain it, it was still miraculous.

They conquered the city, taking no booty as commanded by God, which makes it clear that this was not the typical type of conquest with bloody warfare, rape, and pillage, such as we read about in secular history. God had said, "Nothing like that here. And, if you follow My instructions, all will go well."

After the easy-as-pie conquest of Jericho, they moved onto the next city-state, a place called Ai. But here things didn't go so smoothly. In fact, they met with a terrible defeat, with many killed. Traumatized by this experience, they pleaded to know why God had abandoned them and quickly learned the terrible truth — that one person, Achan, had stolen some items back in Jericho. One person out of three million didn't listen to God and everyone had to suffer!

The fascinating thing here is that the Bible seems to be saying that obedience to God's commands is paramount, and that as far as the Jews are concerned, it is all for one and one for all. Every Jew is a guarantor for his or her fellow Jew.

As an outgrowth of that lesson, Judaism teaches that there is such a thing as collective responsibility as well as individual responsibility — no person is an island; each exists as part of the whole and is responsible for the actions of others as well as his or her own.

In today's world, the motto seems to be "Mind your own business," or "It's not my problem." If people operated today according to this standard, most of the world's problems would disappear.

Life in the Land

After most of the land was conquered — with some notable exceptions, such as Jerusalem — it was divided into separate tribal portions via a divinely guided lottery.

But life in the land was far from calm, particularly after the death of Joshua. The Bible relates that they had only themselves to blame:

> And the children of Israel did that which was evil in the eyes of God... and the anger of God was kindled against Israel and He delivered them into the hands of plunderers...and He gave them over into the hands of their enemies.[119]

From a simple reading of the text, one might assume that the entire Jewish people abandoned the Torah and started worshipping idols. But this, in fact, was not true. As with the incident of the Golden Calf, only a small percentage of the people sinned, yet the entire nation was held accountable.

As mentioned previously, the hypercritical nature of this passage is typical of others which makes the Bible a unique document — a holy book of a people, but also a chronicle of the sinful history of this people. The exaggerated focus on the mistakes — and the self-criticism within the text — gives added emphasis to the lessons that the Jewish people must learn from their sins.

In addition, there are good reasons why the slightest offense by a small group of people is condemned so strongly:

First, every Jew is responsible for every other Jew, and what one does reflects on all. Second, it's such an obvious point in the moral history of the world that as soon as people begin to tolerate something, it becomes bearable, and before long it will become common and acceptable. Therefore, here God is driving home an important point to the Jews: You're on a very high spiritual level. If you tolerate even small indiscretions by a few, eventually these few are going to pollute the nation, as is seen in the "Time of Judges."

15.
THE TIME OF THE JUDGES

The Talmud calls the Book of Judges the "Book of the Straight."[120] Why?

Because the ultimate goal of every Jew is to use his or her free will to work out what is wrong and right, using the Torah as a guide, and this is what happened in the time of Judges:

> In those days, there was no king in Israel, everyone did what was right in his eyes.[121]

You might think that this verse sounds like a description of anarchy. But there was no anarchy; the vast majority of Jews were totally dedicated to Torah, were making proper decisions and didn't need someone tell them what to do. The tribes functioned as a loose confederation of states, with strong central leadership arising only when the nation was threatened by an external enemy.

Of course, the lack of central authority following the death of Joshua did have negative consequences — a small minority took it as a license to slip into idolatry and immorality. This happened largely because the Jews did not get rid of all of the Canaanites, as they were commanded to do, deciding to tax some of the people they subjugated.[122] Little by little the Canaanite pagan influence was felt: "And they forsook the Lord, the God of their fathers, and they went after other gods."[123]

Whenever the Jews abandon God, the repercussions are immediate.

This is one of the most important and oft-repeated patterns in Jewish history. When the Jews betray their covenant with God — be it worshipping idols or failing to love their neighbor — bad things happen. Usually, an enemy comes and attacks.

God says over and over again — keep the Torah, all facets of it, and no one will bother you. You will live in peace in your land. You will prosper, and not only that, the whole world will come to learn from you, and you will be a light to the nations.

But if you don't, a big fist will not come out of heaven and swat you, because God acts within history. What will happen instead is a physical enemy will appear, or a famine will hit the land, and all will suffer. These negative events will serve as a wake-up call and will only intensify if ignored, until they reach the level where they are impossible to ignore.

Repercussions

From Mount Sinai onward the Jewish people were always aware of their covenant with God, the responsibilities it entailed, and the consequences of not adhering to their side of the bargain. Because of this awareness, any calamities were always viewed as symptoms of deeper problems in the Jewish people's relationship with each other and/or with God.

When bad things happen to Jews, it is never by chance. It is always a consequence of Jewish actions, and therefore, the remedy is never to deal solely with the external threat. If an enemy attacks, defense is in order, but so is introspection; the presence of an enemy is only a symptom of a deeper problem that must be dealt with. This cause-and-effect relationship repeats itself over and over again throughout the time of the Judges and continues throughout Jewish history until today.

The time of the Judges extended from 1242 B.C.E. to 879 B.C.E. During this period, "God raised up Judges, and they saved them [the Jews] from the hands of those who had oppressed them."[124] Who were these Judges?

The Judges were various Jewish leaders who arose during this time, unified the people, got them to repent, dealt with the spiritual problems of the nation, and also dealt with the physical threat. While many were great military leaders who knew how to mobilize the nation for war against an enemy, their real power lay in their Torah knowledge and their ability to adjudicate Jewish law.

The narrative for this period appears chiefly in the Book of Judges, authored by the last great personality in the time of the Judges — Samuel the prophet. During this time there were sixteen different judges. Some led the Jewish people for decades while others only for a few years. The Book of Judges goes into great detail for some of the Judges (for example, Deborah, Gideon, and Samson) while others get only the briefest mention (Ibzan, Elon, Abdon).

CHRONOLOGY FROM JOSHUA TO SAMUEL

JUDGE	LENGTH OF RULE	FOUND IN BOOK OF
Joshua	28 years	Joshua
Othniel	40 years	Judges 3:7–11
Ehud	80 years	Judges 3:12–29
Shamgar	½ year	Judges 3:31
Deborah	40 years	Judges ch. 4–5
Gideon	40 years	Judges ch. 6–8
Abimelech	3 years	Judges 9
Tola	23 years	Judges 10:1–2
Jair	22 years	Judges 10:3–5
Jephthah	6 years	Judges 11–12:1–7
Ibzan	6 years	Judges 12:8–10
Elon	10 years	Judges 12:11–12
Abdon	8 years	Judges 12:13–15
Samson	20 years	Judges ch. 13–16
Eli	39 years	1 Samuel ch. 1–4
Samuel	11–13 years	1 Samuel ch. 1–8

While all were great leaders, some were greater than others. Tradition tells us that the level of any given Judge depended on the collective level of the Jewish people. Every generation got the leadership it deserved. We will look at some of the most famous ones.

Deborah

As it does with the other Judges, the story of the Deborah,[125] who was both a prophetess and judge, begins with an assessment of the spiritual state of the Jewish people:

> The Children of Israel continued to do what was evil in the eyes of God.... So God gave them into the hands of Jabin, King of Canaan, who ruled in Hazor. His general was Sisera.... The Children of Israel cried

> out to God for he [Jabin] had 900 iron chariots, and he oppressed the Children of Israel harshly for twenty years.[126]

However, God heard the cry of the Jews and made victory possible through the guidance of Deborah.

She was famous for sitting under a palm tree where anyone could seek her advice, and from where she issued battle orders. Barak, Israel's top warrior during that time, refused to go into battle without her. Together they led the troops against the much larger Canaanite force backed up by iron chariots, of which Israel had none.

The Book of Judges describes a key battle with the Canaanites led by Sisera. On the eve of the battle, Barak was doubtful that Israel's warriors could ever beat such a strong opponent, but Deborah stood firm. An unexpected storm was unleashed in the heavens, and the resulting downpour turned the ground to mud; the heavy iron chariots got stuck and the Canaanites panicked.

Deborah's prophecy that "This is the day on which God will deliver Sisera into your hands..." was thus fulfilled.

Gideon

The story of Gideon[127] has a similar-sounding beginning:

> The Children of Israel did what was evil in the eyes of God, and God gave them into the hands of Midian for seven years. The hand of Midian was harsh on Israel...if Israel would plant, Midian and Amalek and the people of the east would come up upon it. They came upon them and destroyed the produce of the land as far as Gaza...Israel became very poor because of Midian, and the Children of Israel cried out to God.[128]

Gideon was a farmer, and one day as he was threshing wheat, an angel appeared to him telling him that God wanted him to rescue Israel from its oppressors. Gideon at first demurred, but was persuaded that this was his mission.

His first order of business was to destroy a local altar to the idol Baal. After that he mobilized a force of 32,000 men, but this was a weak force compared to 135,000 troops amassed by the enemy. However, God told him that he had too many soldiers and he should send some of them home, because God wanted to make a point:

> The people that are with you are too numerous for Me to give Midian

> into their hands, lest Israel glorify themselves above Me, saying, "My own hand saved me."[129]

Gideon asked all those who were afraid to leave — immediately 22,000 packed up. Still too many, said God, advising Gideon to devise a test as to which of the remaining men were worthy of going to battle. As part of the test, the soldiers were taken to water — those who knelt down to drink water were eliminated. Thus Gideon was left with 300 men. And, though outnumbered 450 to 1, he easily won the battle.

After the victory, there was peace for forty years. But....

> When Gideon died, the Children of Israel again went astray.... [And they] did not remember the Lord, their God, who had saved them from the hands of all their enemies all around.[130]

Samson

So another chapter begins:

> The Children of Israel continued to do what was evil in the eyes of God, and God gave them over into the hands of the Philistines for forty years....[131]

This time the hero is Samson. Samson was the judge famous for his super-hero strength, and for leading the struggle against Israel's archenemy, the Philistines.[132]

The Philistines were a seafaring people who probably migrated from the area of the Aegean near Greece about 3,200 years ago. They settled along the eastern Mediterranean Coast from southern Israel to Lebanon. In the southern coastal area of Israel they established a confederation of five city-states (Gaza, Ashkelon, Ashdod, Gat, and Ekron). During the period of the Judges, they were constantly at war with the tribes of Israel, pushing them away from the sea and into the hilly, inland regions of the country.

Excavations show that the Philistines — despite what the word "Philistine" now means in the English language — were very sophisticated culturally. They had perfected iron tools and iron weapons, gaining an important technological advantage over their neighbors. Samson, who judged Israel for twenty years, was one of the people who dared to take on the Philistines.

Samson was a *nazir*. Generally, a *nazir* is an ascetic who for a set period of time refrains from cutting his hair and abstains from wine as part of his penitence. But Samson's *nazir* status was unusual in that he was a *nazir* from birth and remained one his entire life. In addition, his status gave him superhuman strength.

To undermine the Philistines, Samson pretended to join them by deliberately taking a Philistine woman as his wife. She was killed by her own people, and he then married another Philistine woman (who had first converted) — Delilah. This proved to be a mistake.

Delilah realized that Samson was a major threat to her people. After many failed attempts and much pleading, she finally succeeded in getting Samson to reveal the secret of his superhuman strength, and while he was asleep she cut off his hair. As a result, the Philistines were able to capture him. They then blinded him and threw him in prison.

Finally, the Philistines decided to execute Samson in a public display at the temple of Dagan, one of their gods. As the masses gathered to watch the execution, blind Samson asked a slave boy to position him next to the columns supporting the temple. It is a climactic moment in the narrative:

> Samson called to God and said, "My Lord and Master! Remember me and strengthen me just this one time, O God, and I will extract vengeance from the Philistines for one of my two eyes." Samson grasped the two central pillars upon which the building rested, and he leaned on them; one with his right hand and one with his left hand. Samson said, "Let my soul die with the Philistines!"[133]

With his renewed superhuman strength he overturned the columns and collapsed the building, killing all inside.

He died giving his life for the Jewish people, and the Bible says he killed more Philistine enemies in that moment than he had vanquished during the rest of his life.

Samuel

The last great personality of the period of the Judges is the prophet Samuel, who is one of the most important prophets in Jewish history, and who is also famous for anointing the first two kings of Israel — Saul and David.[134] He authored the Book of Judges and, together with the prophets Gad and Nathan, the Book of Samuel as well.

By the time Samuel appeared on the scene, almost 400 years had passed without strong central leadership. During this time, the Jewish people had to live up to a very high level of individual responsibility or else God would let them know they were off course via the Canaanites, or the Philistines, or the Midianites. This was a very difficult way to live. In the final analysis, they could not maintain this level of self-scrutiny without stronger guidance.

When Samuel was younger, he would travel the land adjudicating Jewish law and giving people advice, but when he had grown old, he couldn't do it anymore. Meanwhile, his two sons, who had taken over for him, proved unpopular with the people. So a delegation was dispatched to ask Samuel to anoint a king instead:

> And they said, "Behold, you have grown old and your sons do not walk in your ways. Now set up for us a king to judge us like all the nations. And the thing was displeasing in the eyes of Samuel...."[135]

Samuel was not happy about this request, but God told him to go ahead and find a king for the people. Even so, it is clear that God acceded reluctantly: "Listen to the voice of the people according to all that they say to you, for they have not rejected you but they have rejected Me from reigning over them."[136]

Why are Samuel and God displeased, especially since Moses had predicted this turn of events,[137] and there is even a Torah commandment to do appoint a king? The answer lies in the way the people asked: And they said [to Samuel]: "Now set up for us a king to judge us *like all the nations....*"[138]

A Jewish king was not supposed to be *like* the kings of other nations. A Jewish king was supposed to be a model of an ideal Jew — a model for the rest of his nation to emulate.

To ask for a king "like the rest" suggests that the Jews wanted a strong ruler like other nations had — an all-powerful leader who would make all the decisions so that they could sit back and throw off the heavy burden of responsibility that they had to deal with on a day-to-day basis. It's much easier in many respects to have someone decide for you, which is why the Talmud says that "a slave is happier being a slave."[139] A slave who is well treated will give up his freedom in exchange for being taken care of and having his decisions made for him.

The Jewish monarchy, as described in the Bible, was meant to be a unique institution. A Jewish king was meant to have real power and tremendous responsibility, but he could never be a tyrant or a dictator. He was to be a model for the rest of the nation to emulate: a leader, a scholar, pious, righteous, and God-fearing. He was meant to act as a catalyst to enable the Jewish people to fulfill their national historic mission as a light to the nations.[140] As spelled out in the Book of Deuteronomy:

> Only he [the king] shall not have too many horses for himself...and he shall not have too many wives...and he shall not greatly increase silver and gold for himself.... It shall be that when he sits on the throne of his kingdom, he shall write for himself two copies of this Torah.... It shall be with him, and he shall read from it all the days of his life, so that he will learn to fear the Lord his God to keep all the words of the Torah...so that his heart does not become haughty over his brethren.[141]

We are about to see how the Jewish kings measured up to the standard God set for them.

16.
KING SAUL

In the year 879 B.C.E., 393 years after the Jewish people first entered the Land of Israel, Saul was anointed as the first king by the prophet Samuel, in accordance with the wishes of the people.

The story of Saul's anointment tells us much about the functioning of Jewish society at this time. For one thing, there were many prophets around. So many, in fact, that the Talmud estimates that from the time of Moses to the destruction of the First Temple, there were over a million prophets.[142] The people turned to them for everything. You have a profound question? Ask a prophet. You needed advice on marriage? Ask a prophet. You've lost your donkey? Ask a prophet.

The Bible itself mentions that prophets were originally called seers (*ro'eh* in Hebrew) precisely because their higher spiritual level enabled them to see things that others couldn't, including lost objects.[143]

Indeed, this is how Saul and the prophet Samuel met. The seer that Saul encounters while searching for his donkeys happened to be the Judge of Israel and the greatest prophet of his generation.

It's an odd story. A man goes to the greatest prophet alive and asks, "Where are my donkeys?" The prophet answers, "Don't worry, your donkeys have been found, and by the way, you're king of Israel."

To seal the deal, Samuel took out a flask of oil and poured some on Saul's head. The oil he used was comprised of a special mixture of olive oil and spices.[144] This special oil was used by Moses to anoint and consecrate the sanctuary and its vessels, as well as Aharon and his sons, the *kohanim*, for priestly service in the *Mishkan*. From the reign of King Saul until the destruction of the First Temple, it was used by prophets to anoint the kings of Israel. The prophets' use of this special anointing oil designated an object or individual as chosen by God for a special purpose.

When Saul returned home, he did not tell his family what happened, and when Samuel gathered the nation to announce that Saul had been chosen as king, Saul hid in embarrassment. Some people mocked his actions, calling him unsuitable for kingship, yet in face of such outright disrespect, Saul remained silent.

The Talmud is very clear that Saul was not only head and shoulders above everyone physically, he was head and shoulders above everyone morally and ethically. He was an exemplary human being, but he had one weakness — his sense of humility interfered with his duty as king. It was good that Saul had no desire for honor or power, but true leadership requires the leader to take the initiative and distinguish between honor due him and the honor due his position.[145]

As great as Saul was, his innate modesty and humility inhibited his ability to properly lead the Jewish people. To lead the Jews requires a unique combination of iron will and diplomacy — as we saw with the difficulties Moses faced in the wilderness. If the leader is not strong enough, they will walk all over him, but if he's too aggressive or tries to bully them, they'll rebel. The problem of flawed leadership is something that will plague the Jewish people throughout history, as will become glaringly apparent.

When the Ammonites invaded the Land of Israel, Saul finally rose to the occasion and accepted the kingship. He went on to lead the nation in a series of victories against the enemy and thus established his authority as king.

However, Saul's reign lasted only two years, and he died a tragic death. Indeed, his brief reign was itself flawed and tragic.

His misplaced modesty at the beginning of his kingship caused him to make a fatal mistake: He disobeyed the commandment of God to wipe out the nation of Amalek.

Amalek Redux

One of the key commandments that the Jewish people were given upon entering the Land of Israel was "to wipe out Amalek."

As was explained in chapter 6, the nation of Amalek has been the ultimate enemy of the Jews in history. This is a people that symbolize evil, and there is a commandment in the Bible to wipe them off the face of the earth, because their pathological hatred of the Jews is so great that, if they have a chance, they will try to wipe the Jews off the face of the earth.

Amalek's major ambition was to rid the world of the Jews and their moral influence and return the planet to idolatry, paganism, and barbarism.

Since this is a cosmic war between good and evil which cannot be settled with treaties, God commanded the Jews to destroy Amalek — the entire nation, down to the last cow.[146]

Saul had the opportunity to do so. He waged war against Amalek as commanded and won, but when it came to fulfilling the decree, he faltered. Oddly, he killed everyone, but spared some of the cows, and worst of all, through misplaced mercy, he also spared Agag, the king of the Amalekites. Thus, the Amalekite nation survived, because Agag lived long enough to father a child before he was killed by the prophet Samuel.

To this day, history continues to struggle with the consequences of Saul's mistake.

Although we have no way of identifying the descendants of Amalek since they have been mixed in among the nations, we do know that the Amalekite ideology lives on. There has been more than one occasion when people have arisen bent on exterminating the Jews. The Bible itself mentions that the battle with Amalek represents the ultimate struggle in history between good and evil, with total victory achieved only at the End of Days.

> God said to Moses, "Write this as a reminder in the book and repeat it carefully to Joshua. I will totally obliterate the memory of Amalek from under the heavens." Moses built an altar, and he named it *Hashem Nissi* ("God is my banner"). He said..."God shall be at war with Amalek for all generations."[147]

One example of Amalek was Haman (a descendant of Agag) who, while wielding power as a Persian minister, tried to annihilate the Jews in the time of Queen Esther (355 B.C.E.), giving rise to the Jewish holiday of Purim.

And Hitler certainly espoused Amalekite ideology:

> Yes, we are barbarians! We want to be barbarians. It is an honorable title to us.... Providence has ordained that I should be the greatest liberator of humanity. I free man from...the degrading self-mortification of a false vision called conscience and morality.... Conscience is a Jewish invention.[148]

Looking at Hitler and the Holocaust, we can understand that such intense hatred as the Bible ascribes to Amalek can exist in the world. The Nazis wanted to kill every Jew. A Jew could have been assimilated, intermarried with Christians for three generations, but that didn't matter; the Nazis were bent on killing anyone with the slightest bit of Jewish heritage — they were bent on wiping out any trace of the Jewish people and Jewish influence.

The End of Saul

Saul's failure to obey God's command and wipe out Amalek earned him severe rebuke from the prophet Samuel:

> God sent you on the way, and He said, "Go, destroy the sinner Amalek and wage war with him until you have exterminated him." Why did you not obey the voice of God? You rushed after the spoils, and you did what was evil in the eyes of God.[149]

And then the prophet Samuel delivered God's verdict:

> "I shall not return to you for you have rejected the word of God and God has rejected you as king over Israel." And Samuel turned to go and he [Saul] seized the hem of his robe and it tore. And Samuel said to him, "God has torn the kingdom of Israel from you today and has given it your fellow who is better than you."[150]

With this critical mistake, Saul was finished. He didn't get a second chance. God doesn't mess around when it comes to the kings of Israel.

If this seems harsh, we must keep in mind the guiding principles of the relationship between God and the Jewish people which we have spelled out in chapters 12 and 14:

According to your level of knowledge is your level of responsibility. According to your level of responsibility is your level of accountability. The mistakes of people in positions of power have huge consequences; the greater they are, the bigger the impact of their decisions; therefore, they must be held to an extremely high standard. As we saw previously, with Moses hitting the rock, even the smallest mistakes of great Jewish leaders are severely punished.

Although Saul was finished as king, he was not immediately deposed; he understood, however, that his line would not carry on the monarchy. Meanwhile, following this declaration to Saul, Samuel went out looking for another king to anoint, and he found him in the most unlikely place.

17.
DAVID: THE SHEPHERD, THE WARRIOR

One sunny day, the prophet Samuel arrived in the town of Beit Lechem (today's Bethlehem) to pay a call on a man named Jesse, among whose sons God had told him the next king would be found.

Obligingly, Jesse presented six of his sons, and Samuel saw that all were amazing men — physically fit, well-educated in Jewish law, dedicated to God. But they were not good enough.

The Bible relates that as Samuel was admiring one of Jesse's sons, he got a message from God: "Do not look at his face and at his tall stature, for I have rejected him. For it is not as man perceives; a man sees what is visible to the eyes, but God sees into the heart."[151]

So Samuel asked Jesse: "Don't you have any more sons?" A little flustered, Jesse responded: "Well, there is still the little one, but he is out tending sheep."

The "little one" was David.

Samuel demanded that Jesse summon him and as soon as redheaded David appeared, Samuel knew he was the one. Despite the fact that he was not physically impressive, he had the necessary qualities to be the strong leader that Israel needed.

This teaches us a very important lesson about how we should judge people. In contrast to the superficial world we live in, where people are judged by their looks (which is why plastic surgery and looking eternally young is such a big thing), the Bible says that true greatness is not measured by outward appearance; true greatness resides in the soul.

Samuel took a flask of oil, poured it on David's head and "anointed" him — in Hebrew *mashach*, which is where the word *Mashiach* or Messiah (literally, "anointed one") comes from. When Samuel anointed David, this did not mean that David instantly became king. It just meant that he had been designated by God as next in line.

Meanwhile, Saul continued to reign, not knowing what had happened, although previously he had been told by Samuel that his days were numbered.

The Bible relates that the moment David was anointed, "the spirit of God left Saul," and he fell into a deep depression. To help relieve his angst, his advisors decided to bring in a harp player, reasoning music would make the king feel better. And this is how David, still the shepherd, was brought to the palace — he played the harp beautifully and his playing lightened Saul's dark moods, though the king was unaware that this youth would soon replace him.

David and Goliath

During this time Israel was constantly at war with the Philistines (as we saw in chapter 15).

We know that ancient warfare was highly ritualized. In Homer's *Iliad*, we read how battles were conducted in ancient times in the epic story of the siege of Troy.[152] Each side would send out its great champion, who would fight on behalf of his people. Often the battle would end with that encounter, because whichever champion won, the other side would be so demoralized it would retreat.

This was the same situation at this time in Jewish history — the Philistines had a champion who was an awesome guy. His name was Goliath and he was huge. (In the world of wrestling there used to be a guy by the name of Andre the Giant. He was 7' 5" and weighed 450 lbs. He used to wrestle three opponents at the same time. Goliath was even bigger.)

The problem was that the Jewish forces had no champion at all.

The Jewish forces were stationed just south of Jerusalem, on one side of the Elah Valley — a place you can visit today in Israel — and the Philistines were on the other. Goliath was marching in front of the Philistine lines, shouting curses at the Jews and challenging someone to come and fight him:

> "Choose yourself a man and let him come down to me! If he can fight me and kill me, we will be slaves to you; if I defeat him and kill him, you

will be slaves to us and serve us."[153]

The mortified Israelite army had to listen daily to these taunts, because no one was willing to take on Goliath.

One day, David — who was still a shepherd and sometime musician, but not a soldier — arrived at the battlefield, bringing food for his brothers and he was shocked by what he saw. Outraged at Goliath's insults to the warriors of Israel, David volunteered to go out and fight, though he had a hard time convincing everybody to let him do it. Finally, he convinced King Saul with his steadfast faith in God:

> And David said: God who saved me from the claws of the lion and the claws of the bear, He will save me from the hands of the Philistine.[154]

To that Saul answered: Go, and may God be with you.

David went out to meet Goliath without even a sword, armed only with his slingshot, a few stones, and his deep, abiding faith in God. Seeing him, Goliath burst out in laughter: "Am I a dog that you come to me with sticks?" But David was undisturbed:

> "You come towards me with a sword, a spear, and a javelin, but I come to you with the name of the Lord, Master of Legions, the God of the battalions of Israel whom you have insulted. This day God shall deliver you into my hand...and this entire gathering shall know that it is not with a sword or with a spear that God saves...."[155]

As Goliath advanced toward him, David used his sling to hurl a rock at the giant's face. It hit Goliath in the forehead and he fell to the ground, flat on his face. David then removed Goliath's sword and cut off his head.

The stunned Philistines ran away, pursued by the Israelite army. The end result was a tremendous victory for the Jews.

"Not by Might"

The words that David spoke on the battlefield are very powerful. He emphasized that the true strength of the Jewish people — indeed, of all people — is God. We saw this in the story of Gideon in chapter 15, and the same message will later be famously echoed by the prophet Zechariah: "Not by strength, not by might, but with My spirit," says God, the Master of Legions.[156]

Jews have to remember that they will win if God is with them, but as soon as they lose sight of that, they are in trouble. (We'll see this when we get to modern Israeli history — specifically, the great victory in the Six Day War of 1967 and the terrible losses of the Yom Kippur War of 1973.) The Jewish people must always remember where the source of their strength comes from. David was one Jewish leader who knew that, even though overnight he became a national hero. A song was even composed about him, and it became very popular: "Saul has slain his thousands, but David his tens of thousands."

This kind of comparison did not sit well with Saul, and it gave rise to the king's jealousy of David.

> Saul grew very angry, and this matter was disturbing in his eyes. He said, "They have attributed to David tens of thousands, while to me they have attributed thousands! He is lacking only the kingship." And Saul eyed David with suspicion from that day on.[157]

It happened that the next day Saul was overcome by his black mood and David was called in to play the harp and soothed him. However, on this occasion, the music did not help. Saul raved incoherently around the house and threw his spear at David, but David ducked just in time.

This was the beginning of Saul's intense hatred of David, and of his many attempts to kill David off.

One of Saul's plots was to see David killed in a war against the Philistines. He demanded that David produce 100 Philistine foreskins in exchange for the hand of his daughter, Michal. But David brought back 200 foreskins.

Jonathan, Saul's son who loved David, tried to intercede on his behalf. For a time, Saul calmed down, but then his jealousy flared up again. Finally, helped by Michal, David had to flee, and, from then on, he led a life on the run from the king's wrath. This is when he composed some of his most famous Psalms.

Meanwhile, the Philistines attacked yet again — near Mount Gilboa, in northern Israel and near the city of Beit Shean. It is amazing how far the Philistines managed to encroach into the country. No longer content to hug the coastline, they had actually reached deep into the eastern part of Israel along the area of the major trade route in the ancient Middle East.

Marching out against the Philistines, Saul was very nervous, but he had no one to reassure him because the prophet Samuel had recently died. Using necromancy (a practice strictly forbidden by the Torah), he nevertheless managed to contact the dead prophet in a séance, only to be told that he stood no chance in battle as God had turned away from him.

Resigned to his fate, Saul went into battle, only to see his own sons killed before his eyes. With defeat certain, and not wanting to be captured by the enemy, the wounded Saul fell on his sword and died on the battlefield.

Gleefully, the Philistines seized his corpose and removed the head, which they displayed all around the country. The body they hung on the wall of the city of Beit Shean, but the Jews managed to retrieve it under the cover of darkness and bury it.

Such was the end of Saul. After his death and the death of his sons — which David mourned greatly — David ceased his nomadic life and assumed the monarchy at last.

18.
DAVID: THE KING

King David was one of the most important figures in Jewish history. Born in 906 B.C.E., he reigned as king of Israel for 40 years, dying at age 70 in 836 B.C.E.

Once King David assumed the throne, it was to be his — and his descendants — forever.[158] He came from the line of Judah, who was blessed by Jacob to be the ruler of Israel. Thus, from David came all the legitimate kings of Israel and, ultimately, at the end of history, will come the Messiah.

(We will see that this idea of a God-ordained monarchy will be copied by many other nations throughout history and will serve as the basis for the concept of the divine Right of Kings in Medieval and Renaissance Europe.[159])

There is so much that can be said about King David. Some historians like to focus on the warrior aspect — the great hero fighting for God — but when his persona and accomplishments are considered as a whole, it is his spiritual greatness that shines most of all. David's first and foremost drive was to have a relationship with God. We get the glimpse of the beauty of his soul when we read the Book of Psalms, most of which he wrote. Who doesn't know:

The Lord is my shepherd, I shall not want (Psalm 23).

The Lord is my light and my salvation, whom should I fear (Psalm 27).

I lift my eyes to the mountains — from where will my help come? My help comes from God, the Maker of heaven and earth (Psalm 121).

Even when we consider his military conquests, we see that the driving force behind them was his attachment to God, as was certainly the case in his drive to conquer Jerusalem and make it the spiritual center of Israel.

The Conquest of Jerusalem

We know historically that the story of Israel during this entire period — from the Exodus onward — is the story of a tiny nation sandwiched between the two great ancient civilizations, Egypt and Mesopotamia (which at the time of King David was ruled by the Assyrians).

When David took the throne, Egypt and Assyria were both in a temporary decline. They were in no position to expand, which left a vacuum in the middle where Israel was located, and Israel was allowed to exist unmolested by these empires.

Thus David was able to subdue, at long last, the Philistine threat and to take over the remaining Canaanite city-state — Jerusalem — that the Israelites had thus far not been able to conquer.

For 440 years — since the Jewish people first entered the Land of Israel until the time of King David — Jerusalem had remained a non-Jewish city in the heart of a Jewish country. A city-state inhabited by Canaanite tribesmen called the Jebusites, it was heavily fortified, yet despite its seemingly impregnable appearance, Jerusalem had one weakness — its only source of water was a spring (the Gihon Spring) outside the city walls. The spring was accessed from inside the city by a long tunnel carved into rock.

The Book of Samuel and the Book of Chronicles describe how David's general, Yoab, climbed up a *tzinor* (literally, "pipe"), entered the city and conquered it. Some archaeologists speculate that this might refer to the tunnel of the city's ancient water system (which to this day is a great tourist attraction in "David's City," just outside the walls of today's Jerusalem).

Right after he occupied the city, David made it his capital. (Up to then, he had ruled out of Hebron.[160]) And here we have to pause and ask: Why Jerusalem?

Certainly, there were more suitable sites for the capital of Israel. Jerusalem did not adjoin any important body of water, nor was it located on any significant trade route. Virtually all the capital cities in the world are built near oceans, seas, rivers, lakes, or at least near a major trade route.

(There were two major trade routes traversing Israel at this time. There was the King's Highway, which was one of the major trade routes in the ancient Middle East, running from the Gulf of Aqaba on the Red Sea to Damascus. And there was also the Via Maris, the "Way of the Sea," which ran from Egypt along the Mediterranean coast then through Israel and on to Syria.)

Logically, the capital of Israel should have been on the Mediterranean Sea.

Ideally a place like Jaffa (next to today's Tel Aviv) would have made the most sense. So why Jerusalem?

The reason has to do with a very unique aspect of the Jewish people, and why the Children of Israel became a nation in the first place. As noted in chapter 11, normally nations become nations by occupying a piece of real estate for a long period of time, and developing a common language and a common culture. But the Jews became a nation shortly after escaping slavery in Egypt — long before they entered the Land of Israel — when they were camping out in no-man's land in the desert, at the foot of Mount Sinai. The Jews became a nation there, when they made a covenant with God, promising "We will do and we will hear." And the nationhood of Israel was defined, first and foremost, by its communal relationship with God and by the Jewish people's historic mission.

And, it turns out, there was no better place to relate to God than Jerusalem.

Mount Moriah

After David made Jerusalem his capital, he bought the upper part of a hill above the northern boundary of the city from its owner Aravnah the Jebusite. The purchase is recorded in the Bible in two places — in the Book of Samuel and the Book of Chronicles.[161] This hill was Mount Moriah, and what it lacked in physical size, it made up in spiritual greatness.

From the earliest period of Jewish history, the patriarchs of the Jewish people recognized the tremendous spiritual power of Mount Moriah. This is where Abraham, sensing God's presence, went up to offer Isaac as a sacrifice, and where Jacob dreamt of a ladder going up to heaven. No wonder this is a spot that so many conquerors have wanted to own. (Jerusalem has been the center of more than 100 known conflicts and only once has it changed hands without bloodshed.[162])

Today on this spot stands an Islamic structure known as the Dome of the Rock. Under this golden dome is an exposed piece of the bedrock of Mount Moriah — metaphysically known as the *even shetiah*, or "foundation stone." According to Judaism, the world is spiritually nourished from this spot, from this stone which is the metaphysical center of the universe. This is the place where God's presence can be felt more intensely than in any other place on planet Earth. Therefore, this was the logical place to build a permanent resting spot for the most holy object the Jewish people had — the Ark of the Covenant.[163]

King David wasted no time bringing the Ark to Jerusalem. And it was an occasion of great communal happiness. In ecstasy, David danced wildly at this celebration. For this he was condemned by his wife, Michal, the daughter of Saul, who had backed him through thick and thin and who even saved his life when King Saul wanted to kill him.

Although David brought the Ark of the Covenant to Mount Moriah, he was not allowed by God to build the Temple there. A number of reasons are given. One is that the Temple is a house of God and a house of peace and David had a lot of blood on his hands from subduing the enemies of Israel. However, he was promised that his son would build it.

Now David had a number of sons by several wives, some of whom gave him serious trouble. One, Amnon, raped his half-sister, Tamar. Another, Absalom, plotted against David and tried to have him deposed. But there was one special boy, Solomon, born from David's relationship with the beautiful Bathsheba.

David and Bathsheba

The story of David's relationship with Bathsheba[165] is one of the most misread stories in the Bible, and we have to be careful not to think of it as some kind of soap opera. In summary, however, this is what happened:

Restless one night, David was pacing the roof of his palace from where he had a view of the homes and gardens in the city below. And he noticed a beautiful woman bathing. She was the wife of one of his generals, Uriah the Hittite, who was away at war.

David sent for Bathsheba. When she became pregnant, he commanded that Uriah be placed on the front lines, where he died in battle. David then married Bathsheba.

At this point, the prophet Nathan was sent by God to rebuke David. Nathan said that he had come to inform the king of a great injustice in the land. A rich man with many sheep, stole the one beloved sheep of a poor man, and had it slaughtered for a feast.

Furious at what he heard, King David, declared, "As God lives, the one who has done this deserves death."

Responded the prophet, "You are that man!"

David understood immediately. "I have sinned before God," he said.

This is an enormously complex story and there is much more here than meets the eye. Technically, Bathsheba was not a married woman since David's troops always gave their wives conditional divorces, lest a soldier be missing in action, leaving his wife unable to remarry.[166] However, the Bible states clearly that David sinned, and the sages explain that while David did not commit adultery in the literal sense, he violated the spirit of the law.[167]

As noted earlier, the Bible takes a hypercritical view of Jewish leaders. It never whitewashes anyone's past, and in that sense it stands alone among the records of ancient peoples which usually describe kings as descendants of gods without faults.

David's greatness shone in his ability to take responsibility for his actions, the humility of his admission and the repentance that followed. This is part of the reason that the ultimate redeemer of the Jewish people and the world will descend from David's line — he will be "Messiah son of David."

Shortly thereafter, Bathsheba gave birth, but the child became deathly ill, as the prophet Nathan had predicted. David prayed and fasted, but the child died nevertheless. David realized that the death of the baby was divine punishment and also served as atonement for his actions. David "paid his dues," repented for many years and was ultimately forgiven by God.

And, before long, Bathsheba became pregnant again. And this time, she bore a healthy child who was named Solomon. He would be a golden child, gifted with unusual wisdom.

Solomon’s Temple

19.
KING SOLOMON

Before David died, he appointed as king his twelve-year-old son, Solomon, with these words:

> I go the way of all the earth. You shall be strong, therefore, and show yourself a man, and keep the charge of the Lord, your God to walk in His ways, to keep His statutes and His commandments and His testimonies, as it is written in the Law of Moses, so that you may prosper in all that you do and wherever you turn.[168]

This classic blessing is often quoted by fathers to their sons on the day of their bar mitzvah. It restates the cardinal rule that has guided the Jewish people since the giving of the Torah at Mount Sinai — in order to prosper, keep the Torah.

Shortly after Solomon was anointed king, God appeared to him in a dream in which He invited Solomon to make a request for himself. Solomon answered:

"I am but a small child.... Give, therefore, your servant an understanding heart to judge your people...." His request pleased God, who told him: "Because you have not requested riches and honor but only that which would benefit all the people, I will give you not only an understanding heart like none other before or after you...but also riches and honor like no other king in your days."[169]

Born in 848 B.C.E., Solomon died at age fifty-two in 796 B.C.E., ruling as king for forty years of peace and prosperity — the best years in all of Israel's history.

During his reign, he was known as "the wisest of all the men." The Bible relates that kings from all over the world came to hear his wisdom, which included not only Torah wisdom, but also wisdom in secular knowledge and science.[170]

> His fame spread through all the surrounding nations. He composed 3,000 parables and 1,005 poems. He discoursed about trees, from the cedars of Lebanon to the hyssop that grows from the wall. He also discoursed about animals, birds, creeping things and fish. Men of all nations came to hear Solomon's wisdom, as did all the kings of the earth who had heard of his wisdom.[171]

One of those who came on a much-celebrated visit was the Queen of Sheba,[172] who wished to test the king with her most difficult questions. What was she so curious about? Jewish tradition[173] relates that she had come armed with provocative riddles, one of which went like this: "A woman said to her son, 'Your father is my father, your grandfather is my husband, you are my son, and I am your sister, who am I?'" King Solomon promptly answered, "A daughter of Lot" (who, together with her father, tried to repopulate the world after the destruction of Sodom and Gomorrah). The queen went home highly impressed with the king and his kingdom.[174]

The Temple

The crowning achievement of Solomon's reign was the building of the Temple which his father, King David, had dreamt about.

The Bible devotes several chapters[175] to the construction of this most important building to the nation of Israel — the place of communion between man and God. It statess that the entire Temple, both inside and outside, including floors and doors, was overlaid with gold. Besides this there were bronze structures such as columns, an immersion tank, and basins. This magnificent edifice took seven years to build.

When it was finished, Solomon dedicated the Temple with this prayer to God:

> Behold, the heaven and heaven of heavens cannot contain You — how much less this house that I have built? Yet, have regard for the prayer of Your servant, and for his supplication, Lord my God, listen to the cry and to the prayer, which Your servant prays before You today, that Your eyes may be open toward this house night and day, toward the place of which You have said, 'My name shall be there,' that You may listen to the prayer...of your people Israel....[176]

This was the pinnacle of Solomon's reign and of Jewish history. Everyone was united. Their neighbors didn't bother the Jews — in fact, they came to learn from them. There was peace and prosperity. This was as good as it would ever get for Israel, the closest that it came to achieving the ideal of creating a nation that is "a light unto the nations."[177] This was the zenith. So why didn't it last?

Too Many Wives

Solomon made one serious mistake. In violation of the Torah's prohibition, he took too many wives. In fact, he had 700 wives and 300 concubines.

If we go back to the Book of Deuteronomy, where the idea of a Jewish king is first discussed, Moses warns that the king should not have too many horses nor too many wives.[178] The great eleventh century Torah commentator Rashi tells us that this means no more than eighteen, and that King David had only six.

The Torah places limits on the number of wives and on the amount of wealth the king can have to insure that he stays focused on his responsibilities and does not get distracted and corrupted by materialism and power. Solomon was certainly aware of these prohibitions, but felt that his great wisdom and spirituality would enable him to handle these challenges and be an even greater king. Unfortunately, he did not foresee the problems that some of his many foreign wives would cause.[179]

Why did Solomon "need" so many wives? The answer has nothing to do with love. Throughout history the overwhelming reason for marriage among nobility and royalty was to create political alliances. The Middle East in Solomon's time was made up of many city-states, and all the kings of these city-states wanted to send their daughters to marry King Solomon and, in this way, form an alliance with him. Solomon himself had an additional reason — his marriages to these foreign wives were his way of bringing these nations closer to God.[180]

Obviously, the foreign wives were required to convert to Judaism. Now, the motivation to convert should come solely out of a love of truth and a sincere desire to join the Jewish people despite the tremendous obligations that a Jewish lifestyle entails and the external dangers that the Jewish people have always faced. In short, the prospective convert must demonstrate total commitment, in spite of any difficulties or danger. The reigns of David and Solomon were unique, idyllic periods when the Jewish people enjoyed peace, prosperity, and a unique leadership role among the nations. During these periods, there were many people who wished to convert, not out a desire for truth, but rather for personal benefit. Such insincere conversions were not accepted, and the Talmud states that during this time all conversions were suspended.[181] However, an exception was made for the wives of the king, and a special court was set up to handle their conversions. It is certain that, despite claims to the contrary, not all Solomon's wives completely abandoned their idolatrous practices.

Again, note the incredible level of accountability that great Jewish leaders must meet. For a wife of King Solomon, who was prophet, wisest of all men, king of Israel, to worship idols was inexcusable, and Solomon was held directly accountable for it. The Bible states:

> In his old age, his wives turned away Solomon's heart after other gods.... And Solomon did what was sinful in the eyes of God and did not follow after God as his father David had done.[182]

This does not mean that Solomon became an idolater, but the Bible uses these harsh words because, as king, he did not prevent his wives from carrying on their idolatrous practices.

One of the greatest leaders of the Jewish people, a man on the highest spiritual level — who wrote the Song of Songs, the Book of Ecclesiastes, and the Book of Proverbs — must be suffering eternal pain knowing what has been written about him in the Bible.[183]

Not only is criticism of Solomon harsh, but as with other great Jewish leaders, so are the consequences of his mistakes. The Bible ends Solomon's story relating that God was angry with him and told him:

> "Since you are guilty of this, and you have not kept My covenant and My laws...I will tear the kingdom away from you.... But I will not do this in your time, for the sake of your father David. Instead, I will tear it away from your son.... [But] I will give your son one tribe for the sake of My servant David, and for the sake of Jerusalem, which I have chosen."[184]

It is clear from this how much God loved King David and how completely He had forgiven him for his faults. It is also clear that hard times are coming for the Jewish people, as the kingdom of Israel is about to be torn in half.

20.
A NATION DIVIDED

Although at the time of King Solomon's death in 796 B.C.E., Israel was still a united country, there was already some tension between the north and the south. We have to keep in mind that the biblical kingdom of Israel was comprised of twelve tribes, but the king came from the tribe of Judah (and Jerusalem sat on Judah's tribal border), which could be viewed by the other tribes as unfair. A wise king would have to be especially aware of the sensitivities of the other tribes.

Following the death of Solomon, his son Rehoboam became king and, in response to the political situation, went up north to the city of Shechem to have himself crowned. At this time, the northern tribes sent a delegation to tell the king their complaints. Chief among these was the toll that King Solomon's building projects — the Temple in Jerusalem, his palaces, etc. — had taken on the people in terms of taxes and forced labor. The northern tribes, in effect, asked the new king for a tax cut.

Rehoboam consulted his advisors. The elders who had served under Solomon told him to ease up on the people: "Speak to them gently, and they will be your servants forever."[185] But the younger upstarts advised him to show the people who is boss. Rehoboam took the latter advice and announced, "If you think my father was tough on you, just watch me! I'm going to be even tougher."

Big mistake!

Rehoboam forgot that even God had called the Jews a stiff-necked people. Jews are stubborn. In response to Rehoboam's arrogance, in the year 796 B.C.E., the northern tribes seceded, creating a new kingdom called Israel. Rehoboam was left with just the southern part of the country and Jerusalem — his kingdom was called Judah. (The terminology we use today — Judea and Samaria, which was the capital of the northern kingdom of Israel — has its origins in the split of the country after Solomon's death.)

Rehoboam considered waging war, but the prophet Shemaiah warned him against it, telling him that he could not possibly win as this rending of the nation had been brought about by God. While the immediate cause of the split was the weakness and bad judgment of Rehoboam, the prime cause was rooted in idolatry of Solomon's wives, which the king had failed to stop.

The split was clearly bad news for many reasons, both spiritual and geopolitical. The once strong, unified nation was now a weak, divided nation, and it was easy prey to the empires of Egypt, Assyria, and later, Babylon.

King Jeroboam

The king of the northern country of Israel was Jeroboam ben Navat. He was a great man, a great leader, and a great scholar who once stood up to King Solomon.[186] But unfortunately, the old saying — "power corrupts and absolute power corrupts absolutely" — proved true. Soon, Jeroboam was worrying less about leading the people and more about hanging onto his throne.

Jeroboam saw that the Jewish people in the north were still very strongly connected to Jerusalem. After all, that was where the Temple stood with its Holy of Holies and the Ark of the Covenant; that was where the presence of God was most strongly felt. On the three big festivals — Pesach, Shavuot ("Weeks"), and Sukkot ("Booths") — the people continued to stream to Jerusalem. He saw that this commonality with the south could bring about a reunification, in which case he would no longer be king.

So Jeroboam hatched a scheme. What did he do? He decided to set up an alternative place of worship in the north. He built two other temples — one in Bet El and one in Dan (where Tel Dan stands today). Worse yet, he set up golden calves in these temples and even used the same language as in the Golden Calf story: "These are your gods, O, Israel, who brought you up from the land of Egypt!"[187]

Once you open the door to idolatry by introducing alternative sites and alternative modes of worship, it means trouble. And there began a terrible period in Jewish history. In the next 220 years after Jeroboam, there were nineteen different kings of the northern kingdom of Israel — all bad, but some much worse than others. They were idolaters, corrupt and evil, and they led the Jewish people into idolatry.

Some of these kings were potentially great leaders, but spiritually they were lacking. As we know — if the Jews don't get their act together spiritually, they're not going to have their act together physically either. So, we see a time period of great political instability and palace intrigue, when kings came and went, and the succession was usually very bloody.

King Ahab and Jezebel

Of all the bad kings of Israel, the one who stands out as the worst is King Ahab. He married the infamous Jezebel and built a temple to the Canaanite deity Baal, popularizing this form of idolatry among the Jewish people. Of him the Bible says: "Ahab son of Omri did what was evil in the eyes of God, more than all who had preceded him."[188]

When you're reading the Books of Kings and looking at what the Jewish people were doing then, it's important to understand that the ancient people of the world were very religious and were always looking for ways to heighten their "spirituality." This is why idolatry was such a powerful draw and an ever-present obstacle that stood between the Jews and God.

A basic tenant of Judaism is that there is only one power in the world — God. There is no devil or other power competing with Him for control of the universe. The impure spirituality of idolatry was placed in the world by God to enable people to make the ultimate choice of living with, or ignoring, Him. In the ancient world, the attraction to idolatry was real and very powerful. This may be hard to fathom today, because we don't have the same drive for spirituality (as will be explained later). Much of the Jewish people's drive to worship idols came out of a misguided desire to "enhance" their spiritual experience by mixing Judaism with paganism. On a practical level it meant that they were still keeping kosher and observing other Jewish laws, but they wanted "to have their cake and eat it too" — they wanted both God and the spiritual high of idolatry.

The prophet of note at this time was Elijah. During this period of the divided monarchy, the primary function of the major prophets was to urge the Jews of both Judah and Israel to turn away from their idolatrous and evil ways and return to God before it was too late. Elijah yearned to have the Jewish people repent. To this end, he decided to have a showdown with the priests of Baal and to physically demonstrate the lie of idolatry to the Jewish people. So, Elijah went up north to Mount Carmel.

(Today, the modern city of Haifa sits on the western edge of the Carmel Mountain Range. On the eastern side of the range is a place called Mukhraka, where there is a Carmelite monastery. In front of the monastery, there stands a statue of Elijah which commemorates the site where Elijah took on the priests of Baal.)

Elijah wanted the Jewish people to see that idolatry is nonsense and that there is only one God. So he challenged 450 priests of Baal to a contest. He proposed that each side offer a sacrificial bull to their deity and whichever deity sent a fire from heaven to consume the offering in full sight of the people would be accepted as the true God.

The priests of Baal readily agreed. They put up their bull on the altar, and they beseeched Baal, shouting to the skies. But after nearly a full day of trying, nothing happened and the animal carcass was only attracting flies. Meanwhile, Elijah mocked them:

"Shout louder! After all, he is a god, but he may be in conversation, he may be detained, or he may be on a journey, or perhaps he is asleep and will wake up."[189]

They shouted louder, but still got no response. So they started slashing their heads with knives. It was an ancient form of worship, based on the idea that blood excites the gods. Still nothing. It was really embarrassing for them to have no response with all the Jewish people watching.

Toward the end of the day, Elijah finally gave orders for the preparation of his own offering. He had it doused with water three times so it would be even more difficult to set aflame. He even had a water-filled ditch built around the altar. Then he said one short prayer:

"Lord, God of Abraham, Isaac and of Israel, let it be known this day that you are God in Israel, and that I am your servant, and that I have done all these things at your word. Hear me, Lord, hear me, that this people may know that you are the Lord God, and that you have turned their hearts back again."[190]

With that, a fire came down from the heavens consuming the sacrifice, the wood pile, the stones, the dust and even the water in the ditch.

The gathered multitude responded in awe: "The Lord, He is God, the Lord, He is God!" (This is the very phrase Jews shout at the end of the Yom Kippur liturgy every year; this is where it comes from.)

The priests of Baal were put to death, and it seemed that the nation would now reject idolatry. But the story does not end there.

Hearing what had happened, Jezebel sent a message to Elijah: "Tomorrow I will kill you." She knew that the memory of miracles did not last long. Today, the Jews might be shouting, "The Lord, He is God," but tomorrow is another day.

Sure enough, idol worship resumed, and Elijah had to flee for his life; the impact of his miracle quickly faded from the memory of most of the population and the northern kingdom sank even lower spiritually.

Eventually, God was going to get tired of this. There was a covenant after all, and the Jews were not keeping their part of the bargain. The covenant clearly specified that the Land of Israel, along with its bounty, was given to the Jewish people on certain conditions. If they violated those conditions, they would be expelled from the land. And this was about to happen to the northern kingdom, though not yet to the southern kingdom.

21.
ASSYRIAN CONQUEST

At a time when the Jewish people of the northern kingdom of Israel were weakening spiritually — which is to say, they were also weakening physically/militarily — the Assyrians were growing stronger. They occupied the territory immediately north — what is today's Syria, Iraq, and Turkey — and they continued to build their empire.

If you visit the British Museum in London, you can see some fascinating Assyrian artifacts from this period.[191] You can see the four-sided black obelisk of the Assyrian King Shalmaneser III. The black obelisk depicts the tribute paid to Assyria by King Jehu of the northern kingdom of Israel. You can also see there a bas-relief stripped by the British from the walls of the magnificent palace at Nineveh, Assyria's capital city. That palace belonged to King Sennacherib, and the relief depicts the siege of the Israelite city of Lachish; it was conquered by Sennacherib, who then boasted about it on his palace walls.

In the sixth century B.C.E., Assyrian king Tiglathpileser III strengthened Assyria and established it as a great empire to be reckoned with. (Eventually, Assyria would even challenge the mighty Egypt.) He also introduced a very interesting way of dealing with conquered peoples. It's called exile.

To pacify the lands they invaded, the Assyrians moved the indigenous people someplace else and brought in others to take their place. By the time the exiles adjusted to their new surroundings, decades had passed, and rebellion was no longer a problem.

Starting around 575 B.C.E., in order to take control of the northern kingdom, Tiglathpileser invaded the lands belonging to the tribes of Zebulun and Naphtali, and exiled them. Then, Shalmanaser V, another Assyrian emperor, took over the lands belonging to the tribes of Reuben, Gad and Manasseh, and exiled them. Finally, in 555 B.C.E., Sargan II, one of the great emperors of Assyria, completed the job, and the whole northern part of the country ceased to exist as a Jewish state. As the Book of Kings relates:

> In the ninth year of [the reign] of Hoshea, the King of Assyria took Samaria and exiled the Israelites to Assyria, and he settled them in Halah at the [River] Habor, at the River Gozan, and in the cities of Media. And so it was that the Israelites sinned against the Lord their God...they worshipped other gods and followed the customs of the nations.... God had issued warnings in Israel and Judah through the hand of all the prophets of any vision saying, "Repent from your evil ways and observe My commandments and decrees...." But they did not listen and they stiffened their necks.... Then God became very angry with Israel and removed them from His Presence; none remained except the tribe of Judah.[192]

The important and obvious lesson to be learned from this quotation is that while the superficial reason for the fall of the northern kingdom was linked to the geopolitical realities of the ancient Middle East, the real cause was violation of the Torah.

With the Jews driven out, who took their place? The Assyrians brought in a group of people from someplace else, who — because they were now living in Samaria — came to be known as the Samaritans.

The Samaritans were people who more or less adopted Judaism, but not properly or for the right reasons. Because their conversion was incomplete or insincere, they were never accepted by the Jewish people, and they were very resentful of this. Indeed, the Samaritans have had a long history of animosity towards the Jews, and while many people are familiar with the story of the "good Samaritan" from the Christian Gospels, the Jewish perception and experience of the Samaritans has rarely been favorable.

Today, there are only about 600 Samaritans left; their cult site is in Mount Grizim, which is adjacent to the city of Shechem, called Nablus in Arabic.

Ten Lost Tribes

Meanwhile, the Jewish people of the north had been settled in various locations throughout the Assyrian empire. What happened to those ten tribes?

They assimilated and are known today as the Ten Lost Tribes. There are numerous people throughout the world, especially in the Middle East and Asia, who claim to be descended from the Ten Lost Tribes. Some scholars have dedicated much time and effort to identify and authenticate them. One such person is Dr. Tutor Parfitt of London University. He has made it his specialty to track and trace different exotic peoples who claim to be of Jewish origin. He has written a book called *The Thirteenth Gate* in which he presents his research.[193]

It's amazing how many people, few of whom know anything about Judaism, claim to be descendants of ancient Jews. For example, many of the Pathans, Muslim fundamentalists who reside in Afghanistan and Pakistan, say they are descended from the Ten Lost Tribes.

The Midrash[194] states the lost tribes live "over the River Sambatyon," a mystical river flowing with sand and stones, that cannot be crossed. This is an allegorical way of saying the tribes are gone and they can't come back — not yet anyway.

There is a Jewish tradition that during the Messianic Era all the lost tribes will return. The great eighteenth century sage, the Vilna Gaon, taught that converts are lost Jewish souls who are trying to find their way back to the Jewish people. But for now, the ten tribes are gone.

With the Jewish people dispersed from the northern kingdom of Israel, the Assyrians set their sights on the southern kingdom. But this one did not prove so easy.

22.
THE END OF JUDAH

Judah, the southern kingdom of Israel, lasted 133 years longer than the northern kingdom. This was largely because it was nowhere near as unstable, nor as corrupted by idolatry.

In the north there was a king every dozen years or so, but in the south the average reign lasted about twice as long.

Unlike the kings of the northern kingdom, some of the kings of the southern kingdom were actually good and holy men. The one who stood out above the rest was the fourteenth king after David, Hezekiah (who, incidentally, was married to the daughter of prophet Isaiah). The Bible says about him:

> And he did what was right in the eyes of God, like all that his [forefather David had done. And he trusted in the God of Israel. There was none like him among all the kings of Judah who were after him nor before him.[195]

Now that's pretty high praise.

It was during Hezekiah's reign that the northern kingdom of Israel was destroyed by the Assyrians and the ten tribes exiled. So Hezekiah fortified Jerusalem in expectation of the Assyrian invasion of Judah. And some of his handiwork we can see today.

By Hezekiah's time, the city of Jerusalem was no longer confined to the original "city of David." Much of the population lived in a new neighborhood on the western side of the Temple Mount. But this part of the city was defenseless, so Hezekiah enclosed it with a wall, which has been excavated by archaeologists and can be seen today — it's called the Broad Wall.

Another achievement attributed to Hezekiah was a major improvement of the water supply system to the city (which, as we saw in chapter 18, depended on the Gihon Spring outside the city walls). Hezekiah organized two teams of diggers to dig a tunnel from Gihon to a reservoir within the city. One team started at the spring, the other within the city walls, and they met somewhere in between. Considering the limited technology of the day, the tunnel they dug is an amazing piece of work — 533 meters long.

Today you can go to David's City, just outside the walls of Jerusalem's Old City, and walk through this tunnel (the water reaches only up to your ankles). There, you can see the tool marks of the ancient diggers. You can also see where the two sets of marks meet. There used to be an ancient plaque there, but unfortunately it was removed during the Ottoman period, and it's now in a museum in Istanbul, Turkey.

The city was fortified just in the nick of time before the Assyrians, led by Sennacherib, come to lay siege. This was in the year 547 B.C.E.

We mentioned in chapter 21 that many of the treasures of the Middle East now sit in the British Museum. One of those items is a clay hexagon describing Sennacherib's military campaigns. An inscription on it reads: "Hezekiah, King of Judah, I locked in Jerusalem like a bird in a cage." Noticeably absent is the description of Jerusalem falling, because it didn't fall. The Book of Kings[196] tells us what happened:

The mighty Assyrian army besieged the city and things looked grim, but the prophet Isaiah assured the people that the city would not fall. True to Isaiah's prediction, a plague hit the Assyrian camp, and their army was decimated overnight. Sennacherib packed up and ran back home to Assyria, where he was murdered not long after by his children.

One can understand Sennacherib, the bloodthirsty emperor of Assyria, having bad children. But unfortunately, the saintly king Hezekiah did not fare much better in the offspring department.

Bad Seed

The son of Hezekiah, Manasseh, assumed the throne after his father died. He was as bad as his father was good. Of him the Bible says:

> He did what was evil in the eyes of God.... He erected altars to Baal... he passed his son through fire, practiced astrology and read omens, performed necromancy and conjured spirits. He did much that was evil in the eyes of God to anger Him.[197]

Manasseh was so bad that he even had the prophet Isaiah — his own grandfather — put to death. The ultimate downfall of Jerusalem was blamed by God on the evil behavior of Manasseh:

> Because Manasseh, King of Judah has committed these abominations... and he caused even Judah to sin with his idols.... I will wipe out Jerusalem as one would wipe a plate thoroughly, and then turn it upside down.[198]

The next king — Amon — was as bad as Manasseh. But then came Josiah, who truly loved God and instituted a round of impressive religious reforms. Unfortunately, when he died, these reforms died with him, and the spiritual decline continued.

(There is a tradition that Josiah anticipated this. He knew that the southern kingdom would soon be invaded and fall as had the northern, so he decided to hide the Ark of the Covenant in order that it not fall into enemy hands.)[199]

In the meanwhile, the Assyrian empire — which had been such a great threat to Israel — had been overrun by a new world power called Babylon. And it was the Babylonians who invaded Judah in 434 B.C.E.

The Babylonians marched on Judah as part of their campaign to stake claim to the former Assyrian empire. Their aim was to impose their rule and make Judah a vassal state. In this, they largely succeeded. They pillaged Jerusalem — though they did not destroy it at this time — taking into captivity 10,000 of the best and brightest Jews (the prophet Ezekiel among them). They also removed the king, whose name was Jehoiachin, and took him to Babylon.

The exile of the 10,000 best and brightest seemed like a terrible disaster, but it turned out not to be so. In fact, it proved to be a blessing in disguise, as we shall see in the next chapter.

The Babylonians then appointed their own puppet king from among the Jews — Zedekiah. Although Zedekiah was a weak ruler, he was also foolishly ambitious, and eventually he decided to rebel against his Babylonian overlords. In instant response, Babylonian emperor Nebuchadnezzar ordered a siege of Jerusalem.

Make no mistake about it. This did not happen because Jews rebelled against Babylon. This happened because Israel rebelled against God. When the Jews had a good relationship with God — as in the days of King Hezekiah or King Josiah — they were invincible. Sometimes, they didn't even need to fight, as when God sent a plague to vanquish their enemies. But if they betrayed God, no matter how mighty the Israelite army, it could not withstand the enemy.

But, as always, God gave the Jews plenty of time to mend their ways. While the Babylonians laid siege to Jerusalem, the prophet Jeremiah called for all to repent but his message went unheeded. Instead, he was beaten and thrown into prison!

Years earlier, Jeremiah had written the Book of Lamentations, predicting in great detail the destruction of the Temple and of Jerusalem, but the king at that time — King Jehoiakim (the father of Jehoiachin) — tore it to bits and threw it into the fire.[200]

Today we read the Book of Lamentations every year on the ninth of Av, the horrible day when these predications came true. This is the Jewish date that continues to live in infamy. As we saw in chapter 13, the ninth of Av — Tishah B'Av — is the catastrophic day in Jewish history when the spies sent by Moses to look over the Land of Israel came back advising the Israelites not to enter, and God doomed that generation to forty years of wandering in the desert; when the First Temple was destroyed by the Babylonians; when the Second Temple was destroyed by the Romans; when the Jews of Spain were given an ultimatum by the Inquisition — leave, convert, or die; when World War I, the prelude to the Holocaust, began; and when many other calamities were visited upon the Jewish people.

The Siege of Jerusalem

There is clear archaeological evidence for the siege of Jerusalem — which lasted two years — that you can see today in the Old City of Jerusalem. Near the remains of Hezekiah's Broad Wall, you can visit the Israelite Tower Museum. It's about 60 feet under ground, and you can see there the remains of a three-door gate in the northern defensive wall of the city. (Archaeologists call it the "E Gate.") At this site, archaeologists digging in the early 1970s found clear evidence of the Babylonian siege.

Among the artifacts they found there were Israelite and Babylonian arrowheads. How did they know? The arrowheads have names on them, because in ancient times, arrowheads were very valuable. They also found a layer of charred earth, attesting to the burning of the city as is related in the Book of Kings.[201] Other fascinating evidence was also found in area "G" of David's City, including a clay seal inscribed with the name of Gemariah son of Shaphan, a scribe mentioned in the Book of Jeremiah.[202]

After two years of siege, the Jews couldn't hold out anymore. They had been starved into submission, as Jeremiah had so vividly predicted:

> The tongue of the suckling infant cleaves to its palate from thirst; young

> children beg for bread, no one extends it to them. Those who once feasted extravagantly lie destitute in the streets; those who were brought up in scarlet clothing wallow in garbage.... Their appearance has become blacker than soot, they are not recognized in the streets; their skin has shriveled on their bones, it became dry as wood.... Hands of compassionate women have boiled their own children; they became their food when the daughter of my people was shattered....[203]

On the seventeenth of Tammuz of the year 422, the Babylonians breached the walls of the city. They poured in and carried out a mass slaughter. A month later, on the ninth of Av, the Temple Mount fell into their hands.

During the mayhem, Zedekiah tried to flee to the Dead Sea through a secret tunnel that led out of Jerusalem. But he got caught and it's very interesting how.

According to the Midrash,[204] Nebuzaradan, Nebuchadnezzar's captain was out hunting while his men were pillaging the city. He saw a deer, and he began following it. The deer just happened to run above the tunnel. (This, of course, was God's way of assuring that Zedekiah was not going to escape punishment.) When Zedekiah came out of the tunnel, the deer was standing there, and so was Nebuzaradan right behind the deer. This is how Zedekiah got caught. He met a horrible fate, along with the rest of the Israelites, as the Bible relates:

> And they...put out the eyes of Zedekiah and bound him with fetters of bronze and carried him to Babylon. And in the fifth month, on the seventh day of the month, which is the nineteenth year of King Nebuchadnezzar, king of Babylon, came Nebuzaradan, captain of the guard, a servant of the king of Babylon, to Jerusalem. And he burned the house of God [the Temple], and the king's house, and all the houses of Jerusalem, and every great man's house burned he with fire.[205]

With the destruction of the Temple, the special connection that the Jewish people had with God was severed. As with the fall of Israel in the north, there was a superficial cause for the destruction of Jerusalem (i.e., the revolt against Babylon), but the Bible makes it clear that the real cause was the immoral behavior of the Jews.[206]

Here is when it all came crashing down. Where previously the Babylonians had been satisfied in making Israel into a vassal state, this time their punishment was much worse. They decide to carry on the Assyrian policy of exile and remove the Jews from the Promised Land, the land flowing with milk and honey.

KINGS OF ISRAEL
(THE UNITED KINGDOM)

KING	REIGNED
Saul	2 years
Ishboshet	2 years
David	40 years
Solomon	40 years

SPLIT OF KINGDOM

KINGS OF JUDAH
(RULING IN JERUSALEM)

King	Reigned
Rehoboam	17 years
Abijam	3 years
Asa	41 years
Johoshaphat	25 years
Johoram	8 years
Ahaziah	1 year
Athaliah	6 years
Jehoash	40 years
Amaziah	29 years
Uzziah	52 years
Jotham	16 years
Ahaz	16 years
Hezekiah	29 years
Manasseh	55 years
Amon	2 years
Josiah	31 years
Jehoahaz	3 months
Jehoiakim	11 years
Jehoiachin	3 months
Zedekiah	11 years
EXILED	422 B.C.E.

KINGS OF ISRAEL
(NORTHERN TEN TRIBES)

King	Reigned
Jeroboam	22 years
Nabad	2 years
Baasa	24 years
Elah	2 years
Zimri	7 days
Tivni	5 years
Omri	12 years
Ahab	22 years
Ahaziah	2 years
Jehoram	12 years
Jehu	28 years
Jehoahaz	17 years
Jehoash	15 years
Jeroboam	41 years
Zechariah	6 months
Shallum	1 month
Menahem	10 years
Pekahiah	2 years
Pekah	20 years
Hoshea	19 years
EXILED	555 B.C.E.

PART III
ADRIFT AMID THE EMPIRES

23.
BABYLONIAN EXILE

By the rivers of Babylon, we sat down,
And we wept when we remembered Zion.
Upon the willows, we hung our harps,
For there, our captors demanded of us words of song,
And our tormentors mocked us: "Sing for us a song of Zion."
How can we sing the song of God in a foreign land?
If I forget you, O Jerusalem,
May my right hand forget [to play its song],
May my tongue be stilled if I do not remember you,
If I do not hold Jerusalem as my highest joy.
Remember, God, the day Jerusalem [fell]
And the words of the sons of Edom:
"Destroy it! Raze it down to its foundation!"
O daughter of Babylon, it is you who will be destroyed.
Happy is he who repays you in kind
For what you have done to us:
Happy is he who seizes your infants
And dashes them against a rock.[207]

The destruction of the Temple and the exile to Babylon was a tremendous shock to the Jewish people. It may be hard to imagine today what it must have meant back then, because we really have no basis of comparison.

In those days, normative Judaism meant living with the constant presence of God, which was always accessible at the Temple. Miracles occurred there daily and could be witnessed by anyone. For example, whichever way the wind was blowing, the smoke of the sacrifices always went straight up to heaven. Spiritual feelings today do not begin to compare to those felt in the Temple. With such intense spirituality, it was clear that God was with the Jewish people.

The same thing could be said for the land. One miracle of the land was that every six years there was such a bumper crop that the Jews could take the seventh year — the sabbatical year — off from work. It was amazing.

Now all of that was gone. The land, the Temple, the sense of God's presence. No wonder they wept by the rivers of Babylon. However, God still looked after the Jewish people in exile, even if His presence was concealed. We see this with the preparation God laid for the exile.

In the previous chapter we noted that when the Babylonians first attacked Israel, they took away 10,000 of the best and the brightest with them. That seemed like a disaster at the time, but when the Jews arrived in Babylon it turned out to be a blessing. Why? Because a Jewish infrastructure was already in place. Yeshivas had been established; there was a kosher butcher and a *mikveh*. Jewish life could continue, and as a result, we see hardly any assimilation during the Babylonian exile.[208]

If we jump ahead 2,500 years to the Jewish migration to America, we see how different it was. Starting at around 1882, millions of Jews fleeing from persecution in Czarist Russia started coming to the New World, but they didn't find yeshivas and synagogues there. And what was the consequence? The single greatest mass assimilation of Jews in history.

Therefore, this turn of events in Babylon proved to be a tremendously positive thing. It was a great example of God putting the cure before the disease, which we see over and over in Jewish history.

Surviving Exile

God made a promise to the Jewish people at the time of Mount Sinai that they would be an "eternal nation," and He means to keep it:

> Thus, even while they [the Jewish people] are in the land of their enemies, I will not reject or obliterate them, lest I break my covenant with them by destroying them. For I am the Lord their God; I will remember them because of the covenant I made with their original ancestors whom I brought out from the land of Egypt, in the sight of the nations, so that I might be their God.[209]

In all of human history, exiles of an entire people from their country have been very rare. It's a highly unusual phenomenon to take a whole people and throw them out of their country. Multiple exiles are unheard of, since, after the first one, the people generally disappear — they simply become assimilated among other peoples. As a matter of fact, in all of human history, multiple exiles and dispersions are unique to the Jewish people.[210]

And yet the Jews survived despite exile, because God had promised that they would be an "eternal nation."

It helped somewhat that life in Babylonia was tolerable. [211] The Babylonians could be very cruel in their wars and conquests, but their attitude toward the exiled Jewish community was "live and let live." They even appointed a leader whose job was to represent the concerns of the Jewish community to the Babylonian authorities. He was given the Aramaic title of *Reish Galusa*.[212]

(By the way, Aramaic was the international language of the ancient Near East. It is a Semitic language, and it is closely related to Hebrew. It is the language in which most of the Talmud is written. The Jews of Babylon spoke Aramaic, and even when they returned to the Land of Israel, they continued to speak Aramaic.)

This Aramaic word *Reish Galusa* means "Head of the Diaspora." (Diaspora, incidentally, is a Greek word, meaning "dispersion.") The *Reish Galusa* was a person who was a direct descendant of the House of King David. Even though he was not a king in the Land of Israel, he was recognized not only as being the representative of the Jewish community in Babylon, but also as having noble status. Over the next 1,500 years, forty-three people would hold that title. And they would all trace their ancestry back to King Jehoiachin (second to last of the kings of Judah) and all the way back to King David. This was a noble line that has always been preserved in Jewish history.[213]

The oldest Diaspora community in the world is the Babylonian community. There's no question that Jews have lived in Babylon long before the Iraqis. And when the Jews came back to the Land of Israel in the late 1940s and early 1950s, there were many so-called Bavli Jews coming in from Iraq who could trace their ancestry back to this time of the Babylonian exile.

Why did they stay there so long? Because the Babylonians, and later the Persians and the Ottomans, made life in that part of the world relatively easy. (For example, when the Jews were expelled from Spain, the Ottomans welcomed them with open arms.)

This is not to say, however, that all was peaches and cream. The Book of Daniel tells the story of young Jewish men who were thrown into a fiery furnace by Nebuchadnezzar because they refused to eat non-kosher food or to bow to idols. They miraculously survived, causing Nebuchadnezzar to issue an edict forbidding anyone to blaspheme the God of Israel.

Writing on the Wall

The last king of Babylon was Belshazzar, son of Nebuchadnezzar. Like many of the other neighboring kings, Belshazzar was well versed in Jewish prophecy. Why? Because, in the polytheistic world, the God of Israel had a reputation. He had to be reckoned with, and therefore the rulers kept up with Jewish beliefs and took Jewish prophets and their prophecies seriously.

Belshazzar knew what the prophet Jeremiah had prophesied at the time when Nebuchadnezzar conquered Israel:

> And this whole land [of Israel] shall be a ruin, and a waste, and these nations [the tribes of Israel] shall serve the king of Babylon seventy years. And it shall come to pass, when the seventy years are fulfilled, that I will punish the king of Babylon....[214]

Naturally, this was something that worried Belshazzar, and so he kept count. But he miscalculated.[215] When the year 371 B.C.E. arrived, Belshazzar thought the prophecy would not be realized — God had abandoned the Jews and would not restore them to Israel as promised in Jeremiah prophecy:

> For thus said God: After seventy years for Babylonia have been completed, I will attend to you, and I will fulfill for you My favorable promise — to return you to this place.[216]

In celebration, Belshazzar threw a huge feast and brought out the Temple vessels that Nebuchadnezzar had stolen from Jerusalem for all to see. He ordered his consorts and concubines to drink from Temple cups and to praise "the gods of gold and silver, copper, iron, wood and stone."[217]

At that moment, a large, unattached hand appeared and started to write on the wall. Belshazzar was shaken to the core, but no one could tell him what the strange message on the wall meant.

Finally, the queen recommended that they send for a man who had a reputation for "extraordinary spirit, intelligence, and understanding." This man — of whom it was said that "the spirit of God was in him" — was the prophet Daniel.

Daniel had no trouble reading the writing on the wall. It said:

> God has numbered the days of your kingdom and brought it to an end...your kingdom has been divided and given to the Medes and Persians.[218]

That very night, invading hoards of Persians and Medes attacked. The king and all his party were killed. Only Nebuchadnezzar's granddaughter, Vashti, survived. She would come to marry the King of Persia, Ahasuerus, and unwittingly start in motion one of the great sagas of Jewish history, which happened in the days of the Persian Empire.

24.
PURIM IN PERSIA

The armies of Medes under Darius and the armies of Persia under Cyrus marched into Babylon and conquered it. The Babylonian Empire ceased to exist, and Babylon was absorbed by the new Persian Empire.

So who do we have in that part of the world, just to keep it straight? First Assyria, then Babylon, then Persia — they were all great Mesopotamian empires, one after the other, all interacting with the Jewish people.

Following the brief reign of Darius came Cyrus of Persia. In 370 B.C.E., Cyrus issued a decree allowing all the indigenous peoples that had been exiled by the now-defunct Babylonian empire to go back to their homelands. One copy of this decree — known as the "Cyrus Cylinder" — is on display at the British Museum, and although this version does not specifically mention the Jews, they are included, as we learn from the Book of Ezra:

> In the first year of Cyrus, king of Persia, upon the conclusion of God's prophecy, by the mouth of Jeremiah, God aroused the spirit of Cyrus, king of Persia, and he issued a proclamation throughout his kingdom, as well as in writing, saying, "Thus said Cyrus the king of Persia: All the kingdoms of the earth has the Lord, God of heaven, given to me and He has commanded me to build Him a Temple in Jerusalem, which is in Judah. Whoever is among you of His entire people, may his God be with him, and let him go to Jerusalem which is in Judah and build the Temple of God....[219]

You would think that the Jews would jump up, pack up and go. But that's not what happened. Of what was probably between 500,000 to one million Jews living in the empire, only 42,000 went back[220] — that is, only between 5 and 10 percent of those that went into exile seventy years earlier went back. The remaining 90 to 95 percent stayed put.

It may sound strange, but we will see that this pattern repeats itself in Jewish history. The same thing happened in 1948 when the State of Israel was declared. There were about 12 million Jews in the world at that time and only 600,000 — or 5 percent — settled the land. The remaining 95 percent preferred to stay in exile. Why?

The answer is the same for 370 B.C.E., for 1948, and for today.

After decades living outside of Israel, many of the Jews were settled into a comfortable existence abroad. Life in the Diaspora can be very pleasant. There are many places outside Israel with strong Jewish communities and a lifestyle that is often more comfortable than that in Israel. This attitude has been repeated many times in Jewish history, and it is a problem. While God might give the Jews a little breathing space in Diaspora from time to time, in the long run, He's not going to allow them to stay there.

One of the great patterns we're going to see over and over again is the higher the Jews rise in the Diaspora, the lower they fall. The nicer the Diaspora seems to be at first, the worse the subsequent reaction against the Jews. We see it first in Egypt. Jews are invited in, they do well and prosper, and look what happens — they end up slaves. We see this in Spain and Poland. We see this in Germany. All the places that once welcomed the Jews eventually turn on them. Therefore, Jews make a mistake if they ever think that the Diaspora is their permanent home. Israel is the only home for the Jews, because the Diaspora never works as a long-term solution. Ironically, the greatest explosions of anti-Semitism have taken place in countries that were the most accommodating to the Jews.

The 42,000 Jews, led by Zerubabel ben Shaltiel (a descendant of King David), arrived back in Israel in the year 370 B.C.E. and immediately started rebuilding Jerusalem, beginning what is known as the Second Commonwealth. And, of course, the first thing in Jerusalem that they wanted to rebuild was the Temple, because a Jew can't live a complete Jewish life without a Temple.

The Samaritans, who never liked the Jews and who hated this new influx, immediately sent a message to Persia demanding that the Jews be forbidden to continue building. They said that if the Jews were allowed to rebuild the Temple, they were going to rebel. As a result of their threats, Persia froze the building permit. For eighteen years no construction was allowed. And it was during this period that the Purim story, related in the Book of Esther, took place.

Meanwhile, Back in Persia...

Back in Persia, a new king had replaced Cyrus. His name was Ahasuerus, and he was married to Vashti, a survivor of the bloodbath in the royal palace of Belshazzar during the Persian invasion.

Ahasuerus threw a party reminiscent of the one that Belshazzar had thrown some years before. He, too, had been calculating, and he had decided that the seventy years allotted in Jeremiah's prophecy for the Jews to regain the Land of Israel was up.[221]

(The reason why both Belshazzar and Ahasuerus miscalculated was that neither was sure when the seventy years began. Belshazzar assumed that the clock began to tick when Nebuchadnezzar came to power, while Ahasuerus assumed the seventy years began with the initial exile of 10,000 Jews from Jerusalem before the Babylonian destruction of the city. Both were wrong. In truth, Jeremiah's prophecy began with the actual destruction of Jerusalem and the First Temple.)

To this feast, Ahasuerus invited the Jews and, possibly because they were afraid to decline, they came — strangely enough — to "celebrate" their own end. This gives you an idea of the negative impact the Diaspora had on them. Though years before they had "sat by the rivers of Babylon and wept," they had gradually adapted to the point that they were enjoying themselves in exile. Clearly, these were not the Jews who rushed back to resettle the Land of Israel when first allowed to do so.

After some drunken revelry featuring (yet again) the Temple vessels, the king ordered his wife to appear wearing nothing besides the royal crown. She refused to come, and he had her executed.

Queenless, the king sent his scouts to round up all the eligible women in the land — and this is how Esther was taken to the palace. No one knew she was Jewish, and her uncle Mordechai, who happened to be the leading Jewish scholar of his generation, told her to keep her identity secret. The king fell in love with her and, from among all the women taken to the palace, Esther became queen.[222]

Haman, the Amalekite

Ahasuerus's chief minister was a man named Haman HaAgagi. If that doesn't ring a bell, it should. Agag was the king of the nation of Amalek whom King Saul neglected to kill as commanded. Haman was an Amalekite, and he harbored a pathological hatred of the Jewish people. (We covered Amalekite ideology in chapters 6 and 16.)

And so it came to pass that Haman convinced the king to issue a secret decree to annihilate the Jews of Persia on the thirteenth day of the month of Adar. And how he decided on the best date for genocide is very interesting: Haman threw lots, called *purim*.

Why? It is part of Amalekite ideology that everything is a random occurrence — everything happens by chance. There is no God running the show. It's the ultimate denial of reality. So this holiday, which we call Purim (or "Chance"), comes to illustrate that, in fact, nothing happens by chance.

From the day that Haman threw his lots — flipped the dice, so to speak — everything began to flip on him. Expecting honors from the king, Haman found himself forced to bestow these honors on his archenemy Mordechai. Invited along with the king to the queen's feast, Haman was preening with pride, only to discover that the queen was Jewish. And that now he was accused of plotting to murder her along with her people. Begging for mercy, he threw himself onto the queen's divan, only to be caught by the king in this precarious position and accused of attempted rape.

When things couldn't possibly look worse for Haman, then came the clincher. Having erected a gallows for Mordechai, he found them put to an unexpected use when he himself was sentenced to death. And the Jews, whom he had wanted to wipe off the face of the earth, were given the king's permission to annihilate their enemies.

The most fascinating thing about the Book of Esther, which relates this incredible story, is that in the entire text the name of God is never mentioned. We learn from this that after the destruction of the First Temple the presence of God was concealed in the world, but that we could still see God acting through history — delivering one hidden miracle after another to help the Jews survive, keeping His promise that Israel would remain an "eternal nation."

We learn from the Talmud that this state of affairs was actually prophesied in the Book of Deuteronomy, where God says: "I will surely conceal My face on that day...."[223] The Hebrew word for "conceal," *hester* — because of its identical root letters with Ester, that is Esther — is read as an allusion to this time.

When the First Temple stood, you could sense God's presence. You could feel God in Jerusalem. God was always there. But since the Temple's destruction, the level of spirituality in general has been lower and the Jews' ability to relate to God from that period of time onward has been much less direct. From the time of the destruction, God has not acted in history in the open manner He had previously. But God is always here, nevertheless. He's the master puppeteer behind the scenes, putting everything into place.

The Book of Esther is the ultimate story of God putting the cure before the disease.[224] Everything that's a seeming disaster works out in hindsight, so at the end of the story the Jewish people look back and see how incredible it all was.

This is why, on Purim, Jews get drunk so that they can't tell the difference between "Blessed be Mordechai" and "Cursed be Haman." This illustrates that, even when we're not in control, God always is, and that even the worst evil is really serving His will. Everything is not what it seems, which is why on Purim it is a custom to wear masks.

The phrase in the Book of Esther that best describes Purim is *venahafoch hu*, meaning "flipped-over." Whatever bad had seemed to be happening by chance was, in fact, intricately planned for the good. Nothing happens by accident. There's a design to it all.

This, in fact, sums up Jewish history since the destruction of the First Temple. Just as in the story of Purim, when it's over, we look back and see how everything fits into place. Nothing is by chance. Everything has a reason, and God will make sure that even in the worst circumstances the Jews are always going to have a way out, so that they can accomplish their mission in this world.

The next part of their mission proved to be rebuilding the Temple.

Darius II succeeded Ahasuerus as king of Persia. Jewish tradition tells us that he was Esther's son, and he allowed the Jews to finish the job they had started under Cyrus.

This was a very special time in Jewish history when the Jews made a second attempt at getting it right.

CHRONOLOGY OF BABYLONIAN EXILE

HEBREW DATE	B.C.E.	EVENT
3318	442	Nebuchadnezzar assumes throne of Babylon
3319	441	Nebuchadnezzar makes Judah vassal state of Babylon
3327	433	Nebuchadnezzar exiles Jehoiachin, king of Judah, and 10,000 leading scholars
3338	422	Nebuchadnezzar destroys the Temple and exiles Jewish nation
3389	371	Belshazzar, counting from Nebuchadnezzar's ascent to the throne, counts 70 years wrong, holds a banquet and sees writing on the wall; that night Persians and Medes conquer Babylon
3390	370	Persian ruler Cyrus allows Jews to return to Israel, but only 42,000 take up his offer; he allows the rebuilding of the Temple, but Samaritans stop it
3392	368	Ahasuerus becomes the king
3394	366	Ahasuerus counts to 70 again and holds another banquet; Esther becomes queen
3405	355	Purim victory
3406	354	Ahasuerus dies and is succeeded by Darius II, son of Esther
3408	352	Darius allows construction of Temple to begin; it is 70 years since the fall of Jerusalem

25.
THE SECOND TEMPLE

The rebuilding of the Temple was completed in 352 B.C.E. and the Temple rededicated. But it was not the same.

The intense spiritually of the First Temple cannot be compared to the Second. The constant open miracles were gone. Prophecy was rapidly disappearing, and it would soon be gone. The Ark of the Covenant was also gone, and although there was a Holy of Holies, it stood empty.

The Ark — the special gold-lined cedar chest which had contained the tablets of the Ten Commandments — was the place where the Shechinah, the Presence of God, descended from heaven between the outstretched wings of the two golden cherubs. What happened to it?

The Talmud talks about it and presents two opinions.[225] One opinion states the Babylonians took it into captivity. The other opinion states that it was hidden by King Josiah, who had anticipated the impending invasion and destruction (as we mentioned in chapter 22).

There's a well-known story told in the Talmud of a *kohen*, a priest, who finds a loose stone on the Temple Mount and realizes that is where the Ark is hidden. On the way to tell others about it, he dies.[226] The point of the story is that the Ark is not meant to be found. Not yet.

Ezra and Nechemiah

The Jews who rebuilt the Temple in Jerusalem were faced with many challenges and difficulties. Strong leadership would be essential for them to reestablish a strong community. Two individuals played a critical role in this task. The first was Ezra.

A scribe, scholar, and a Jewish community leader in Persia, Ezra, a *kohen*, heard that the Jewish community in the Holy Land was floundering with neither king nor prophet. So, he took with him 1,496 well-chosen men with leadership abilities and came to the rescue.

Ezra is so well thought of in the Talmud that it is written of him that "the Torah could have been given to Israel through Ezra, if Moses had not preceded him."[227] This high praise goes to Ezra for the spiritual rebuilding of the Jewish people and his efforts to reinstate Torah law in the land.

Among his most dramatic reforms was his war against assimilation and intermarriage. Indeed, the Book of Ezra condemns all the men living in Israel who had married non-Jewish wives and gives their names — all 112 of them.[228]

You might ask: What's the big deal? After all, only 112 men strayed. Today, millions of Jews are intermarrying — the intermarriage rate in America is over 50%. The difference is that 2,500 years ago, even one Jew intermarrying was an outrage. Now society accepts it as normal. So-called "progressive" congregations in America are even shopping for rabbis who will officiate at mixed marriages — to lend legitimacy to something which the Bible repeatedly condemns and which spells the death of the Jewish people.

Through Ezra's efforts, these mixed marriages were dissolved. All the people then gathered in Jerusalem — men and women from all over the country — and the Torah was read out loud to all. At the end, all present pledged not to intermarry, to uphold the Torah, and to strengthen themselves spiritually.[229]

The other major personality dominating this period was Nechemiah, a leader of the Jewish community in Babylon and an official in the court of the Emperor Darius II. While Ezra had succeeded in spiritually strengthening the returnees, Jerusalem remained unwalled and unprotected. Thirteen years after the arrival of Ezra, Nechemiah arrived, having been appointed governor by Darius. After surveying Jerusalem he announced:

"Come, let us build the walls of Jerusalem so that we will no longer be an object of scorn."[230]

Despite the efforts of the surrounding peoples to hinder construction, the walls were completed. Spiritually and physically fortified, Jerusalem could prosper and its population expand.

Of course, neither the city nor the Temple were as splendid as what had been destroyed. But the returnees from Babylon did not have the resources of King Solomon. Eventually (circa 18 B.C.E.), the Temple would be rebuilt again by Herod the Great, and made into a spectacular structure, but although it would be physically beautiful, it would be spiritually empty. Even the institution of the priesthood would become corrupt.

According to the Talmud, during the First Temple period of about 410 years, there were only eighteen High Priests. During the Second Temple period of 420 years, there were more than 300 High Priests![231] We know that the first three High Priests of the Second Temple held their position for a total of 130 years — Jonathan was High Priest for eighty years, Simon was High Priest for forty years, and Ishmael ben Pabi was High Priest for ten years. That means in the remaining 290 years there were at least 300 High Priests — one every year or so. What accounts for that?

The Talmud tells us that the Holy of Holies was forbidden ground, except for Yom Kippur. On that one day only, the High Priest entered to perform special rites before God. But if he himself was not spiritually pure, he would not be able to withstand the intense encounter with God and would die on the spot. We know that during the Second Temple period, a rope had to be tied to the High Priest, so that in case he died, he could be pulled out of the Holy of Holies.

Because the whole priesthood was a corrupt institution for most of the Second Temple period, the High Priests died or were replaced every year. And yet people clamored for the job, which went to the highest bidder. So the question has to be asked: If he was going to die on Yom Kippur, who would want the position? One possible answer is that many of the candidates strongly believed that their violation of the Temple service was actually the correct way to do it.[232] That is how bad things got.

Loss of Prophecy

Why did things get so bad? Because prophecy disappeared from the land and strong central authority was largely lacking.

When the prophets were around and leadership was strong, heresy was unthinkable. A prophet talked to God, and he was able to deal with a heretic. No one could deny basic tenets of Judaism in the face of prophecy and open miracles. In the period of the Judges and the First Temple, an individual could always make a free-will decision to reject Judaism, worship idols and even use the impure spirituality of idolatry to perform magic and divination, but the presence of prophets and strong leadership made it virtually impossible to undermine the philosophy and practices of Judaism itself. But when prophecy disappeared and central authority was weakened, it became easier for people to stray and for various holy institutions (like the priesthood) to become corrupt.

Prophecy disappeared because the Jewish people had damaged their relationship with God. They were spiritually weaker and could not do the same intense spiritual work required to achieve the high level of communication with God that defined prophecy.[233]

According to Judaism, prophecy is not just the ability to predict the future; it is a state of transcendence of the physical world. This means the prophet has entered such a high plane of understanding that he or she is able to communicate with God and access information and understanding inaccessible to a normal person.

As we saw in chapter 11, Moses was the ultimate prophet — that is, he reached the highest level of prophecy that is humanly possible. But there were many others who achieved lesser levels of prophecy. In chapter 16, we talked about how the Jewish people consulted the prophets on everything, including lost objects. But that trend disappeared during the early years of the Second Temple. Says the Talmud: "After the later prophets, Haggai, Zechariah, and Malachi, had died, the prophetic spirit disappeared from the Jewish people...."[234]

If anyone is interested in how to become a prophet, there is an instruction book available. It called *The Path of the Just*, and it was written in the eighteenth century by the great kabbalist, Rabbi Moshe Chaim Luzzatto, also known as the Ramchal. This guidebook tells you how to get complete control of yourself physically, emotionally, and spiritually so you can transcend this world and become a prophet. In another of his books, *The Way of God*, Rabbi Luzzatto clearly defines the concept of prophecy:

> The main concept of true prophecy is, therefore, that a living person achieves such an attachment and a bond with God. This in itself is certainly a very high degree of perfection. Besides this, however, it [prophecy] is often accompanied by certain information and enlightenment. Through prophecy one can gain knowledge of many lofty truths among God's hidden mysteries. These things are perceived very clearly.... Part of a prophet's career may include being sent on a mission by God.[235]

But even if you master both these books, you will not be a prophet because the gates of prophecy are closed to us. And why is that? Because prophecy is only possible if the rest of the Jewish people are also spiritually elevated.

As an individual you can reach a tremendously high level, but you can only reach so high. To get all the way to the top and break through the threshold, you've got to "stand on the shoulders" of the Jewish people, because there has to be a minimum level of spirituality of the entire nation in order for you to reach the level of prophecy. If the nation drops below that threshold, it doesn't matter how much you stand on your tippy-toes and reach up, you're not going to succeed.

During the Second Temple period, we see the Jewish people dropping below a certain threshold of spirituality, which they're never going to attain again. As we saw from the Purim story, by the time we arrive at the period of the Second Temple, God's presence is hidden, the Ark of the Covenant is hidden, and so is prophecy.

The Talmud says there were definitely individuals living at this time, who, had they lived earlier, would most certainly have been prophets: There is one among you who deserves that the Shechinah [divine Presence] should rest on him as it did on Moses, but his generation is not deserving.[236]

The door to prophecy had been slammed in the face of the Jewish people. And we are told that it will not be opened again until the Messianic Era.

PROPHETS & PROPHETESSES OF ISRAEL			
IN ALPHABETICAL ORDER			
Abigail	Elkanah	Jahaziel	Nathan
Abraham	Esther	Jehu	Neriah
Aharon	Ezekiel	Jeremiah	Obadiah
Ahijah	Gad	Joel	Oded
Amos	Habakuk	Jonah	Pinhas
Amotz	Haggai	Joshua	Samuel
Azariah	Hanani	Malachi	Sarah
Baruch	Hannah	Mehseiah	Seraiah
David	Hosea	Micah	Shemaiah
Deborah	Huldah	Michaiah	Solomon
Eli	Iddo	Miriam	Urijah
Eliezer	Isaac	Mordechai	Zechariah
Elijah	Isaiah	Moses	Zephaniah
Elisha	Jacob	Nahum	

26.

MEN OF THE GREAT ASSEMBLY

The Men of the Great Assembly — in Hebrew *Anshei Knesset HaGedolah* — were an unusual group of Jewish personalities who assumed the reigns of Jewish leadership between 410 B.C.E. and 312 B.C.E. They first came together in Babylon following the destruction of the First Temple, when it became apparent that the Jewish people were growing weaker spiritually, and continued in the Land of Israel during the early days of the Second Temple period.

They defined Judaism in this tumultuous time when prophecy was all but gone from the Jewish people. This group of wise leaders expanded the Sanhedrin, the Jewish Supreme Court, from 70 to 120 members, with the goal of preserving and strengthening Judaism in the Diaspora and afterward.

(Today's Israeli Parliament, which is called the Knesset, also has 120 members in imitation of the Great Assembly, although the Knesset of today serves an entirely different function than did the *Anshei Knesset HaGedolah* of 2,400 years ago.)

Among the Great Assembly we count the last of the prophets Haggai, Zechariah and Malachi, as well as the sages Mordechai (of the Purim story), Nechemiah (the chief architect of rebuilding of Jerusalem), and Simon HaTzaddik (the High Priest).

Keep in mind that at this time the Talmud has not yet been compiled. Knowing how to live a Jewish life depends on knowing the commandments of the Torah and their interpretations and applications, which have been passed down orally — in short, knowing the Written Torah and the Oral Torah, both of which date back to Moses' teachings at Sinai.

It is impossible to understand the Written Torah without its Oral Torah complement. For example, when the Written Torah states: "And these words which I command you today shall be upon your heart...and you shall write them upon the doorposts of your house and upon your gateways," it is the Oral Torah that explains which "words" the Written Torah is referring to, and that these words should be penned on a small scroll and affixed to the door frame. Without the Oral Torah we wouldn't know about the mezuzah and countless other practices of day-to-day Judaism.

The destruction of the First Temple and the ensuing exile were incredibly traumatic experiences for the Jewish people. They found themselves in an alien land with none of the normative institutions fundamental to Judaism. As they struggled with the aftermath of exile, accurate transmission of this oral tradition became essential. And here is where the Men of the Great Assembly made the greatest contribution.[237]

As we see in history, to the extent that the Jews stop living according to Jewish law and Jewish tradition (i.e. that which makes them Jewish), to that extent they assimilate and disappear. Therefore, the contributions of these men can be said to account in large measure for Jewish survival. The Talmud pays them great homage:

> Moses received the Torah from Sinai and conveyed it to Joshua, Joshua to the Elders, the Elders to the Prophets, and the Prophets to the Men of the Great Assembly.... Simon HaTzaddik was one of the last of the Great Assembly. He used to say, "The world stands on three things: on the Torah, on the service of God, and on acts of loving-kindness."[238]

Contents of the Bible

In addition to ensuring the accurate transmission of the Oral Law, the Men of the Great Assembly decided which of the multitude of Jewish holy writings should be in the Bible. The Jewish people had produced hundreds of thousands of prophets (both men and women), but which of their writings should be preserved for future generations and which had limited applicability?

The Men of the Great Assembly made this decision and gave us what is known as the Hebrew Bible today (i.e., the *Tanach*).

The word *Tanach* is an acronym for the Bible's three essential parts — Torah, *Nevi'im* (Prophets), and *Ketuvim* (Writings). The Torah includes the Five Books of Moses — Genesis, Exodus, Leviticus, Numbers, and Deuteronomy. *Nevi'im* include the works of the prophets such as Samuel, Isaiah, Jeremiah, Ezekiel, etc. *Ketuvim* include other writings such as the Psalms, the Proverbs, the Book of Esther, the Book of Ruth, etc.

The Hebrew Bible is what the Christians call the "Old Testament," but traditionally Jews have never called it that. The word "testament" is derived from the Latin word *testari,* meaning "to testify/be a witness." The Hebrew Bible was named the Old Testament by the Christians because of their belief that God cancelled the covenant He made with the Jews and made a new covenant, or the "New Testament," with the followers of Jesus. Since Jews deny that God would ever "change His mind" after promising the Jews they would be His "eternal nation" (a promise He clearly kept), they find that term insulting.

BOOKS OF HEBREW BIBLE & THEIR AUTHORS

BOOKS OF THE TORAH	BOOKS OF THE PROPHETS	BOOKS OF WRITINGS
Genesis	Joshua (Joshua)	Psalms (David)
Exodus	Judges (Samuel)	Proverbs (Solomon)
Leviticus	Samuel (Samuel)	Job (Moses)
Numbers	Kings (Jeremiah)	Song of Songs (Solomon)
Deuterononomy	Isaiah (Isaiah)	Ruth (Samuel)
	Jeremiah (Jeremiah)	Lamentations (Jeremiah)
	Ezekiel (Ezekiel)	Ecclesiastes (Solomon)
	Hosea (Hosea)	Esther (Mordechai & Esther)
	Joel (Joel)	Daniel (Daniel)
	Amos (Amos)	Ezra (Ezra)
	Obadiah (Obadiah)	Nehemiah (Nehemiah)
	Jonah (Jonah)	Chronicles (Ezra)
	Micah (Micah)	
	Nahum (Nahum)	
	Habbakuk (Habbakuk)	
	Zephaniah (Zephaniah)	

Prayer

The last thing that the Men of the Great Assembly did was formalize prayer. They actually only began a process which was not finished until the second century C.E., after the destruction of the Second Temple, but they laid down the key principles and basic structure of formalized prayer.[239]

During the First Temple period, there was no need for formalized Jewish prayer liturgy, because God's presence was manifest. It was much easier for the individual to have a close, intense, personal relationship with God. Additionally, a great deal of what is now the object of prayer was formally accomplished through the offering of sacrifices and the Temple service. Of course, when the Second Temple was rebuilt, sacrifices resumed, but most of the Jews had not returned to the Land of Israel and, therefore, had no access to this medium of connecting to God via the Temple. In addition, as mentioned previously, even with the Temple rebuilt, the connection with God during the Second Temple period was much weaker.

Therefore, the times of the formalized prayer were designed to correspond to times when things were done in the Temple: the morning prayer corresponded to the *Shacharit* service in the Temple; the afternoon prayer corresponded to the *Mincha* service; the evening prayer, *Ma'ariv* or *Aarvit* corresponded to the nightly duties (as there were no sacrifices as night).

The centerpiece of each selection of prayers (repeated three times a day) was the *Shemoneh Esrei*, "The Eighteen Blessings." Each "blessing" was stated in the plural ("we") to underscore the interdependency of the Jewish people.

The mystical depth of this prayer — a masterpiece of writing by the Men of the Great Assembly — is astounding to this day. For example, the blessing for healing is composed of twenty-seven words, corresponding to the twenty-seven words in the Book of Exodus[240] where God promises to be the healer of the Jewish people. It is said that the text of the *Shemoneh Esrei* is so spiritually powerful that even when recited without intention, feeling, or understanding, its words have a great impact on the world.[241]

Through divine inspiration and sheer genius, the Men of the Great Assembly were able to create a spiritually thriving people out of the ashes of a physically destroyed nation. Their work defined and anchored Jewish religious and national identity and created focus, unity, and uniformity for the Jewish people, no matter where in the world they might be scattered.

The last surviving member of the Great Assembly was Simon HaTzaddik, who was the High Priest in the Second Temple. Under him, according to the ancient historian Josephus, the Jews of Israel prospered and Jewish population in the Land of Israel reached 350,000.[242]

It helped the Jews physically (if not spiritually) that, during the time of Simon HaTzaddik, the Persians were the rulers and they were benevolent dictators. But the picture changed when the Greek Empire took over.

27.
THE GREEK EMPIRE

The fourth century B.C.E. had been eventful for the Jewish people:

Exiled to Babylon, they witnessed the fall of a mighty Babylonian Empire before their very eyes as the Persians invaded.

Permitted to return to the Land of Israel by the Persian Emperor Cyrus in 370 B.C.E., they reluctantly took up the offer, with only 42,000 of their number actually returning.

The returnees' attempts to rebuild the Temple in Jerusalem were aborted early as their angry neighbors, the not-so-good Samaritans complained to the emperor.

In Persia, Haman, the chief minister to King Ahasuerus, hatched a plot to annihilate the Jews. But Queen Esther (who was secretly Jewish) came to the rescue in 355 B.C.E.

The next Persian monarch, Darius II, Esther's son, allowed the rebuilding of the Temple in 370 B.C.E.

The Jewish people living in the Land of Israel were reenergized spiritually thanks to the leadership of Ezra and the Men of the Great Assembly.

By the year 336 B.C.E., when the last of the Men of the Great Assembly, Simon HaTzaddik, was High Priest, a new threat was looming on the other side of the Mediterranean. It was called Greece.

The Rise of the Greek Empire

The origins of Greece are shrouded in mystery and date back to the time of

Abraham, eighteenth century B.C.E., or perhaps even earlier. Historians disagree as to where the Greeks came from — they could have been people migrating down from Asia through Europe and settling in the Greek Isles, or they could have been seafaring people who settled along the coast.

Whoever they were, the earliest inhabitants of mainland Greece (called Mycenaeans after excavations found at Mycenae) developed an advanced culture. But, around 1100 B.C.E., the Mycenaeans were invaded by barbarians called Dorians and their civilization disappeared. Greece went into a "Dark Age," to reemerge hundreds of years later.

The classical Greek period began as early as the seventh century B.C.E., though we tend to be more familiar with its history in the fifth century B.C.E. when Greece consisted of a group of constantly warring city-states, the most famous being Athens and Sparta. The Greek victory at Marathon (490 B.C.E.),[243] the destruction of the Persian fleet at Salamis (480 B.C.E.), and the victory at Plataea (479 B.C.E.) brought an end to the Persian Empire's attempts to conquer Greece.

During the last three decades of the fifth century B.C.E., Athens and Sparta waged a devastating war called the Peloponnesian War, which went on from 431 to 404 B.C.E. and which culminated in the surrender of Athens. More inter-Greek fighting followed in the fourth century, but later in that century all of Greece succumbed to Phillip II of Macedon, who paved the way for his son, Alexander the Great, to spread the Greek civilization across the world.

The late fifth and the fourth centuries B.C.E. were as eventful for the Greeks as for the Jews. Despite constant warfare, this was also the golden age of classical Greek culture — the birth of democracy, the time of Aristotle, Socrates, and Plato.

Today, it is easy — while admiring the Greek contributions to civilization with its politics, philosophy, art and architecture — to forget what Greek society was really like. For example, we've heard of the "Spartan lifestyle," but what did that mean in practice? Well, for starters, at the age of seven, Spartan boys were separated from their parents, they lived in military barracks where they were beaten, and they were not even given minimal food in order to encourage them to steal. To be Spartan meant to be tough.

The Athenians, though not as tough as the Spartans, were not what you'd describe as "soft" either. For example, they thought nothing of killing infants (a common practice in all ancient civilizations, even the "elevated" ones). One of the most influential thinkers in Western intellectual history — none other than Aristotle — argued in his *Politics* that killing children was essential to the functioning of society. He wrote:

> There must be a law that no imperfect or maimed child shall be brought up. And to avoid an excess in population, some children must be exposed [i.e. thrown on the trash heap or left out in the woods to die]. For a limit must be fixed to the population of the state.[244]

Note the tone of his statement. Aristotle isn't saying "I like killing babies," but he is making a cold, rational calculation: overpopulation is dangerous, and this is the most expedient way to keep it in check.

In warfare, the Greeks invented the "pitched battle" — with thousands of foot soldiers colliding with the enemy, slaughtering and being slaughtered as they advanced. (The eighty pounds of armor and weaponry carried by the average Greek hoplite, or infantry man, necessitated a pitched battle, since after about 30–45 minutes the soldiers were all exhausted.) While we tend to think today of the Greeks as cultured and noble, it is shocking to learn how brutal their civilization (like all ancient civilizations) could be.[245]

The other great Greek innovation was the phalanx. Instead of the undisciplined "free-for-all" combat common in ancient warfare, the Greeks fought in disciplined battle lines. Infantry advanced with shields "locked" together and spears pointing straight ahead. A well-disciplined phalanx created a formidable wall of shields and spears which was used with deadly efficiency.[246]

But the one who took the Greek conquests to new heights was, of course, Alexander the Great.

Alexander the Great

Alexander, born in 356 B.C.E., was the son of Phillip II, the king of the northern Greek province of Macedonia (who was considered a barbarian by the southern Greek city-states). Phillip had created a powerful, professional army which forcibly united the fractious Greek city-states into one empire. His son Alexander displayed tremendous military talent from an early age and was appointed as a commander in his father's army at eighteen.

Having conquered all of Greece, Phillip was about to embark on a campaign to invade Greece's archenemy, the Persian Empire. Before he could act, however, he was assassinated, possibly by Alexander, who then became king in 336 B.C.E. Two years later, Alexander crossed the Hellspont (in modern-day Turkey) with 45,000 men and invaded Persia.

The backbone of Alexander's army was his infantry. They carried extremely long pikes (spears which may have been as long as 21 feet, or 7 meters). These pike-men moved in giant squares called a phalanx, with shields locked together, sixteen men across and sixteen deep — the first five rows of pikes pointed straight ahead creating a lethal wall of spear heads.

In three colossal battles — at Granicus, Issus, and Gaugamela — that took place between 334 and 331, Alexander brilliantly (and often recklessly) led his army to victory against Persian armies that may have outnumbered his own as much as ten to one. His chief tactic was always to be on the offense and always do the unexpected. In battle, he would lead his Campanion Cavalry right at the strongest (rather than the weakest) point of the enemy line. When he fought the Persians, he went for the most heavily protected point of the Persian force surrounding the Persian emperor, aiming to destroy the leadership.

When the Persian Emperor Darius III fled from the battle site, the Persian army collapsed. By 331 B.C.E., the Persian Empire was defeated and Alexander was the undisputed ruler of the Mediterranean. His military campaign lasted twelve years and took him and his army 10,000 miles to the Indus River in India. Only the weariness of his men and his untimely death in 323 B.C.E. at age 32 ended the Greek conquest of the known world. It is said that when Alexander looked at his empire he wept, for there was nothing left to conquer.

At its largest, Alexander's empire stretched from Egypt to India. He built six Greek cities in his empire, all named Alexandria. (Today the best known is the city of Alexandria in Egypt on the Nile Delta.) These cities, and the Greeks who settled in them, brought to the oldest civilizations of Mesopotamia a new way of being — Greek culture, which was called Hellenism because Greece was then called Hellas. Only later did the Romans dub it Greece.

Hellenism

The Greeks were not only military imperialists, but also cultural imperialists. Greek soldiers and settlers brought their way of life — their language, art, architecture, literature, and philosophy — to the Middle East. When Greek culture merged with the culture of the Middle East, it created a new cultural hybrid-Hellenism whose impact would be far greater and last for far longer than the brief period of Alexander's empire. Whether through the idea of the pitched battle, art, architecture, or philosophy, Hellenism's influence on the Roman Empire, Christianity, and the West was monumental.

The Greeks showcased all human talents — literature, drama, poetry, music, architecture, sculpture, etc. They glorified the beauty of the human body, displaying athletic prowess in their Olympics. Nothing regarding the human body was considered embarrassing, in need of hiding, or private.

(Athletic competitions, performed in the nude, were the norm in Greece. Our modern word "gymnasium" is derived from the Greek word *gumnos,* which means "naked." Public toilets often consisted of a bench on a main street with holes in it; people sat there and did their business as others walked by.)

Even Greek gods were described in human terms and were often bested by human beings in Greek mythology; with time, it became the style of intellectual Greeks to denigrate their gods and speak of them with biting cynicism and disrespect.

In short, the Greeks introduced into human consciousness an idea which is going to come into play as one of the most powerful intellectual forces in modern history — humanism. The human being is the center of all things. The human mind and its ability to understand and observe and comprehend things rationally is the be-all and end-all. That's an idea which comes from the Greeks.

Above all, the Greeks thought that this was enlightenment, the highest level of civilization. They had a strong sense of destiny and believed that their culture was ordained to become the universal culture of humanity.

Of course, the Jews had a different vision. The Jews believed that a world united in the belief in one God and ascribing to one absolute standard of moral values — including respect for life, peace, justice, and social responsibility for the weak and poor — was the ultimate future of the human race. This Jewish ideology was wedded to an extreme, uncompromising exclusivity of worship (as demanded by the belief in one God) and a complete intolerance of polytheistic religious beliefs or practices. There is only one God and so only one God can be worshipped, end of story.

To the Jews, human beings were created in the image of God. To the Greeks, gods were made in the image of human beings. To the Jews, the physical world was something to be perfected and elevated spiritually. To the Greeks the physical world was perfect. In short, to Greeks, what was beautiful was holy; to the Jews what was holy was beautiful.

Such disparate views were bound to clash.

The Greeks versus the Jews

During his military campaign against Persia, Alexander took a detour to the south, conquering Tyre (in today's Lebanon) and then Egypt via what is today Israel. Alexander was planning to destroy the Temple, egged on by the Samaritans who hated the Jews. But he didn't.

There is a fascinating story about Alexander's first encounter with the Jews of Israel, who were until his time the subjects of the Persian Empire. The narrative concerning Alexander's first interaction with the Jews is recorded in both the Talmud and by the ancient historian Josephus.[248] In both accounts, the High Priest of the Temple (in the Talmudic narrative he is identified as Simon HaTzaddik, the last surviving member of the Men of the Great Assembly), fearing that Alexander would destroy the city of Jerusalem, goes out to meet him before he arrives at the city gates. The narratives then describe how Alexander, upon seeing the High Priest, dismounted and bowed to him. (Alexander rarely, if ever, bowed to anyone!)

In Josephus's account, when asked by his general, Parmenio, to explain his actions, he answered:

> I did not bow before him but before that God who has honored him with the High Priesthood, for I saw this very man in a dream, in this very apparel...he exhorted me to make no delay, but boldly to pass over the sea there, for that he would conduct my army and would give me the dominion over the Persians.

Because of this dream, Alexander spared Jerusalem and did not destroy the Temple as he had planned, and he listened when Simon HaTzaddik told him that the Jews were not enemies of the Greeks, while the Samaritans were. The Talmud relates the interaction between Alexander and the Jewish delegation:

> They [the Jews led by Simon HaTzaddik] asked, "Is it possible that these idol worshippers should fool you into destroying the House [of God] where prayers are offered for you and your kingdom that it should never be destroyed?" Alexander said to them, "What idol worshippers do you mean?" They replied, "We are referring to the Samaritans who are standing before you now." Said Alexander, "I am handing them over to you to do with them as you please."[249]

As a result, the Jews were given free rein to subdue the Samaritans, which they promptly set out to do, and Israel and Jerusalem were peacefully absorbed into the Greek Empire. As tribute to his benign conquest the rabbis decreed that the Jewish firstborn of that time be named Alexander (which is a Jewish name until today), and the date of the meeting (twenty-fifth of Tevet) was declared a minor holiday.

At first, everything went well. The Greek authorities preserved the rights of the local Jewish population and did not attempt to interfere with Jewish religious practice. The Jews continued to flourish as a separate and distinct entity for 165 years — a rare phenomenon in the Hellenistic world, because the vast majority of the peoples conquered by Alexander the Great had willingly allowed themselves to be Hellenized. The fact that the Jews (with the exception of a small minority) rejected Hellenism was a strong testament to that ever-present Jewish drive and sense of mission.

The famed classical historian, Michael Grant, in his book *From Alexander to Cleopatra*, explains:

> The Jews proved not only unassimilated, but unassimilable, and... the demonstration that this was so proved one of the most significant turning-points in Greek history, owing to the gigantic influence exerted throughout subsequent ages by their religion....[250]

But with time, Judaism, with its intractable beliefs and bizarre practices, began to stand out as an open challenge to the concept of Hellenistic world supremacy. For the generally tolerant Greeks, this challenge became more and more intolerable. It was only a matter of time before open conflict would arise.

It did not help matters that Alexander's vast empire did not survive his death in 323 B.C.E., but fragmented into three large entities centered in Greece, Egypt, and Syria, each controlled by his former generals. These smaller empires were known as: (1) Seleucid or Assyrian Greece (which also included Persia); (2) Ptolemian or Egyptian Greece; and (3) Macedonian or Greece proper (which included the independent city-states of Athens, Sparta, etc.).

Initially, Israel fell under the Ptolemies of Egypt. They were generally liberal and open-minded, in keeping with the spirit of their capital city of Alexandria, which was the world's cultural center. But this changed in 198 B.C.E. after the Battle of Panias (or Banyas) in northern Israel, which took place between the Ptolemies and the Seleucids, and which the Seleucids won.

After their victory at Panias, the Seleucids of Assyria, led by the King Antiochus III, took over Israel, but they were insecure about their control over the region. The next Seleucid king, Antiochus IV Epiphanes, found himself under a lot of pressure, as he tried to hold back the Ptolemies and worried about the rising might of Rome. He decided that the weak link in his defenses was Israel.

Why? Because Israel was bordered by Ptolemic Egypt and the Mediterranean Sea (from whence the Romans could come), and, worst of all, the majority of Jews were not into Greek culture.[251] This situation he promptly moved to remedy.

28.
GREEK PERSECUTION

When they first met the Jews, the Greeks — who had conquered the entire known world — were astonished; they'd never encountered people like this before.

The Jews were the only monotheists in the world, and they subscribed to a worldview that was totally different from anyone else's — namely, that everything that exists has been created and is sustained by One infinite, invisible, and caring God. This idea — particularly, that this caring, perfect God busies Himself with the lives of imperfect mortals — the Greeks found just about incomprehensible. The Greek historian, Hecateus, describes the unique monotheism of the Temple in Jerusalem:

> There is no image nor statue nor votive offering therein; nothing at all is planted there, neither grove nor anything of the sort. The priests abide therein both nights and days, performing certain purification rites, and drinking not the least drop of wine while they are in the Temple.[252]

Moreover, the Greeks could not understand the Jewish adherence to the Torah. This was an ancient book, which the Jews claimed they received from God, and which contained rituals, restrictions, and values that were far removed from Greek ideals.

In short, the Greeks didn't know what to make of the Jews.

The Jews were likewise confounded. The Greeks were people who valued education and intellectual pursuits — something the Jews also valued and very much admired. The Greeks spoke a beautiful language, which the Jews appreciated very much.[253]

Indeed, the Torah was promptly translated into Greek (in the third century B.C.E.) at the behest of Ptolemy III — the first such translation in Jewish history. This translation was called the "Septuagint" after the seventy rabbis who translated it. As the Talmud relates:

> It happened that King Ptolemy gathered seventy-two sages and placed them in seventy-two houses without telling them why he had brought them together. He went to each one of them and told him, "Translate for me [into Greek] the Torah of your master Moses."[254]

(This translation is considered a national disaster for the Jewish people. In the hands of the non-Jewish world, the Hebrew Bible has often been used against the Jews and has been deliberately mistranslated. Most Christian Bibles in English today depend on the Greek translation which was then translated into Latin, the language of the Roman Empire, and from there into English. You can just imagine how many interpretations and mistakes and deliberate mistranslations were made along the way.[255])

However, it was inevitable that the Bible would be translated into Greek because Greek became the international intellectual language of the ancient Mediterranean world. It was as common everywhere as English is today! And the Jews, who were mostly speaking Aramaic, thanks to their foray in the Babylonian exile, became conversant in Greek as well. (Hebrew was then a language primarily of prayer and of study but not the spoken language of the street, even in Israel.)

Despite this mutual appreciation between the Greeks and the Jews, the vast differences could not be tolerated by the dominant culture for long.

Jew versus Jew

The Hanukah story is often portrayed as a struggle for national liberation — the Jewish revolt against the Greek occupation of Israel. In reality, it is much more complicated than that. The real conflict was not physical but intellectual. Hanukah was ultimately an ideological-spiritual war between paganism and Judaism. It was also not a struggle purely between Greeks and Jews. It was first and foremost a civil war of Jew versus Jew. The initial impetus for the Greek attack on Judaism came from a certain splinter group of the Jewish people themselves — the Hellenized Jews. These were Jews who had been seduced by Greek culture. And it is no wonder why. Greek culture was the major cultural milieu of the ancient world.

We see this as a pattern in Jewish history. A world culture comes along which is enlightened and progressive and is changing the world, and some of the upper-class Jews always get into it. Why? Because they are rich, sophisticated, and have lots of spare time. Then, they say to the rest of the Jewish people: "Let's get modern. Forget this ancient Jewish stuff." (We will see this pattern repeated in Spain, in Germany, and even today in America and Israel.)

At the time of the Hanukah story, there was a small but very vocal and powerful group of Jews who aligned themselves with the Greek authorities. They became Hellenized, and they imitated the Greeks in every way. They sent their children to the gymnasium, and they reversed their circumcisions — a very painful operation — because so many Greek activities were conducted in the unclothed and the Greeks would consider them mutilated otherwise.

To make matters worse, the schism between the Hellenized Jews and mainstream Jews was paralleled by another schism — between two factions of religious Jews.

It began in the third century B.C.E., when two students named Zadok and Bysos started preaching a new form of Judaism, devoid of belief in the divine origin of the Oral Torah (the importance of which we explained in chapter 26). There is little doubt that Greek thought played a significant role in creating this early break with mainstream Judaism. Their followers were called the Zadukim and Bysosim, though it is the Zadukim — i.e., Sadducees — that have gone down in history.

Ironically, the mainstream observant Jews, who followed the rabbis and kept Jewish law as it has always been practiced, were called "separatists" — Perushim or Pharisees — to distinguish them from the others.

Since the Sadducees did not believe that the Oral Torah came from God, they maintained that they were only obligated to keep the laws of the Written Torah, which they read literally.[256] But so many of the laws of the Written Torah are incomprehensible without the Oral Torah. Their answer? Each man for himself — anyone can decide what it means and act accordingly.

The Sadducees found natural allies among the Hellenized Jews, as modern-day historian, Rabbi Berel Wein, explains:

> The Sadducees were always more acceptable in the eyes of the Hellenist Jews than their rabbinic foes. The alliance of the Hellenists and the Sadducees against traditional Judaism guaranteed constant turmoil in Jewish life throughout the time of the Second Temple and even thereafter.[257]

This is how the ancient historian Josephus describes the beliefs of the Jews at this time:

> The Pharisees are considered most skillful in the exact explication of their laws and are the leading school; they ascribe all to fate and to God and yet allow that to do what is right or to the contrary is principally in the power of men, although fate does cooperate in every action. They say that all souls are imperishable but that the souls of good men only pass into other bodies while the souls of evil men are subject to eternal punishment.
>
> But the Sadducees are those that compose the second order and exclude fate entirely and suppose that God is not concerned with our doing or not doing what is evil. They say that to do what is good or what is evil is man's own choice and that the choice of one or the other belongs to each person who may act as he pleases. They also exclude the belief in immortality of the soul and the punishment and rewards of the afterworld.
>
> Moreover, the Pharisees are friendly to one another and cultivate harmonious relations with the community, but the behavior of the Sadducees towards one another is to some degree boorish, and their conversation with those other than of their own party is barbarous as if they were strangers to them.[258]

You can see how the Sadducees were influenced by Greek thought. They were part of the reason that the priesthood and the Temple service became so corrupt, as many of the priestly class, an upper class at that time, became Sadducees.

(We shall discuss the Sadducees in greater detail in chapter 33, when we come to the Roman Empire and its domination of the Jews.)

Forced Hellenization

Meanwhile, the Greeks under Antiochus IV Epiphanes were taking deliberate steps to Hellenize the mainstream Jews by attempting to destroy Judaism.

The Book of Maccabees calls this period — between 140 B.C.E. and 138 B.C.E. — a "reign of terror" and describes its beginnings:

> Not long after this, the king sent an Athenian senator to compel the Jews to forsake the laws of their fathers and cease to live by the laws of God, and also to pollute the Temple in Jerusalem and call it the shrine of Olympian Zeus....[259]

One of the first actions undertaken by Antiochus was to take control of the Temple by undermining the office of the High Priest. He removed the High Priest from his position and replaced him with a Jew he had in his back pocket. From this point on the High Priesthood became, to a large extent, a corrupt institution (as noted in chapter 25).

In fact, all the basic institutions were corrupted — the monarchy, the priesthood, even the Temple service. Only the Sanhedrin, the Jewish Supreme Court and its rabbis (who will eventually write down the Talmud) remained relatively intact.

After he installed his own High Priest, Antiochus tried to destroy the Jewish calendar. Why was this so important?

By this time Antiochus understood the Jews very well. To him, these people were time obsessed — they were always trying to make time holy. Destroy time and you destroy the Jews' ability to practice Judaism. Therefore, Antiochus forbade the observance of Shabbat, the observance of the New Moon (Rosh Hodesh), and the observance of the holidays — Pesach, Shavuot, Rosh HaShanah, Yom Kippur, Sukkot.

Next, Antiochus forbade keeping kosher and studying Torah. Torah scrolls were publicly burned, and swine were sacrificed over sacred Jewish books to defile them. Knowing that this animal was particularly repugnant to the Jews, Antiochus even forced the High Priest to institute swine sacrifices in the Temple in Jerusalem, and also to permit worship there of a whole array of Greek gods.[260]

Lastly, Antiochus forbade circumcision. To the Jews, this was the physical, tangible sign of their covenant with God. And it was the one thing the Greeks — who worshipped the perfection of the human body — found most abhorrent. To them, circumcision was a mutilation.

Jews resisted, so Antiochus and his henchmen went about driving the point home in a crude and cruel fashion. Rabbi Berel Wein relates this graphically in his book *Echoes of Glory*:

> Women who allowed their sons to be circumcised were killed with their sons tied around their necks. The scholars of Israel were hounded, hunted down, and killed. Jews who refused to eat pork or sacrifice hogs were tortured to death.... Even the smallest hamlet in Judah was not safe from the oppression of the Hellenists. The altars to Zeus and other pagan deities were erected in every village, and Jews of every area were forced to participate in the sacrificial services.[261]

Until then, this type of religious persecution was unknown. No one in the ancient world declared war on other people's religion, because the attitude of polytheism was "I'll worship your god, you worship mine. The more gods the merrier." (Later we will see Greek and Roman mythologies blending — with Zeus becoming Jupiter, etc. — in a display of ultimate pluralism where everyone's religion was as good as the next, and none were taken seriously.)

In the polytheistic world no one died for their religion. No one, except the Jews.

The Jews maintained that some things in this life were worth dying for because they were more meaningful than life itself. Jews were willing to give up their lives for Judaism, not because God needs people to die for Him, but because the ideology of Torah is something without which humanity is doomed. The Jews, who are supposed to be "the light unto the nations," cannot abandon their mission, even when their lives are threatened.

In the early stages of the conflict, many Jews chose the path of "passive resistance" by ignoring the Greek restrictions and continuing to learn Torah and circumcise their infant sons. However, this proved fatal, as many Jews were martyred for their continued loyalty to Judaism. Resistance to Greek persecutions then took on a more active form — the Jews began to actively fight against this type of tyranny. What was most terrible in this fight, however, was that the Jews who were defending Judaism had to fight the Greeks as well as some of their own fellow Jews who had converted to Hellenism.

Finally, the fight erupted into an open revolt against the Greeks and their Jewish collaborators. This open revolt of the Maccabees — which we celebrate today as Hanukah — was as much a story of a civil war between Jews as it was a war against Greece. It was not as much a war for national liberation or a struggle for physical freedom as it was a battle of ideologies.

29.
THE REVOLT OF THE MACCABEES

We know the details of the Jewish fight against the Greeks and Hellenism from the two Books of the Maccabees, as well as the writings of the Jewish historian, Josephus.

(These chronicles are not included in the Bible because, as we learned in chapter 26, the Men of the Great Assembly had decided many years earlier what the Bible should contain and these events occurred much later in time. The Books of the Maccabees were both written in the first century B.C.E. The First Book of Maccabees was originally written in Hebrew, as an official court history for the Hasmonean Dynasty. The Second Book of Maccabees was originally written in Greek and was based on an earlier work, written by the ancient historian, Jason of Cyrene.)

This revolt of the Jews set a precedent in human history. It was the world's first ideological/religious war. As noted in the previous chapter, no one in the ancient world died for their gods; only the Jews thought that their religion — the only monotheistic religion at the time — was worth dying for.

The year was 138 B.C.E.[262] and the horrible persecution of Judaism by the Greeks was in full swing. Greek soldiers came to the town of Modi'in (a site west of Jerusalem which you can visit today off the Jerusalem–Tel Aviv highway) and demanded that the Jews there sacrifice a pig to the Greek gods. The elder of the town, Mattathias, who was a *kohen*, that is of the priestly class, refused:

> "Even if all the nations that live under the rule of the king obey him, and have chosen to do his commandments, departing each one from the religion of his fathers, yet I and my sons and my brothers will live by the covenant of our fathers.... We will not obey the king's word by turning aside from our religion to the right or to the left."[263]

As it happened, there was a Hellenized Jew in the town who was willing to do what was unspeakable in Jewish eyes. As he was about to sacrifice the pig, Mattathias stabbed him, also killing the Greek official present. He then turned to the crowd and announced:

"Follow me, all of you who are for God's law and stand by the covenant."[264]

Those who joined Mattathias and his five sons — named Johanan, Simon, Judah, Elazar, Jonathan — headed for the hills, expecting that the Greeks were going to come back and wipe out the whole village as a reprisal. In the hills, they organized a guerilla army, led primarily by the oldest of the sons named Judah, nicknamed Maccabee, which means "the Hammer." Maccabee is also an acronym for *Mi Kamocha Ba'eilim Hashem*, "Who is like You among the powers, O God" — the battle cry of the Jewish people.

We don't know exactly how large this Maccabee army was, but even the most optimistic estimates put the number at no more than 12,000 men. This tiny force took on the fighting Greek army of up to 40,000 men.

But the Greeks were not just numerically superior. The Greeks were professional soldiers — they had equipment, they had training, and they had a herd of war elephants, which were the tanks of the ancient world. The Jews were vastly outnumbered, poorly trained and poorly equipped (not to mention, they had no elephants), but what they lacked in training and equipment they made up for in spirit.

Most of the battles took place in the foothills leading from the coastal plain area (Tel Aviv) to Jerusalem. The Greeks were trying to march their armies up the natural canyons that led into the mountain areas, the stronghold of the Jewish forces. There were only a few places where the Greeks could actually ascend, and these were the places where the Maccabees challenged them.

Now, when we read about the revolt of the Maccabees today, it seems like it was over in a few weeks — the battles were fought, the Jews won, and the Greeks went home. But, in fact, it took twenty-five years of off-and-on fighting and a great many casualties on both sides until the Greeks finally reached a peace agreement with the Jews.

Hanukah

After the first three years, the Jews were able reconquer Jerusalem. They found the Temple defiled and turned into a pagan sanctuary, where pigs had been sacrificed on the altar. When they reentered the Temple, the first thing they did was to try to light a makeshift menorah (as the real gold one had been melted down by the Greeks), but only one vial of pure lamp oil with the special seal was discovered. They used this vial to light the menorah and, miraculously, it stayed lit for eight days, by which time fresh pure oil has been pressed and delivered to the Temple.

The miracle of the oil lasting for eight days (which is not mentioned in the Book of the Maccabees) is described in the Talmud:

> And when the royal Hasmonean House gained the upper hand and vanquished [the Greeks], they searched and found only one flask of oil... with the High Priest's seal, and it contained only [enough] oil to burn for one day. A miracle occurred and it burned for eight days.[265]

The Maccabees then purified the Temple and rededicated it on the twenty-fifth of Kislev, which is the date on the Hebrew calendar when we celebrate the first of the eight days of Hanukah. (The Hebrew word Hanukah means "dedication" or "inauguration.") The Book of Maccabees relates:

> Early in the morning of the 25th day of the ninth month, which is the month of Kislev...they [the priests] rose and offered sacrifices, as the law directs, on the new altar of burnt offerings which they had built... it was dedicated with songs and harps and lutes and cymbals.... So they celebrated the dedication of the altar for eight days....[266]

Hanukah — one of two holidays added to the Jewish calendar by the rabbis — celebrates two kinds of miracles: (1) the military victory of the vastly outnumbered Jews against the Greeks; and (2) the spiritual victory of Jewish values over those of the Greeks. It is this spiritual victory which is symbolized by the lights of Hanukah.

If we look at these two miracles, clearly the military victory was greater, yet the miracle of the oil is commemorated during the festival of Hanukah. The military victory may have been more impressive, but as we already mentioned, the real battle was spiritual and not physical. Precisely this spiritual victory is what is symbolized by the light of the menorah. (Fire, the soul, and spirituality are all connected in Jewish thought.)

The light of Hanukah is symbolic of the inner spiritual strength of the Jewish people that, despite all odds, is never extinguished. It is precisely this inner spiritual strength that has enabled the Jews to outlast the greatest empires in history and have a monumental impact on humanity.

The rededication of the Temple did not end the fight, however. A Greek garrison remained stationed in Jerusalem, and the Greek armies besieged the city in an attempt to reconquer it. Many more battles were fought over many years before the conflict finally ended.

In fact, it was not until 113 B.C.E., during the reign of Seleucid monarch Demitrius II, that the Greeks finally had enough of the fighting and signed a peace treaty with Simon, the last survivor of the five sons of Mattathias:[267]

> In [that] year, Israel was released from the gentile yoke; the people began to write on their contracts and agreements: "In the first year of Simon, the great High Priest, general and leader of the Jews."[268]

Thus, Jewish sovereignty over the Land of Israel was officially restored.

The Reign of the Hasmoneans

As noted above, Mattathias was a *kohen*, and so it is not surprising that his son, Simon, should become High Priest. But Simon also took upon himself the title of *Nasi,* meaning "prince/president." He did not call himself king, because he knew full well that a Jewish king could only come from the line of David, but for all practical purposes he assumed the role of kingship.

(The line of David — the line of kings — comes from the tribe of Judah, whereas the line of the *kohanim*, the priests, comes from the tribe of Levi, as per the blessing of Jacob on his twelve sons, the twelve tribes of Israel.)

This was a bad choice on the part of Simon, because his descendants did not respect his distinction. They started a new ruling dynasty in Israel — the Hasmonean dynasty — which lasted for 103 years and which was marked by great territorial expansion, but also by a terrible moral and religious decline. They should not have been kings in the first place, and then they became corrupted by their own power.

The next ruler was Simon's son, Johanan Hyrcanus, a powerful and ambitious man. Among his many errors, Johanan Hyrcanus did a terrible, anti-Jewish thing. As part of his effort to expand the borders of Israel and strengthen the country, he forcibly converted the newly conquered peoples. This was something never done in Judaism before or since — Jews discourage converts rather than the other way around.

One of the peoples forcibly converted at this time were the Idumeans. And this error cost the Jews dearly.

In Israel, not far from Beit Shemesh, there is a fascinating archaeological site open to tourists called Beit Guvrin Maresha. It consists of thousands of man-made caves that are mostly cut into the soft limestone. This was one of the major cities of the Idumeans. And you can even play archaeologist and go there and dig for a day. This is one of the places that the Hasmoneans conquered, giving the people a terrible choice (that would later be given to the Jews) — convert or leave. Many of the inhabitants chose to destroy their houses and leave the country.

One of the Idumean families that was forcibly converted would become very significant for its role in the drama some years later during the Roman invasion. A descendant of this family — Herod — will be appointed Jewish king and he will be a schizophrenic ruler. He will murder the High Priest, forty-five members of the Jewish Supreme Court, as well as several members of his own family, but he will also embark on a series of fantastic building projects that will include the city of Caesarea, the fortress at Masada, and a total rebuilding of the Temple. As we will see, Herod (who was only nominally Jewish) will have a bizarre relationship with the Jews.

Decline of Jewish Rule

After the death of Johanan Hyrcanus, his son, Judah Aristobulus, declared himself king, not being satisfied with the title of "prince." Naturally, the Sanhedrin — which had been willing to have Johanan as prince — objected to this and earned his ire. Writes Rabbi Berel Wein in *Echoes of Glory*:

> [He] persecuted the rabbis and their Pharisee followers. He ruthlessly exiled many of them, and hundreds of Pharisees were painfully and violently executed.[269]

The next ruler, Alexander Yanni (the brother of Judah Aristobulus) was another chip off the old block. Like his brother, he could not tolerate Pharisee opposition, and he had 800 Pharisees executed after first forcing them to watch the slaughter of their families. During the executions, Alexander Yanni hosted a Greek-style feast.

After Yanni's death, his widow, Queen Salome, ruled for nine years. She was the only ray of light in this dismal period. Her brother was Simon ben Shatach, the leading rabbi of his generation, and during her reign there was peace between the leadership and the rabbis, the last period of tranquility and stability for a very long time.

The history of the Hasmonean Dynasty is a tragic case of a great family starting off illustriously and ending disastrously, in the process bringing the Jewish people to ruin.[270]

The last two Hasmonean rulers were the sons of Salome, Hyrcanus and Aristobolus, both of whom were totally Hellenized. Hyrcanus was the weaker of the two, but he had a strong advisor by the name of Antipater, a descendant of Idumean converts to Judaism (who just happened to have a baby boy named Herod).

The brothers were fighting with each other as to who should be king. The obvious answer was neither. But tell that to morally corrupt, power-hungry men. They hit on the idea of asking Rome to mediate in their dispute.[271]

Inviting the Romans in was not like inviting a multinational peace-keeping force or international mediation team. We're talking about people with an incredible energy to conquer and gain all the territory they could.

The year was 63 B.C.E. and the great Roman general, Pompeii, was cleaning up the last of the Greek Empire. He was more than happy to oblige and move his armies into Israel.

CHRONOLOGY OF THE HASMONEAN DYNASTY

HEBREW DATE	B.C.E.	NAME/EVENT
3622	138	Revolt of the Maccabees begins, led by the Hasmoneans – Mattathias and his five sons: Johanan, Simon, Judah, Elazar, and Jonathan
3624	135	Hasmoneans reclaim the Temple in Jerusalem; miracle of Hanukah
3625	133	Death of Antiochus IV, ruler of Seleucid arm of the Greek Empire, who persecuted the Jews
3626	132	Antiochus V besieges Jerusalem
3627	131	Demetrius I rules; Alcimus appointed High Priest
3628	130	Judah the Maccabee killed in battle, Jonathan becomes leader of Jewish forces
3629	130	Alcimus dies, Jonathan becomes High Priest
3636	122	Alexander I rules
3641	117	Alexander I deposed; Demetrius II rules
3644	114	Demetrius II deposed, Tryphon rules
3646	112	Tryphon kills Jonathan, Simon becomes High Priest and proclaims himself "Prince of the Jews"
3646–3657	112—101	Rule of Simon; treaty made with Greek forces
3657	101	Rule of Johanan Hyrcanus who forcibly converts conquered peoples to Judaism
—	—	Judah Aristobulus (son of Johanan Hyrcanus) rules, declares himself king
—	—	Alexander Yanni (Judah Aristobulus' brother) rules
3683	76–67	Queen Salome (Alexander Yanni's widow) rules
3693–3697	67–63	Hyrcanus and Aristobulus (Salome's sons) rule; they invite Roman general Pompeii to Israel
3697	63	Pompeii enters Jerusalem, slaughters Jews, makes Hyrcanus nominal ruler

30.
THE ROMANS

Before we tell the story how the Second Commonwealth of Israel met its sad end at the hands of the Roman Empire, let us step back in time and delve into what Rome was about, and how it became a power that challenged the mighty Greeks.

Rome started out as a city-state, dating its history to 753 B.C.E. The founding of the city is rooted in a famous legend:

It was common practice of the settlers of the banks of the Tiber River to keep "vestal virgins" on whom they believed their fate rested. These young women had to stay pure and chaste, and if any vestal virgin strayed, she was put to death by being buried alive. According to legend, in the eighth century B.C.E. one vestal virgin, named Rhea Silvia, found herself pregnant, by the god Mars!

(Here we have a familiar story, that predates the Christian one by some 800 years — a woman who has a physical relationship with a god, *ergo est*, as they say in Latin, she remains a virgin yet she gives birth.)

Rhea Silvia gave birth to twins — Romulus and Remus — but the local king, jealous of their semi-divine status, had them thrown into the Tiber River. Miraculously, they floated ashore, were nursed by a she-wolf, and then reared by a shepherd. When they grew up, these boys established the city of Rome on seven hills overlooking the Tiber, near the very place where they had been rescued from drowning. (Later, Romulus killed Remus and became the god Quirinus.)

Interestingly, Jewish tradition holds that the Romans were the descendants of Esau, the red-haired and bloodthirsty twin brother of Jacob. Judaism calls Rome "Edom" — another name given Esau in the Book of Genesis[272] — from the Hebrew root which means both "red" and "blood." When we look at the Jewish-Roman relationship later on, we will see that the Romans were the spiritual inheritors of the Esau worldview.

The Roman Republic

If we skip ahead a few hundred years from the time of Romulus, we find that, circa 500 B.C.E., the residents of Rome have overthrown the monarchy ruling them and have established a republic ruled by a senate. An oligarchy, the senate was made up of upper class, land-owning male citizens called the "patricians."

As any healthy and strong ancient civilization, the Romans went to war to expand their sphere of dominance. Roman ambitions met the like-minded Carthaginians, unleashing a titanic struggle known as the Punic Wars, which lasted from 264 to 146 B.C.E., and in which Rome was victorious.

The Romans went on to conquer the Greek colonies and Greece itself, and to become the great power of the Mediterranean. To a large extent they inherited the Greek view of the world. We call their culture Greco-Roman because — although Greece and Rome were two different peoples, different civilizations, and different cultures — the Romans viewed themselves, to a large extent, as the cultural inheritors of the Greeks.

Later on in Roman history, many Romans would literally see themselves as the reincarnation of the Greeks. The Greeks influenced Roman architecture and much of the Roman worldview in many respects. But the Romans made their own unique contributions as well.

For one thing, Rome was a much more conservative, patriarchal society than was Greece. The Romans were also very hard-working and extremely well organized, and this is what made them masters of empire building. We see their ability to organize in all spheres:

We see it in their feats of engineering. Everywhere we look where the Romans dominated, we find Roman aqueducts, Roman roads, Roman fortifications, Roman walls still standing today. They were incredible builders and had amazing knowledge of how to build.

We see it in their government and law. They institutionalized a system of law that was used throughout the entire Mediterranean basin.

We see it in their ability to administer and collect taxes.

And most of all, we see it in their ability to systematically wage war and conquer. Conquest and empire building were the greatest feats of Roman organization.

The Romans revolutionized warfare. Unlike the Greeks, they did not conscript citizens; instead, they developed the world's first professional army. Their soldiers were paid to fight, and they made a lifelong career of it. Soldiering for Rome was not just a job — it was a way of life and a commitment which lasted for twenty-five years. The Roman motto was captured in a famous saying of Julius Caesar, arguably Rome's greatest general: "*Veni, vidi, vici* — I came, I saw, I conquered."

Because they made a career of fighting, Roman soldiers were extremely well-trained and very disciplined in battle. And they were also extremely well equipped. The art of warfare was perfected through constant drilling and tactical training, discipline, and state-of-the-art military technology. This gave the Romans a huge advantage in battle that was unparalleled in human history.

Instead of the big, unwieldy Greek phalanxes that could not move quickly, the Romans created what they called legions — of about 5,000 men each — which were further subdivided into ten smaller and more mobile cohorts. The legion became the basic unit of the Roman army. The Romans had between twenty-four and twenty-eight legions — that is 120,000 to 140,000 men — plus an equal number of auxiliary troops, mostly infantry with a little cavalry.

The organizational structure of the legions gave the Romans tremendous flexibility on the battlefield. The smaller units (i.e. the cohorts) that comprised each legion could maneuver independently in ways that the Greek phalanx could never do, which is how the Romans vanquished the Greeks. They simply slaughtered them, like they slaughtered everyone they encountered.

This brings us to another key feature of the Roman culture. Although the Romans were very sophisticated people, they were also very brutal, perhaps the most brutal civilization in history.

Their brutality can, of course, be seen in their warfare. They were an incredibly aggressive people, a people with seeming unbridled ambition to conquer everything. (This fits with the Jewish understanding of the descendants of Esau, who was gifted with the power to dominate physically; whereas Esau's twin-brother Jacob was gifted with the power to dominate spiritually.) But even more strikingly, their brutality can be seen in their forms of entertainment.

At 200 different locations throughout the empire, the Romans built amphitheaters where they would spend the day eating, relaxing, and watching people being grotesquely butchered. (The practice was extremely popular and Emperor

Augustus in his *Acts* brags that during his reign he staged games where 10,000 men fought and 3,500 wild beasts were slain.)

(This brings up a very interesting lesson in human history. We often will find the most advanced cultures to be the most brutal, despite their sophisticated legal systems. We see it with Rome and later with many others, most recently with Nazi Germany.)

The Roman Empire

While the Roman armies were mightily victorious abroad, the republic wasn't doing so well at home.

In the first century B.C.E., Rome had to contend with internal strife and class struggle, of which the slave revolt led by Spartacus (in 72 B.C.E.) is perhaps the most famous. The so-called "Social War" forced Rome to extend citizenship widely, but the republic was nevertheless doomed.

The general Pompeii emerged as a popular champion and found allies in Crassus and Julius Caesar, forming the First Triumvirate in 60 B.C.E. But within ten years Pompeii and Julius Caesar had a falling out, and Julius Caesar become the master of Rome, laying the foundation for the Roman Empire.

This is the point in time where we left off the story back in the Land of Israel.

As noted, the last two Hasmonean rulers were brothers — Hyrcanus and Aristobolus. Quarreling with each other as to who should be king, they asked Rome to mediate in their dispute. And thus, in 63 B.C.E., Pompeii was invited to move his armies into Israel.

The historian Josephus explains what happened next in great detail: The Romans came in, slaughtered many Jews and made Hyrcanus, the weaker of the two brothers, the nominal puppet ruler of the country.

This was part of the Roman system. They preferred to rule by proxy, allowing the local governor or king to deal with the day-to-day problems of running the country, as long as the Roman tax was paid and Roman laws were obeyed!

Roman intervention in Israel had effectively ended Jewish independence and ushered in one of the bleakest periods of Jewish history. Rome ruled, not Hyrcanus — or any Jew, for that matter. (The Sanhedrin's authority was abolished by Roman decree six years after Pompeii's conquest.)

The independent state of Israel ceased to exist and became the Roman province of Judea. Pompeii split up much of the land, giving large chunks to his soldiers as a reward for their prowess in battle. Gaza, Jaffa, Ashdod, and other Jewish cities were now a part of the map of the Roman Empire, while Hyrcanus, though he might call himself king, ruled only Jerusalem, along with a few pieces north and south. Even this small area was overseen by the Roman proconsul in Damascus.

As we mentioned in the previous chapter, a key role in the Roman takeover of Israel was played by Hyrcanus' chief advisor — the Idumean general Antipater. The Idumeans bore testimony to an unprecedented lapse in observance among the Jews — they were the people whom Johanan Hyrcanus forcibly converted to Judaism.

Antipater, the real strength behind the weak Hyrcanus, made sure, of course, that he positioned his own family in power while he had a chance. He continued to guide Hyrcanus and — when in 49 B.C.E., Pompeii and Julius Caesar became engaged in internal struggle — he helped him choose the winning side. Soon, Antipater was the man in power.

The Romans judged correctly that this forcibly converted Jew did not identify with Jewish values or nationalism, and that with him in power, "militant monotheism" would not again rear its dangerous head.

While Antipater did not go down in history as a household name, his son, Herod — who took after his father and then some — did. Coming from a family of forced converts that was only nominally Jewish, he nevertheless became one of the most famous kings of the Jews. He went down in history as Herod the Great.

31. HEROD THE GREAT

Herod the Great (not to be confused with Herod Antipas who figures famously in the Christian Gospels later on) was one of the most important characters in Jewish history. He was ambitious, cruel, and paranoid to be sure, but, nevertheless, he remains a very significant person in terms of understanding this period of Roman domination of the Jewish people.

Herod's rise to power[273] happened against the backdrop of the Roman civil war that would transform Rome from a republic into an empire ruled by the caesars/emperors. In 44 B.C.E., Julius Caesar was murdered by Brutus and Cassius, and these two were, in turn, defeated by Anthony and Octavian a few years later. By 31 B.C.E., Octavian emerged as the unrivaled victor,[274] changing his name to Augustus and becoming the first Roman emperor.

Herod had originally sided with Anthony but switched allegiance at the last minute and backed Octavian. His last-minute support earned him the new emperor's confirmation as king of Judea.

Herod would rule from 37 B.C.E. until his death in 4 B.C.E., a very long reign of more than thirty years, and in many ways a good period for the Jews in terms of development of the country and social stability. Part of the reason for the stability was that, during this time, the Romans took a backseat role in the day-to-day life of the Jews.

The general Roman attitude was one of tolerance — meaning, Jews were granted exemptions from the official Roman state religion. A very interesting point to remember is that religion and state went together in all empires in the ancient world, but more so in Rome than almost anywhere else, because Rome also practiced emperor worship — that is, the Romans deified their emperors posthumously.

Linking state and religion obviously gave the rulers added legitimacy. The connection between temporal power and spiritual power gave them complete control over the physical and spiritual existence of their subjects. (Later, we are going to see the Roman Catholic Church doing the same thing in Medieval Europe.)

While accepting that the state religion was a vital part of Roman identity and loyalty to the empire, the Romans were also pragmatists. They had learned from the Greek experience that Jews could not be forced to worship idols. And they saw for themselves that the Jews were not like other pagan peoples — they were not going to conform. So the Romans granted the Jews an official exemption status from the Roman state religion.

On the one hand, it was a very smart and very tolerant policy. On the other hand, with that policy also went a punitive tax specifically instituted for the Jews called *fiscus Judaicus*. You want to be exempt from the state religion? Okay, as long as you pay for the privilege.

So, it might have happened that the Jews simply paid the tax and did their own thing. But it didn't go as smoothly as that (as we shall see).

Herod, the Builder

Herod's rule was also characterized by a period of unprecedented growth and construction, thanks in large part to his amiable relationship with Rome.

Herod had Rome's complete support in administering a very important territory which included several major trade routes. Everything moved through Judea, which was the great way-station for the incense trade coming from Yemen up the Arabian Peninsula and out to the Mediterranean. Additionally, this was one of the most agriculturally productive pieces of land in the Middle East, famous for its olive oil (which was used as a main source of light, and not just for cooking), for its dates (the chief sweetener in the times before sugar), and for its wine.

Herod used the huge profits from trade — and money acquired through the crushing taxes he levied upon his subjects — to satisfy his obsession with mammoth construction projects. As a matter of fact, if they hadn't closed the list of the wonders of the ancient world before his time, Herod would probably have added three more to it. Almost all archaeologists and students of architecture of the ancient world appreciate that he was one of the greatest builders in human history. He built relentlessly — cities, palaces, and fortresses, some of the most magnificent in the world, a few of which still stand, like the fortresses at Masada, Antonia and Herodium; the port city of Caesarea; the huge edifice at the top of the Cave of the Patriarchs in Hebron; the massive fortifications around Jerusalem as well as three towers at the entrance to the city.

At Herodium, in an incredible feat of engineering, Herod built an artificial mountain and, on top of it, a huge palace. Unfortunately, this palace was destroyed in 70 C.E. during the Great Revolt.

He built another fortress, Masada, on top of a rock plateau in the desert. Complete with all creature comforts, Masada had an incredible water supply system that irrigated gardens for growing agricultural staples and three bathhouses. (Masada is open to tourists today and IS a sight to behold.)

The port city of Caesarea deserves special mention — not only because it was a center of trade, the Roman administrative capital of Judea and one of the largest ports in the Empire, but because it became a symbol in Jewish eyes of everything that was pagan, Roman, and antithetical to Judaism.[275] Here, Herod created an amazing artificial port (one of the two largest in the empire) with a beautiful amphitheater, a hippodrome for chariot races, bathhouses, and a huge temple dedicated to the Roman god-emperor, Augustus Caesar. (Today you can visit the excavations of Caesarea, and they are most impressive.)

The most ambitious of Herod's projects was the rebuilding of the Temple, which was almost certainly an attempt to gain popularity among his subjects — who, he knew, held him in contempt — and also to make amends for his cruelty toward the rabbis.[276]

It took 10,000 men ten years just to build the retaining walls around the Temple Mount (on top of which the Muslim shrine, the Dome of the Rock, stands today). The Western Wall (formerly known as the Wailing Wall) is merely part of that 500-meter-long retaining wall designed to hold a huge, manmade platform that could accommodate more than twenty-four football fields. When completed, it was the world's largest functioning religious site and until today it remains the largest manmade platform in the world.

Why did he make the Temple Mount so large?

There's no question that Herod had a huge ego and liked to impress people with grandiose building projects. But there was also another, more practical reason. Historians estimate that there were between six and seven million Jews living in the Roman Empire (plus another one million in Persia), many of whom would come to Jerusalem for the three pilgrimage festivals: Pesach, Shavuot and Sukkot. So you had to have a huge space able to accommodate such a large number of people. Hence the size of the platform.

When it came to building the Temple atop this platform, Herod truly outdid himself, and even the Talmud acknowledges that the end result was spectacular: "He who has not seen Herod's building has never in his life seen a truly grand building."[277]

The Holy of Holies was covered in gold; the walls and columns of the other buildings were of white marble; the floors were of carrara marble, its blue tinge giving the impression of a moving sea of water; the curtains were tapestries of blue, white, scarlet, and purple thread, depicting "the whole vista of the heavens," according to Josephus who describes how incredible it looked:

> Viewed from without, the Temple had everything that could amaze either mind or eyes. It was covered all over with plates of gold of great weight, and, at the first rising of the sun, reflected back a very fiery splendor, so that those who endeavored to look at it were forced to turn away as if they had looked straight at the sun. To strangers as they approached it seemed in the distance like a mountain covered with snow; for any part not covered with gold was dazzling white....[278]

Herod saw fit, however, to place at the main entrance a huge Roman eagle, which the pious Jews saw as a sacrilege. A group of Torah students promptly smashed this emblem of idolatry and oppression, but Herod had them hunted down and dragged in chains to his residence in Jericho, where they were burned alive.

Herod the Tyrant

Once the Temple was complete, Herod took pains to make sure it would function without problems. He appointed his own High Priest, having by then put to death forty-six leading members of the Sanhedrin, the rabbinical court.

Herod's persecutions were infamous, and they even extended to his own family. Knowing that his Jewish credentials were suspect, Herod had married Miriam — the granddaughter of Hyrcanus and therefore a Hasmonean princess — largely to gain legitimacy among the Jewish people. But he also loved her madly. As Josephus relates:

> Of the five children which Herod had by Miriam, two were daughters and three were sons. The youngest of these sons was educated in Rome and died there, but the two eldest he treated as those of royal blood on account of the nobility of their mother, and because they were not born until he was king. But what was stronger than all this was his love he

> bore for Miriam which inflamed him every day to a great degree....

The problem was that Miriam hated him as much as he loved her, largely because of what he had done to her brother, Aristobulus. Herod had made Aristobulus High Priest at the age of seventeen and watched with trepidation as the young man became hugely popular. This was not surprising as Aristobulus was a Hasmonean with a legitimate right to be High Priest — a genuine Jew and a genuine *kohen*.

The adulation of Aristobulus threatened Herod too much, so he had him drowned. Indeed, Herod later became jealous of his own sons for the same reason and had them murdered as well. He even had his own wife murdered in a fit of jealousy. Josephus again:

> His passion also made him stark mad and leaping out of his bed he ran around the palace in a wild manner. His sister Salome took the opportunity also to slander Miriam.... Then out of his ungovernable jealousy and rage he commanded [her] to be killed immediately. But, as soon as his passion was over, he repented of what he had done, and as soon as his anger had worn off, his affections were kindled again.... Indeed, the flame of his desire for her was so strong that he could not think she was dead, but he would appear under his disorders to speak to her as if she were still alive....[279]

He was not a stable man, to say the least. Even Augustus said of him: "It is better to be Herod's dog than one of his children."

Herod's paranoia, his interference with the Temple hierarchy, and his dedication to the Hellenization of the Jewish people all contributed to the growing discontent that would erupt in a revolt against Rome some seventy years after his death. Beneath the surface events, there was a deeper spiritual battle raging — a battle between paganism and Judaism. Additionally, Jewish nationalistic feelings were rising to the surface.

It didn't help matters that Hellenism dominated Judea. A significant number of Greeks, as well as other non-Jews who adopted the Greek lifestyle, had lived there since the days of the Greek Empire and now, encouraged by the Romans, more Hellenist outsiders came to settle the land. Additionally, the Jewish upper classes, though a minority, subscribed to this "higher" culture. And, of course, the king was an avowed Hellenist. Seeing himself as an enlightened leader who would bring his backward people into the modern world, Herod did what he saw necessary to accomplish this end. His way of going about it included the persecution and murder of all rabbis, whom he viewed not only as threats to his authority, but as obstacles to the mass Hellenization of the Jews.

As a result of Herod's interference and the ever-spreading Hellenistic influences among the Jewish upper classes, the Temple hierarchy became even more corrupt that it already was. The Sadduccees, a religious group of the wealthy who collaborated with the Romans in order to maintain their power base, now controlled the Temple, much to the chagrin of the mainstream Jewish majority, the Pharisees, and of the extreme religious minority, the Zealots.

The cauldron was beginning to boil and soon it would erupt.

32.
HILLEL AND SHAMMAI

In chapter 28, we discussed the rift between the Pharisees (the mainstream Jews) and the Sadducees (the Jews who only followed the Written Law, making up their own interpretations). In chapter 31, we saw how Herod's massacres of rabbis and interference with the Temple hierarchy (not to mention his efforts to further Hellenize the Jews) contributed to widespread corruption within the priesthood. But we didn't cover what was right with Judaism.

For one thing, all the normative institutions — the yeshivas, etc. — were all run by the mainstream Jews and were functioning well. There was still a Sanhedrin (a Jewish Supreme Court), though its power had been severely curtailed. Most importantly, the teachings of the rabbis and the chain of transmission remained undisturbed.

The very opening of *Pirkei Avot* (*Ethics of the Fathers*) records how the chain of transmission was maintained, starting with Moses, going on to Joshua, the Elders, the Prophets, the Men of the Great Assembly, and so forth. When Simon HaTzaddik, the last member of the Great Assembly died in 312 B.C.E. — one thousand years after Mount Sinai — prophecy ended and, shortly thereafter, began a period known as that of the *zugot*, meaning "pairs."

From that time on, for almost 300 years, there were always two rabbis at the helm of the Jewish tradition. One was called the *Nasi* (the prince/president); the other was called the *Av Beit Din* (the chief justice). These pairs are all listed in *Ethics of the Fathers*.

The last pair was perhaps the most famous — Hillel and Shammai.

Hillel, who came to Israel from Babylon, was very poor. The Talmud tells some interesting stories about how poor he was and how much he loved learning Torah. For example, he was so poor that he couldn't even afford the couple of coins that it cost to enter the *beit hamidrash*, the study hall. So in order to learn, he would sit up on the roof and listen through the skylight.

One day, he was doing this in a terrible cold and became so frozen he passed out. The students down below were suddenly aware that something was blocking the skylight; they went up onto the roof, found him, revived him and invited him inside.[280]

Despite his poverty, which had no impact on how much people respected his wisdom, Hillel achieved the position of *Nasi*. At that time, Shammai held the position of *Av Beit Din*.

The schools (i.e. followers) of Hillel and Shammai are famous for their disputes in Jewish law. One of these concerned whether one should tell a bride on her wedding day that she is beautiful even if this was not true. The school of Shammai held that it would be wrong to lie. The school of Hillel held that a bride is always beautiful on her wedding day. The school of Hillel won the dispute.[281]

Indeed, Jewish law today almost always agrees with the school of Hillel. The Talmud explains why:

> A heavenly voice declared: The words of both schools are the words of the living God, but the law follows the rulings of the school of Hillel.[282]

So why does the law follow the rulings of the school of Hillel? The Talmud explains that the disciples of Hillel were gentle and modest, and studied both their own opinions and the opinions of the other school, and humbly mentioned the words of the other school before their own.

Dangerous Time

We might recall that in the days of the First Temple, while the rabbis debated points of Jewish law, they did not engage in lengthy disputes. So why were things different in the days of Herod's Temple?

By that time, around 1,300 years had passed since the revelation at Mount Sinai. The Jewish people had been exiled from the Land of Israel and, upon their return, faced many struggles. The influence of the Greeks, the fight against Greek domination, and the corruption of the Hasmonean rulers, all left their wounds. More recently, there was the Roman occupation and the corruption that came with Herod. As a result of this unrest, scholarship declined among the Jewish people, resulting in an increasing lack of clarity. Indeed, the oral transmission process was starting to fray around the edges, as it became harder for the rabbis to reach a consensus on certain legal issues.[283] (The Talmud had not yet been written, but the time was coming soon when the rabbis would decide that the Oral Law must be written down because it might be lost.)

Of course, if you read these disputes in the Talmud today — and the Talmud contains thousands of them — you see that the rabbis were not arguing about anything big, like "Can Jews eat pork?" The disputes usually dealt with the details of how to apply the law. A small number of these disputes had no actual ramifications in the practical application of Jewish law; they were arguments about theoretical cases which impacted upon important principles that needed to be understood.

A very important point to make clear here — although there were disputes, there were also red lines which no mainstream, traditional, Orthodox Jew ever crossed. All the disputes concerned small details, which meant that on the major issues everyone agreed.[284]

But even if these disputes were small, we have to see them as bad news, because they signified not just a decline in scholarship, but even more importantly, a decline in the spiritual state of the Jewish people. This is called *yeridat hadorot*, "decline of the generations." The closer Jews were to Mount Sinai, chronologically speaking, the clearer things were to them; the farther away, the more murky.

It's very important to understand how the Jewish people traditionally have looked at the transmission process. Modern man thinks that the later we get in history the more technology we have, and the better we are. This has never been a Jewish idea — not in history, not in spirituality, not in Jewish law. According to Jewish thought, ancient man was spiritually more sophisticated. And in the realm of the transmission process, the closer one was to Mount Sinai, the clearer things were.

The entire transmission process of the Jewish people is one of the most amazing aspects of Jewish history. The fact that the Oral Torah has been passed down for thousands of years and has been applied to all kinds of new scenarios — yet the basic body of Jewish law has not changed — is amazing.

But the closer the Jews were to Mount Sinai, the more spiritual they were, and the more clearly they understood the will of God. Today, we are much further removed and that much more confused. This is why we do not have the authority to uproot Jewish law laid down by the sages who came before us.

That's fundamental to the whole order of transmission.

The disputes marked the beginning of a process that would make Judaism that much more complicated. More and more arguments and debates were coming. This period of time highlights a significant problem plaguing the Jewish people — that of discord. Says the Talmud:

> Originally, there were not many disputes.... However, with the increase in the number of students of [the schools of] Hillel and Shammai who did not have adequate training, unresolved disputes increased and the Torah became like two Torahs.[285]

The discord that existed between the schools of Hillel and Shammai was mirrored in triplicate by the discord among the Sadducees, Pharisees and the Zealots. All this tension created an atmosphere of "senseless hatred" which undermined the unity of the Jewish people at a point when they had decided to revolt against Rome.

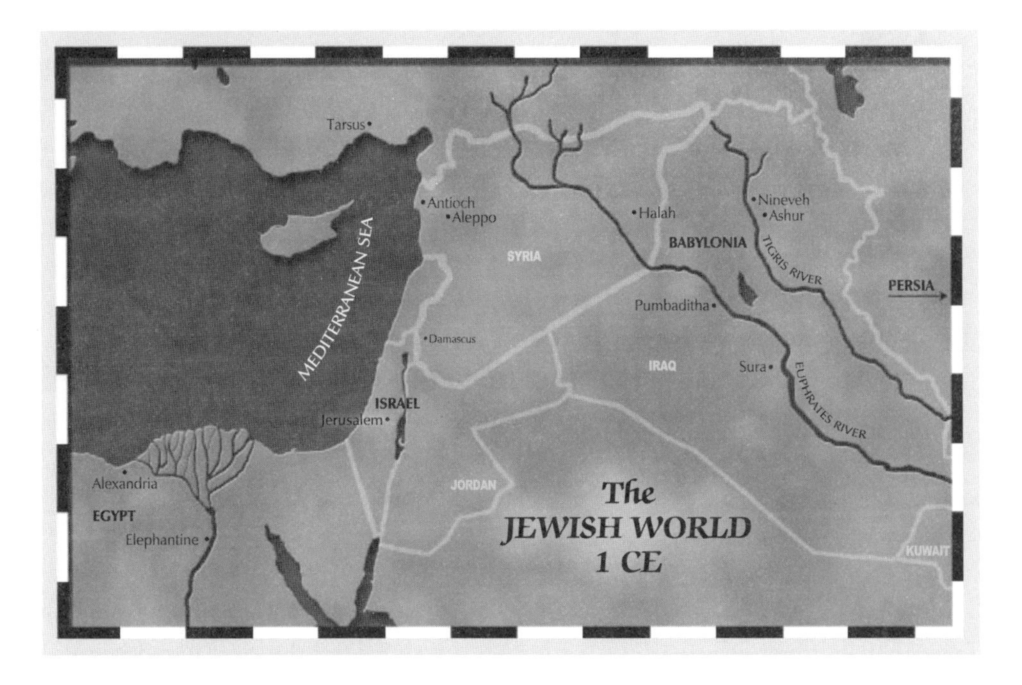

33. THE GREAT REVOLT

A rebellion against Rome in the first century C.E. would be the equivalent of Israel declaring war on NATO today. That's how mighty Rome was. So how did the Jews decide to take on such a seemingly suicidal challenge? This question has no single answer. Into the equation enter:

- Ideological differences between the pagan Greco-Roman world and the monotheistic Jewish world
- Jewish response to the Roman domination which led to strife among the various Jewish factions: the Pharisees, the Sadducees and the Zealots
- Roman persecution of Jews which started with taxation and ended with outright slaughter

We will look at these one by one.

Ideological Differences

Like the Greeks, the Romans worshipped many gods. Not only that, whenever they conquered a swath of land, they simply added the conquered peoples' gods to the Roman pantheon. The Roman historian Varro writes that by the first century B.C.E. they had in excess of 30,000 gods.[286]

The Jewish idea of one, invisible God, who demands exclusive worship and could not be added to the big pot, was totally incomprehensible to the Romans.

But more importantly, along with Jewish beliefs went a lifestyle of obedience to a host of commandments that countered the Roman worldview. For example, the Jewish insistence on respect for life was bound to irk a people who built amphitheaters just so the public could be amused by watching their fellow human beings butchered, the more grotesquely the better. The Talmud captures the difference in a very interesting statement:

> Caesarea and Jerusalem: If someone will tell you, "Both are destroyed," do not believe it; if someone will tell you, "Both are standing," do not believe it. But if someone will tell you, "Caesarea is destroyed and Jerusalem is standing," or "Jerusalem is destroyed and Caesarea is standing" that you can believe.[287]

Now we know for a historical fact that Caesarea and Jerusalem were standing at the same time. When Herod was alive, he built the city of Caesarea, and for sure he didn't destroy Jerusalem. So what does this mean?

In making this statement, the rabbis were making a theological, historical, and political point about the reality of the relationship between Israel and Rome — between the descendants of Jacob and the descendants of Esau.

What they meant is that, in terms of the cosmic struggle, one can't be on top without the other being down. When the Jews are up and Jewish values are strong, then Roman values are going to be down and vice versa. That's the cosmic struggle for the soul of humanity.

Strife Among Jews

The Jewish reaction to the presence of the Romans had many faces:

Hellenized and assimilated Jews. They welcomed the Roman presence and profited by it. They were angry with other Jews who resisted Roman domination.

The Sadducees. For the most part, these were wealthy Jews who denied the divine origin of the Oral Law. They dominated (and corrupted) the Temple hierarchy and were willing to cooperate with the Romans to keep their power base. They saw other Jewish factions as troublemakers.

The Pharisees. These were mainstream Jews who wanted nothing to do with the Romans, but they were pragmatic. They wanted Judaism to survive and, short of giving up their religious principles, were willing to make the best of the Roman domination. They disapproved of the other Jewish factions — those that tried to curry favor with the Romans and those that advocated open rebellion.

> **The Zealots.** They were comprised of several different groups of nationalistic extremists. Among the Zealots was a group called the Sicarii (meaning "daggermen") who derived their name from the concealed daggers they carried to murder their political opponents; they were incensed at the Roman presence and were angry with other Jews whom they saw as actively or tacitly cooperating with the Romans. Also masquerading under the guise of nationalism was a criminal element called Biryonim (meaning "wildmen"). They, too, sided with the Zealots.
>
> **Splinter sects.** These religious groups (such as the Essenes) held extreme views and opposed both the Sadducees and the Pharisees. For example, the Dead Sea Sect (famed for the Dead Sea Scrolls) expected the world to end shortly and went off to live in the desert to escape the depravity and corruption of city life and to prepare for the End of Days.

Jewish sources list twenty-four separate factions. Their conflicting views were a symptom of a disease afflicting the Jewish people at this time. The rabbis call this disease *sinat chinam,* "senseless hatred" of one Jew for another Jew.

Unfortunately, we are seeing a very similar situation today. You don't need to be a scholar of political science or have a doctorate in sociology to realize that by far the biggest problem in the Land of Israel, and the Jewish world as a whole, is lack of unity which leads to divisiveness, infighting, and even hatred. There are factions of Ashkenazim, Sephardim, secular, religious; among the religious there are the Hassidim, the *Mitnagdim*, and the religious Zionists. A weakened, disunited Jewish nation is easy prey for both anti-Semites and the enemies of Israel.

The paradigm for all that is happening today can be found in the Roman era.

Roman Persecution

Adding fuel to the ideological fire was the way the Romans tried to extract money — by taxation and sometimes outright looting — from the local population. This was especially true of several of the governors (procurators) of Judea, who were exceptionally cruel and avaricious. Josephus provides us with numerous examples of Roman mistreatment of the Jewish inhabitants of Judea:

> Pilate, who had been sent as procurator into Judea by Tiberius [in 26 C.E.], sent images of Caesar called "standards" into Jerusalem by night.

> This aroused a very great tumult among the Jews when day broke, for those who were near them were astonished at the sight of the images as indications that their law was trampled underfoot, for those laws do not permit any sort of images to be brought into the city.... After this, he caused another disturbance by expending that sacred treasure which is called *korban* (funds to be used for offerings in the Temple) on aqueducts....
>
> [After this, Gaius Caesar, who represented himself as a god] sent Petronius [governor of Syria] with an army to Jerusalem to place his statue in the Temple and commanded that in case the Jews would not admit him, he should kill the opposition and carry all the rest of the nation away into captivity.[288]

Historian Paul Johnson in his *History of the Jews* explains why this proved a particularly incendiary element in the conflict:

> The Hellenized gentiles...[who] constituted the local civil service and the tax collectors...were notorious in their anti-Semitism.... Foolishly, Rome insisted on drawing its Judean procurators from Greek-speaking gentile areas — the last and most insensitive of them, Gessius Florus came from Greek Asia Minor.[289]

Florus persuaded Nero to strip the Jews of Caesarea of their citizenship, making them effectively aliens in the city and totally at the mercy of the Greco-Roman population. The Jews revolted, and their protest was viciously put down, with many people killed and synagogues desecrated. The riots spread to other cities, where the Hellenized population seized the opportunity to get rid of the Jews — Jewish homes were invaded, looted, and burned down.

Jewish refugees, vowing vengeance, began to stream into Jerusalem. But Florus only escalated the conflict, first by giving Roman soldiers free rein to massacre more than 3,600 Jews who had jeered him, and then by arresting Jewish elders, having them publicly flogged and crucified (the standard Roman punishment for rebellion). Josephus relates:

> Florus...called out aloud to the soldiers to plunder that which was called the Upper Market Place, and to slay those that they encountered. So the soldiers — taking this exhortation of their commander in a sense agreeable to their greed — did not only plunder the place they were sent to, but forcing themselves into every house, they slew its inhabitants; so the citizens fled along the narrow lanes, and the soldiers slew those that

> they caught, and no method of plunder was omitted; they also caught many of the quiet people and brought them before Florus, whom he first whipped and then crucified.[290]

Now there was no turning back. The Jews took up arms.

To go up against the might of the Roman Empire was nothing short of suicidal, and indeed, the Jewish War would end in great tragedy. But when it began in 66 C.E., it had some astonishing successes, with Florus fleeing from Jerusalem for his life and the Roman garrison isolated and overwhelmed.

But such insults to its might Rome could not abide. Jewish historian Rabbi Berel Wein relates graphically what happened next:

> The success of the Jews in driving Rome from Jerusalem sent shock waves throughout the Roman Empire. It also unleashed a wave of bloody pogroms against Jews, especially in Caesarea, Alexandria, and Damascus. Thousands of Jews were slaughtered in these riots, and thousands more were sold into the slave markets of Rome.[291]

The sages and rabbis advised a reconciliation with the Romans, seeing that, if irritated any further, Rome would retaliate with even greater force and then surely destroy the whole country and decimate the Jewish people. Considering that the Sadducees were already pro-Rome and the Pharisees held generally moderate views, their wisdom might have prevailed. But the Zealot extremists would have none of it.

Vowing to fight to the death, they went up against a new Roman contingent making its way toward Jerusalem and killed 6,000 Roman soldiers. Coincidentally, the victory was won on the very same spot where the Maccabees had vanquished the Greeks, and the Zealots — seeing a divine hand helping them — were encouraged further.

But the might of Rome would not sit still for such a challenge.

34.
THE WAR FOR JERUSALEM

In response to the revolt of the Jews, in 67 C.E. Rome dispatched the empire's most experienced commander, Vespasian, at the head of four legions. This was a massive force. Each legion had 5,000 fighting men plus an equal number of auxiliaries for a total of some 40,000 Roman soldiers. (One of these four legions, the tenth, was the most famous. It was commanded by Vespasian's own son, Titus, and had a boar as its symbol. We will see its importance shortly.)

The Roman goal: the annihilation of those Jews who dared to rise against the empire and who had heretofore (unbelievably) succeeded. Shrewdly, Vespasian began his campaign in the north. Any city or town that resisted his advance was utterly destroyed, its population slaughtered or taken into slavery, the women raped, property pillaged. Then, the surrounding area was denuded of trees and the fields strewn with salt to ensure that nothing would grow there again — at least, not for a very long time.

While always brutal in warfare, the Romans surpassed themselves when it came to suppressing the revolt in Judea. Their aim was to send a message throughout the empire: any resistance against Rome would end in total and complete devastation.

Vespasian hoped that by the time he turned to Jerusalem, the Jews would have seen that resistance was futile and would have surrendered. Instead, even with four legions at his disposal, Vespasian faced a tough fight.

Josephus

One of the first to resist was the fortress of Jotapata, built on the slopes of Mount Atzmon. Here, the commander of the Jewish forces in the Galilee, Joseph ben Mattathias — better known to us as Josephus Flavius — made a heroic stand, but he could not withstand the Roman onslaught.

When defeat seemed certain, the Zealots of the group decided that it was better to die at their own hands than to be sold into slavery or to be forced to watch their families mercilessly butchered by the Romans. So, they made a pact to kill their own wives and children and then themselves. Josephus was one of the few survivors; rather than kill himself, he surrendered to the Romans.

Vespasian realized immediately that Josephus could be useful to the Romans and employed him as guide/translator and later as a chronicler of the war. Josephus' works have survived to this day. Among the best known are *Antiquities* and *The Jewish War*, the latter of which describes the events taking place before, during and after the Great Revolt, from 66 C.E. to 70 C.E.

His account is unique, as far as historical accounts go, because he was an eyewitness to much that he wrote about. (He differs in this regard from other Roman historians — like Deo Cassius, for example — who lived later and merely repeated what they had read in official records.)

Of course, Josephus had his own slant on things — he was writing for the Romans (which is probably why his works have survived intact), yet he was born and raised a Jew, so he seemed to be trying to please everyone at the same time. For this reason he has to be read very cautiously and very critically.

Despite the extreme subjectivity of much of his writing and his tendency to exaggerate and be melodramatic (which is typical of historians of this period), his works are an invaluable source of information about the entire Second Temple period and the Great Revolt. Even his critics agree that he is very accurate concerning the physical descriptions of places and structures in the Land of Israel. Archaeology has verified many of his accounts.

Gamla

All during the summer and autumn of 67 C.E. Vespasian marched through northern Israel suppressing Jewish resistance. Some cities surrendered without a fight — like Tiberias, for example. Others fought to the end. One of the most heroic stories concerns the city of Gamla in the Golan Heights.

Partially excavated and the center of a beautiful nature reserve, Gamla is a must-see spot in Israel today. This site is unusual, because unlike most cities in Israel that were destroyed, Gamla was never rebuilt by anyone and is therefore considered to be one of the best-preserved Roman battle sites in the world. The excavations show the city exactly as it looked on the day of its destruction in 67 C.E. (Gamla stood covered by the sands of time for exactly 1900 years until Israel won back the Golan Heights in 1967.)

Anticipating the Roman advance, the citizens of Gamla minted coins with the imprint "To the Redemption of Jerusalem, the holy." They believed that the future of Jerusalem depended on the outcome of their resistance. Sadly, they were right.

The Romans totally annihilated Gamla, killing some 4,000 Jews. The remaining 5,000 inhabitants, rather than waiting to be brutally slaughtered by the Romans, jumped to their deaths off the cliffs surrounding the city. (This is why Gamla is called the Masada of the north.)

Jerusalem

In the summer of 70 C.E., having liquidated virtually all the other pockets of resistance, the Romans finally worked their way to Jerusalem. They surrounded the city and besieged it.

The Romans knew that if they could destroy Jerusalem, they would destroy the soul of rebellion, because Jerusalem was the center of Israel's spiritual life.

Before the Great Revolt began, Jerusalem had somewhere between 100,000 and 150,000 inhabitants (prior to its destruction, the walled city of Jerusalem was considerably larger then the Old City of today, which has only 30,000 inhabitants), but with refugees from other places flocking in, the population was two to three times its normal size. It was concentrated in two enclaves:

The Lower City, south of the Temple Mount (this section of Jerusalem is today outside the current city walls and is called the "City of David" or *Silwan* in Arabic).

The Upper City, west of the Temple Mount, inhabited by the wealthier folks and the priestly class (excavations of this part of the city can be seen in the underground Wohl Archaeology Museum under Yeshivat HaKotel in today's Jewish Quarter).

The city was massively fortified. It also had huge storehouses of food. It had a good water supply. Jerusalem could hold back the Romans for a long time.

So it seemed like the Romans were in a very bad situation. They were trying to besiege one of the largest cities in the ancient world, which was remarkably well fortified, had a huge amount of food and water, and a lot of determined people who were not afraid to die.[292]

Jerusalem could have gone done down in history as the only city that the Romans couldn't take by laying siege. But it didn't. The reason that it did not was *sinat chinam*, "senseless hatred" among the Jews.

While the Romans were besieging the city outside, the Jews were waging a civil war inside. Forces of the various factions were occupying various parts of the city. Most importantly, the Sicarii and the Zealots, led by Johanan of Gush Halav, had control of the Temple Mount. An unlikely alliance of Sadducees and Pharisees made up the bulk of the moderate forces which ruled the rest of the city.

When the moderates attempted to remove the extremists from the Temple Mount, Johanan of Gush Halav brought in non-Jewish mercenaries, the Idumeans, who slaughtered the moderate Jews. As if that was not enough, the Zealots destroyed the great storehouses of food so that the people would have no choice but to fight or starve.

When famine broke out in the city, desperate people tried to sneak outside the walls to forage for food. Anyone who was caught by the Romans was immediately put to death via the standard Roman form of execution — crucifixion. So many died that the city was surrounded by thousands of crucified Jews. Writes Josephus:

> So the soldiers out of the wrath and hatred they bore the Jews, nailed those they caught, one after one, and another after another, to the crosses, by way of jest; when their multitude was so great, that room was wanting for the crosses, and crosses wanting for the bodies.[293]

Meanwhile, the Romans continued their systematic destruction of the city's defenses, layer by layer.

Johanan Ben Zakkai

The leader of the Pharisees and the head of the Sanhedrin, Rabbi Johanan ben Zakkai, saw that Jerusalem could not hold out. It was too late, yet the Zealots were bent on continuing their suicidal fight. So he formulated a plan.

At this time the Zealots were not allowing anyone to leave the city (as if anyone wanted to flee to be crucified), except for burials. In a desperate bid to salvage something from the impending disaster, Rabbi Johanan ben Zakkai had himself put in a casket and taken to Vespasian.

He greeted Vespasian as if he were the emperor, to which Vespasian replied that he ought to be executed for his remarks. Not exactly a friendly welcome.

But Rabbi Johanan ben Zakkai persisted, telling Vespasian that God would allow only a great ruler to take Jerusalem.

Just then, a messenger arrived from Rome with a message for Vespasian: "Rise, because Caesar has died and the prominent men of Rome have decided to seek you as their head. They have made you Caesar."

Impressed with Rabbi Johanan's ability to predict the future, Vespasian asked him to name a wish. And the rabbi asked Vespasian: "Give me the city of Yavneh and the sages." Vespasian did. He gave Rabbi Johanan a safe escort for the Torah sages of the day to leave Jerusalem and to convene a Sanhedrin at Yavneh.

Could Rabbi Johanan have asked Vespesian to spare Jerusalem? Not likely. By then, the Romans had to prove a point. They would never have spared Jerusalem. But Rabbi Johanan's quick thinking spared Judaism.[294]

The Jewish people can always survive physical destruction, but the much bigger danger is spiritual destruction. Had the Sanhedrin been wiped out, the transmission process of the Oral Law would have been severed. Without the Oral Law there is no Judaism. Because the Romans granted Rabbi Johanan's wish, the sages survived, the chain of transmission survived, and the Jewish people survived.

Meanwhile, now that Vespasian was emperor, he was obligated to return to Rome. He turned the siege over to his son, Titus, and he told him to finish the job.

35.
DESTRUCTION OF THE TEMPLE

Titus attacked Jerusalem just after Pesach in the year 70 C.E., battering the city with his catapults which propelled a rain of stone, iron, and fire onto the population. By then, the city defenders were weakened from hunger and, perhaps even more so, from internal strife. Even so, it took Titus two months of intense fighting before he was able to breach the outer city walls and reach the Temple Mount.

The date for this event is seventeenth of Tammuz.[295] To this day, Jews fast on the seventeenth of Tammuz in commemoration of this event. Roman historian Deo Cassius reports:

> Though a breach was made in the wall by means of engines, nevertheless the capture of the place did not immediately follow even then. On the contrary, the defenders killed great numbers [of Romans] who tried to crowd through the opening, and they also set fire to some of the buildings nearby, hoping thus to check the further progress of the Romans. Nevertheless, the soldiers, because of their superstition, did not immediately rush in but, at last, under compulsion from Titus, they made their way inside. Then the Jews defended themselves much more vigorously than before, as if they had discovered a piece of rare good fortune in being able to fight near the Temple and fall in its defense.[296]

A horrific slaughter ensued, with the Romans taking the city, literally house by house. One of the excavations that testifies to the destruction is the famous "Burnt House" which is open to visitors in the Old City of Jerusalem today.

Here the skeletal remains of a woman's arm were found on the doorstep of her house, a spear still lying nearby.

Despite the determined resistance of the Jewish defenders, Titus slowly worked his way to the Temple Mount. Now a duel to the death ensued, and finally, five months after the Romans had begun their attack, Titus ordered the Second Temple razed to the ground. The date was the ninth of Av, the very same day on which the First Temple was destroyed.

Deo Cassius again:

> The populace was stationed below in the court, and the elders on the steps, and the priests in the Sanctuary itself. And though they were but a handful fighting against a far superior force, they were not conquered until part of the Temple was set on fire. Then they met their death willingly, some throwing themselves on the swords of the Romans, some slaying one another, others taking their own lives and still others leaping into the flames. And it seemed to everybody and especially to them that so far from being destruction, it was victory and salvation and happiness to them that they perished along with the Temple.

All of the neighboring countryside was denuded of whatever trees remained from the siege to create a giant bonfire in order to burn the Temple buildings to the ground. The intense heat from the fire caused the moisture in the limestone and marble to expand, and it exploded like popcorn, producing a chain reaction of destruction. In a day's time, the magnificent Temple was nothing but rubble.

Josephus describes the destruction of the Temple:

> While the Holy House was on fire, everything was plundered that came to hand, and ten thousand of those that were caught were slain; nor was there a commiseration of any age...but children and old men...and priests were all slain in the same manner.... The flame was also carried a long way and made an echo, together with the groans of those who were slain...one would have thought the whole city would have been on fire. Nor can one imagine anything greater and more terrible than this noise.[297]

History as Destiny

The destruction of the Second Temple is one of the most important events in the history of the Jewish people, and certainly one of the most depressing. It is a sign that God had withdrawn from (though certainly not abandoned) the Jews. Although the Jews would survive — in accordance with the promise that they would be an "eternal nation" — the special relationship with God they enjoyed while the Temple stood was gone.

Sadly, this period of time, perhaps more than any other, reflects the maxim that Jewish past is Jewish future, that Jewish history is Jewish destiny.

There's no period of time that more closely reflects what is going on today in Israel and among the Jewish people worldwide. Jews are still living with the consequences of the destruction of the Second Temple, spiritually and physically. And the problems they had then are the same problems they have now, as noted in chapter 33. States the Talmud:

> Why was the Second Temple destroyed? Because of *sinat chinam* — senseless hatred of one Jew for another.[298]

What is the antidote to this problem, which is so rampant in the Jewish world today? The answer is *ahavat chinam* — Jews have to learn to love their fellow Jews. There's no hope for the Jewish people until all learn how to communicate with each other and respect each other, regardless of differences.

God has no patience for Jewish infighting. It's extremely important to study this period of time carefully because there are many valuable lessons about the pitfalls that need to be avoided.

Judea Capta

Before setting fire to the Temple, the Romans removed everything of value. Then they forced a group of Jewish slaves to take these priceless artifacts to Rome. Their arrival in Rome is memorialized in the engravings on the Arch of Titus, still standing there today near the Forum and depicting the parade held by Roman legions to celebrate their victory and display the spoils of war.[299]

It had been the tradition in the Roman Jewish community that Jews would never walk under that arch. On the night of May 14, 1948, when Israel was declared a state, the Jews of Rome had a triumphant parade and marched under the arch. Their message: "Rome is gone, we're still around. Victory is ours."

But at the time it was a horrible disaster. Hundreds of thousands of people died, and many more were enslaved. There were so many Jews flooding the slave market after the Great Revolt that you could buy a Jewish slave for less than the price of a horse. Israel was in despair.

Congratulating themselves on asserting Roman might against the defiant

Jews, the Romans minted coins depicting a weeping woman and proclaiming "*Judea Capta* — Judah Is Captured."

But it was not over yet.

Masada

A group of about 1,000 Zealots escaped and made their way into the desert, near the Dead Sea, where they took refuge in the great fortress on top of a mountain plateau called Masada, more than 1,200 feet above the shores of the Dead Sea.

Masada was built by Herod the Great as his place of refuge. As such, it was practically self-sufficient, with its own water collection system and storage houses that could feed an army for years. What's more, the fortress was practically inaccessible from below and easy to defend. Indeed, the Zealots managed to survive there for three years.

If you visit the ruins of Masada, you will see the remains of the fortress as well as the siege-wall, camps, and ramp that the Romans built (using Jewish slave labor), in order to capture Masada.[300]

Josephus reports on the capture of Masada in 73 C.E. and his narrative resembles the capture of his home town. Here, too, the Zealots killed their own families and then each other until, finally, there was only one man left, and he committed suicide. Josephus gives his account of the final speech of the Zealot leader, Elazar ben Yair:

> "Since we, long ago, my generous friends, resolved never to be servants to the Romans, nor to any other than God Himself, Who alone is the true and just Lord of mankind, the time has now come that obliges us to make that resolution true in practice.... It is very clear that we shall be taken within a day's time; but it is still an eligible thing to die in a glorious manner, together with our dearest friends.... Let our wives die before they are abused and our children before they have tasted slavery; and after we have slain them, let us bestow this glorious benefit upon one another mutually and preserve ourselves in freedom, as an excellent funeral monument to us. But first let us destroy our money and the fortress by fire...and let us spare nothing but our food, for it will be a testimonial when we are dead that we were not conquered for want of provisions, but that, according to our original resolution, we have preferred death before slavery."[301]

(For the modern State of Israel, Masada is a symbol of Jews who chose to die as free men rather than be enslaved or executed by the Romans, and it is held up as a Zionist ideal. Until recently, Israeli soldiers would climb up to Masada to be sworn in and would call out for the mountain to hear the stones echo back: "Masada will never fall again!")

Back in 73 C.E. when Masada, the last Jewish stronghold, fell, the Romans could finally declare an end to the revolt. The Jewish Revolt had been totally and finally put down and Judah was truly captive.

But was it?

True, the land was no longer under Jewish control, but it had not been since the days of the Hasmoneans anyway. True, the Temple, the center of Jewish worship and the symbol of Judaism's special connection to the one God, was gone. But Judaism — along with all its unique value system — was alive and well.

Thanks to the foresight of Rabbi Johanan ben Zakkai, the center of Torah learning at Yavneh thrived. It was here that the rabbis put together the legal/spiritual infrastructure which would allow the Jewish people to survive without many of the normative institutions which were the backbone of Judaism: Temple and its service, the High Priesthood, the monarchy. It was here that the rabbis institutionalized public prayer as a replacement for the Temple service and made the synagogue the center of Jewish communal life.[302]

But most importantly, it was here that the rabbis devised a way of making sure that Judaism lived on in every Jewish home. In the coming years, when the Jews would be dispersed the world over — doomed for 2,000 years to have no common land, no centralized leadership, and no common language aside from Hebrew scriptures — they would carry with them their Judaism undiminished.

But that was yet to come.

36.
THE BAR KOHBA REVOLT

The Temple was no more. Jerusalem had been conquered. Rome had asserted its might and crushed the Great Revolt of the Jews. Now there would be quiet.

Hardly.

Virulent anti-Semitism continued unabated throughout the Roman Empire, generated by the Hellenists who, not happy to leave well enough alone, seemed determined to pour salt onto Jewish wounds.

(This same need for overkill would be exhibited by later enemies of the Jews, who, having exterminated entire Jewish communities and having no more Jews left to slaughter, would then go on to desecrate Jewish cemeteries and mutilate Jewish corpses.)

The level of hostility and mistreatment of the Jews escalated until it became unbearable, and the Jews revolted several times more. Each time thousands of their number were killed. As a result, the average Roman looked at every Jew as a person hostile to Rome. Jews were officially designated as having "enemy status" — *deditici* in Latin.

Here we are not talking about the Jews in the Land of Israel who had been crushed in the Great Revolt and who did not have the strength to fight — at least, right after the destruction of the Temple. But a considerable number of Jews were living outside Israel at this time. In fact, historians estimate that there were between five and seven million Jews living in the Roman Empire, and at least sixty percent of that number were living outside the Land of Israel. Alexandria, Egypt (one of the most cosmopolitan cities of that era) alone had a

Jewish population of about 250,000 and boasted the largest synagogue in the world.

The War of Kittos

In 114 C.E. the Emperor Trajan embarked on a military campaign to crush the Parthian (Persian) Empire in the east (today, Iraq and Iran). After initial successes, Trajan's legions suffered a series of defeats, and he was forced to retreat (he died while on this campaign). The Jews of the Parthian Empire fought side by side with their Persian allies and embarked on a series of behind the lines guerrilla actions. As well, many Jewish communities in the eastern Roman Empire rose up in revolt, hoping that the Persians would succeed.

The Roman response, with the help of anti-Semites of the region, was to slaughter the Jews. Several major Jewish communities in the Diaspora — in Cyprus, Libya, Alexandria, and Mesopotamia — were decimated. This slaughter was known as the War of Kittos, after the Roman military governor of Judea, Lucious Quietus, who brutally persecuted the Jewish population of Israel.[303]

Now it must be noted that while the Romans could be absolutely vicious and brutal in the heat of battle, they did not embark on any kind of policy to exterminate the Jewish people. At the time, it wasn't seen as in the Roman interest to attempt a total massacre of the Jews. This would have caused concern among the people living in other conquered territories, and it might have led them to rebel in fear that they might be next. The Romans were very practical, and this is not something they wanted.

Hadrian

When Publius Aelius Hadrianus, known to us as Hadrian, took the reigns of power in 117 C.E., he inaugurated — at least at first — an atmosphere of tolerance. He even talked of allowing the Jews to rebuild the Temple, a proposal that was met with virulent opposition from the Hellenists.[304]

Why Hadrian changed his attitude to one of outright hostility toward the Jews remains a puzzle, but historian Paul Johnson in his *History of the Jews* speculates that he fell under the influence of the Roman historian Tacitus, who was then busy smearing the Jews.

Tacitus and his circle were part of a group of Roman intellectuals who viewed themselves as inheritors of Greek culture. (As noted earlier, some Roman nobles actually considered themselves the literal descendants of the Greeks, though there is no historical basis for this myth.) It was fashionable among this group to take on all the trappings of Greek culture. Hating the Jews for representing the antithesis of Hellenism went with the territory.

Thus influenced, Hadrian decided to spin around 180 degrees. Instead of letting the Jews rebuild, Hadrian formulated a plan to transform Jerusalem into a pagan city-state on the Greek polis model, with a shrine to Jupiter on the site of the Jewish Temple. Hadrian was seemingly attempting to follow in the footsteps of the Selucid Greek Empire 300 years earlier, by trying to destroy Judaism. Specifically he targeted Shabbat observance, circumcision, the laws of family purity, and the teaching of Torah.

An attack against such fundamental commandments of Judaism was bound to trigger a revolt — which it did.

Bar Kohba

Jewish outrage led to one of the single greatest revolts of the Roman Era. Simon Bar Kosiba led the uprising, which began in full force in 132 C.E. His entire guerilla army was Torah-observant, and his soldiers hid out in caves in the Jerusalem area and in the Judean desert. (Some of these caves have been found — full of belongings of Bar Kosiba's people. These belongings — pottery, shoes, etc. — are on display in the Israel Museum, and the caves, though bare, are open to tourists.)

For many years, historians did not write very much about Simon Bar Kosiba. But then, archaeologists discovered some of his letters in Nahal Hever near the Dead Sea. These letters contain a tremendous amount of historical facts and are absolutely fascinating. From the letters and other data, we learn that in 132 C.E., Bar Kosiba organized a large force and succeeded in actually throwing the Romans out of Jerusalem and Israel and establishing, albeit for a very brief period — only two-and-a-half years — an independent Jewish state.[305]

Bar Kosiba's success caused many to believe — among them Rabbi Akiva, one of the wisest and holiest of Israel's rabbis — that he could be the Messiah. He was nicknamed "Bar Kohba" or "Son of a Star," an allusion to a verse in the Book of Numbers: "A star shall come out of Jacob."[306] This star is understood to refer to the Messiah. Bar Kohba did not turn out to be the Messiah, and later the rabbis wrote that his real name was Bar Kosiva or "Son of a Lie," highlighting the fact that he was a false Messiah.

At the time, however, Bar Kohba — who was a man of tremendous leadership abilities — managed to unite the entire Jewish people around him. Jewish accounts describe him as a man of tremendous physical strength, who could uproot a tree while riding on a horse. This is probably an exaggeration, but he was a very special leader and undoubtedly had messianic potential, which is what Rabbi Akiva recognized in him.

Jewish sources list Bar Kohba's army at 100,000 men. But even if that is an overestimate and he had only half that many, it was still a significant number. United, the Jews were a force to be reckoned with. They overran the Romans, threw them out of the Land of Israel, declared independence, and even minted coins. That was a pretty unique event in the history of the Roman Empire.

Naturally, Rome could not let this be. Such boldness had to be crushed and those responsible punished — brutally and totally.

But the Jews were not easily overcome. Hadrian poured more and more troops into Israel to fight Bar Kohba until the Romans had enlisted almost half of their entire army, sending as many as twelve of the twenty-four legions of the empire to Israel (three times as many as they had sent in to crush the Great Revolt sixty-five years earlier).

Heading this mammoth force was Rome's best general, Julius Severus. But even with all this might behind him, Julius Severus was afraid to meet the Jews in open battle. This fact alone is very telling, because the Romans were the masters of open battle. But they feared the Jews because they saw them as being willing to die for their faith — a mentality the Romans thought suicidal. So what happened?

The Roman historian Deo Cassius tells us:

> Severus did not venture to attack his opponents in the open at any one point in view of their numbers and their desperation, but by intercepting small groups. Thanks to the numbers of soldiers and his officers, and by depriving them of food and shutting them up, he was able — rather slowly to be sure, but with comparatively little danger — to crush, exhaust and exterminate them. Very few of them in fact survived. Fifty of their most important outposts and 985 of their most famous villages were razed to the ground, and 580,000 men were slain in various raids and battles, and the number of those who perished by famine, disease and fire was past finding out.
>
> Thus nearly the whole of Judea was made desolate, a result of which the people had had forewarning before the war. For the tomb of Solomon, which the Jews regarded as an object of veneration, fell to pieces of itself and collapsed. And many wolves and hyenas rushed howling into the cities. Many Romans, however, perished in this war.

> Therefore, Hadrian, in writing to the Senate, did not employ the opening phrase commonly affected by emperors: "If you and your children are in health, it is well and I and my legions are in health."[307]

This account of Deo Cassius — even if he is exaggerating the numbers — is very interesting. He tells us that the revolt was very bloody and very costly.

Indeed, the Romans lost an entire legion in battle. The twenty-second Roman legion walked into an ambush and was slaughtered and never reconstituted.

Apparently the Jews came very close to winning the war. Indeed, they did win for a time. Why did they lose in the end? The sages say they lost because they were too arrogant. Having tasted victory, they adopted the attitude of "By my strength and my valor I did this."[308] Judaism teaches that while people must make the effort, it is God who wins the wars. It is not human strength nor human might that does it.

Bar Kohba, too, became arrogant. He saw himself winning, and perhaps he heard people calling him the Messiah. Certainly, if Rabbi Akiva thought so, then he had the potential to be Israel's ultimate leader. He also became corrupted by his power and even beat his uncle, the great Rabbi Elazar HaModai, to death, after hearing false accusations that he was a Roman spy.[309] Because of these faults, he began to lose battles and was forced to retreat into guerrilla warfare.

The Fall of Betar

Bar Kohba made his final stand in the city of Betar, which is southwest of Jerusalem. You can visit it today, though ancient Betar has not been excavated as its ruins lie under the Arab village of Batir. The Talmud relates what happened:

> They had the custom in Betar that when a baby boy was born they planted a cedar tree and for a baby girl they planted a pine tree, and when they would marry they would cut them down and make a marriage canopy of the branches. One day the daughter of Caesar was passing and the shaft of her litter broke. They cut down a cedar and brought it to her. The Jews of Betar fell upon them and beat them. They reported to Caesar that the Jews were rebelling and marched against them...they killed [Jewish] men, women, and children until their blood flowed into the Mediterranean Sea.... It was taught that for seven years the non-Jews

> cultivated their vineyards with the blood of Israel without requiring manure for fertilization.[310]

In the year 135 C.E., the city fell on the saddest day in the Jewish calendar — the ninth of Av — the same date as both the First and the Second Temple fell.

The Romans, in their fury, did not want to allow the Jewish bodies to be buried; they wanted to leave them out in the open to rot. According to tradition, the bodies lay in the open for months but did not rot. Today, when Jews say *Birkat HaMazon*, the Grace after Meals, they add a special blessing as a way of thanking God for this act of mercy in Betar.

Exhausted, the Romans had enough of the Jews, who had caused them more manpower and material losses than any other people in the history of the empire. At the end of the Bar Kohba revolt, Hadrian decided that the way to avoid another one was to cut off the Jews from connection to their beloved land.

CHRONOLOGY OF ROMAN DOMINATION

HEBREW DATE	B.C.E./C.E.	NAME/EVENT
3697	63 B.C.E.	Roman general Pompeii enters Jerusalem
3728	32 B.C.E.	Time of Hillel and Shammai
3742	18 B.C.E.	Herod the Great renovates the Temple
3794	34 C.E.	Beginnings of Christianity
3826	66 C.E.	The Great Revolt of the Jews begins
3827	67 C.E.	Gamla falls
3830	70 C.E.	Jerusalem falls, Temple is destroyed by the Romans
3833	73 C.E.	Masada falls
3870	110 C.E.	Time of Rabbi Akiva
3874	114 C.E.	War of Kittos
3892	132 C.E.	Bar Kohba revolt begins
3890	130 C.E.	Jerusalem rebuilt as Aelia Capitolina
3895	135 C.E.	Betar falls
4085	325 C.E.	Constantine: Roman Empire becomes Christian
4236	476 C.E.	Fall of Western Roman Empire – Byzantine rule of Israel

PART IV
IN EXILE

37.

EXPULSION

No people had revolted more or caused the Romans greater manpower and material losses than the Jews. But they had done so at a great price to themselves as well. The Roman historian, Deo Cassius writes that more than half a million Jews died in the fighting. Even if this figure is exaggerated, there is no doubt that hundreds of thousands of Jews did die and the country was devastated.

The Jewish challenge to Rome that began in 66 C.E. had lasted almost seventy years. How such a comparatively small group could take on the might of Rome over and over again, and for so long, is hard to fathom. But perhaps the answer lies in the reason behind the conflict. It was not so much a fight over territory or property as it was a fight over the very way of life. Monotheism and the laws of the Torah were so deeply ingrained in the Jews that any attempt to separate the people from the essence of Judaism was seen as the death of the very soul of the nation. The Jews found reserves in themselves beyond normal human boundaries, like a mother who is capable of superhuman feats of strength to defend the life of her child.

In the end, the Jews were crushed, and the Romans did everything in their power to make sure that they would stay crushed. They wanted to make sure that no Jew was ever in a position to rally his brethren again.

Their solution: separate the Jews from their land.

Aelia Capitolina

As part of this policy of erasing the Jewish presence from Israel, Hadrian leveled Jerusalem and on top of the rubble rebuilt the pagan city he had planned, which he named Aelia Capitolina — Aelia in honor of his own name, Pulbius Aelius Hadrianus, and Capitolina in honor of the god Jupiter, whose temple was located on the Capitolene Hill in Rome.

Through the heart of the city, he built a columned esplanade called the Cardo. (Today, the excavated Cardo, albeit in its later sixth century C.E. Byzantine form, stands in the Old City of Jerusalem as a reminder of that time.)

The few Jews remaining in the area were strictly forbidden to enter Aelia Capitolina. The only day that Jews were permitted to enter the city was on the ninth of Av, so that they could be reminded of their greatest disaster and weep over the ruins of the Temple, of which nothing remained save some of the retaining walls surrounding the Temple Mount. (The Kotel — a section of the retaining wall that was dubbed the "Wailing Wall" — was a section of those walls that Jews could access for hundreds of years. And this is where they came and wept and prayed.)

For the first time since King David made it Israel's capital a thousand years earlier, Jerusalem was empty of Jews. It's ironic that the first city in history to be made intentionally and completely *Juden rein*, "Jew free" (to borrow a term later used by the Nazis), was their very own Jerusalem.

But that was not all.

To further squelch any nationalistic feeling, Hadrian renamed the land Philistia (Palestine) after the Philistines, an extinct people who once occupied the Mediterranean coastal area and who were among the most bitter enemies of the Jews described in the Bible.

This name survived in Christian writings, to be resurrected in 1917 after World War I, when the British took over the Middle East after conquering the Ottoman Empire. They named the lands east and west of the Jordan River — including the country of Jordan which the British created in 1923 — the British Mandate for Palestine.

Rabbi Akiva

The Roman plan sought not only to separate Jews from the Land of Israel; it also sought to separate them from Judaism.

Writes Rabbi Berel Wein:

> Their [the Roman] plan was to eliminate the scholars and sages of Israel, who were, after all, the true leaders of the Jews, and to forbid the practice of Judaism, the lifeblood of Israel, thus guaranteeing the Jews' de-

> mise as a counter-force to Roman culture and hegemony. The Shabbat, circumcision, public study and teaching of Torah, as well as observances of all Jewish ritual and customs, were forbidden.[311]

One of the great rabbis of the time, who simply refused to abide by these decrees, was Rabbi Akiva. Although other rabbis did likewise and were killed by the Romans for their acts of disobedience, Rabbi Akiva deserves special mention because of his stature in the Jewish world and the particular way he met his death.

It is fascinating to note that Rabbi Akiva did not even begin to study Torah until age forty. Until that time, he had been an uneducated shepherd, but then he fell in love, and his beloved Rachel said she would marry him only if he studied Torah. He thought the task impossible until he saw a stone that had been hollowed out by dripping water. He said: "If water, which is soft, can hollow out a stone, which is hard, how much more can the words of the Torah, which are hard, cut through and make an impression on my heart, which is soft."[312]

Thus he began his studies and in a short period of time was considered one of the wisest men of Israel. Students from all over flocked to learn from him, and at one point, he headed a chain of schools totaling 24,000 students.

The Talmud abounds with stories about Rabbi Akiva. One of the most famous is the story of four great sages who entered *pardes*, the "orchard" — that is they engaged in mystical meditative techniques. Of the four, three met terrible fates as a result of their mystical foray — one died, another went insane, and the third became a heretic. Only Rabbi Akiva "entered in peace and emerged in peace."[313]

A person like Rabbi Akiva, who lived on such a high spiritual level and who possessed an uncompromising dedication to Torah, could not be silenced by Roman decrees.

When the Romans learned that Rabbi Akiva was openly teaching Torah they decided to make a public example of his punishment. They arrested him and took him (most likely) to the stadium in Caesarea[314] where on (or around) Yom Kippur in 136 C.E., they staged a prolonged torture of the great sage. This horrible spectacle included having Rabbi Akiva's skin flayed with iron combs.

Rabbi Akiva, along with many other great Rabbis, went to his death sanctifying God's name, with the words of the Shema on his lips: "Hear O Israel, the Lord is our God, the Lord is One." Rabbi Akiva's spirit exemplified the spirit of the sages who against the greatest odds sought to keep Judaism alive. We shall see next how they succeeded.[315]

38.
TALMUD

At various times during the Hadrian persecutions, the sages were forced into hiding, though they managed to reconvene at Usha in 122 C.E., and again at Yavneh in 158 C.E. With so much persecution and unrest and with the Jewish people fleeing the Land of Israel, the rabbis knew that they would not be able to keep a central seat of rabbinic power alive for long. Yet, during these great periods of chaos, some of the finest rabbinic minds made their mark. Among them:

Rabbi Akiva (who we discussed in the previous chapter);

Rabbi Akiva's chief disciple, Rabbi Meir, husband of the legendary Bruria;

Rabbi Simon Bar Yochai, the author of the *Zohar*, the central text of the Kabbalah;

Rabbi Simon Bar Yochai's son, Rabbi Eliezer;

Rabbi Simon Ben Gamliel II, the descendant of the House of Hillel and a direct descendant of King David.

Judah HaNasi

Now, another man was to emerge and impact the Jewish world in a major way; he was the son of Rabbi Simon Ben Gamliel II and his name was Rabbi Judah HaNasi ("Judah, the Prince").

Rabbi Judah HaNasi is one personality who is absolutely fundamental to understanding this period of time, and one of the greatest personalities of Jewish history. So great was he that he is now affectionately referred to in Jewish scholarship as only "Rebbe."

He had a unique combination of attributes — being both a great Torah scholar and a strong leader — that gave him the power to lead the Jewish people at this chaotic time. He was also a man of tremendous personal wealth, and his high position enabled him to deal effectively not only with the Jews in the Land of Israel, but with the Roman authorities as well.

Hadrian died in 139 C.E. and with his death came an improvement in the treatment of the Jewish community in Israel. During a period of relative quiet, Rabbi Judah HaNasi managed to befriend the Roman emperors who succeeded Hadrian, particularly Marcus Aurelius. Writes historian Rabbi Berel Wein:

> Providentially, in the course of the Parthian war, Marcus Aurelius met Rabbi [Judah HaNasi], and they became friends and eventually confidants. Marcus Aurelius consulted with his friend in Judea on matters of state policy as well as on personal questions.... The years of Marcus Aurelius' reign, ending in his death in 180 C.E., was the high-water mark in the intercourse between Rome and the Jews. The Jews, under the leadership of Rabbi [Judah HaNasi] would use this period of blissful respite to prepare themselves for the struggle of darker days surely lurking around the corner.[316]

At this time — circa 188 C.E. — the Mishnah was born.

Mishnah

What is the Mishnah?

In previous chapters we discussed the fact that at Mount Sinai the Jewish people received the Written Torah and the Oral Torah. The Oral Torah was the oral explanation of how the written laws should be executed and followed.

The Oral Torah was transmitted from generation to generation and was never written down.[317] Why? Because the Oral Torah was meant to be fluid. The principles stayed the same, but they were constantly applied to all types of new circumstances.

This worked exceptionally well as long as the central authority — the Sanhedrin — remained intact and the chain of transmission was not interrupted. (That is, teachers were able to freely pass on their wisdom to the next generation of students.) But in the days since the destruction of the Temple, the Sanhedrin had been repeatedly uprooted and teachers had to go into hiding.

Rabbi Judah HaNasi realized that things would not get better any time soon. He foresaw that the Temple would not be rebuilt in his generation and possibly for many generations to come; that the Jews would continue to flee the land as a result of the constant persecutions and impossible living conditions; and that central rabbinic authority, which was already weaker than ever, would cease altogether. To make sure that the chain of transmission would never be broken, he decided that the time had come to write down the Oral Torah.[318]

This was a mammoth undertaking. Although much of the work may have already been done by previous generations of rabbis, the monumental task of editing, explaining, and organizing this vast amount of material was left to Rabbi Judah. The end result of this massive undertaking was a definitive, yet cryptic (the basic principles were all there, yet a teacher was still required to elucidate the material) version of the entire Oral Law called the Mishnah. (Incidentally, the word *mishnah* means "repetition" because it was studied by repeating — *mishnah* then, by extension, means "learning.") Maimonides, in the introduction to his *Mishneh Torah*, explains it as follows:

> He gathered together all the traditions, enactments, interpretations, and expositions of every position of the Torah, that either came down from Moses, our teacher, or had been deduced by the courts in successive generations. All this material he redacted in the Mishnah, which was diligently taught in public, and thus became universally known among the Jewish people. Copies of it were made and widely disseminated, so that the Oral Law might not be forgotten in Israel.

The Mishnah, which is written in Hebrew, is divided into six basic sections or "orders" and further subdivided into sixty-three tractates with a total of 525 chapters. The six segments deal with six basic areas of Jewish law:

Zeraim, literally "seeds," covering all agricultural rules and laws for foods as well as all blessings.

Moed, literally, "holiday," dealing with the rituals of Shabbat and other Jewish holidays.

Nashim, literally "women," examining all the issues between men and women such as marriage, divorce, etc.

Nezikin, literally "damages," covering civil and criminal law.

Kodshim, literally "holy things," concerning laws of the Temple.

Taharot, literally "pure things," concerning laws of spiritual purity and impurity.

Rabbi Judah HaNasi finished the Mishnah in 190 C.E. in the town of Tzipori in the Galilee. You can visit the site today, and the area is very interesting from an archaeological perspective. At a site called Beit She'arim (where the Sanhedrin had been located prior to its move to Tzipori), there is a vast number of burial caves carved into the side of a mountain. Based on evidence found at the site, archaeologists believe that one of these caves contains the grave of Rabbi Judah HaNasi, along with many other great scholars of that time.

Writing the Talmud

During the centuries following the completion of the Mishnah, the chain of transmission of the Oral Law was further weakened by a number of factors. Economic hardship and increased persecution of the Jewish community in Israel caused many Jews, including many rabbis, to flee the country. Many of these rabbis emigrated to the Babylon region (today's Iraq) of the Persian Empire.

As a result, the role of the rabbis of Israel as the sole central authority of the Jewish people came to an end. This decentralization of Torah authority led to further weakening of the transmission process. Thus it became clear to the sages of this period that the Mishnah alone was no longer clear enough to fully explain the Oral Law. It was written in shorthand fashion and in places was cryptic. This is because it was very concise and written on the assumption that the person reading it was already well-acquainted with the subject matter. As questions arose, the rabbis began to have discussions about it and to write down the substance of these discussions.

At this time a significant portion of the Jewish population was living in Babylon, outside the bounds of the Roman Empire, and the rabbis there assembled their discussions, the end product of which was called "Talmud Bavli" or the Babylonian Talmud. Even before this process had begun in Babylon, another set of discussions took place in the Land of Israel, and the end result was "Talmud Yerushalmi" or the Jerusalem Talmud. (Incidentally, the Jerusalem Talmud was not written in Jerusalem; it was written in Tiberias, the last place where the Sanhedrin sat, but it was called the Jerusalem Talmud in deference to the Sanhedrin's rightful home.)

Due to persecution of the Jewish community in Israel, the Jerusalem Talmud, completed in the mid-fourth century C.E., is much shorter (it contains only four of the six sections of the Mishnah) and is harder to understand than the Babylonian Talmud. The situation of the Jews in Babylon was much more stable, and the rabbis there had considerably more time to edit and explain the subject matter.

Although there are two Talmuds, they are not really separate. The rabbis of Babylon had access to the Jerusalem Talmud while they were working on their text. But in case of a dispute, the Babylonian Talmud is followed.[319] Because the Babylonian Talmud is considered more authoritative and the Jerusalem Talmud is more difficult to study, Jewish students poring over the Talmud in yeshivas today are using chiefly the Babylonian Talmud.

The Talmud is more than just an application of the details of the Jewish law as expounded in the Mishnah; it's the encyclopedia of all Jewish existence.

The Talmud also contains *aggadata*, stories that are meant to illustrate important points in the Jewish worldview. These stories contain a wealth of information on a huge range of topics. You name it, it's in there.

This information has always been vital to the Jewish people, because Jewish law was never applied by reading a sentence in the Torah and executing it to the letter. Take for example the biblical prescription, "An eye for an eye, a tooth for a tooth." This statement was never taken literally in Jewish law. It was always understood on two levels: (1) that justice must be proportional (it's not a life for an eye), and (2) that in the matter of injuries compensation is required — i.e. the value of an eye for the value of the eye.

To read the Talmud is to read a lot of arguments. On every page it seems that the rabbis are arguing. This kind of argument — the purpose of which was to arrive at the kernel of truth — is called *pilpul*. This word has a negative connotation outside the yeshivah world, as to the uneducated eye it often seems that the rabbis are merely splitting hairs, and that some of the arguments have absolutely no basis in everyday life. But this is not so.

The reason why the rabbis argued about matters that may not have any application to everyday life was to try to arrive at the truth in an abstract way — to understand the logic and to extract the principle. These rabbis were interested in understanding reality and in doing the right thing. Reality is what Judaism is all about — the ultimate reality being God.

Another important point is that much of the dispute is focused on relatively minor points while the larger issues were generally not disputed. You never see an argument as to whether or not you can eat pork, or whether or not you can light a fire on Shabbat. These things were given and totally agreed upon. Only small points were subject to discussion. And these rabbis were wise enough to know that a day would come when the principles established by striving for truth would have far-reaching implications.

Gemara

If you look at a page of the Babylonian Talmud today, you will find that the Hebrew text of the Mishnah is featured in the middle of the page. Interspersed between the Hebrew of the Mishnah are explanations in both Hebrew and Aramaic, which are called the Gemara.

מאימתי פרק ראשון ברכות ב

A page of the Babylonian Talmud

The Aramaic word Gemara means "tradition." In Hebrew, the word Gemara means "completion." Indeed, the Gemara is a compilation of the various rabbinic discussions on the Mishnah, and as such completes the understanding of the Mishnah.

The texts of the Mishnah and Gemara are then surrounded by other layers of text and commentaries from a later period.

The text of the Mishnah quotes rabbis who lived circa 100 B.C.E. to 200 C.E. These rabbi are called the *Tanaim*, or "teachers." In this group are included such greats as Rabbi Johanan Ben Zakkai, Rabbi Simon Bar Yochai, Rabbi Akiva, and of course Rabbi Judah HaNasi. (In the Gemara, they usually have the title *Rebbi* before their first names, although there are many exceptions such as the names: Hillel, Shammai, Ben Azai, and Ben Zoma.)

The text of the Gemara quotes rabbis who lived circa 200 C.E. to about 500 C.E. These rabbis are called *Amoraim*, "explainers" or "interpreters." In this group are included Rav Huna, Rav Ashi, etc. (Names of the Babylonian *Amoraim* are usually preceded by the title *Rav* as opposed to the Israeli *Amoraim* who continued to use the title *Rabbi* or *Rebbi*. This is because the authentic institution of rabbinic ordination was only done in the Land of Israel.)

THE TRANSMISSION OF THE ORAL TRADITION

PERIOD	CIRCA	CHAIN OF TRANSMISSION
Mount Sinai	1312 B.C.E.	Moses > Joshua
The Elders	1260 B.C.E. to 800 B.C.E.	>Pinhas and the 70 Elders > Eli > Samuel > King David > King Solomon
The Prophets	800 B.C.E. to 410 B.C.E.	> Ahijah > Elijah > Elisha > Jehoiada > Zechariah > Hosea > Amos > Isaiah > Micah > Joel > Nahum > Habakuk > Zephaniah > Jeremiah > Baruch
The Great Assembly	410 B.C.E. to 310 B.C.E.	> 120 Men of the Great Assembly > Simon HaTzaddik > Antigonos of Soho
Zugot ("Pairs")	260 B.C.E. to 10 C.E.	> Jose b. Joezer & Jose b. Johanan > Jehoshua b. Perahiah & Nittai of Arbel > Judah b. Tabbai & Simon b. Shatach > Shemaiah & Avtalion > Hillel & Shammai
Tanaim ("Teachers")	10 to 200 C.E.	> R' Simon b. Hillel, R' Johanan b. Zakkai > Rabban Gamliel the Elder, R' Eliezer b. Hyrcanus, R' Jehoshua b. Hananiah, R' Simon b. Netanel, R' Elazar b. Arakh > Rabban Simon b. Gamliel I, R' Akiva, Rebbe Tarfon, R' Simon b. Elazar, R' Johanan b. Nuri > Rabban Gamliel II, R' Meir, R' Ishmael, R' Judah, R' Jose, R' Simon Bar Yochai > R' Simon b. Gamliel II > R' Judah HaNasi (codifier of the Mishnah)
Amoraim ("Explainers")	200 to 475 C.E.	> Rav Samuel, Rabbi Johanan (compiler of Jerusalem Talmud) > Rav Huna, Rav Judah, Rav Nachman, Rav Kahana, Rabba Bar Hanna, Rav Ami, Rav Asi > Rabbah, Rav Josef, Rav Hisda, Rabba Bar Huna > Abaye, Rava > Rav Ashi and Ravina (compilers of the Babylonian Talmud)
Savoraim	475 to 589 C.E.	> Rav Yose, Rav Aha
Geonim	589 to 1038 C.E.	Achai Gaon, Amram Gaon, Dodai ben Nahman, Hai Gaon, Saadia Gaon, Sherira Gaon
Rishonim	1038 to 1500 C.E.	Rabenu Gershon, Rashi, R' Yitzchak Alfasi, R' Yehuda Halevi, Ibn Ezra, Maimonides, Nachmanides, R' Yaakov ben Meir
Achronim	1500 C.E. to present	Abarbanel, Bartenura, R' Yosef Karo, R' Isaac Luria, R' Chaim Vital, Maharal, R' Moshe Isserles, Ramchal, R' Chaim Volozhin, R' Moshe Sofer, Chafetz Chaim

The surrounding text of today's Talmud also quotes *Rishonim*, literally "the first ones," rabbinic authorities (circa 1000 C.E. to 1500 C.E.) who predated

Rabbi Joseph Karo, the sixteenth-century author of the code of Jewish law known as the *Shulchan Aruch*. Among the most prominent *Rishonim* are: the eleventh-century commentator Rashi, his students and descendants who were the chief authors of the commentary called *Tosafot*, and the twelfth-thirteenth century philosophers Maimonides and Nachmanides. We will discuss the contributions of these rabbis in chapters 43 and 46.

Just how important was the work of Rabbi Judah HaNasi and those that followed him would become very clear in the next hundred years when the Jewish people would face another threat to their religion. This is when the Roman Empire decided to convert its entire population to Christianity.

39.
ORIGINS OF CHRISTIANITY

The century and a half that followed the completion of the Mishnah corresponds to a period in history when the Roman Empire adopted Christianity — a move that had a severe impact on the Jews. However, before we tell that story, we must go back in time to the first century C.E., when the Temple still stood.

As we might recall from chapter 31, from the time of the invasion of the Romans and particularly following the persecutions of the sages by King Herod the Great, the Jewish people were in turmoil. Soon nationalistic feelings would erupt in the Great Revolt, and the Jews would be fighting the Romans as well as each other.

In this atmosphere of tension — when the Jewish people were yearning for a leader who would help them throw off the Roman yoke — the seeds of what would later become known as Christianity were first sown.

Messiah

When Jews yearn for a savior, they are yearning for the Messiah.

It is important to realize that the notion of the Messiah was not invented by Christianity. It is an ancient Jewish idea — one of the Thirteen Principles of Faith within Judaism.[320] This idea is recorded numerous times in the various books of the prophets, including Isaiah, Micah, Zephaniah, and Ezekiel.

(Indeed, throughout Jewish history, strong leaders arose and for a time were mistaken for the Messiah. But when the so-called Messiah did not fulfill the prophecies — by bringing world peace, etc. — it became clear he was not the right one.)

The English word Messiah comes from the Hebrew verb *mashuach,* which means "anointed."[321] The Mashiach, then, is God's "anointed one." This, for example, is how the Book of Samuel relates the anointing of David as king:

> Samuel took the horn of oil and anointed him [David] in the midst of his brothers, and the spirit of God rested on David from that day on.[322]

Throughout the Bible we see numerous examples where God would designate individuals for kingship by sending a prophet to anoint them with oil. While numerous personalities in the Bible are called "anointed," there is only one who is called *the* anointed — the Messiah. The Jewish definition of Messiah is a Jewish leader (without question, a human being), descended from the line of King David (that is, from the tribe of Judah), with the the Torah knowledge and the leadership ability to bring all the Jewish people back from exile to the Land of Israel. His task is to rebuild the Temple, bring world peace, and elevate the entire world to the realization of One God. The great medieval scholar Maimonides gives a concise description of the Messiah:

> The king Messiah will arise and restore the kingship of David to its former state and original sovereignty. He will rebuild the sanctuary and gather the dispersed of Israel. All the ancient laws will be reinstituted in his days.... Do not think that the king Messiah will have to perform signs and wonders, bring anything new into being, revive the dead, or do similar things. It is not so.... If there arise a king from the House of David who meditates on the Torah, occupies himself with the commandments...observes the precepts prescribed in the Written and Oral Law, prevails upon Israel to walk in the way of Torah...fights the battles of the Lord, it may be assumed that he is the Messiah. [But] if he does these things and succeeds, rebuilds the sanctuary on its site, and gathers the dispersed of Israel, he is beyond all doubt the Messiah. He will prepare the whole world to serve God together.[323]

The prophet Isaiah, whose prophecy on this subject is perhaps the best known, describes the Jewish messianic vision with these words:

> In the days to come, the mountain of God's house shall stand firm above the mountains and tower above the hills. And all the nations shall stream to it. And the many peoples shall go and say: "Come, let us go up to the Mount of God, to the House of the God of Jacob, that He may instruct us in His ways, that we may walk in His paths." And they shall beat their

> swords into plowshares and their spears into pruning hooks; nation shall not lift up sword against nation. Neither shall they learn war anymore.... [At that time] the wolf shall dwell with the lamb, the leopard lie down with the kid, the calf and the beast of prey shall feed together with a little child to herd them.[324]

Since the notion of a person who will redeem the Jewish people is a fundamental, philosophical part of the Jewish worldview, it is not surprising that the expectation of that redemption always appears at times of crisis.

Indeed, the sages say that the Messiah will be born on the ninth of Av, the worst date in the Jewish calendar, when terrible disasters (including the destruction of the First and Second Temples) befell the Jewish people.

The Book of Ezekiel, for example, talks of a final showdown — the war of Gog and Magog — a terrible war, when all the nations turn against the Jews.[325] According to one possible scenario, this is when the Messiah is expected to come and usher in the final redemption.

This is why, when times are very bad, the Jewish people are prone to think that the final showdown is now. It's always darkest before the dawn. If it looks like things can't get worse, then the Messiah must be right around the corner.

Dark Time

The Roman occupation was such a dark time in Jewish history. Some of the most brilliant of the rabbinical sages had been murdered by Herod. Corruption had crept into the Temple hierarchy. Jews had split into three major groups: the wealthy Sadducees (many of whom were *kohanim*, the priests) who denied the authority of the Oral Law, pledging allegiance to Rome; the fanatically religious and nationalistic Zealots, ready to battle Rome to the death in a suicidal war; and the mainstream Pharisee majority, still loyal to Torah and Oral Law, caught in between.

Out of this chaotic time — marked by virulent anti-Semitism and cruel oppression of the Jews — arose a number of splinter sects whose members believed that the Apocalypse was at hand. Finding a receptive ear among the disillusioned, these sects preached that the ultimate battle of good versus evil would soon be fought, followed by the messianic redemption of humanity.

The Dead Sea Sect — which became famous in modern times after the discovery of the Dead Sea Scrolls at Qumran, and which may or may not have been associated with the Essenes — was one such sect, but there were many others.

The teachings of these sects did not attract many Jews. In the same way that the Jews usually rejected foreign religions, they also rejected attempts to tamper with the inner workings of Judaism. Nevertheless, at this tumultuous time, the Jews were more susceptible than ever before. The countryside was alive with charismatic healers and preachers, and people flocked to them, hoping to hear prophecy that the years of strife and suffering were at an end.

The one who would become most legendary was Joshua, or Jesus, who later in history came to be called Christ, which is Greek for Messiah.

It is beyond the scope of this book to describe the beginnings of early Christianity under Jesus. Currently, there exist approximately 2,700 books in print on the subject, many of them written in recent years discussing the issue of the historical Jesus versus the legendary Jesus, and debating what he said or did not say and what can be said of him with any certainty.

(For those interested, one good source is a highly readable book by the award-winning British biographer A. N. Wilson, *Jesus: A Life*, which thoroughly analyzes all the data and throws in a fair amount of fascinating speculation as well.)

Historically speaking, very little is known. The authors of the Christian Gospels, beginning with Mark (generally dated at around 60 C.E.), all lived after the accepted date of Jesus' death (generally dated between 30 and 34 C.E.). There are several references in the Talmud to various personalities of whom the rabbis disapproved, and some have speculated that one or more of these references are to Jesus. The closest possibility is Yeshu HaNotzri,[326] but there are several problems with this idea:

First, there are at least two characters in the Talmud with the name Yeshu HaNotzri. Second, according to Jewish chronology, these two individuals lived about 300 years apart and neither lived at the time of Jesus. The first Yeshu lived at the time when Joshua Ben Perahjah led the Sanhedrin (circa 150 B.C.E.) and, therefore, predated Jesus according to Christian chronology by at least 150 years. The second Yeshu lived sometime during the second century C.E. about 100 years after the death of Jesus. Finally, the limited narrative we do find in the Talmud[327] about Yeshu does not match anything from the Christian Gospels.

One would expect — if Jesus was at all influential in his time — that the great historian Josephus would have devoted considerable space to him. In all of Josephus's writings there is but one mention of Jesus,[328] and this single reference is considered by virtually all scholars to have been inserted into the original text by Christian monks who copied such texts for church libraries.[329]

The best we can say with certainty is that the Christian world does agree that Jesus was a Jew who was familiar with the Torah, observed the "Law of Moses" and taught many of its precepts, though he also departed from some of them.

One of the most famous of his teachings, which consists of two Torah quotations that were staples of Judaism, echoes the emphasis of the rabbinic teachings of his era. Asked to name the greatest commandment, Jesus, as cited by Matthew, replies:

"Love the Lord, your God, with all your heart and with all your soul and with all your mind. This is the first and greatest commandment. And the second is like it. Love your neighbor as yourself. All the law and the prophets hang on these two commandments."[330]

Of course, "love the Lord, your God, with all your heart and with all your soul and with all your might" is a quotation from the Book of Deuteronomy.[331] "Love your neighbor as yourself" is from the Book of Leviticus.[332] These teachings predated Jesus by some 1,300 years.

As already mentioned, the Christian Gospels, which are said to record the teachings of Jesus, were written in Greek many years after his death, which took place some forty years before the destruction of the Temple.

Jewish Followers

Who were the Jewish followers of Jesus?

The members of the Jesus sect were clearly religious Jews who believed that Jesus was the Messiah. They could not have believed that Jesus was "god" and remained part of the Jewish community. Such a belief would have been complete idolatry in Jewish eyes and would have appeared closer to the Greco-Roman pagan beliefs, where gods took on human form and had relations with humans.

At any rate, the Jesus sect, like numerous other sects in the Land of Israel, would certainly have died out even if its members had survived the revolts against Rome in the first and second centuries. (The Pharisees survived and evolved into the Orthodox Jews of today in part due to the vision of their leader, Rabbi Johanan ben Zakkai, as we saw in chapter 34.)

So where did all the Christians comes from? Indeed, where did Christianity come from?

For the answer, we must look at another colorful personality who appeared on the scene after the death of Jesus, and who is given the credit by virtually every historian of Christianity for spreading the message of Jesus worldwide and fashioning the Christian message for the consumption of the pagan world.

He was a Jew — originally known as Saul — who became famous in Christianity as "Saint Paul."

40.
FROM PAUL TO CONSTANTINE

The Jesus sect in Jerusalem remained small and was simply not spreading among the Jews. Indeed, it had become offensive in Jewish eyes, and the Jesus followers were considered heretics.[333] The attitude of the rabbis was that these people — Jews though they may be — were pursuing an ideology that was wrong, and their skewed beliefs were going to pollute the Jewish people. Thus, this splinter sect had no place in Judaism, and, therefore, had to be driven out.

One of those who took the driving-out part seriously, according to his own account, was a Jew named Saul from Tarsus (a city in Asia Minor, today's Turkey). But, as he later wrote in his epistles or "letters," after participating in persecutions of the Jesus sect, Saul had a sudden change of heart. He claimed that Jesus appeared to him in a vision and dissuaded him from persecuting his followers.

Following this "mystical" encounter, Saul disappeared from the scene to re-emerge some thirteen years later (circa 47–60 C.E.) as Paul, "missionary to the gentiles."

When he reemerged on the world scene, Paul introduced some revolutionary ideas, which at first caused some furor among the more seasoned Jesus followers. During a dramatic meeting with the Jesus sect in Jerusalem, his viewpoint won: the new religion would separate from Judaism.

Paul embarked on a series of missionizing journeys in which he was highly successful, attracting many converts to the new religion — Christianity. He preached monotheism, to be sure, but with one radical innovation. The way of salvation for non-Jews was now much simpler: belief in Jesus replaced observance of the commandments.

Through Paul's efforts and the zeal of his early disciples, Christianity experienced a meteoric rise in popularity. Its initial successes were all in places where the non-Jewish inhabitants had had significant exposure to Jewish ideas.

Roman Attraction to Judaism

We have previously described the tensions in the Greco-Roman world that pitted Hellenism against Judaism. But we neglected to mention that there were Romans who were very much attracted to Judaism.

This was especially true in the first century C.E., in the time of Nero, when the decay of Rome began, and thoughtful, intelligent people saw the empire turning into a cesspool of decadence, violence, and immorality. Such people were looking for stability, for a universal moral view of the world, and they were receptive to more exotic forms of worship than the official state religion.

Their search brought to Rome many alien religious cults — in particular the worship of Mithra, the Persian god of light and wisdom, who became identified with Helios, the Greek sun god, as well as Sol, the Roman sun god. This cult became so popular that the Romans named a day of the week — Sunday — in honor of Mithra and celebrated the sun god's birthday in late December in conjunction with the Winter Solstice.

Loyalty to the state gods was further weakened by the Roman policy of stealing the gods of conquered peoples. The "captured gods" were then incorporated into the official pantheon. As the empire grew, the number of gods multiplied wildly. According to the Roman writer Varro, at one point Rome had in excess of 30,000 gods and 157 holidays a year.[334] Who could keep them straight, or, for that matter, take them seriously?

Another important factor was the constant threat of internal rebellion and external invasion with which the Romans lived. The feeling that merciless fate and a cruel death lurked around the corner made them anxious and fearful. (Perhaps all those hours of watching minor criminals butchered at the Coliseum created a subconscious concern that "there but for the grace of one of the 30,000 gods go I.")

The atmosphere of impending doom was only heightened by all of the murderous intrigue in politics, by the general corruption and by the apparent state of moral decline. Historian Michael Grant, in *The World of Rome*, sums it up as follows:

> The Roman age was a time of not only uncontrolled blood lust but pessimism and nerve-failure regarding the powers of man to work his

> own future. The existence and propaganda of the imperial government claiming support of the old gods did not remove the deep-seated feeling that every man was adrift and everything hazardous. So the presiding deity of nerve-failure was Fortune. "Throughout the whole world," says Pliny the Elder, "at every place and hour, by every voice, Fortune alone is invoked and her name spoken.... We are so much at the mercy of chance that chance is our god."[335]

In such an atmosphere, the Jewish view that one is not lost at sea in a random and hostile universe, but is looked after by One, Omnipotent and loving God, who orders and runs the world, was likely to get a receptive hearing.

The Jewish people were also a unique and sizeable minority dispersed throughout the major cities of the empire. Not only was their idea of one God unique, they also possessed a unique sense of community, a highly developed social welfare infrastructure, and a very high level of literacy. Michael Grant again:

> Numerically...[the Jews] were fewer in those days than they are now, perhaps eight million...but no less than seven million of these eight million were in the Roman empire, where they constituted between six and nine percent of the population — in the eastern provinces, the percentage was perhaps as high as twenty. Comprising, as they did, such a high proportion of the total number of inhabitants, they could scarcely fail to exercise an influence upon events; given their highly distinctive beliefs and customs, so divergent from the Greco-Roman way of life which surrounded them, it was predictable that their relationship with their neighbors would become both dramatic and explosive.[336]

Conversion to Judaism (generally discouraged by the Jews) has always been a major undertaking, one which has historically required the prospective convert to demonstrate his or her sincere desire to follow the Torah's teachings. Nevertheless, Roman historical records show us that Judaism won many converts. Among them was Onkelos, a nephew of one of the Roman emperors (possibly Nero), who subsequently translated the Hebrew Bible into Aramaic. Josephus describes Nero's wife, Poppea, as being very supportive and interested in Judaism,[337] and there is much speculation among historians about other important Romans who were sympathetic to Judaism and may even have converted.

During this time, the best-known exporter of Jewish ideology was Philo Judeas, who lived and taught between 20 B.C.E. and 50 C.E.. Strongly influenced by Hellenism, he sought to fuse Greek philosophy with Judaism and to export this mixture to the world. Philo was a prolific writer with a considerable following, especially in major cultural centers such as Rome and Alexandria.

It cannot be denied that the message and lifestyle of Judaism was very attractive to many Romans. Historian Howard Sachar, in his *A History of Israel*, suggests an explanation for why this was so:

> The conditions were highly favorable. The old paganism...was decaying, and sensitive minds were repelled by it. The clear-cut monotheism and the rational practices of the Hebrews, expounded with charm by the Hellenized Jewish writers, made a deep impression. There were great numbers of converts, if not officially to Judaism, at least to Jewish practices and ideals.[338]

So great was the impact of Judaism on the empire that the Roman writer Seneca complained, "This abominable nation has succeeded in spreading its customs throughout all lands — the conquered have given their laws to the conquerors."

But the fact that some citizens of the empire converted and many more openly sympathized with the Jews does not mean the religion of Moses was taking Rome by storm. The reason why not was simple: Jewish laws, restrictions, and rituals were difficult to follow. While certain commandments, such as Shabbat rest and dietary laws, were very popular and relatively easy to observe, other rituals of Judaism were seen as too extreme and too difficult — for example circumcision and the laws of family purity.

Additionally, many saw Judaism as a national religion of a specific people — that is, being Jewish meant not only ascribing to a religious faith, but also adopting a different national identity. Naturally, if you were born in Rome, you surely did not want to appear to be giving up your Roman citizenship. It didn't help that Judea was one of the most rebellious and troublesome provinces in the empire, and that Jews in general were viewed with suspicion and hostility. This, no doubt, caused many Romans to think twice about joining Jewish ranks.

But this is where Paul stepped in.

Paul's Revolution

Paul's shrewd move was to retain the parts of Judaism that appealed to the Roman world, while dropping the "objectionable" components.

Paul preached that belief in Jesus replaced the laws of the Torah — that is, all the commandments that Romans attracted to Judaism found so cumbersome. By converting to Paul's new religion, a Roman was able to subscribe to the Jewish view of One, loving God, as well as to the Torah's moral vision of peace, justice, and love of one's neighbor. A Roman could subscribe to these ideas without having to become "different" in the way Jews were "different."

Thus, Paul removed the barriers and opened the floodgates. Writes John G. Gager in *Kingdom and Community: The Social World of Early Christianity*:

> Christianity preserved all the advantages of its Jewish heritage but without the only two factors that might otherwise have inhibited its growth: the obligation of the ritual law and the close connection between religion and national identity. By proclaiming that the Christ was "the end of the law" and by presenting itself to the world as "the new spiritual Israel," Hellenistic Christianity was able to reap the political and social fruits that had been sown by three centuries of Hellenistic Judaism.[339]

Needless to say, observant Jews objected to Paul, a Jew whom they saw as the worst kind of heretic. Indeed, because of Jewish complaints against him, Paul was arrested by the Roman authorities, held for a time under house arrest, and finally executed in or around 66 C.E. — the year of the start of the Great Revolt against Rome in Israel. (Christian tradition has it that Paul and the chief apostle of Jesus, Peter, were buried on Vatican Hill, the current seat of the Roman Catholic Church.)

After the death of Paul, Christianity continued to evolve and grow. Many controversies arose as the new religion struggled to develop its core theology.

As this is a book about Jewish history and not a treatise on Christianity, we are not going to get involved in discussing the development of the various Christian dogmas (such as the Trinity, Virgin Birth, Resurrection, etc.), nor of the various "heresies" which flourished in early Christian Church. For those interested in the subject, the premier work is *A History of Christianity* by Christian historian Paul Johnson.

Suffice it to say that it took some 300 years for the early Christian Church to refine its core dogma, which turned out to be a synthesis of Jewish ideals and Greek/pagan concepts. With the growth of Christianity came stiff resistance from official Rome. The new religion was proving so popular that it was threatening the state religion and, therefore, the stability of the state. Christianity was outlawed in Rome, and those who were caught practicing it were regularly crucified or fed to the lions in the Coliseum. These persecutions — which came in waves, depending on the tolerance level of the Roman emperor in power

— actually served to make Christianity stronger. In this regard, the Christians were following the precedent-setting behavior of the Jews in the days of the Greek Empire. (Back then, no one died for their religion — no one, except the Jews.)

And then, suddenly, in 306 C.E., a remarkable thing happened which dramatically changed Christian fortune and led, within a dozen years, to the elevation of Christianity to the state religion of the Roman Empire. The remarkable event was the "conversion" of Constantine, who would become the Emperor of Rome.

Constantine

On the eve of a battle with his rival for the throne of Rome, Constantine reported that he had a dream of Jesus, followed by a vision of a cross superimposed on the sun.

Constantine was prone to visions. A few years before, he claimed to have seen the sun-god Sol in a grove of Apollo in Gaul. The juxtaposition of the two — cross and sun — was an omen for victory and, when Constantine won the battle, he credited his newfound god and converted to Christianity.

Oxford scholar, David L. Edwards, Provost of London's Southwark Cathedral and author of *Christianity: The First Two Thousand Years,* openly doubts the sincerity of Constantine's conversion, and some scholars wonder if he converted at all. But such are the quirks of history. Soon, Constantine was emperor, and he established his capital in the east, in Byzantium, which was renamed Constantinople. And Christianity became the official state religion of the new order — the Byzantine Empire.

Constantine had initiated a unique way of seeing Christianity by merging pagan and Christian symbols (sun and cross). Over the next few hundred years much more such synthesis followed.

Though Christians like to characterize Christianity as "the religion of love" and Judaism as "the religion of law," a Jew looking at Constantine's record might well ask: "What's love got to do with it?" Writes Paul Johnson in *A History of Christianity*:

> [Constantine] had no respect for human life, and as emperor he executed his eldest son, his own second wife, his favorite sister's husband and 'many others' on doubtful charges.... He was much criticized for condemning prisoners of war to mortal combat with wild beasts at Trier and Comar and for wholesale massacres in north Africa.[340]

What followed was a bitter struggle for wealth and power that was all but inevitable once Christianity was declared the sole official religion. With the aim of eradicating paganism, Christian mobs scoured the lands of the empire, smashing idols and burning temples. Writes Johnson: "[The Church] transformed itself from a suffering and victimized body, begging toleration, into a coercive one, demanding monopoly...."[341]

Cynics have charged that once it became a state power, the Christian Church turned the cross into a sword, and its ability to convert the Western world had less to do with its message than its methods. By the late fourth century C.E. the official government efforts at intimidation through laws and decrees — aided by mob terrorism — succeeded in imposing Christianity on the majority of the empire.

With the disappearance of paganism, Judaism began to stick out like a sore thumb. As always, it was strange and separate, and it wouldn't compromise. The stubborn Jews, as they had done with every other religion that had assaulted their belief system previously, were obstinately refusing to bow to the new order. This presented a special problem, as William Nicholls explains in *Christian Anti-Semitism: A History of Hate*:

> The very presence of the Jewish people in the world, continuing to believe in the faithfulness of God to the original covenant...put a great question against Christian belief in a new covenant made through Christ. The presence of this question, often buried deep in the Christian mind, could not fail to cause profound and gnawing anxiety. Anxiety usually leads to hostility.[342]

Within a short time, Jews living in the empire had lost most of their civil rights. The Jewish Supreme Court, the Sanhedrin, was forbidden to meet, and sermons against the Jews, often inciting violence, were routinely preached. The idea of presenting Jews as the killers of Jesus originated at this time, though it was not popularized until several hundred years later.

By the early seventh century — when the Byzantine Empire began to wobble, facing attacks from the Persians, who seized chunks of its territory including Jerusalem — the Jews were in a very precarious position. Anti-Jewish legislation, heavy taxes, outbreaks of violence, and forced conversions, all had taken their toll on the population. Hoping to find a respite from the Christians, some fled back home to safety. But when the Byzantine Emperor Heraclius reclaimed Jerusalem in 629 C.E., the poor Jews who found themselves there were brutally massacred.

Praying for relief, these Jews could never have dreamed that it would come in the form of a "mixed blessing" from a most unexpected place — from Arabia. There in Mecca — a place that had long been the center of pagan worship at the famed Black Stone of Kaaba — an unusual man named Mohammed was preaching an unusual message.

41. THE RISE OF ISLAM

In the previous chapter, we described the Jewish impact on intellectual Rome prior to the advent of Christianity. Similarly, Jews living on the Arabian Peninsula had an impact on their Arab neighbors.

During the days of Jewish clashes with the Roman Empire, Jews fled to areas outside the control of Rome and founded many towns and villages in Arabia. One very famous town, almost certainly founded by Jews, was Yathrib. Today Yathrib is better known as Medina and is considered Islam's second holiest city (after Mecca).

As in Rome, the local Jews attracted significant numbers of converts to their way of life and many more admirers. M. Hirsch Goldberg, in the *Jewish Connection*, sums up the story before the early seventh century:

> In Arabia, whole tribes converted to Judaism, including two kinds of the Himyarites. French Bible critic Ernest Renan remarked that "only a hair's breadth prevented all Arabia from becoming Jewish."[343]

One of those impressed by the Jews' uncompromising devotion to monotheism was a young trader named Mohammed ibn Abdallah. Although his travels had exposed him to Christianity and he was clearly influenced by it, he found aspects of it troublesome — in particular, the doctrine of the Trinity did not seem strictly monotheistic in his eyes. He is recorded as having said:

> "Unbelievers are those that say, 'Allah is the Messiah, the son of Mary'.... Unbelievers are those that say, 'Allah is one of three.' There is but one God. If they do not desist from so saying, those of them that disbelieve

shall be sternly punished."[344]

However, there is no doubt that in the early stages of his spiritual awakening, Mohammed was greatly impressed by the Jews. Writes S.D. Goiten in *Jews and Arabs*:

> The intrinsic values of the belief in one God, the creator of the world, the God of justice and mercy, before whom everyone high and low bears personal responsibility, came to Mohammed — as he never ceased to emphasize — from Israel.[345]

Mohammed clearly had some knowledge of the Torah; later he would quote Moses (though not always accurately) more than one hundred times in the Koran, the record of his teachings that became the holy book of his newfound religion. Of the twenty-five prophets listed in the Koran, nineteen are from the Hebrew Bible, and many ritual and civil laws of Islam parallel Judaism — for example, circumcision and the prohibition against eating pork.

Children of Ishmael

Mohammed believed that the Arabs were the other children of Abraham — through the line of his son Ishmael by the Egyptian maidservant Hagar — and that they had forgotten the teachings of monotheism they had inherited ages ago. He saw his mission as bringing them back. Paul Johnson, in his *A History of the Jews*, explains:

> What he [Mohammed] seems to have wished to do was to destroy the polytheistic paganism of the oasis culture by giving the Arabs Jewish ethical monotheism in a language they could understand and in terms adapted to their ways. He accepted the Jewish God and their prophets, the idea of fixed law embodied in scripture — the Koran being an Arabic substitute for the Bible — and the addition of an oral law applied in religious courts.[346]

There is no argument that the Arab world of Mohammed's time was badly in need of moral values and social reform. The Mecca of his day was a focal point of pagan worship. The Arab tribesmen of the region worshipped a pantheon of gods there, including Al-Lat, the moon goddess, Al-Uzza, the fertility goddess, and Manat, the goddess of fate, all three of whom were daughters of the chief deity, known as Al-Ilah (Allah) or "the God."[347]

The Kaaba, the shrine enclosing the famous black meteorite which was worshipped in Mecca before Mohammed's time, was also a site for an altar where blood sacrifices were offered to these and other gods.

The morality of the neighboring tribesmen could, charitably, be described as chaotic. Huston Smith, in his classic *The Religions of Man*, goes so far as to call the Arab society before the advent of Mohammed "barbaric."

> Tribal loyalties were paramount; other than that, nothing served to mitigate the blood feuds, drunken brawls and orgies that the harsh life of the desert gave sway to.[348]

Mohammed was repelled by the cruel and crude reality around him. In the year 610, at the age of forty, he escaped to a desert cave where, according to Muslim tradition, he experienced a series of mystical visions, including revelations from the angel Gabriel. He returned from the desert imbued with a spiritual mission to transform the pagan society around him.

Preaching an end to licentiousness and need for peace, justice, and social responsibility, Muhammed advocated improving the lot of slaves, orphans, women, and the poor. He envisioned that tribal loyalties would be replaced with the fellowship of a new monotheistic faith which he called Islam, meaning "surrender to God." (One who submits is a Muslim.) Islam, according to Mohammed, was built on five pillars:

- Faith in one God ("there is no God but Allah")
- Prayer (five times a day)
- Charity (2.5% of one's income)
- Pilgrimage to Mecca called Haj (once in a lifetime)
- Fasting (a fast lasting from dawn to dusk for thirty days during the month of Ramadan)

Initially, Mohammed attracted very few followers. After three years, he had barely forty converts. But, imbued with a passion that has been the hallmark of the great visionaries of the world, Mohammed would not give up. And, little by little, he built a steady following of committed loyalists.

The more followers he attracted, the more attention, and with it, the more hostility. The merchants of Mecca, whose livelihood depended on the pagan sites and rites of the city, weren't going to be easily displaced. A murder plot was hatched, but Mohammed escaped in the nick of time.

While persecution of the Muslims was mounting in Mecca, the city of Yathrib was experiencing problems of internal strife, and a delegation decided that the fiery preacher from Mecca would be the man to bring order to chaos. After winning the pledge of city representatives to worship only Allah, Mohammed agreed to migrate. His journey to Yathrib in the year 622 C.E., the year 1 of the Islamic calendar, has been immortalized as the Hegira.

Thus his life was saved and a new horizon opened for his teachings. It was in Yathrib — hereafter to be known as Medina, "the city of the prophet" — that Islam took hold in a major way.

Once he had made Medina his stronghold, Mohammed mobilized an army of 10,000 men, and in 630 C.E., moved against Mecca, intending to purify the Kaaba and turn it into a center of worship of the one God, Allah. His success is legendary. Two years later when he died, all of Arabia was under Muslim control.

Mohammed and the Jews

The one problem Mohammed had faced in Medina — and elsewhere — were the Jews, who were not prepared to accept his new religion. In the same way they had previously rejected Christianity, so too did they reject Islam.

It must be pointed out, however, that the Jews had fewer problems with Islam than they did with Christianity. Islam was purely monotheistic, whereas Christianity incorporated a lot of pagan mythology. Islam did not claim that Mohammed was "god" or "son of God" or that God came in three parts. Islam followed many Jewish laws and customs, unlike Christianity which disavowed the law of the Torah in favor of faith in Jesus. The most important point of agreement was that Abraham was the father of both the Jews (through his son Isaac) and the Arabs (through his son Ishmael). This made the two peoples half-brothers. But the chief disagreement was whether Mohammed was indeed the last of the prophets to be sent by God and that his word was the final revelation. The Jews found the idea unthinkable; for them prophecy had ended long before and the words of the Torah could never be superseded.

This rejection was painful to Mohammed, who reacted with hostility toward the Jews and took great pains to pointedly separate Islam from its Jewish roots. The holiest day of the week was changed to Friday; direction of prayers was changed from Jerusalem to Mecca; most of the Jewish dietary laws were excised from Islam with the exception of the slaughter rituals and the prohibition against consumption of blood and pork.

Further, Mohammed maintained that the Jews had distorted their own Bible: Abraham did not attempt to sacrifice Isaac to God at Mount Moriah in Jerusalem; rather, Abraham took Ishmael to Mecca, where he offered to sacrifice him to Allah on the Black Stone of Kaaba.

If Jews had previously rebuffed Mohammed's claims to prophecy, they now openly sneered at what they considered a complete fabrication. This only made things worse. Mohammed's anger and curses against the Jews are recorded in the Koran:

> "And humiliation and wretchedness were stamped upon them, and they were visited with wrath from God."
>
> "Of all men you will certainly find the Jews...to be the most intense in hatred of those who believe."
>
> "Vendors are they of error and are desirous that you go astray from the way...But God has cursed them for their unbelief."[349]

Mohammed's anger toward the Jews was not just rhetoric. The period from 622 C.E. until Mohammed's death in 632 C.E. was punctuated by periods of intense anti-Jewish violence, as he systematically expelled, plundered, and even slaughtered the Jews of Nadir, Khaybar, and Banu Qurayza who lived in and around Mecca. Mohammed's victories against the Jews are discussed in great length in the Koran.[350]

After Mohammed's death, some of his followers would interpret his actions and statements as license to purge the world of the Jews. Other Muslims would concentrate more on the commonality of heritage and belief that Mohammed had also emphasized, and they would treat the Jews better.[351]

Jihad

At the time of Mohammed's death in 632 C.E., Arabia was united and poised for *Jihad*, the "holy war" or "holy struggle" to bring the world to Allah. Soon, it moved with a fearsome power against the Byzantine and Persian empires.

From its earliest foundation, *Jihad* was an important principle of Islam. While most people think the term *Jihad* means holy war, the actual meaning is "struggle" and can be used to refer to both the internal struggle between good and evil and the external struggle between the Muslim world (*dhar al Islam*) and the non-Muslim world, which is called the "world of war" (*dhar al hare*). The earliest mention of the term *Jihad* — as used in seventh century Islamic law code called Sharia — refers to the latter, the external struggle against the non-Islamic world.[352]

What did *Jihad* against the Byzantine Empire mean for the Jews? Answers Rabbi Berel Wein in *Echoes of Glory*:

> Most Jewish historians (until the recent revisionist-historians) are convinced that the Byzantine Church would have attempted to eradicate Judaism totally if the Church itself had not been defeated and its plan for hegemony in Asia Minor and the Mediterranean basin thwarted by the rising tide of Islam. Thus, the coming of Islam may be seen as a providential occurrence that allowed the Jews to slip between the cracks Islam made in Byzantine Church persecution. However, as is the case in all historic "gifts" in Jewish history, the rise of Islam would prove to be only a mixed blessing for Israel.[353]

In the Islamic world, Jews were classified as ahl al-dhimma or dhimmi, "protected people," and were allowed to live without being forced to convert. But a whole code of law applied to them, most of it designed to set them apart, humiliate them, and emphasize their inferior status. For example, a Jew could never have his head higher than a Muslim. So, if a Jew was walking along and a Muslim passed by, the Jew had to step into the gutter in deference to the Muslim's superior status. A Jew could never testify against a Muslim in court (which basically meant there was no justice for Jews). Jews could not build a house of worship that was taller than a mosque, which is why, for example, the Four Sephardic Synagogues in the Old City of Jerusalem are subterranean.

It should be noted that these laws were not uniformly enforced, and there were periods when Jews living in Muslim countries were openly persecuted and others when they were treated very well, as we shall see with the Jews of Babylon.

TURKEY
BABYLONIA
IRAN
MEDITERRANEAN SEA
SYRIA
Pumbaditha
Nehardea
Mata Mechasia
Sura
EUPHRATES RIVER
TIGRIS RIVER
ISRAEL
JORDAN
IRAQ
SAUDI ARABIA
KUWAIT
THE
JEWS OF BABYLONIA
422 BCE – 700 CE

42.
THE JEWS OF BABYLON

The story of the Jews of Babylon requires us to go back some 1,000 years in time to recap some information we have previously covered to sum up what has been happening to the Jews living in that region.

In 434 B.C.E., when the Babylonians first marched on Israel as part of their campaign to stake claim to the former Assyrian empire, they did not destroy the Temple, nor send the Jews into exile. However, they did succeed in taking into captivity 10,000 of the best and brightest Jews. While it seemed like tragedy at the time, these brilliant men, Torah scholars all, immediately established a Jewish infrastructure upon arrival in Babylon. A dozen years later when the Temple was destroyed, the Jews who were exiled to Babylon found there yeshivas, synagogues, kosher butchers, etc., all the essentials for maintaining a Jewish life.

Some sixty-five years later, when the Land of Israel fell to the Persians and the Jews were permitted to return to Israel, relatively few did. Of about a million Jews living in the Persian Empire, only 42,000 went back, meaning that the vast majority stayed in Babylon under Persian domination. During the Second Temple period, up until its destruction in 70 C.E., the Jewish community in Babylon — far from the eye of the storm that raged in the Land of Israel — continued to flourish.

Indeed, this is where the center of Jewish rabbinic authority came to rest after the Roman Empire shut down the Sanhedrin. The head of the Jewish community of Babylon — who was officially recognized by the Persian authorities — was called *Reish Galusa* in Aramaic ("Head of the Diaspora" in English).

The *Reish Galusa* was a direct descendant of the House of King David. Even though he was not a king in the Land of Israel, he was recognized as not only the leader of the Jewish community in Babylon, but also as having noble status. During the 1,500-year history of the Jewish community in Babylon, some forty people held that title, all tracing their ancestry back to King David. This was a noble line that was always preserved in Jewish history.

Part of the reason for the stability of the Jewish community in Babylon was that the area was ruled by the Persian Sassanian dynasty from the third century C.E. onward. The Sassanians managed to keep out of their kingdom first the Romans and then the Byzantines. As a result, the Jews of Babylon escaped the harm that the Byzantine Christians inflicted elsewhere.

In this atmosphere, Jewish scholarship was able to flourish in the great yeshivas at Sura (founded by Rabbi Abba Ben Ibo, better known as Rav) and at Nehardea (founded by the great sage Shmuel), which later moved to Pumbedita.

This is where the Babylonian Talmud was written (as we saw in chapter 38), immortalizing the great rabbis of Babylon, especially Abbaye and Rava.[354] As historian Berel Wein relates in *Echoes of Glory*:

> Their stamp of analysis and discussion appears in countless numbers of debates and discussions that form the Talmud. In fact, the surname of the Talmud is "the discussions of Abaye and Rava."[355]

These rabbis are known in Jewish scholarship as *Amoraim*, "explainers" or "interpreters." The *Amoraim* lived from about 200 C.E. to about 500 C.E. during the time when Jewish scholarship thrived in Babylon.[356]

But then the situation changed.

In the middle of the fifth century, the Persian priests, fighting against encroaching Christian missionaries, unleashed anti-Christian persecutions and included Jews in the mayhem. Writes Rabbi Berel Wein:

> The worsening situation in Babylonia came as a shock to the Jewish community, for nothing of this sort had officially been in Babylonia for almost a millennium. Jewish confidence was shattered.[357]

Things went from bad to worse — with the *Reish Galusa* executed at one point — as Babylonia became embroiled in civil war and as the Byzantines continued their encroachments.

In the midst of this chaos, the Muslim conquest of the Middle East in the seventh century brought unexpected benefits to the Jewish community in Babylon.

Caliph Omar

Mohammed had died in 632 C.E., leaving no successor, a situation which led to immediate strife and a split in the nascent Muslim world. The candidates for caliph were two: 1) his cousin Ali, who married Mohammed's daughter Fatima, and 2) his first convert and father-in-law, Abu Bakr.

This struggle gave rise to the creation of two Muslim sects: (1) the Shi'ites, who recognized Ali as Mohammed's rightful successor; and (2) the Sunnis, who recognized Abu Bakr as the rightful successor. Today, the Shi'ites are the minority in the Muslim world, making up 16% of all Muslims. The majority of the Muslims are Sunnis, followers of Abu Bakr and his successor, Omar, who founded the first major Islamic dynasty, the Umayyad (sometimes spelled Omayyad).

Caliph Omar recognized that the road to unity was to have a common enemy. Therefore, he embarked on a series of foreign wars of conquest, in which the Muslims were remarkably successful. As part of his conquests, Caliph Omar invaded Jerusalem in 638 C.E., taking it away from the Byzantines.

To see the remains of Byzantine homes from that period, you can visit the archaeological excavations below the southern end of the Temple Mount in the Old City of Jerusalem. It was this area, in particular, that Omar turned over to seventy Jewish families following his conquest. (Until then the Byzantines had forbidden the Jews from living in Jerusalem at all.)

He found the Temple Mount site in ruins and covered with garbage, as the Byzantines had deliberately decreed that refuse should be dumped there to humiliate the Jews. Omar had the area cleared and may have prayed at the southern end (toward Mecca), which could well be the first time that a small mosque was erected there, though historians are not certain.

It must be made clear that up to this time, Jerusalem had no special significance to Muslims. Already during his lifetime, Mohammed had changed the direction of prayer to Mecca, and the Koran does not mention Jerusalem even once!

A connection with Jerusalem came later in the Islamic tradition, as a result of an Umayyad interpretation of Mohammed's dream, which is recorded in the Koran.[358] In that dream, Mohammed rides his flying horse, Burak — a steed with the body of a woman and the tail of a peacock — to the "farthest place." The "farthest place" in Arabic is Al-Aksa. There he meets Jebril (Gabriel) and goes up to heaven for a forty-day sojourn, meeting all the prophets and talking to Moses and Jesus, etc.[359] The Umayyad leadership decided that Al-Aksa, the farthest place, had to be the edge of the Temple Mount in Jerusalem. And, they decided, the center of the Temple Mount, where a huge stone protruded, must be the spot from which Mohammed ascended to heaven.

In 691 C.E., some fifty years after Omar's conquest, an Umayyad ruler named Abd al Malik built the Dome of the Rock, called Qubbat as Sakrah. It still stands there today and dominates the Jerusalem skyline.

Note that the Dome of the Rock is not a mosque. Rather, it is a shrine built around a huge exposed piece of bedrock, which Jews believe to be the same place where Abraham brought Isaac to be sacrificed, where Jacob dreamed of a ladder to heaven, and where the Holy of Holies once stood. The mosque — Al-Aksa — is a separate structure, built at the southern end of the Temple Mount by Abd al Malik's son, El Walid in 701 C.E. The Dome of the Rock, together with the Al-Aksa mosque, were the first great religious buildings in the Islamic world and predate the building of the Great Mosque in Mecca.

The Dome of the Rock was not always golden as it is today. It was covered with anodized aluminum in 1956, but more recently the late King Hussein of Jordan sold one of his houses in London and used the proceeds to plate it with 80 kg. of gold. Today, this site is the third holiest to Sunni Muslims (after Mecca and Medina in Saudi Arabia) and the fourth holiest to Shi'ite Muslims, who also revere Karbala (in Iraq), the site of the battle in 681 C.E. which gave rise to the Sunni-Shi'ite split. The Temple Mount is known to Muslims as Haram el Sharif, "the Noble Sanctuary." And Jerusalem is known as Al-Quds, "the Holy."[360]

The capture of Jerusalem was a big blow to the Christians, who were reeling from other Muslim conquests that were sweeping the world. Jews greeted it more favorably, as the Christians had been merciless to them. The Muslims might humiliate them, but they would not slaughter them outright.

Indeed, when Omar defeated the Persians and took over Babylonia, he immediately reinstituted the authority of the *Reish Galusa* to head the Jewish community. As a matter of fact, Omar was so fond of the *Reish Galusa*, Bustenai Ben Haninai, that when he decided to marry the daughter of the Persian king, he insisted that Bustenai marry her sister. Thus, in a bizarre twist of fate, the *Reish Galusa* became brother-in-law to the caliph.

(After the death of Bustenai, his sons by an earlier wife sought to delegitimatize his sons by the Persian princess, claiming that she never converted to Judaism. However, this was unlikely as the *Reish Galusa* marrying a non-Jewish woman without conversion would have caused a furor and public condemnation. Indeed the *Gaonim* of the day, the rabbis who headed the famed yeshivas of Babylon, ruled that all his children were legitimate Jews.)

The Karaites

During the long history of Babylonian Jewry, sometimes the *Reish Galusa* wielded more power, sometimes the *Gaonim*. Much depended on the political climate and the personalities involved. Generally, however, the position of the *Gaon* was determined by scholarship, while the position of *Reish Galusa* was depended on lineage (as the *Reish Galusa* was traditionally the descendant of King David). And it was a dispute over lineage that gave rise to a splinter sect in eighth century Baghdad — a splinter sect that came to be known as the Karaites.

When Shlomo, the *Reish Galusa*, died childless in 760 C.E., two of his nephews — Hananiah and Anan — vied for the position. Hananiah got the job and Anan went off to start his own religion.

(This is another example of an old pattern — a split among the Jews due to pride and ego. We saw it, for example, in chapter 20 with Rehoboam and Jeroboam.)

The sect that Anan founded was similar in some ways to the Sadducees. Like the Sadducees, the Karaites didn't recognize the authority of the Oral Torah, and hence they read the Written Torah literally. (Their name, Karaites, comes from the Hebrew verb *kara*, meaning "read.")

As noted earlier, it is impossible to live a Jewish life without the Oral Torah, as so much of the Written Torah is not specific enough. For example, where the Torah commands "And you shall write them [these words] upon the doorposts of your home," how can anyone know which words of the Torah, or indeed, if the entire Torah is to be written on the doorpost? It is the Oral Torah that explains that this passage refers to the words of the Shema prayer, which are to be written on a parchment scroll and then affixed in a specified place and manner on the doorpost. The mezuzah!

As a result of their literal reading of the Torah, the Karaites came to observe Shabbat in total darkness, unable to leave their homes all day except to go to the synagogue. They did away with the observance of Hanukah because it is not mentioned in the Written Torah, as well as with the separation of meat and milk for the same reason. Ironically, because so many statements in the Bible cannot be explained without the Oral Law, the Karaites had to create their own "Oral Law" as a way of translating the Torah's injunctions into practical applications.

One might think that this sect would have little appeal, but this was not the case. The Karaites began to attract those Jews who wanted to dismiss the opinions of the rabbis — this turned out to be a huge draw.[361]

That is, until the great sage Sa'adiah Gaon entered the picture.

Sa'adiah Gaon

Sa'adiah Gaon is famed for his writings, particularly the *Book of Belief and Opinions*, and for his critiques of the Karaites which made mincemeat of their beliefs. In addition to being the head of the great yeshiva of Sura, he was one of the greatest Jewish legal and philosophical minds of the period.

His arguments stopped the spread of Karaitism which could have overwhelmed the entire Jewish world. It was so popular at one point that in the tenth century the majority of Jews in the Land of Israel may well have been Karaites.

The Karaites never recovered from the assault of Sa'adiah Gaon on the logic of their beliefs. Their numbers shrunk with time although, unlike the Sadducees, they never completely disappeared.

During the nineteenth century in the Russian Empire, the Karaites were legally considered to be a religion totally separate from Judaism. During World War II, the large Karaite community in the Crimea was spared by the Nazis who also did not consider them to be Jewish.

Today, there are few Karaites left; they live chiefly in Israel, though no one is sure how many there are exactly, as the Karaites forbid census-taking. Their population has been variously estimated at between 7,000 and 40,000. Until recently, the Karaites were reputed to be very religious people and outwardly indistinguishable from Orthodox Jews, though they are forbidden to marry Jews and marry only each other.

When Sa'adiah Gaon died in 942 C.E., the period of the *Gaonim* of Babylon was almost over. (It would officially end in 1038 with the death of Chai Gaon.) By then, a great many Jews had left Babylon, following the opportunities that were opening up for them in other parts of the world conquered by the Muslims — especially in Spain.

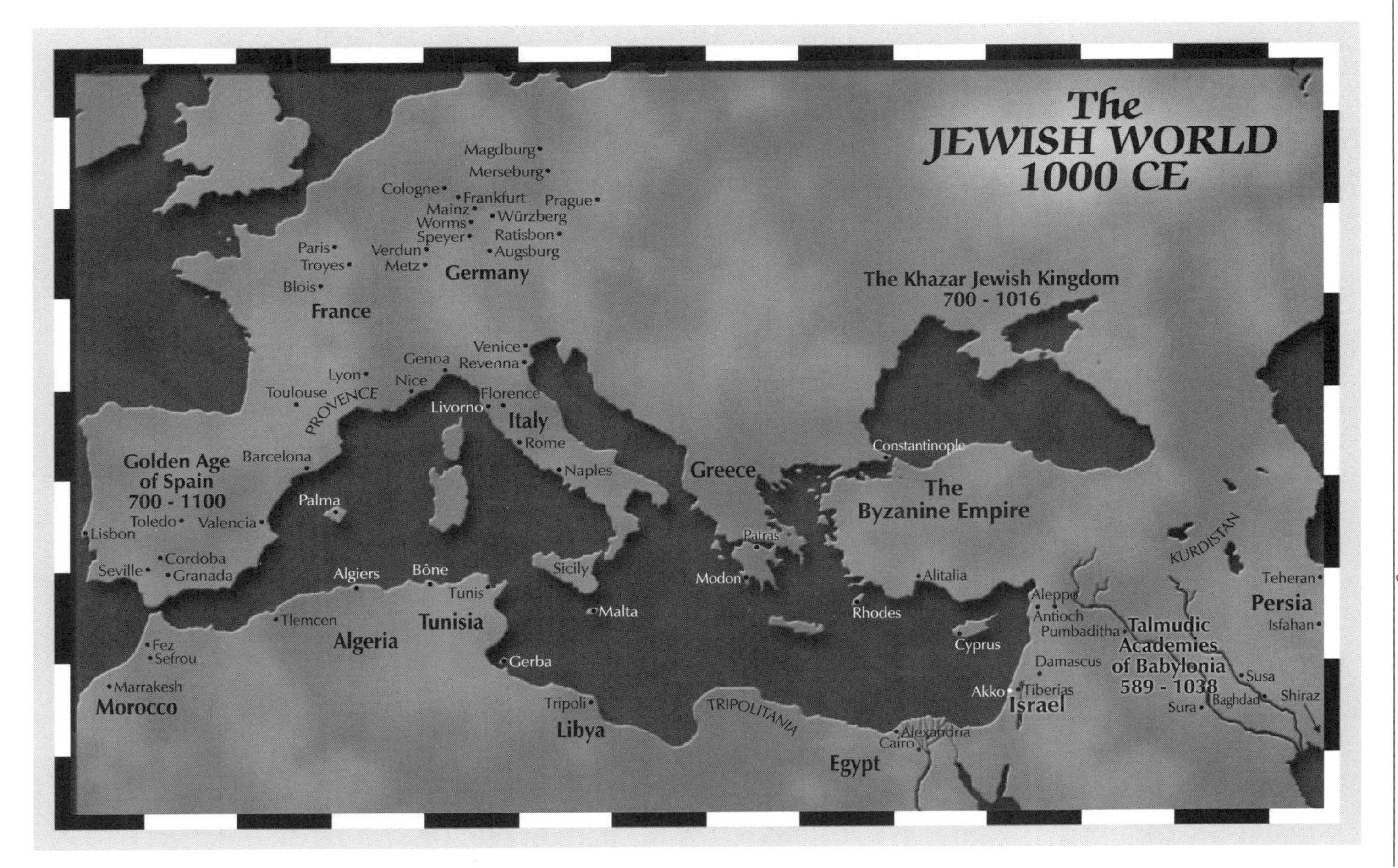
The
JEWISH WORLD
1000 CE
Magdburg
Merseburg
Cologne
Frankfurt
Prague
Mainz
Würzberg
Worms
Ratisbon
Speyer
Augsburg
Paris
Verdun
Troyes
Metz
Germany
Blois
France
The Khazar Jewish Kingdom
700 - 1016
Venice
Genoa
Revenna
Lyon
Nice
Toulouse
PROVENCE
Florence
Livorno
Italy
Rome
Constantinople
Golden Age
of Spain
700 - 1100
Barcelona
Naples
Greece
The
Byzanine Empire
Palma
Toledo
Valencia
Lisbon
Patras
KURDISTAN
Cordoba
Seville
Granada
Algiers
Bône
Sicily
Modon
Alitalia
Teheran
Tunis
Aleppo
Persia
Malta
Rhodes
Antioch
Tlemcen
Tunisia
Pumbaditha
Talmudic
Isfahan
Algeria
Academies
Fez
Sefrou
Cyprus
Gerba
Damascus
of Babylonia
Susa
Marrakesh
Akko
Tiberias
589 - 1038
Morocco
Tripoli
TRIPOLITANIA
Israel
Sura
Baghdad
Shiraz
Libya
Alexandria
Cairo
Egypt

43. THE JEWS OF SPAIN

As the armies of Islam conquered larger and larger swaths of Europe, the Jews of the Middle East saw new opportunities opening up for them in Muslim Europe. One of the best opportunities proved to be Spain, starting with the Muslim conquest of 711 C.E. Indeed, things were so good for Jews there, that to this day, half the Jewish world is known as *Sephardi*, meaning "Spanish." (The other half would later become known as *Ashkenazi*, meaning "German.")[362]

In Muslim Spain, Jews found a symbiotic relationship emerging between them and the non-Jewish world that surrounded them.

The Muslims impacted on the Jews, and some of the greatest Jewish scholars wrote in Arabic. But the impact was much greater the other way around. Indeed, there can be no question that the Islamic world, especially in Spain, did remarkably well because of the large number of Jews who were allowed to operate freely there. The positive impact of the Jews of Muslim Spain is yet another example of the fulfillment of the prophecy: "I will bless you and make your name great. You shall be a blessing. And I will bless those who bless you and curse those who curse you."[363]

To quote the great Jewish historian, Cecil Roth:

> The essential contribution of the Jews, as Jews, to the cultural life of the medieval world, and of medieval Europe in particular, depended basically upon two factors. They were literate, and they were international.... Their work as intermediaries between the two mutually-exclusive cultural worlds [Muslim and Christian] was without any doubt the charac-

teristic Jewish function in the Middle Ages: it was a function that they performed by virtue of their specific position and circumstances as Jews. That did not, however, preclude them from making memorable contributions to European civilization as individuals.[364]

Jewish Contributions

The Jewish contributions came in every sphere — whether economic or intellectual. For example:

Jews excelled in skilled crafts. Jews were excellent tanners, metalworkers, goldsmiths, silversmiths, and jewelers. (We see some of these skills surviving today. Yemenite Jews continue their reputation as silversmiths and Jewish diamond merchants are famous the world over.)

Jews excelled in the sciences, particularly in medicine. Jewish doctors were everywhere, among the most famous was Maimonides (who we will speak about later) and Hasdai ibn Shaprut, the tenth century physician to two caliphs who was considered one of the most influential people in Spain.

Jews excelled in trade. Jews were the middlemen between the Muslim and Christian worlds, which at this time were engaged in huge rivalry and were not communicating directly with each other. As a result Jews became traders who covered the Far East, the Middle East, and Europe.

Jews excelled in scholarship. The Muslims were fascinated by classical knowledge, but since they did not know either Greek nor Latin, the Jews filled the gap by translating these works into Arabic. The Jews also helped to disseminate Arabic scholarship and much of the classical scholarship of the ancient world (some of which had been lost after the collapse of the Roman Empire) to Christian Europe, translating Arabic texts first into Hebrew, then sending these translated texts to Europe, where other Jews translated the Hebrew into Latin — the language of the Roman Empire that was still the language of scholarship in Western Europe.

Some of the greatest Jewish writers and philosophers came from this time period. Three deserve special mention:

Abraham ibn Ezra, the famed scientist, philosopher, astronomer, and biblical commentator.

Bachya ibn Pakuda, the famed moralist who authored *Duties of the Heart* (a book that continues to be a highly popular text in Jewish ethical studies today), examining the obligations of one's inner life and presenting a system to assess one's true religious commitment.

Judah HaLevi, the famed author of *The Kuzari*, a philosophical novel based on the story of the king of Khazaria. Basing himself on this reportedly true story, Judah HaLevi imaginatively recreated the debate before the king in his novel, which continues to be popular to this day.

(In the eighth century, the king of Khazaria — a kingdom located between the Black Sea and Caspian Sea — undecided whether he should affiliate with the Christians or Muslims, had great scholars argue before him the merits of the world's religions, and because of this debate converted to Judaism, as eventually did a goodly portion of his country; the history of Khazaria ended in eleventh century when it was destroyed by a Byzantine-Russian coalition.)

The Jewish paradise in Spain ended abruptly when a cruel Muslim Berber Dynasty — the Almohades — came to power in the twelfth century. When the Almohades seized southern Spain, they gave the Jews three choices: convert to Islam, leave, or die.

Of the many Jews fleeing Spain at this time was none other than the famed Maimonides (often known as Rambam, the acronym of his full name, Rabbi Moses ben Maimon).

(Incidentally, many of the famous Jews were known by their acronyms. This is because Jews until this time did not have last names. While Sephardic Jews assumed last names more than 500 years ago, most Ashkenazi Jews did not use surnames until forced to by Christian authorities in the late eighteenth and early nineteenth centuries. Jews were traditionally known by their first names and their father's names, sometimes by their tribal names, such as Kohen or Levi, or places of their origin, and therefore, it was easier to shorten so many words to an acronym.)

Maimonides

Maimonides was born Moses ben Maimon on the eve of Pesach in 1135 in Cordoba, Spain, to a prominent rabbinical family. In his family tree figured King David and Rabbi Judah HaNasi, who had compiled the Mishnah (as we saw in chapter 38). His primary teacher was his father, Rabbi Maimon ben Joseph, a Jewish judge, who taught him not only the Talmud, but also the fundamentals of mathematics, astronomy, and philosophy.

Maimonides was only thirteenth when his family was forced to leave Spain. After wandering homeless for many years — wanderings during which his father died — Maimonides and his brother, David, finally settled in Fustat near Cairo, Egypt. There, Maimonides continued his Torah studies, while David, a dealer in gems, supported the family. When David perished in a sea voyage in 1166, the burden fell on Maimonides.

Maimonides refused to make money from his Torah knowledge, and therefore, in order to earn a living, he became a physician, having begun his study of medicine years earlier. Within a short time, he was so famous as a healer that he was appointed physician to the Court of Sultan Saladin in Cairo. He was also appointed the chief rabbi of Cairo.

In addition to being a famous doctor and healer, Maimonides was a prolific writer.[365] Of his voluminous works — most of which were composed in Arabic but written with Hebrew characters — four stand out as perhaps the most famous:

Commentary on the Mishnah, his explanation of the Mishnah;

Mishneh Torah — his greatest accomplishment, a monumental compendium covering all of the Oral Law, also known as *Yad HaHazakah;*

Guide to the Perplexed — a philosophical treatise which discusses traditional Jewish thought and compares it to classical Greek philosophy, considered the single greatest philosophical work ever produced by a Jew;

Discourse on the World to Come — his explanation of the Messianic Age which includes the Thirteen Principles of Faith.

During his time, some writings of Maimonides were highly controversial. Some of his statements were deemed too radical; others were simply misunderstood. At one point, his works were banned, and after his death in 1204, burned at the instigation of some rabbis. However, when nine years later, the French king Louis IX ordered the Talmud burned, Jews interpreted this as a "measure-for-measure" punishment from God for the burning of the works of Maimonides. Indeed, the rabbi who instigated the ban and burning, Rabbi Jonah Gerondi, subsequently repented for doing so and authored the book *Sha'arei Teshuvah* ("Gates of Repentance") as a form of atonement for his derogatory statements about Maimonides.

Today the works of Maimonides are universally accepted and revered. Indeed, Maimonides is known in the Jewish world as one of most important of the *Rishonim* or "the First Ones," who between 1038 and 1440 added significantly to Jewish scholarship.

It is far beyond the scope of this overview to discuss the dozens of great rabbinic personalities who were the *Rishonim.* Despite the very difficult time of Jewish history in which they lived, they ensured that it became also one of the greatest periods of Torah scholarship. The impact of the *Rishonim* was monumental and, together with the rabbis who created the Talmud, they played a pivotal role in transmitting the Torah and shaping the law and practice of Diaspora Judaism.

However, there is one whom we must mention. In addition to Maimonides, he was among the most famous of the *Rishonim* — he was the French rabbi, Solomon ben Isaac, known the world over by his acronym: Rashi.

Rashi

A question may be asked here, How did Jews end up in France?

First of all, Jews were living in France when it was a far-flung outpost of the Roman Empire, but for a long time these Jewish settlements were small. The expansion came through some interesting quirks of fate.

Jewish tradition has it that in the eighth century Charlemagne, the King of the Franks, seeing how helpful Jews were to the Muslims, asked the caliph to send him a few rabbis, knowing that once he had rabbis more Jews would follow.

Additionally, Jews were frequently kidnapped by pirates, who knew that their fellow Jews would pay handsomely to redeem them. There is a legend concerning four captives, rabbis from the Babylonian community, each of whom was ransomed by a different Jewish community. According to the legend, a small group of French Jews put up a lot of money to redeem Rabbi Nosson HaBavli in just such circumstances on the condition that he come and start a yeshiva in their community in France — and he did.[366]

Rashi, the most famous of the French rabbis, was born Solomon Ben Isaac in 1040 in France, though he was sent to study in a yeshiva in Germany.

After he completed his studies, Rashi returned to France and settled in his hometown of Troyes. Just like Maimonides, he refused to profit from his Torah knowledge, instead earning a living from several vineyards that he owned.

Rashi had an absolutely encyclopedic knowledge of the Written and Oral Law. He took it upon himself to answer some of the most obvious questions that arise when reading the text of the Torah; this is why today so many editions include his explanations alongside the text.

Another of Rashi's accomplishments was a commentary on the entire Babylonian Talmud. Today, this commentary appears on the inner margin of virtually every Talmudic page. We find his explanations indispensable because it becomes harder and harder to understand the nuances of Jewish law as we move further and further away from Mount Sinai.

Rashi did not have sons, but he did have two very famous daughters, Miriam and Yocheved, whom he educated in the Talmud. Rashi's daughters married great scholars and fathered great scholars. Rashi's sons-in-law, his students and his descendants became part of a group of scholars that is known as the *Ba'alei HaTosafot*, meaning "Masters of Addition." The Ba'alei HaTosafot added commentary to the Talmud which is featured on the outer margin of every Talmudic page. The best known of this group is Rashi's grandson, Rabbi Jacob ben Meir, also known as Rabbeinu Taam.

Rashi lived until 1105, and he survived the first Crusade, which saw the slaughter of about a third of the Jews of Europe.

According to Jewish tradition, he met one of the leaders of the Crusade, the Norman nobleman, Godfrey de Bouillon. As Godfrey embarked on the Crusade to liberate the Holy Land from the Muslims, Rashi told him that he would succeed, but that he would come back home with only two horses. In response, Godfrey vowed that if Rashi's prediction was wrong, he'd kill him upon his return.

As it happened, Godfrey came back home from the Crusade with only three horses. As he entered the archway to the city of Troyes, the center stone of the arch fell and killed one of the horses.

In the next chapter, we will see just what role Godfrey de Bouillon played in the Crusades, and how this shameful period in history came about.

44.
THE CRUSADES

As long as the Byzantine (Eastern) Empire, with its seat in Constantinople, dominated the Christian Church, it maintained the balance of power between the bishop of Constantinople and the bishop of Rome. But when it began to crumble, the balance of power shifted to Rome, and it is from Rome that the Crusades originated. However, before we can discuss these bloody escapades and how they impacted the Jews, we must first set the stage and go back in history some 600 years.

In 476 C.E., the Western (Roman) Empire, undermined by the Goths and the Franks, ceased to exist. The resulting vacuum in the economic, legal, and administrative infrastructure led to a state of chaos. The Church, aligning itself with the Franks, stepped in to restore order.

Consciously modeling its bureaucratic framework on the model of the old, the Church created titles and administrative positions which people were used to. It's not by accident that the pope (from the Latin *papa* or "father") was called the pontiff (from *pontifex maximus* or "chief priest") — a title previously reserved for the Roman emperor.

Today, we remember the period of time when the Church ruled Western Europe with an iron hand as the "Dark Ages," although more charitable historians call it the "Middle Ages."

Feudalism

With its well-organized bureaucracy, the Church found itself assuming a position of paramount importance in the evolution of feudalism in European society.

Feudalism had its roots in all the warfare that was common during this period. To support the cavalry, the kings gave their soldiers estates of land farmed by dependent laborers. It was a huge pyramid, with the majority of the population at the bottom, working as serfs, or virtual slaves. Feudal serfs were engaged in backbreaking labor from dawn to dusk. They usually lived in absolute filth and squalor. It is impossible for us to imagine today the conditions and the deprivations of this time.

The Church's role in the feudal system was quite ironic. It did nothing to fight the injustice; in fact, the Church helped to create it and profited handsomely from it.

The Church supported the inequality of the feudal system through its various dogmatic formulations, which strongly implied that God Himself endorsed the spiritual value of poverty, and that the king was a divinely ordained human being whose authority could not be questioned.

Why? Because the Church was a major player in the feudal game. Early in its history, the Church started to acquire land. At first, it took over the properties of pagan temples and temple priests. Then, it continued to expand its holdings, until it became by far the biggest landowner in Europe, collecting huge taxes from the hapless peasants.

Oxford scholar Henry Phelps-Brown in *Egalitarianism and the Generation of Inequality* suggests that the Church, while it embodied monotheism, never eliminated its old Hellenistic-pagan tendencies:

> Thus Christianity itself, and the views on wealth and power that came down from it, did not challenge the inequality of the secular world. They rather upheld it.... In this way they followed the main drift of the pagan philosophies. The inequality of human capacity was obvious, the need for subordination inescapable.[367]

As the Church's empire grew in size, so did its need for more revenue. While the Crusades were launched in part to curb the growth of the Islamic Empire — which by then had conquered Spain and challenged France, as well as Constantinople itself — a key motivation was to gain new land and wealth for the growing population of Europe. Clearly, the Crusades offered an outlet for the ambitions of land-hungry knights and noblemen. They also greatly enhanced the power and prestige of the Church (and especially of the Pope) by enabling the Pope to galvanize much of the nobility of Europe for a Church-sponsored military campaign.

The reason given at the time, however, was the reclamation of the Church of the Holy Sepulcher in Jerusalem from the Muslims. This church had been originally built on the site identified in the fourth century by Empress Helena, the mother of Constantine, as the site where Jesus was buried following his crucifixion.

(The church still stands today, after being rebuilt by the Crusaders; it is a focal point of Christian pilgrimages to Jerusalem, although Protestant Christian denominations contend that it is not the site of Jesus' burial.)

The "Noble" Quest

To our Western minds, reared on the Hollywood version of so much history, the Crusades mean noble knights rescuing damsels in distress. *Oy vey* — is that ever a lie.

Now, it's true that there were knights, and there were kings, and there was a chivalric ideal. And that King Richard the Lionhearted, a Crusade leader (who was incidentally one of the worst kings England ever had) was definitely a macho warrior. But that's pretty much where it ends.[368]

The Crusades turned into campaigns of slaughter, rape, and pillage, and woe to the poor Jews in the way. Indeed, the Crusades mark the first large-scale European mob violence directed against Jews which, unfortunately, became the pattern for the next few hundred years. The later pogroms were merely a repeat of this idea.

The Jews were not the only — and, in fact, not the primary — victims of the Crusaders. Muslims were. All the brutality directed toward them devastated the Arab peoples economically, caused the Islamic world to be more reactionary and closed, and contributed to Arab hatred of the West.[369]

(Why do Arabs paint the doors of their houses blue to this day? To ward off the evil eye. Why blue? One explanation is that it was the color of the blue-eyed northern Europeans that came to slay them.)

Altogether, ten Crusades took place between the eleventh through the thirteenth centuries:

The First Crusade, 1095–1099, saw the capture of Jerusalem from the Muslims, the slaughter of both the Muslim and Jewish populations of the city, and the establishment of the Crusader-run Latin Kingdom of Jerusalem (which lasted only until 1187).

The Second Crusade, 1147–1149, was organized to help the Christians to recover lands which they lost to the Turks, but it ended in dismal failure.

The Third Crusade, 1189–1192, began after Saladin, the Sultan of Egypt, recaptured Jerusalem. This is the Crusade in which King Richard the Lionhearted figured, and it was a failure.

The Fourth Crusade, 1202–1204, saw the capture of Constantinople, which at the time was occupied by Greek-speaking Eastern Orthodox Christians, who did not recognize the authority of the Roman Pope.

The Children's Crusade, 1212, sent thousands of children to the Holy Land, where they were captured by Muslims only to be sold as slaves or to die of hunger or disease.

The Fifth Crusade, 1217–1221, was aimed at Egypt, but failed.

Four more Crusades mounted in the thirteenth century failed to reverse the Muslim gains. In 1291, the last Crusader stronghold at Acre (Acco) fell.

That's the picture in a nutshell. Now we can look in greater detail at those aspects of the Crusades which most impacted on the Jews.[370]

Infidel Cleansing

Pope Urban II mounted the first campaign, in part in response to a plea for help from Christians in Constantinople who were besieged by the Muslims. Its aim was to beat back the "infidels" (as Christians called their fellow monotheists) and to recapture the Holy Land. In his sermon the Pope declared:

> A grave report has come from the lands of Jerusalem and from the city of Constantinople that a people from the kingdom of the Persians, a foreign race, a race absolutely alien to God...has invaded the land of those Christians [and] has reduced the people with sword, rapine, and fire.... Let those who in the past have been accustomed to spread private war so vilely among the faithful advance against the infidels.... Let those who were formally brigands now become soldiers of Christ; let those who once waged war against their brothers...fight lawfully against barbarians; let those who until now have been mercenaries for a few coins achieve eternal rewards.[371]

To sweeten the pie, the Pope promised those that signed up that there would be plenty of booty, not to mention the spiritual benefit of having all your sins forgiven by God.

The Pope received an enthusiastic response. An armed force of 15,000 — including 5,000 knights and the rest infantry — set off, wearing large red crosses on their outer garments (hence their name *Crusaders* from the Latin word *crux* meaning "cross," though they called themselves "pilgrims").

A peasant force also joined in. As these peasants started marching through Europe (in advance of the knights and their army), they needed to eat, and eat they did by pillaging the countryside. As they were marching along, they got the idea that they might as well get rid of the infidels in their midst — namely, the Jews.

Here is one eyewitness account of an attack on the Jewry of Mainz in May of 1096 written by a Jew who survived:

> The Jews of the city, knowing of the slaughter of their brethren fled in hope of safety to the Bishop of Ruthard. They put an infinite treasure in his guard and trust having much faith in his protection. He placed the Jews in a very spacious hall in his own house that they might remain safe and sound in a very secure and strong place. But...the band held council, and after sunrise attacked the Jews in the hall with arrows and lances, breaking down the bolts in the doors. They killed the Jews, about 700 in number who in vain resisted the force of an attack of so many thousands. They killed the women also and with their sword pierced tender children whatever age and sex....[372]

This is how about 30%-50% of the Jewish community of Europe met its end. Some 10,000 Jews of an estimated population of about 20,000-30,000 were slaughtered by Crusader mobs.

After conquering Antioch in Turkey, the Crusaders reached Jerusalem, many of their number lost due to the heavy fighting along the way. At the gates of Jerusalem, fighting in the bright sunlight that scorched their heavy impregnable armor, many more of the knights died.

The French nobleman Godfrey du Bouillon — plus Raymond of Guilles, Raymond of Flanders, and Robert of Normandy — besieged the gates of Jerusalem which at that time had a significant population of Jews. Their forces breached the walls and poured into the city.

(Incidentally, the Crusader cry of "Hep! Hep!" may well have originated at this time. It was an acronym for *Hierosolyma Est Perdita*, meaning "Jerusalem Is Lost." With time it became "Hip, Hip, Hooray!" — a cheer that Jews never use.)[373]

What happened after the Crusaders entered the city?

We have one account from Ibn Al Kalanisi, the Muslim chronicler, describing hair-raising behavior of unimaginable brutality with thousands of Muslim men, women, and children slaughtered. The poor Jews had all huddled together in a synagogue, and this is where the Crusaders found them, set the place on fire, and burned them alive. One of the Crusaders, Raymond of Aguilers, joyfully recounted:

> With the fall of Jerusalem and its towers, one could see marvelous work. Some of the pagans were mercifully beheaded, others pierced by arrows plunged from towers, and yet others, tortured for a long time, were burned to death in searing flames. Piles of heads, hands and feet lay in the houses and streets, and men and knights were sunning to and fro over corpses.[374]

Once the Crusaders conquered Jerusalem, they embarked on a vast building effort all over Israel. The ruins of some of the massive fortresses and churches they built can be visited today, though most were destroyed by the Muslims once they reclaimed their earlier holdings, for fear that the Crusaders would return.

The Crusaders established special orders of military monks to look after their kingdom. Those that interest us in particular are the Knights Templars and the Knights Hospitalers.

The Knights Templars were stationed on the Temple Mount (hence their name). Interestingly, Knights Templars did not destroy the Dome of the Rock (though the Crusaders did destroy all the mosques that they did not turn into churches). Why? They thought it was the "Temple of Solomon," and that the nearby Al-Aksa mosque was the "Palace of Solomon."[375]

So what did they do? They removed the crescent from the top of the Dome of the Rock, replaced it with a cross, and called the place Templum Domini, "Temple of God." They converted the Al-Aksa mosque, as well as the vaulted space below the mosque, into a monastery. Consistent with their other errors, they called this space, which had been built by Herod, "Solomon's Stables." (These so-called stables have recently been renovated by the Muslim religious authority, the Wakf, and transformed into another mosque amid enormous archaeological devastation, which the government of Israel felt powerless to stop.)

The Knights Hospitalers were supposed to provide hospitality to the large numbers of Christian pilgrims who would visit the Christian holy sites, and to care for the sick among them. (Thus we see the word for hospitality became synonymous with a place of care for the sick — hospice or hospital.)

The Knights Hospitalers built their main complex near the Church of the Holy Sepulcher, a logical place for it. Another complex — consisting of church, hospice, and hospital — was built in what is today the heart of the Jewish Quarter of the Old City of Jerusalem, near the main staircase going down to the Western Wall. This ruin has been preserved and is a tourist attraction. Nearby Crusader buildings have been renovated and are in use as apartments, schools, and shops.[376]

Needless to say, the Knights Hospitalers did not provide hospitality to Jews. In fact, they brought in Christian Arab tribes to help populate the city with Christians. But Jews always yearned to be part of the Holy City. One such Jew, who braved the Crusader occupation of the Holy Land, was none other than the famed poet and writer Judah HaLevi (author of *The Kuzari* mentioned in chapter 43). Judah HaLevi managed to reach the city, but he was trampled to death by a Christian-Arab horseman just outside one of the city gates. As he lay dying, he is said to have recited one of his own poems, "Zion, Shall I Seek You":

I shall cherish your stones and kiss them,
And your earth will be sweeter than honey to my taste.[377]

Sultan Saladin

The reign of the Crusaders over the Holy Land was short-lived. In less than 100 years — in fact, in 1187 — the Crusaders were conquered by Sultan Saladin of Egypt (whose family, by the way, was employing Maimonides as their physician, as noted in chapter 43).

Sultan Saladin defeated the Crusaders in what was one of the most important battles in the medieval history of the Middle East — at the Horns of Hattin, which is northwest of the Kineret lake (also known as the Sea of Galilee). There, Saladin very skillfully managed to lure the Crusaders out into the open. In the burning heat of mid-summer, they found themselves vastly outmaneuvered and outnumbered, and Saladin destroyed them.

Even though they lost Jerusalem, the Crusaders didn't give up. They mounted campaign after campaign to recoup the Holy Land, but they never did get Jerusalem back (although the Muslims did grant them access to Christian holy sites there). Finally, in 1291, the last Crusader stronghold, in Acre (Acco), fell.[378]

Today, we have amazing ruins from the Crusader period all over Israel. Some of the most massive and impressive are in Caesarea, Acre, Tiberias, and in Belvoir (near the battle site of Hattin). If you should happen to visit any of these sites, keep in mind while admiring them, what the Crusaders did to the Jews.

45.
BLOOD LIBEL

In this chapter, we focus on an excruciating period of Jewish history marked by constant and unrelenting Christian persecution. During this period we see:

- the Jews expelled from England (1290)
- the Jews expelled from France (1306 and 1394)
- the Jews expelled from Hungary (1349 and 1360)
- the Jews expelled from German states (1348 and 1498)
- the Jews expelled from Austria (1421)
- the Jews expelled from Lithuania (1445 and 1495)
- the Jews expelled from Spain (1492)
- the Jews expelled from Portugal (1497)

And that's only a partial list. See the Appendix for a complete enumeration.

(As often as not, the Jews were expelled and then, when a significant economic decline was noted in their absence, they were readmitted — only to be expelled again. It was the classic "can't live with them, can't live without them" attitude.)

The story of these persecutions begins around the year 1000 — the first millennium. It seems that people get nervous about some dates, especially Christians, whose Book of Revelations predicts that at the end of a thousand years Satan will be released from prison, and then he's going to wreak havoc on the world.

The first millennium led to a religious revival in the Christian world which historians call the "New Piety." The New Piety focused especially on the historicity of Jesus. Focusing on the life of Jesus meant focusing on his death, and even though the Christian New Testament says that the Romans killed Jesus, the Jews were blamed for wanting him to die. So at this time, we see the notion of Jews as Christ-killers — which first surfaced in the fourth century — really growing in popularity.

But that alone does not explain the vehemence of Christian persecutions. To fully understand the issue, we have to look at other, more complex reasons.

Replacement Theology

To start off, the very existence of the Jews was an irritant to many Christians. And this is why:

Christian theology accepts the Hebrew Bible. It does not quarrel with the statements contained there that the Jews were a special people chosen by God to receive the Torah and bring holiness into the world. But Christian theology says that the Jews failed in their mission. This is why God sent His "son" (i.e., Jesus), but the Jews refused to recognize him as the Messiah. As a result, God abandoned the Jews and replaced them with the "new chosen people" — the Christians. (Hence, the Christian segment of the Bible is called the "New Testament," while the Hebrew Bible segment — really the bulk of the Christian Bible — is called the "Old Testament.")

According to this line of reasoning, however, there should no longer be any purpose for Jews in the world. They should disappear, as did so many mightier peoples. But, by the first millennium — 1,000 years after the death of Jesus — the Jews were still everywhere.

Christian theology had to devise a response to this contradiction, and it did: Jews are doomed to wander the earth by God as a "witness people" — *teste veritatis* in Latin. The purpose of a witness people is to survive throughout history in order to bear witness at the end of days that Jesus is the Messiah, when he appears again for the so-called "Second Coming."

But the explanations of Christian theology could not remove the irritant that the presence — at times, strong and prosperous presence — of the Jews represented. At the heart of the matter was the Christian view of Judaism as a direct competitor for the soul of humanity. The hostility that the Christians felt toward the Jews can be readily seen from the writings of the early fathers of the Christian Church.[379]

From John Chrysostom, the Patriarch of Constantinople, we get this:

> Jews are the most worthless of men — they are lecherous, greedy, rapacious — they are perfidious murderers of Christians, they worship the devil, their religion is a sickness.... The Jews are the odious assassins of Christ and for killing God there is no expiation, no indulgence, no pardon. Christians may never cease vengeance. The Jews must live in servitude forever. It is incumbent on all Christians to hate the Jews.

From Gregory of Nyssa, we get more of the same:

> Slayers of the Lord, murderers of the prophets, adversaries of god, haters of god, men who show contempt for the law, foes of grace, enemies of the father's faith, advocates of the devil, brood of vipers, slanderers, scoffers, men whose minds are in darkness, leaven of the Pharisees, assembly of demons, sinners, wicked men, stoners and haters of righteousness.

In some places, such calumny incited people to violence. (We saw in chapter 44, for example, how the Crusader mobs devastated the Jewish population of Europe, slaughtering 10,000 Jews of an estimated population of about 20,000–30,000.) In other places, such calumny bred other forms of persecution.

Money Lenders

If you were a reasonable Christian listening to your Church fathers speak of the Jews, you might quite naturally conclude that such a people had no place in a decent society.

And this is a conclusion that was drawn over time.

Around the first millennium, we see the rise of the Christian trade guilds from which Jews were pointedly excluded. No more Jewish goldsmiths and silversmiths and glass-blowers. Jews were also excluded from owning land, holding office, and from being doctors and lawyers. They were forced to wear "a distinguishing garment" — either a badge or a sign or a silly-looking hat — which set them apart. This was not only to make them look different but also to humiliate them.

Then, beginning in 1123, when the bishops of the Church undertook a series of meetings — called Lateran Councils — to decide Church policy, the Jews were assigned a new function in Christian society. Along with a decree that priests must be celibate, the bishops decided that Christians were not allowed to lend each other money. (This came from a misunderstanding of the biblical commandment that forbids one from charging one's brother interest when making a loan.) As for the Jews, the bishops promulgated a doctrine decreeing them servants of Christians, and then assigning to them the degrading task of lending money — called usury — with which the Christians were forbidden to sully their hands.

The bishops were not stupid. They were well aware that you have to charge interest in order to have banking, and you have to have banking to have economic development; otherwise, there is no growth and the economy stagnates. So, someone has to lend money. And that someone, the bishops decided, would be the Jews.

What happened next is that the Jews were not allowed to live in various cities in Europe unless they supplied a certain number of money-lenders. However, lending money was a very precarious job, which often bred animosity. After all, who likes to pay back loans? And what happened if the local nobleman or bishop decided not to repay his loan? He would accuse the Jew of doing something terrible — like killing a Christian baby. That way he could renege on his loans, confiscate all Jewish property, and then expel or even kill the Jews.

This happened over and over again.

Some have claimed that it was Jewish money-lending practices that engendered such actions and, indeed, were responsible for a great deal of anti-Semitism. This is a total myth. At that time Jews charged an average interest rate of between 33 to 43 percent on loans. And while this may seem high by today's standards, consider that the Lombards, the Christian-Italian bankers living under the nose of the Vatican, charged rates as high as 250 percent. So we see that the Lombard money-lending practices were many times worse and yet no one persecuted them.[380]

Persecutions of the Jews, on the other hand, knew no bounds.

Baby Killers

It is next to impossible to explain the accusations that were hurled at the Jews during this time. Jews were persecuted not only for being "Christ-killers" but as "baby killers."

The first such accusation — better known as a "blood libel" — was leveled in 1144 in Norwich, England. There, Jews were charged with kidnapping a Christian baby and draining it of blood. The charge became so popular that it would sweep, in various forms, through Europe and then spread to other parts of the world.

The most famous of all blood-libel legends is that of the ritual murder of the child named Hugh of Lincoln, England in 1255. The story was immortalized in a ballad so well-known in England and Scotland that it was included in the standard cannon of English and Scottish ballads compiled by Francis James Child in the nineteenth century. Likewise, the best-known tale of ritual murder is "The Prioress' Tale," found in Chaucer's fourteenth-century classic work of early English fiction, *Canterbury Tales*. One verse of that tale goes like this:

> From that time forward, these Jews conspired to chase this innocent child from the earth's face. Down a dark alleyway, they found and hired a murderer who owned that secret place, and as the boy passed at his happy pace, this cursed Jew grabbed him and held him, slit his little throat and cast him in a pit. [381]

Now why did Jews need blood, according to Christian opinion? This is a multiple-choice question:

(a) Jews suffered from hemorrhoids as a punishment for killing Jesus, and drinking blood was the best cure for hemorrhoids at the time.

(b) All Jewish men menstruate and need a monthly blood transfusion.

(c) Jewish men, when they're circumcised, lose so much blood because of that surgical procedure that they need to drink Christian babies' blood.

(d) Blood is the chief ingredient in matzah, and therefore prior to every Pesach Jews would be requiring a large supply.

(e) All of the above.

The correct answer? Shockingly, it's (e) — "all of the above."

This is a very important lesson in anti-Semitism. You can say anything about the Jews, and people will believe it.

It's ironic that Jews, who are prohibited by Jewish law from consuming any blood whatsoever (kosher meat is carefully washed and salted to remove all traces of blood) were precisely the people accused of drinking blood.

The blood libel makes even less sense when you consider that in the thirteenth century the Church adopted the doctrine of transubstantiation. This is a mystical idea which maintains that when the priest says mass over the wafer and wine, these objects change into the body and blood of Jesus. Christians who consume the wafer and drink the wine are said to be mystically eating the flesh of Jesus and drinking his blood.[382]

It's ironic that the Christian world, while engaged in the ritual of drinking "the blood of Jesus," would accuse the Jews — who are forbidden to drink blood — of this totally fabricated, hideous crime.

But then the accusations became even more ridiculous.

Starting in Switzerland and Germany in the thirteenth century, Jews were accused of kidnapping communion wafers from churches. Why would the Jews do this in Christian view?

To torture it.

Medieval documents tell stories describing how a Jew (usually called Abraham) steals a wafer from a church, sticks a knife in it, and blood starts pouring out. And then he cuts it up into pieces and sends it to different Jews who all torture it.

This would be funny if not for a fact that thousands of Jews were slaughtered as a result of such stories. For example, the entire Jewish community of Berlitz, near Berlin, was burned alive based on the accusation of torturing a wafer![383]

Jew Taxes

Throughout this time, the Jews were physically marginalized — beaten, burned, raped. And they were economically marginalized — pillaged, robbed, taxed nearly to death. Indeed, their money was one of the reasons they were tolerated at all. Jews were a good source of income to the crown through special punitive "Jew taxes."

We will see later in Germany that thirty-eight special taxes were imposed on the Jews. There was a tax to be born, a tax to die, a tax to wear a yarmulke, a tax to be married, a tax to be circumcised, a tax to buy Shabbat candles, a tax to be exempt from the German army (in which a Jew was not allowed to serve anyway). If you want to know why Jews are so good at evading taxes and why so many Jews are into accounting, it comes from literally 1,500 years of trying to avoid being taxed to death by their enemies.

And eventually, once Jews were drained of their money, they would be expelled. In 1182, King Philip II of France, out of the need to acquire some quick-and-easy money, expelled the Jews of his kingdom and confiscated all their property. The lure of future Jewish tax revenue caused him to rethink his policy and invite the Jews back to France in 1198.

This is also what happened in England, where heavy taxation of the Jewish population of about 5,000 supplied the crown with almost 20 percent of all of its income. In 1290 — on the ninth day of Av, which, as we have seen, is the same day that the Temple in Jerusalem was twice destroyed and which is therefore the worst day in Jewish history — the Jews were expelled from England, after first being drained of their wealth by crushing taxation. (They were not permitted to return for almost four centuries.) King Edward I decreed that all debts owed to the Jews were cancelled and that the principal was to be paid directly to him. As the Edict of Expulsion stated:

> We, in requital of their crimes and for the Honor of the Crucified, have banished them from our realm as traitors. We...do hereby make totally null and void all penalties and usuries and whatsoever else...may be claimed on account of Jewry...pay the amount to us at such convenient times as may be determined by you."[384]

Other countries would soon follow suit, but first would come another twist in the persecution of the Jews.

46.
THE BLACK DEATH

In the fourteenth century, the bubonic plague — known as the "Black Death" — devastated Europe. At that time, people had no idea of what caused disease and no idea that lack of hygiene was responsible for the spread of bacteria.

Some historians have cynically pointed out that bathing defined the difference between the Classical Age and the Dark Ages. The Greeks and Romans were very clean people and public baths were everywhere. Medieval Europeans, on the other hand, didn't bathe at all. Sometimes they didn't change their clothes for an entire year. The tailors or seamstresses would literally stitch new clothes onto people around Easter time, and that was it for the year. They kept their windows closed because they thought that disease traveled through the air, which they called "bad ether."

Needless to say, when any new disease arrived in Europe, the unsanitary conditions helped it spread. Such was the case with the "Black Death" — a bacteria carried by flea-ridden rats. It is estimated to have killed almost half the population of Europe, or about 25 million people.

Although they didn't know what caused the disease, the Europeans had no trouble figuring it out — it had to be the Jews! They decided that the Jews must be getting poison from the devil and pouring it down the wells of Christians (or spreading it through the air) to kill them all off.

To be fair, the Church, specifically Pope Clement VI, said this was not so, but the masses didn't want to hear it. The Church's message that the Jews killed "god" but meant no harm to the Christian world just didn't add up.

During the time of the bubonic plague (chiefly 1348–1349), there were massacres of Jews in various European communities. For example, Jews of Strasbourg were burned alive. The collection of documents of Jewish history, *Scattered Among the Nations* (edited by Alexis Rubin) contains this account:

> On Saturday that was St. Valentine's Day, they burnt the Jews on a wooden platform in their cemetery. There were about 2,000 of them. Those who wanted to baptize themselves were spared. Many small children were taken out of the fire and baptized against the will of their fathers and mothers. Everything that was owed to the Jews was cancelled....[385]

(Note in particular the last sentence above.)

In Basle, Switzerland, in January of 1349, the entire Jewish community of several hundred Jews was burned alive in a wooden house specially constructed for the purpose on an island in the Rhine River.[386]

When we look at these ridiculous accusations against the Jews, we have to keep in mind that they were not limited to the Dark Ages. The ignorant, superstitious masses of Medieval Europe were not the only ones to believe such things. This phenomenon has recurred in every age — including modern times. For example, an aide to the Mayor of Chicago claimed in 1990 that the high incidence of AIDS in the black community was caused by Jewish doctors deliberately contaminating the blood supply. The Palestinian Authority has made the same claim several times. The PA has made other outrageous accusations against Israel, such as that the Israeli government puts hormones in all the wheat sold to Gaza to turn all Arab women into prostitutes and poisons the chewing gum sold to Arab children. In the presence of Hillary Clinton, Suha Arafat, Yasser Arafat's wife, stated that Jews were poisoning the Palestinian water supply.

Professor Michael Curtis of Rutgers University summed it up:

> Anything and everything is a reason to hate the Jew. Whatever you hate, the Jew is that.[387]

Ghetto

Needless to say, when you believe a people are capable of poisoning your wells, you do not want them anywhere near you.

Indeed, as part of the general physical and economic isolation of the Jews throughout the eleventh to the sixteenth centuries, special living areas for Jews were set aside. They were called "ghettos," a name of Italian origin. The Italian word *ghetto* means "foundry" or "ironworks," and refers to a place where metal was smelted — a really disgusting, smelly part of town, full of smoke and polluted water. In other words, the perfect place for undesirable people.

Although the term "ghetto" as a place for the Jews was first used in Venice in 1516, the herding of Jews into areas specifically designated for them began several hundred years earlier.

These areas were usually fenced off by a moat or a hedge to designate the boundaries. Jews were allowed outside during the day, but at night they had to stay in. A good example is the 1412 decree of King John I of Castile, Spain, ordering both Jews and Muslims into a ghetto:

> In the first place from now on all Jews and Jewesses, Moors and Moorish women of my kingdom and dominions shall live apart from the Christian men and women in a section or part of the city or village.... It shall be surrounded by a wall and have but one gate through which one could enter it.[388]

The ghetto was a mixed blessing for the Jews. While they were kept apart from the rest of society, which was humiliating, they were also kept together. Living together helped them preserve a sense of community and, since there was no socializing with non-Jews, it was also a guard against assimilation.

The worst part of living in the ghetto was that whenever the masses got it in their heads to kill the Jews — as they often did around Easter — they knew exactly where to find them.

Of course, the Christians always offered the Jews a way out of the ghetto — through conversion to Christianity.

Nachmanides

It was during one of these efforts to pressure the Jews to convert to Christianity that the great Kabbalist and Torah scholar known as Nachmanides came to prominence.

Nachmanides, Rabbi Moses ben Nachman, better known as *Ramban* (not to be confused with Rambam or Maimonides) was born in Christian Barcelona in 1194. He became the defender of the Jews in the great disputation of 1263 — the most famous of the debates in which Christians attempted to prove to Jews their religion was wrong in order to get them to convert.

Jews tried to avoid these debates like the plague. Every debate was a nonstarter, as Jews were not allowed to make Christianity look bad in any way — in other words, they were not allowed to win.

In 1263, a debate was staged in front of the Spanish King James I of Aragon, and Nachmanides was given royal permission to speak without fear of retribution. He took full advantage of this opportunity and didn't mince his words.

His primary opponent was a Jew who had converted to Christianity named Pablo Christiani (a name he adopted after his conversion). As we will see later in history, there were no bigger anti-Semites than those Jews who were trying to out-Christian the Christians. In fact, it was Pablo's idea to challenge the great scholar to this debate, which was a little bit like a high school physics student challenging Einstein. Realizing that Pablo might need some help, the Church sent the leaders of the Dominican and Franciscan orders as his advisors. But even they couldn't stand up to Nachmanides.

The debate revolved around three questions:

- Has the Messiah come, as the Christians say, or has he yet to come as the Jews say?
- Is the Messiah divine, as the Christians say, or human as the Jews say?
- Do the Jews practice the true law, or do the Christians?

Nachmanides answered that had the Messiah come the biblical prophecies of his coming would have been fulfilled. Since the wolf wasn't lying down with the lamb and peace did not rule the planet, clearly the Messiah had not come. Indeed, noted Nachmanides, "from the time of Jesus until the present the world has been filled with violence and injustice, and the Christians have shed more blood than other peoples."[389]

As for the divinity of Jesus, Nachmanides said that it was just impossible for any Jew to believe that "the Creator of heaven and earth resorted to the womb of a certain Jewish woman...and was born an infant...and then was betrayed into the hands of his enemies and sentenced to death.... The mind of a Jew, or any other person, cannot tolerate this."

At the end of the debate, which was interrupted as the Church scrambled to minimize the damage, the king said, "I have never seen a man support a wrong cause so well," and gave Nachmanides 300 solidos (pieces of gold) and the promise of continued immunity.

Unfortunately, the promise did not hold. The Church ordered Nachmanides to be tried on the charge of blasphemy, and he was forced to flee Spain. In 1267, he arrived in Jerusalem, where there were so few Jews at the time that he could not find ten men for a minyan in order to pray.

Determined to set up a synagogue, he went to Hebron and imported a few Jews. His original synagogue was outside Jerusalem city walls on Mount Zion, though after his death in 1270 it was moved inside.

(After the Six Day War, the synagogue — which in the meantime had been turned into a dumpsite — was restored and today is a vibrant place of worship. Incidentally, the Ramban Synagogue is a subterranean synagogue, because at the time Muslim law forbade any Jewish place of worship to be taller than any Muslim place of worship, as noted in chapter 41.)

Meanwhile, back in Europe, the Church was still trying to undo the damage of Nachmanides' tour de force. The consequences, unfortunately, were not good for the Jews.

For one, the Church continued its policy of censorship of all Jewish books (especially the Talmud) containing any references perceived to be anti-Christian. If any such books were found — without the pages ripped out or otherwise obliterated — they were burned.

For another, Pope Clement IV issued a special document, called a papal bull, entitled *Turbato Corde*, which later became the basis for the Inquisition's policy of persecuting "Judaizers," as we shall see in the next chapter.

Judensau **— "Jewish Pig." Early 17th century engraving on the entrance of bridge in Frankfurt, Germany. Note the circular coin emblem on all the figures, including the Devil, which was the badge that all Jews were forced to wear in Medieval Europe.**

47. THE INQUISITION

In chapter 44, when we discussed the Crusades, we covered the war of the Church against the Muslims in the Middle East. Now we turn to the war of the Church against Muslims in Europe.

This war went on in fits and starts for quite some time — from the time the Muslim Moors arrived in Spain in 711 C.E. It took a long time for the Christians to vanquish them. The first Muslim stronghold to fall was Toledo in 1085; the last was Granada in 1492.

As the Christians gained momentum against the Muslims, Jews in the newly reconquered territories began to suffer from increasingly harsher Christian persecutions.

In their bloodthirsty vengeance against the Muslims, the Spanish Christians included the Jews, whom they put in the category of infidels.

In fourteenth-century Barcelona, for example, the whole Jewish community was murdered by a rioting mob. Initially given shelter by some Christians, these Jews were pressured to convert. Those who refused were denied protection. Writes Professor Benzion Netanyahu in his 1,400-page work, *The Origins of the Inquisition*, quoting an eyewitness account of the time:

> Those of them who refused to accept baptism were immediately slain, and their corpses, stretched in the streets and the squares, offered a horrendous spectacle.[390]

Just how many Jews converted in these forced mass conversions that accompanied the Christian conquest of Spain? Estimates rage between tens of thousands to as many as 600,000.[391]

Many of those who converted did so only outwardly, continuing to practice Judaism in secret. In due time, the Christians caught on to these phony conversions and decided to root out the heretics.

The Spanish Inquisition

The Spanish Inquisition began officially with a papal bull issued by Pope Sixtus IV on November 1, 1478, that sought to punish Jews who had converted to Christianity but whose conversions were not "sincere."[392]

There is a great deal of irony in this. First you tell people they have to convert or die, then, when they do convert, you decide to kill them anyway because their conversions are not "sincere."

There was another reason for the Inquisition, which had little to do with the sincerity of conversions. Once Jews converted to Christianity they had open access to the playing field, economically and politically. And, of course, they prospered mightily. This engendered considerable hostility from the Christians — a pattern we have seen in Jewish history ever since the enslavement of the Israelites by the Egyptians. The Christians began to call the converted Jews "New Christians" to distinguish them from the "Old Christians," i.e. themselves. Derogatorily, Jewish converts to Christianity were called *conversos,* meaning "converts," or worse yet, *marranos*, meaning "pigs."

The basic accusation of the Inquisition was that these Jewish conversos were not real converts to Christianity because they were secretly practicing Judaism. That was certainly often the case.

Until this day, there exists Christian communities with obvious Jewish roots dating back to this time. There are people in the United States (in New Mexico and Arizona) as well as in South and Central America, who are descended from Spanish or Portuguese settlers, and who have strange customs they cannot explain. For example, even though they are Catholics, on Friday night they go down to the cellar to light candles. They don't know the origins of this custom, but they do it. These people are clearly descended from Jews who pretended to be Christians and yet were practicing Jewish rituals in secret.

The job of the Inquisition was to find such people, torture them until they admitted their "crime," and then kill them.

Ferdinand and Isabella

Every American child knows about King Ferdinand and Queen Isabella — they were the monarchs who backed Christopher Columbus in his discovery of America. However, here are a few facts that most people don't know about them.

The marriage in 1469 of Ferdinand V and Isabella I unified Spain, in some measure making the final victory over the Muslims possible. Prior to their reign, Spain was a collection of provinces — the two most important being Aragon and Castile. When Ferdinand of Aragon married Isabella of Castile, these two provinces were united by marriage into a mighty kingdom.

Isabella was a "fervent" Christian and, in 1478, she asked the pope for permission to weed out heresy in the Christian world. The pope obliged, issuing on November 1, 1478, a papal bull called *Exigit Sincere Devotionis*. Ferdinand and Isabella followed that with a royal decree on September 27, 1480.

One might think that ridding Christianity of heretics should involve targeting other groups, not just false Jewish converts. However, the royal decree mentioned no one else. Writes Professor Benzion Netanyahu:

> The royal decree explicitly stated that the Inquisition was instituted to search out and punish converts from Judaism who transgressed against Christianity by secretly adhering to Jewish beliefs and performing rites and ceremonies of the Jews. No other group was mentioned, no other purpose indicated — a fact that in itself suggests a close relationship between the creation of the Inquisition and Jewish life in Spain. Other facts, too, attest to that relationship.[393]

Although the first inquisitors got to work a few months after the decree, it was not until 1483 — when Tomas de Torquemada, a Spanish Dominican monk, was appointed Grand Inquisitor — that the Inquisition got its bloody reputation. Torquemada, who was descended from Jewish converts to Christianity, outdid the worst anti-Semites with his brutality.

One of the most fascinating and depressing sub-plots of this drama is that many of the major Christian personalities had either Jewish ancestry or were actually Jews according to Jewish law. In addition to Torquemada, Jewish blood also flowed through the veins of: King Ferdinand and Queen Isabella; Diego de Raza, Grand Inquisitor who came after Torquemada; Hernando de Talavera, Isabella's personal confessor (whose mother was a converso); Pedro de la Caballeria and Alanso de Cabrera (both conversos) who helped arrange the wedding of Ferdinand and Isabella; Gabriel Sanchez (converso) chief treasurer of Aragon; Luis de Santangel (converso), Ferdinand's budget minister. (Incidentally, Sanchez and Santangel were responsible for financing the voyage of Christopher Columbus, who was almost certainly also of Jewish ancestry, as we will see shortly.)[394]

How did the Inquisition work?

Jewish conversos would be arrested and accused of being false Christians. They would never know who accused them; evidence would be presented against them in secret. Then they would be tortured until they confessed to being heretics. Then, once they confessed, they would be killed. The usual method was burning at the stake, though if they were willing to kiss the cross, they would be spared the horrible pain of burning and would be strangled instead.

The key point is that, whether or not they repented, they were put to death.

What if some people refused to confess even under torture? Or worse, what if some people admitted right away to practicing Judaism secretly, but even when tortured refused to concede the truth of Christianity? If they survived the horrendous tortures, they would be burned at the stake in a ceremony called auto-da-fé, meaning "act of faith."

This went on until 1834, when the Inquisition was finally abolished, by which time every Spaniard came to fear its power. By then, the Inquisition's operations had spread to Christian heretics, Protestants sects, witches, and even people who read the wrong books. The Inquisition was even able to reach into territories outside of the Spanish Empire. When Jewish conversos fled to other, more friendly countries, the Inquisition followed them, even as far as Brazil, where the last person was burned at the stake in the nineteenth century.

Expulsion Edict

The year 1492 marked the fall of Granada, the last Muslim stronghold on the Iberian Peninsula, bringing to an end the Muslim domination of Spain which had lasted nearly 800 years. Spain was again a completely Christian country.

Shortly thereafter, Ferdinand and Isabella decided to evict all the Jews from Spain. This time, the monarchs were not targeting Jewish converts to Christianity; rather, they were targeting Jews who had never converted.

Why? The main reason stated in the Edict of Expulsion, signed on March 31, 1492, was to keep Jews from re-Judaizing the conversos. Another consideration was that Jewish money was needed to rebuild the kingdom after the costly war against the Muslims. Rather than slowly squeezing the money out of the Jews through taxation, it was easier to expel them all at once and confiscate the wealth and property they would leave behind.

The Edict of Expulsion declared:

> Whereas, having been informed that in these kingdoms, there were some bad Christians who Judaized and apostatized from our holy Catholic faith, the chief cause of which was the communication of Jews with Christians...we ordered the said Jews in all cities, towns, and places in our kingdoms and dominions to separate into Jewries [ghettos] and place apart...hoping by their separation alone to remedy this evil.... But we are informed that neither that, not the execution of some of the said Jews...has been sufficient for a complete remedy.... Therefore, we... resolve to order all the said Jews and Jewesses to quit our kingdoms and never return...by the end of the month of July next, of the present year 1492...if they do not perform and execute the same, and are found to reside in our kingdoms...they incur the penalty of death.... We likewise grant permission and authority to said Jews...to export their wealth and property...provided they do not take away gold, silver, money, or other articles prohibited by the laws of kingdom.[395]

The Jews tried to get the edict reversed, of course, through the intercession of Don Isaac Abarvanel. A Torah scholar and rabbi, Don Abarvanel was the most powerful Jew in Spain, having served as the royal treasurer. He tried very hard to rescind the expulsion order, at one point offering the monarchs 300,000 ducats for a reprieve. He almost succeeded. Unfortunately, his efforts ignited the ire of the Grand Inquisitor, Tomas de Torquemada. According to legend, Torquemada — who had an enormous amount of influence over Queen Isabella — walked in while Abarvanel was pleading his cause. Incensed, he threw the cross at the Queen, hitting her in the head, and yelled: "Judas sold his master [Jesus] for 30 pieces of silver. Now you would sell him anew!"

And so, Don Isaac Abarvanel lost. But he was so important to the monarchs that they offered him a special dispensation to stay; they even agreed that another nine Jews could stay with him so he could pray with a minyan. He refused. In fact, he became the leader of the Jews of Spain when they went into exile.

The six months between the issuing of the edict and the actual expulsion were catastrophic for the Jewish community. Having lived in Spain for centuries they were now being told that they all had leave! Where would they go?

To add insult to injury, they had to liquidate all their assets but could not take most of their wealth with them. They were forced to sell a massive amount of real estate, personal goods, and other valuables at a fraction of their actual worth. In short, most of them lost virtually everything.

Now, on what day was the Jewish community sent into exile?

August 2, 1492. (The original date was July 31st, but Torquemada extended it by a few days.) This day "just happened" to be the ninth of Av, the same date as the destruction of the first and second Temple in Jerusalem (and many other disasters, as we have already seen). On that day the Jews of Spain (some 150,000 to 200,000 people) were forced to abandon their vast possessions and leave. The remainder — around 60,000 conversos though it's unknown exactly how many — stayed behind.

Christopher Columbus

The day after the expulsion, August 3, 1492, Christopher Columbus left on his famed voyage of discovery. His diary begins:

"In the same month in which their Majesties issued the edict that all Jews should be driven out of the kingdom and its territories, in the same month, they gave me the order to undertake with sufficient men my expedition of discovery of the Indies."

Many people like to speculate that Columbus was of Jewish ancestry, and there is a good case for it.[396] Here is some of the evidence:

Although he was born in Genoa, Italy, his first language was Castilian Spanish. Many Jews had been forced to leave Castile about a hundred years before his birth and some went to Genoa. (Incidentally, fourteenth-century Castilian Spanish is the "Yiddish" of Spanish Jewry, known as "Ladino.")

When he wrote, Columbus made funny little marks in his journal, resembling the marks that religious Jews put on top of the written page even to this day — an abbreviation of *b'siyatta diShmaya*, which means "with the help of heaven" in Aramaic.

He talked a great deal about Zion in his writings.

In his crew, he had five known Jews, including his doctor, navigator, and translator.

Columbus hired the translator, Louis de Torres (who had converted to Christianity the day before he set sail), because he spoke twelve languages including Hebrew, and Columbus was sure he was going to bump into Hebrew-speakers. He thought he was heading to the Far East, and he expected to find at least one of the Ten Lost Tribes there, which is why he needed a Hebrew speaker.

Furthermore, there's no question that Columbus' voyage to America was spiritually linked to the expulsion. Just as one of the greatest Jewish communities of Medieval Europe was being destroyed, God was opening the doors to America, which would eventually become the greatest Diaspora refuge for Jews in history. This is another great pattern we see in history: God preparing the cure before the disease.

Incidentally, Isabella did not finance Columbus' voyage by selling her jewels as is often stated. As mentioned earlier, the major financiers were two court officials — both Jewish conversos — Louis de Santangel, chancellor of the royal household, and Gabriel Sanchez, treasurer of Aragon. The first letter Columbus sent back from the New World was not to Ferdinand and Isabella, but to Santangel and Sanchez thanking them for their support and telling them what he found.

The voyage of Columbus stands as a landmark in the Age of Exploration, a time when numerous adventurers opened up the New World. While none of the others is believed to be Jewish, their discoveries were, to a significant extent, made possible by Jewish inventions or Jewish improvements to existing inventions.

For example, the navigational instruments — the quadrant and the astral lobe used in that period — were of Jewish manufacture. In fact, the quadrant then in use was called "Jacob's Staff"; it had been invented by Rabbi Levi ben Gershon, also known as Gershonides.

The famous atlas that Columbus and the other explorers used was known as the Catalon Atlas; it was the creation of the Cresca Family, Jews from Majorca, Spain. Not only was the Catalon Atlas considered the best collection of maps then available, it had no competition to speak of. Jews had a virtual monopoly on map making then, culling information from Jewish merchants from all over the known world.

A Treasure

While Columbus was off discovering America, what was happening to the Jews newly displaced from Spain?

Most made their way across the border to Portugal, but five years later, the King of Portugal offered them the same choice as Spain: Convert, leave, or die. Just as they started to pack their bags yet again, a strange thing happened.

Rather than follow through with his threat and expel them — which would have caused him a massive loss of valuable Jews — the king first forcibly baptized all Jewish children and then orchestrated a mass, forced conversion of virtually the entire Jewish population. He then forbade these "New Christians" from emigrating.

Thousands of Jews who fled Spain went to Turkey, which historically has been very nice to the Jews. Opening his doors to them, the Sultan of the Turkish Ottoman Empire, Bayezid II, declared: "They tell me that Ferdinand of Spain is a wise man, but he is a fool. For he takes his treasure and sends it all to me."[397]

How did the movement of the Jews affect these countries?

Spain, which having discovered and colonized the New World should have been the wealthiest of countries, was bankrupt within 100 years of the expulsion. Turkey, on the other hand, prospered. The Ottoman Empire became one of the greatest powers in the world. The next two sultans, Selim I and Suleiman I, expanded the empire as far as Vienna, Austria.

(Incidentally, it was Suleiman — known as "Suleiman the Magnificent" — who, in 1536, rebuilt the walls of Jerusalem, the same walls that stand today and define the Old City.)

If we recall the lesson of chapter 4, God had given Abraham and his descendants a special blessing: "I will bless those who bless you, and curse those who curse you, and through you, will be blessed all the families of the earth."[398]

God said to Abraham that he and his descendants — the Jews — would be under His protection. The nations and peoples that were good to the Jews would do well. Empires and peoples that ill-treated the Jews would do poorly.

This is another of the great patterns of Jewish history that we have seen and that we will continue to see in coming chapters. We can literally chart the rise and fall of many of the countries and empires of the Middle East and the West according to how they treated the Jews.

One such country, surprisingly, was Poland.

48.
THE JEWS OF POLAND

The Dark Ages, which were dominated by the repressive policies of the Church in Rome, are now behind us, as we begin to examine a time period associated with individual expression, self-consciousness, and worldly experience, and accomplishments in scholarship, literature, science, and the arts. That period, which historians generally date from about 1350 to about 1650, was called the Renaissance. Renaissance means "rebirth" — that is, the rebirth of knowledge.

During the Renaissance, some powerful kings emerged in England and in France, while the power of the Church began to wane. The famous personalities of this period of time were Michelangelo, Leonardo da Vinci, Shakespeare, Machiavelli, Petrarch, Rabelais, Descartes, Copernicus, just to name a few.

This was also the time when Jews made their way into Poland. Today, we tend to think of Jewish life in Poland as being confined to the shtetl, but that did not happen until the eighteenth century. We also tend to think of Poland as synonymous with anti-Semitism, pogroms, etc. But, during the Renaissance, the picture was quite different.

Before we begin the fascinating story of the Jews of Poland, we have to keep in mind the pattern that is constantly repeated in Jewish history. The places where the Jews are the most successful are almost always the same places where the Jews will suffer the most in the end.

This was the case in Spain, and we will see this pattern repeated in Poland and later in Germany. It's the same pattern we saw when the Jews were invited into Egypt and then enslaved there.

So how did the Jews come to Poland?

A Polish Invitation

Poland became Christian very late, only at the turn of the eleventh century, and only then did it join the European community of nations (so to speak). Thereafter, it was a few hundred years before Poland started to emerge as a nation-state with strong potential.

If you want to develop your country economically and culturally, who do you need?

You need Jews.

Why were the Jews so necessary? First, they could read and write. Jews were always highly educated as they had to be literate in order to read and obey the Torah, and general education came along as part of the parcel. Second, Jews were excellent bankers, accountants, and administrators who knew how to keep the economy healthy.

So in 1264, King Boleslav of Poland invited the Jews there. His charter granted Jews unprecedented rights and privileges. For example, it stated that:

> The testimony of the Christian alone may not be admitted in a matter which concerns the money or property of a Jew. In every such incidence, there must be the testimony of both a Christian and a Jew. If a Christian injures a Jew in any way, the accused shall pay a fine to the royal treasury.
>
> If a Christian desecrates or defiles a Jewish cemetery in any which way, it is our wish that he be punished severely as demanded by law.
>
> If a Christian should attack a Jew, the Christian shall be punished as required by the laws of this land. We absolutely forbid anyone to accuse the Jews in our domain of using the blood of human beings.
>
> We affirm that if any Jew cry out in the night as a result of violence done to him, and if his Christian neighbors fail to respond to his cries and do not bring the necessary help, they shall be fined.
>
> We also affirm that Jews are free to buy and sell all manner of things just as Christians, and if anyone hampers them, he shall pay a fine.[399]

This was an amazing document. We saw previously (in chapter 45) that Jews would be brought in as money-lenders (being excluded from other professions), then when a bishop or nobleman wanted his debt annulled, he brought a blood libel against the Jews and had them expelled or killed. King Boleslav boldly promised the Jews that this would not happen in Poland.

Jews did not immediately flock into Poland, though some did settle there to test the waters. But when other countries started expelling Jews — England in the thirteenth century, Germany in the fourteenth century, and Italy and Portugal in the fifteenth century — Poland became an attractive destination point.

About that time, another Polish king, Sigismund II Augustus, issued another invitation. Here is an excerpt from his edict, granting the Jews permission to open a yeshiva at Lublin, dated August 23, 1567:

> As a result of the efforts of our advisors and in keeping with the request of the Jews of Lublin, we do hereby grant permission to erect a yeshiva and to outfit [the] said yeshiva with all that is required to advance learning. All the learned men and rabbis of Lublin shall come together for among their number they shall choose one to serve as the head of the yeshivah. Let their choice be a man who will magnify Torah and bring it glory.[400]

Then, in 1569, Poland unified with Lithuania, and as a result expanded its borders to the east. What we know today as the Ukraine and some of Belorussia became vassal lands of Poland, which was still a semi-feudal country. These lands needed to be managed, and management jobs (at which Jews excelled) sprang up everywhere. Jews also leased tracts of land from the Polish nobility, thus making themselves the middlemen in the feudal economic structure of Eastern Europe. And they prospered.

Golden Age of Polish Jewry

In the early sixteenth century, the Jews of Poland were allowed to have their own governing body called the *Va'ad Arba Artzot*, "The Council of the Four Lands," which was composed of various rabbis from the four major Polish provinces (Great Poland, Little Poland, Volhynia, and Polodia) who oversaw the affairs of the Jews in Eastern Europe. The Poles did not interfere with Jewish life and scholarship flourished.

Some important personalities of this period, which a student of Jewish history should remember, were:

Rabbi Moses Isserles (1525–1572), from Krakow, also known as the Rema. After the Sephardic rabbi, Joseph Karo, wrote the *Shulchan Aruch*, the Code of Jewish Law, Rabbi Isserles annotated it to add the rabbinic decisions from Eastern Europe. His commentary was, and continues to be, critically important in daily Jewish life.

Rabbi Jacob Pollack (1455–1530), from Krakow. He opened the first yeshiva in Poland and was later named the chief rabbi of Poland. He developed a method of learning Talmud called *pilpul*, meaning "fine distinctions." This was a type of dialectical reasoning that became very popular, whereby contradictory facts or ideas were systematically weighed with a view to the resolution of their real or apparent contradictions.

Rabbi Judah Loewe (1526–1609), not from Poland but important to Eastern European Jewry. He was known as the Maharal of Prague and was one of the great mystical scholars of his time. His name has also been associated with the famous Golem of Prague legend, although the legend has been shown to be a fabrication. (The Golem was a Frankenstein-like being supposedly created by the Maharal to protect the Jews of Prague.)

Population Boom

Along with the growth in Torah scholarship came population growth. In 1500 there were about 50,000 Jews living in Poland; by 1650 there were 500,000. This means that by the mid-seventeenth century at least 30% or more of the Jewish population of the world was living in Poland!

Where did all these Jews settle within Poland? Jews of the Diaspora were generally urban people, as they were historically not allowed to own land in most of the places they lived; this was not the case in Poland where they also created their own farm communities called shtetls ("small towns"). Although we tend to think of the shtetl today as a poor farming village (like in "Fiddler on the Roof"), during the golden age of Polish Jewry, many of these communities were actually quite prosperous. And there were thousands of them.

The Jews in these independent communities spoke their own language called Yiddish. Original Yiddish was written in Hebrew letters and was a mixture of Hebrew, Slavic, and German. (Note that Yiddish underwent constant development, and "modern" Yiddish is not like the "old" Yiddish which first appeared in the thirteenth century, nor the "middle" Yiddish of this time.)

Overall, the Jews did well, but working alongside Polish and Ukrainian

Christians (who believed Jews killed Jesus) had its downside.

There were several episodes of Christian rioting against Jews. For example, in 1399 in Poznan, a rabbi and thirteen elders were accused of stealing Church property, and were tortured and burnt at the stake. (The Poles must have forgotten the king's edict.)

Another problem was that Jews worked as administrators and tax collectors for Polish feudal lords. This made them unpopular among the local folk, who needed little encouragement to unleash their anti-Semitic rage.

This was especially true in places like the Ukraine, where the Catholic Poles were viewed as an occupying power in an Eastern Orthodox land, and the Jews — being representatives of the occupiers — were the obvious scapegoats.

In some instances, the Polish soldiers would purposely leave town, abandoning the Jews to the mercy (or lack thereof) of the Ukrainians. This happened, for example, in 1648 in the city of Tulchin. The Polish soldiers made a deal with the Cossacks and left. The Jews defended the city by themselves, until it fell and they were all slaughtered.

Pogroms

When the Ukrainians decided to throw the Poles out of their land, full-scale massacres of Jews began.

The year 1635 saw the first big explosion of violence in the Ukraine against Poles and Jews. This attempt at revolution was crushed, only to return with new vigor thirteen years later.

The second rebellion, beginning in 1648, which succeeded in freeing a large part of the Ukraine from Polish rule, was led by a Ukrainian Cossack named Bogdan Chmielnicki. In large measure, violence was directed at the Jews. Chmielnicki was one of the most violent anti-Semites in human history, on a par with Hitler. His aim was genocide, and his forces murdered an estimated 100,000 Jews in the most horrendous ways. Here is one contemporaneous description:

> Some of them [the Jews] had their skins flayed off them and their flesh was flung to the dogs. The hands and feet of others were cut off and they were flung onto the roadway where carts ran over them and they were trodden underfoot by horses.... And many were buried alive. Children were slaughtered at their mother's bosoms, and many children were torn apart like fish. They ripped up the bellies of pregnant women, took out the unborn children and flung them in their faces. They tore open the

> bellies of some of them and placed a living cat within the belly and they left them alive thus, first cutting off their hands so that they should not be able to take the living cat out of the belly...and there was never an unnatural death in the world that they did not inflict upon them.[401]

Here is another account from Rabbi Shabbetai ben Meir HaCohen, also known as the Shach:

> On the same day 1,500 people were killed in the city of Human [a.k.a. Uman] in Russia on Shabbat. The nobles [i.e. Cossacks] with whom the wicked mob had again made an alliance chased all the Jews from the city into the fields and vineyards where the villains surrounded them in a circle, stripped them to their skin and ordered them to lie on the ground. The villains spoke to the Jews with friendly and consoling words: "Why do you want to be killed, strangled, and slaughtered like an offering to your God Who poured out His anger upon you without mercy? Would it not be safer for you to worship our gods, our images and crosses and we would form one people which would unite together." But the holy and faithful people who so often allowed themselves to be murdered for the sake of the Lord, raised their voices together to the Almighty in Heaven and cried: "Hear of Israel the Lord our God, the Holy One and the King of the Universe, we have been murdered for Your sake so often already. O Lord, God of Israel, let us remain faithful to You." Afterward they recited the confession of sins and said: "We are guilty and thus recognize the divine judgment." Now the villains turned upon them and there was not one of them who did not fall victim.[402]

It's no wonder when Jews hear the word Cossack they break out in a sweat. These people killed tens of thousands of Jews and destroyed hundreds of Jewish communities in the most brutal way one could imagine.

Yet, to this day Chmielnicki is considered a national hero in the Ukraine, where they regard him as a kind of "George Washington." In Kiev, for example, there is a big statue in the square erected in his honor.

These pogroms drove the Jews out of what was then Eastern Poland, ending the Golden Age of Polish Jewry, although Jews in other parts of the country were able to remain. Thus, Poland continued for many years to be the center of the Ashkenazi Jewish world, as we shall see in subsequent chapters.

Before we cover that period of time, however, we will backtrack in order to discuss the Protestant Reformation, which also took place during the Renaissance.

49.
THE PROTESTANT REFORMATION

Jewish history did not take place in a vacuum, and we always have to keep in mind the world events that affected the Jews in a major way. One of those huge events that convulsed Europe was the Protestant Reformation.

What brought it about? Simply put, the corruption of the Church in Rome.

As we saw in chapter 44, with the decline of the Roman Empire, the Church became the great feudal player in the economic system of Europe. This was a system that, while virtually enslaving huge masses of people, made the Church very rich and very powerful, both politically and militarily. "Power tends to corrupt and absolute power corrupts absolutely," said Lord Acton,[403] and this was certainly true of the Church at that time.

Rolling in wealth, the Church built great edifices, fielded its own armies, and sank deeper and deeper into immorality, materialism, and decadence. The list of papal affairs and political intrigues is extensive. For example, Pope Alexander VI bribed some members of the College of Cardinals to ensure his election in 1492, the year the Jews were thrown out of Spain. Once in office, he brought the papacy to new heights of spiritual laxity.[404] A number of popes before him had abandoned celibacy, but Alexander VI openly acknowledged his illegitimate children, who became famous in their own right: Cesare and Lucrezia Borgia.[405]

Giovanni Boccaccio, the great fourteenth-century Italian humanist writer, offers humorous insight into the corruption and decadence of the Church of his day. In his classic work, *Decameron*, a Jew by the name of Abraham is pressured by a Christian friend to visit Rome in the hope that he will be so impressed that he will convert to Christianity. Abraham returns disgusted and reports:

> I say this for that, if I was able to observe aright, no piety, no devoutness, no good work or example of life or other what did I see there in any who was Churchman: nay lust, covetise, gluttony and the like and worse.... And as far as I judge, meseemeth your chief pastor and consequently all others endeavor with all diligence and all their wit and every art to bring to naught and to banish from the world the [values of the] Christian religion....[406]

Those wanting to reform the moral stature of the Church were powerless. Even as the hypocrisy of the situation was becoming intolerable, the Church used its power to stifle any signs of defiance.

The defiance began in the fourteenth century, with challenges to Church doctrine and attempts to translate the Bible into languages other than Latin (the language of the Roman Empire which few spoke). These attempts were brutally put down.

Why didn't the Church want the common people to read the Bible?

Just imagine what might happen if the serfs should read the Bible and discover what it actually said about the obligation of every person (even "his lordship" and "his eminence") to love his neighbor and treat him with equality, since all human beings were created in the image of God.

It was precisely for this reason that the Church opposed translating the Bible into the vernacular. Writes Henry Phelps-Brown in *Egalitarianism and the Generation of Inequality*:

> Despite its anxiety to save man's souls from the perdition of earthly pursuits in order to preserve it for the salvation of the life after death, the medieval Church insulated pupils from the dangerous contamination of Scriptures. Only those entering holy orders were allowed to study theology and delve into Holy Writ. Unsupervised, independent exploration of the Bible was tantamount to heresy and only clerics in good standing were permitted to expound Scripture from a Latin text incomprehensible to the Christian masses.[407]

Martin Luther

In 1506, the Church of Rome undertook one of its grandest and most expensive projects — the construction of a new St. Peter's Basilica as the centerpiece of the Vatican. This church was to be so lavish and so huge that, when completed 150 years later, it was the largest church ever built, and it remained so until 1989.

Such an astronomical project required an astronomical sum of money, and, to raise the funds, the Church turned to the sale of indulgences. The practice of granting indulgences — remission of punishment for sins through the intercession of the Church — already had a long history. But early on, indulgences were granted when a sinner performed some hazardous duty for the Church — like going on a crusade. (A crusade to the Holy Land got you forgiveness for all sins ever committed.) Later, it became possible to buy indulgences on your deathbed. (Thus, you ensured that you would enter heaven immediately, bypassing purgatory.) With the Church engaged in a major fundraising effort, the sale of indulgences took on new significance.

Pope Sixtus IV's fundraising campaign touted indulgences which would free your deceased loved ones suffering in purgatory. Church envoys resorted to imitating the anguished wailing of parents who, in the throes of holy purification fires, pleaded with their children to buy an indulgence and ease their torment. One creative envoy, a Dominican monk by the name of Johann Tetzel, made up a little ditty: "As soon as the coin in the coffer rings, the soul from purgatory springs."

At the height of the indulgence frenzy, Martin Luther, an Augustinian friar from Germany, traveled to Rome and was shocked by what he saw. How could the Church sell heaven to the highest bidder? And how could the bishops and cardinals behave with such moral laxity and worldliness?

Luther returned home and was plunged into a crisis of faith. He resolved his dilemma by coming up with the theory of grace, which would later become part of the Protestant theology. This theory holds that salvation comes by God's grace — or God's indulgence, so to speak. A gift from God could clearly not be sold by the Church.

Full of youthful, idealistic zeal (he was only 34 at the time), Luther posted his protest — the now-famous Ninety-Five Theses — on the door of All Saints Church in Wittenberg, on October 31, 1517.

The long and short of it was that his protest reached Rome, and he was asked, in no uncertain terms, to recant. He refused, proclaiming his famous defense, "Here I stand, I cannot do otherwise." He was excommunicated four years later.[408]

But it was too late to silence him, thanks in part to a remarkable technological advance which would change history forever — the Gutenberg press.

A mere fifty years before Luther's protest, Johann Gutenberg had perfected a system of making metal letters in moulds, setting them in rows, and using the templates thus formed to print multiple copies of a document in minutes, instead of the hours it took to copy it tediously by hand.

When this incredible printing machine was applied to Luther's Ninety-Five Theses — which, in effect, represented an indictment of the Church — all hell broke loose. What might have been a local dispute, with the protestant muzzled by his excommunication, became a public controversy that spread far and wide.

Martin Luther's new religion, called *Protestantism*, was favorably received across northern Europe by nobles who were more than happy to expel the Church from their land and seize the Church's wealth.

Of course, the Church had its allies as well, and Europe was plunged into the Thirty Years War, which lasted from 1618 to 1648. Waged primarily between Protestants and Catholics, this war caused much destruction, bloodshed, and loss of life.[409] And it had a big impact on the Jews.

Luther had seen how shamefully the Church had treated the Jews, and he had a plan to change that.[410] He was certain that the Jews refused to convert to Christianity because they were appalled at the corruption of the Church. Now, the Jews would see that the Protestants were different, and they would convert more readily. As he wrote in his work, entitled *That Jesus Christ Was a Jew*:

> For they [the Church clergy] have dealt with the Jews as if they were dogs and not human beings. They have done nothing for them but curse them and seize their wealth.... I hope that if the Jews are treated [with friendliness] and instructed kindly enough through the Bible, many of them will become real Christians and come back to the ancestral faith of the prophets and patriarchs....[411]

Naturally, the Jews didn't go for Protestantism either. Their allegiance to Judaism and the Torah had nothing to do with the behavior of Christians. To Jews, Christianity was a false religion from the start, and the behavior of the Christians over the years only proved it.

Now Martin Luther would further add to that proof. When the Jews rejected his overtures, Luther, who took this rejection personally, turned into one of the most virulent anti-Semites in history. A few years later, he wrote in his *Concerning the Jews and Their Lies*:

> What shall we do with this damned rejected race of Jews since they live among us and we know about their lying and blasphemy and cursing. We cannot tolerate them even if we do not wish to share their lives, curses and blasphemy. Perhaps we can spare a few of them from the fire and flames. Let me give you my honest advice....[412]

Luther's "honest advice" outlined a plan for dealing with the Jews. It included:

- burn all synagogues;
- destroy Jewish holy books;
- forbid rabbis to teach;
- destroy Jewish homes;
- ban Jews from roads and markets;
- forbid Jews to make loans;
- seize Jewish property;
- force Jews to do hard labor;
- expel Jews from Christian towns.

Some 400 years later, Hitler and the Nazis, using Luther's anti-Jewish writings in their propaganda, would put his plan into action.

PART V

THE LONG ROAD HOME

50.
THE KABBALISTS

In Part IV, we related the events in the history of the Jews during the Renaissance (1350–1650), where we saw saw: a resurgence of classical knowledge and the waning power of the Church; the Spanish Inquisition and the expulsion of the Jews from various countries; the growth of Protestantism as a new offshoot of Christianity; the Golden Age of Polish Jewry, and the Ukrainian massacres of Bogdan Chmielnicki.

Where was the Jewish world as the Renaissance was drawing to a close?

Geographically, about half the Jewish population was located in the Middle East (with a high concentration in Turkey and the lands of the Ottoman Empire) and about half in Europe (with a high concentration in Eastern Europe, primarily in what was then Poland).

That is not to say that all the Jews lived only in these places. In fact, there were Jews literally the world over, including India and China. But for the purposes of a crash course, we are focusing on the large Jewish population centers.

Ottoman Empire

From the year 638 C.E. (six years after the death of Mohammed) when Caliph Omar invaded Jerusalem, the Land of Israel had been in Muslim hands — with the very short exception of the Crusades (1099–1187) — and would continue to be until the end of World War I in 1917.

During the Renaissance (starting from 1516 onward), Muslim power belonged to the Ottoman Empire based in Istanbul. It is important to note that although they were Muslims, the Ottomans were Turks and not Arabs.

Traditionally, the Turks were good to the Jews. As we already saw, following the expulsion from Spain, Jews were welcomed into Ottoman lands by Sultan Bayezid II. As the Ottoman Empire spread, the Turks came to Israel, and it was the greatest of the Ottoman sultans, known as Suleiman the Magnificent, who rebuilt the walls of Jerusalem. (It is fascinating that Suleiman is Arabic for Solomon, and that his walls define the Old City of Jerusalem to this day.)

At this time, many Jews started to return to the Land of Israel, and particularly to the city of Tzfat (sometimes spelled Safed). In less than 100 years the population of Tzfat grew from a mere 300 families to 10,000 people, thus making it the largest Jewish population in Israel in the sixteenth century, when Tzfat gave birth to some amazing contributions to Jewish scholarship.

The first scholar we must mention was Rabbi Jacob Berav (1475–1546), who tried to reinstitute *semichah*, "proper rabbinic ordination." This had not been given in the Jewish world for well over 1,000 years. "Proper rabbinic ordination" is given by a teacher whose own ordination must be traceable all the way back to Moses. *Semichah* had been interrupted during Roman persecutions. Of course, rabbis were still ordained, so to speak, but these ordinations were neither "proper" nor "official" in the way Jewish law intended them to be.

Based on a statement of Maimonides, Rabbi Berav thought it could be done properly again if it was supported by all of the rabbis in Israel. He ordained a few scholars, but his attempt at reinstituting *semichah* was not successful. The rabbis in Jerusalem didn't recognize it, and, to this day, rabbinical ordination is symbolic only.

One of the few that Rabbi Berav ordained was Rabbi Joseph Karo. Rabbi Karo (1488–1575) was among the Jews expelled from Spain, and he had made his way through Europe and Turkey, finally ending up in Tzfat. There he wrote one of the most important books in Judaism — the *Shulchan Aruch,* "The Prepared Table" — the Code of Jewish law which is followed to this day.

Before him, Rabbi Jacob ben Asher (know as the Tur), had attempted to organize Jewish law in a book called the *Arba Turim* ("Four Sections"). Rabbi Joseph Karo took the *Arba Turim* and spent thirty-two years writing a commentary to it, which he called *Beit Yoseph*, "House of Joseph," and which he later condensed into the *Shulchan Aruch*.[413]

While Joseph Karo is today most famous for his book of law, he was a mystic. And it is no coincidence that he made his home in Tzfat, because in his day Tzfat became the center of Jewish mysticism — more popularly known as Kabbalah.[414]

Jewish Mysticism

Kabbalah ("that which was received") is an interpretation of the Torah that focuses on the deepest esoteric teachings of Judaism. According to tradition, this level of understanding of the Torah was revealed at Mount Sinai, but because of its complexity, it was reserved for only a few initiates. With time, that secret interpretation became more widely known and finally published and disseminated generally (though few could understand it).

The key work of Kabbalah is the *Zohar*, the "Book of Splendor." The contents of this book were first revealed by Rabbi Simon bar Yochai in about 100 C.E., while he lived in a cave, hiding out from the Romans. Rabbi Moses de Leon (1240–1305), a Spanish rabbi, was the first to publish the *Zohar*, though he never claimed to be the author. But, because the teachings which he published were not organized into a coherent whole, as before, few could understand them.

Then Rabbi Moshe Cordevero of Tzfat (1522–1570), better known as the Ramak, entered the picture. The Ramak rationally systematized all of Kabbalistic thought up to his time, in particular the teachings of the *Zohar*. In his work, *Pardes Rimonim*, "The Pomegranate Orchard," the Ramak demonstrated the underlying unity of Kabbalistic tradition by organizing the various, often seemingly contradictory, teachings into a coherent system. The core of the Ramak's system consisted of a detailed description of how God created reality through the ten *sefirot*, spheres or channels of divine energy. Understanding these ten forces is key to the study of Kabbalah today.

But perhaps the most famous figure in the development of Kabbalah as we know it today was Rabbi Isaac Luria (1534–1572), called the Ari. The Ari was born in Jerusalem, though he subsequently relocated to Tzfat, arriving there on the day of the Ramak's funeral. He lived there only two years before he died (at age thirty-eight), but in that short interval he revolutionized the study of Jewish mysticism. In fact, his teachings — as recorded by his disciple Rabbi Chaim Vital — virtually dictate the modern study of Kabbalah.

The Ari's system was different from that of the Ramak. Rather than seeing the *sefirot* as one-dimensional points, he visualized them as dynamically interacting *partzufim*, "personae," each with a symbolically human-like character. According to his understanding, human actions can impact on the *sefirot* — which channel divine energy into the world — and can either facilitate or impede the advancement of creation toward its intended state of perfection.

The Ari also advanced the study of reincarnation, which he explained in *Sha'ar HaGilgulim*, "The Gate of Reincarnation."

During this period of time, many people came to study Kabbalah in Tzfat and legends are told of the Kabbalists, all dressed in white, walking out of the city in the fields on the eve of Shabbat, singing the song of welcome: "*Lechah Dodi Likrat Kallah* — Come My Beloved to Greet the Bride." (This famous song/poem was written by Rabbi Solomon HaLevi Alkabetz.) The Kabbalat Shabbat service to welcome the Shabbat on Friday evening was created in Tzfat in the sixteenth century.

Shabbetai Tzvi, the False Messiah

Mysticism, because it often attempts to explain the deeper meaning behind the events of history, is often associated with messianic expectation. But messianic expectation — which is one of the Thirteen Principles of Faith as outlined by Maimonides — can sometimes be misplaced and lead to big problems for the Jewish people.

This happened in the late 1600s, and events of the previous 150 years — the expulsions, the Inquisition, the pogroms — set the scene. Jewish morale was low. It seemed that things could not get any worse. Surely the time had arrived for the Messiah to come to the rescue.

At this time, a so-called mystic named Shabbetai Tzvi became prominent. Born in 1626 in Smyrna, Turkey, he was by all accounts a brilliant, charismatic, if emotionally volatile man. By the age of 20, he was already given the title of *chacham*, "wise man," by the members of his community, though not too long after — when his behavior became erratic and people come to realize that though brilliant, he was also mentally unstable — he was thrown out by them.

He started to wander the Middle East, and in 1651, made his way to Israel, specifically to Gaza. There, he met another so-called mystic by the name of Nathan of Gaza, who became his promoter. It was Nathan who convinced Shabbetai Tzvi that he was the Messiah, and he started sending letters to all Jewish communities that the Messiah had come to Israel.

One account of what happened next comes from a primary source, a Jewish woman living in Germany named "Gluckel of Hamelin," whose memoirs give us insight into the life of European Jewry in the seventeenth century. She writes:

> About this time people began to talk of Shabbetai Tzvi but woe unto us that we have sinned and never lived to see what we heard and I believed. Throughout the world servants and children rent themselves with re-

> pentance, prayer, and charity for two, yeah, for three years my beloved people Israel sat in labor but there came forth naught but wind....
>
> Our joy when the letters arrive from Smyrna is not to be told. Most of them were addressed to Sephardim. As fast as they came they took the letters to the synagogue and read them aloud. Young and old, the Germans, too, hastened to the Sephardi synagogues....
>
> Many sold their houses and lands and all their possessions for the day they hoped to be redeemed. My good father-in-law left his home in Hamelin, abandoned his house and lands and all of his goodly furniture. Full well we know the Most High has given us word and were we not so wicked but truly pious from the bottom of our hearts, I'm certain God would have mercy on us. If only we kept the commandment, "You shall love your neighbor as yourself," but God forgive us for the way we keep it. No good can come from the jealousy and thoughtless hate that rules our lives....[415]

From this account, we see how eager Jews were for the Messiah to come after the many persecutions, and how easily they were swept up by Messianic fervor.

It must be noted, however, that even though Shabbetai Tzvi had a huge following in the Jewish world (much more than Jesus ever had), the majority of the European rabbis, who saw that Shabbetai Tzvi was deviating from Jewish law, were not fooled and warned against him.

Meanwhile Shabbetai Tzvi, believing his own story, went to pay a call on the Sultan of the Ottoman Empire to demand recognition as the Messiah. He also wanted the Sultan to hand over the Land of Israel to him. The Sultan, not impressed, promptly threw him in jail and then threatened to torture him to death if he did not convert to Islam.

So Shabbetai Tzvi converted. For his cooperation, he was even given a royal title, Aziz Mechmed Efendi, and a position, "Keeper of the Sultan's Gate." He continued to claim that he was the Messiah, and the Sultan eventually exiled him.

Of course, as soon as he converted to Islam, the Jewish world stopped believing that he was the Messiah, though some Jews refused to admit they were fooled and converted to Islam along with him. This very small group — the Doenmeh — has survived as a special Muslim sect within Turkey.

As a result of what happened with Shabbetai Tzvi, there was a backlash that continued for many years after his death. The opponents of the Sabbatean movement who had been ignored when Messianic fervor was sweeping world

Jewry — notably Rabbi Tzvi Ashkenazi of Amsterdam, who was known as the Chacham Tzvi, and his son, Rabbi Yaakov Emden — came out blaming Jewish mysticism for the fiasco. This time, people listened to them. As a result of this backlash, some brilliant Kabbalists were unfairly condemned, hounded out of town, and had their books burned.

One of those was the Italian rabbi, Moshe Chaim Luzzatto, known as the Ramchal (1707–1747). A great Kabbalist and a brilliant and profound thinker, he wrote *The Path of the Just*, a book which is still intensely studied today. But because his mystical inclinations aroused fears of more false messianism, he was driven out of Italy; he died in Israel at age forty.

His contribution to Jewish studies was not appreciated until after his death. Rabbi Elijah ben Shlomo Zalman, the Vilna Gaon ("Genius of Vilna"), later said that his understanding of Judaism was perfect, and that if the Ramchal had lived longer, he would have walked from Vilna to sit at his feet and learn.

However, the Vilna Gaon, while praising the Ramchal, opposed some of the teachings of another brilliant rabbi — the famous founder of the Hassidic Movement, the Ba'al Shem Tov, whose story follows.

51.
THE HASSIDIC MOVEMENT

The Hassidic Movement — the movement of the "pious ones," or *Chassidut* in Hebrew — was founded in the eighteenth century in Eastern Europe by Rabbi Israel ben Eliezer, known as the Ba'al Shem Tov ("Master of the Good Name") or Besht.

The Ba'al Shem Tov was born in 1698 in Okup, in Podolia province (of what is now Ukraine) near the Dniester River. He was a poor orphan who worked in the Carpathian Mountains as a laborer. During this time, he studied with a secret society of Jewish mystics, the Nestarim, and eventually became a revered rabbi. He traveled from community to community, developing a reputation wherever he went as a spiritual holy man and mystical healer, and attracting a huge following. His teachings reinvigorated the demoralized, persecuted Jews of Eastern Europe.

After the pogroms and massacres (which we detailed in chapter 48), large parts of Eastern European Jewry had slipped into dire poverty. In addition to the tremendous physical destruction, the huge disappointment caused by the false messiah Shabbetai Tzvi left much of the Jewish population of Eastern Europe in a collective state of deep depression. One victim of this situation was Jewish scholarship, with only an elite few studying in yeshivas while the rest eked out a meager living. As a result, Jewish religious life suffered. The average Jew was not connecting either intellectually or spiritually with God, and this is what the Ba'al Shem Tov sought to change.

His teachings (he left no writings) inspired a movement which emphasized the idea of bringing God into all aspects of one's life through a process called *deveikut* ("cleaving"), achieved via intense prayer and joyous singing. The following parable illustrates how the Ba'al Shem Tov and the early Hassidic masters viewed what was missing in Jewish life:

> An apprentice blacksmith, after he had learned his trade from the master, made a list for himself of how he must go about his craft — how he should pump the bellows, secure the anvil, and wield the hammer. He omitted nothing. When he went to work at the king's palace, however, he discovered to his dismay that he could not perform his duties, and he was dismissed. He had forgotten to note one thing — perhaps because it was so obvious — that first he must ignite a spark to kindle the fire. He had to return to the master, who reminded him of the first principle which he had forgotten.[416]

Besides teaching how to turn on the fire of love for God, the Ba'al Shem Tov also taught that even the deeds of the simplest Jew, if performed correctly and sincerely, were equal to those of the greatest scholars.

The Hassidic brand of fervent spirituality caught on very rapidly — particularly among ordinary Jews. Soon, thousands upon thousands of Jews were drawn to the Hassidic Movement.

Hassidic Dynasties

When the Ba'al Shem Tov died in 1760, he was succeeded by Rabbi Dov Ber (1704–1772), known as the "Maggid of Mezritch," who further developed many of the Hassidic Movement's philosophies. Incidentally, the great psychologist Carl G. Jung, nearing his death, said that all of his advances in psychology were preempted by Rabbi Dov Ber, which says a lot about the Maggid's insights into human nature.[417]

Rabbi Dov Ber's disciples established different branches within the Hassidic Movement and founded their own dynasties. Of the many significant personalities in this group,[418] we will mention the two whose sects are the most well-known today due to the outreach work they do:

Rabbi Shneur Zalman of Liadi (1745–1812) was known as the "Alter Rebbe" or the "Ba'al HaTanya." He wrote the famous work, the *Tanya*, and founded the Lubavitch Hassidic sect, better known as Chabad, which is an acronym for *chochmah* ("wisdom"), *binah* ("understanding") and *da'at* ("knowledge"). According to Kabbalah, these are the three highest intellectual channels of divine energy, and the name hints how much the sect's teachings are steeped in Kabbalah.

Rabbi Nachman of Breslov (1772–1811) was the great-grandson of the Ba'al Shem Tov. He was a gifted storyteller and is perhaps best known for his allegorical tales of beggars and princes through which he tried to teach deep truths to simple people. He founded the Breslover sect of Hassidism.

Hassidic sects have names like Kotzk, Sanz, Belz, Satmar, Gur, Skver. These were all names of communities in places like Poland, Lithuania, and the Ukraine, where these sects were founded. When they moved away, they took their names with them. So today in Israel you have Kiryat Sanz, Kiryat Belz, etc. In New York, you have the New Square sect, which was the Skver sect, whose original name became anglicized to Square.

The Hassidic Movement had a huge impact and spiritually revitalized the Jewish world. It kept a lot of Jews Jewish and put a lot of joy back into Judaism. Writes Rabbi Aryeh Kaplan in *Chassidic Masters*:

> Hassidism uplifted the masses, but it would be wrong to suppose that its teachings were designed solely as a kind of spiritual medicine, necessary when one is ill, but of no value for the healthy. An important teaching of Hassidism is that its insights are important to the spiritual well-being of every Jew. Although its masters aimed much of their energies at helping poor, illiterate Jews, it would be incorrect to say that this was the main characteristic of Hassidism, since the movement also brought new vision and depth to the entire body of Jewish thought.[419]

The Opposition

As it spread, Hassidism also attracted tremendous opposition from those more intellectually-minded rabbis, the majority of whom were against the new movement. The key opponent was Rabbi Elijah ben Shlomo Zalman (1720–1797), known as the "Vilna Gaon" and also as the "Gra" (acronym for the Gaon Rabbi Elijah).

The Vilna Gaon was a brilliant scholar who had an enormous impact on Jewish learning. A person of wide-ranging interests and author of some seventy books on various subjects, the Vilna Gaon excelled in every aspect of scholarship. He knew Jewish law, Kabbalah, mathematics, astronomy, physics, anatomy. He barely slept; he just took short cat-naps throughout the day, and the rest of the time he studied. Whenever he got tired, he'd put his feet in a bucket of cold water to wake himself up. He never wanted to waste a minute. Although he never made it to Israel, he sent many of his students to live there.

What worried the Vilna Gaon was not so much the Kabbalistic aspects of Hassidism (after all, he himself had studied Kabbalah), but its potential for producing another false messiah (like Shabbetai Tzvi, whose story we covered in the previous chapter). The Vilna Gaon also objected to the Hassidic concept that God is "in all things" as too close to pantheism, the idea that everything is equally holy.[420] He was also concerned about the concept of the Rebbe (as the leader of each Hassidic sect was called), as it made each community extremely dependent on one person; he rejected the Hassidic maxim that an individual is elevated spiritually through attachment to a holy leader, because to him it resembled idolatry.

Another significant concern of the Vilna Gaon was de-intellectualization of Torah. The Hassidic Movement was largely composed of simple, uneducated Jews, and he worried that Jewish scholarship was going to be replaced by singing and dancing. A religion that was a synthesis of heart and mind would become all heart and no mind. Finally, the Vilna Gaon and other rabbis strongly objected to the fact that the Hassidic Movement had changed the text of some of the prayers. This was considered a serious break with tradition and, as such, was unacceptable.

The Vilna Gaon was so strongly opposed to the Hassidic Movement that he and others like him came to be called "*Mitnagdim*," which means "those who are against." In April of 1772, the Mitnagdim tried to excommunicate the Hassidim, but the ban did not succeed. The following is an excerpt from their excommunication decree:

> Our brethren, sons of Israel...as you know, new people have appeared, unimagined by our forefathers...and their ways are different from other children of Israel in their liturgy...they behave in a crazed manner and say that their thoughts wander in all worlds...And they belittle the study of the Torah, and repeatedly claim that one should not study much, nor deeply regret one's transgressions.... Therefore, we have come to inform our brethren, Children of Israel, from near and far...and to sound to them the voice of excommunication and banishment...until they themselves repent completely....[421]

While the creation of the Hassidic Movement did initially cause a split in the Jewish world, it did not lead to a real separation. Many of the fears of the Mitnagdim never materialized; for example, Hassidic sects today are quite intellectual and scholarship-minded, with their own yeshivas where the Talmud is studied intensely.

In hindsight, we see that the Hassidic Movement contributed significantly to the revitalization of Eastern European Jewry. It kept a lot of people connected to Judaism who might have been lost because they lacked the time, money, or opportunity to study. At the same time, the pressure brought by the opponents of Hassidism prevented it from going too far. As a result of the Hassidic contribution, Judaism became stronger and more ready to face the assault from a new secular movement in the Western world called "The Enlightenment."

52.
THE ENLIGHTENMENT

The middle of the seventeenth century marked the end of the Renaissance. The new ideology that emerged in the post-Renaissance period — what came to be known as the Enlightenment — is an ideology that still permeates the Western world to a large extent. We have to understand this ideology and the Jewish people's relationship to it in order to make sense out of what happened next in Jewish history.

The Enlightenment, spanning two hundred years from 1650–1850, was a period of time characterized by breakthroughs in thinking which steered the world away from religion and more and more toward secularism, humanism, individualism, rationalism, and nationalism. Of all of these, it was rationalism that, more than any other concept, defined the Enlightenment, which was also called the "Age of Reason."

In previous chapters, we spoke about how the Middle/Dark Ages were dominated by the Church and focused on God. Then came the Renaissance, and the focus shifted to man, with emphasis on the arts and classical knowledge. The Enlightenment sharpened this focus further. At this time the human mind, rational thought, and empirical sciences took center stage. It was an age devoted to the individual.

As a result, we will eventually see many positive ideas and institutions emerging: liberal democracy, the scientific revolution, industrialization. But the focus on man also led to ideological attacks against some of the fundamental institutions of the Western world, including religion. Religion was viewed by many Enlightenment thinkers as an intellectual failing that had been displaced by the ability of science to explain the unexplainable. Thus, a secular culture began to emerge as a very strong alternative to religion. The idea of a world without God took root, with big implications for Europe and the Jewish people.

As odd as it may sound, the less religious the Western world became, the better it treated the Jews. Christian fanatics killed Jews for various reasons as we have seen; the secularists, on the other hand, would do no such thing because the fact that a person was of a different religion did not matter to them. (What did matter more in this period was national, rather than religious identity.)

In tandem with secularism, the Enlightenment popularized the concept of individualism — each individual was valued and important, and along with this came an increased emphasis on civil rights.

On the surface, the emphasis on civil rights was good for the Jews. For the first time, the Western world started to look at the Jew as a human being. Edicts of toleration were issued, granting Jews certain basic (even if not equal) rights. One of the first such edicts, issued by the French National Assembly in 1791, stated:

> The National Assembly — considering that the conditions requisite to be a French Citizen and to become an active citizen are fixed by the constitution, and that every man who, being duly qualified, takes the civic oath and engages to fulfill the duties prescribed by the constitution has a right to all the advantages it insures — annuls all adjournments, restrictions and exceptions contained in the preceding decrees, affecting individuals of the Jewish persuasion, who shall take the civic oath....[422]

As nice as it sounded, problems associated with these ideas would surface, and Jews would again be the victims.

The Big Difference

The world without a God-given standard finds itself in trouble sooner or later. Judaism believes that for an ideal world there must be a focus on both God and man. Without a focus on God, all moral values become relative. Why is this bad? Well, for a while it might be nice to have respect for civil rights, but when it becomes convenient or necessary (for various social or political reasons) to change that focus, then respect for human life becomes just another idea that goes out of style. God-given values are immutable and can never go out of style. Big difference!

This big difference explains how a key figure of the French Enlightenment, Jean Jacques Rousseau — the author of the Social Contract who espoused that human beings are equal — could have been so inhuman to his own children. Rousseau's lofty ideas did not prevent him from practicing a modern version of infanticide by forcing the mother of his five children to drop her newborns on the doorstep of an orphanage where two-thirds of the children died within a year.[423]

Likewise, all the talk of equality of man did not prevent Francoise Voltaire from spewing out vicious anti-Semitic diatribes in his *Dictionnaire Philosophique* and singling out the Jews as "the most abominable people in the world." Although he did state that Jews ought not to be killed, he could not contain his hatred:

> In short we find them only ignorant and barbarous people with long united and most sordid avarice with the most detestable superstition and the most invincible hatred of every people by whom they are tolerated....[424]

In contrast to France, the situation was very different in England (where the Puritan Revolution had a big influence) and in the New World, where, again, the Puritans figured prominently. The American Revolution highlights the synthesis of very religious, Bible-based ideas brought over by the pilgrims and the humanist ideas (such as "the inalienable rights of man") advanced by John Locke. We see this clearly in the opening sentences of the Declaration of Independence:

> We hold these truths to be self evident that all men are created equal, that they are endowed by their Creator with certain inalienable rights, that among them are life, liberty and the pursuit of happiness.

The French Revolution did not have this synthesis. It was purely a secular movement. And it made very apparent the holes in the Enlightenment philosophy.

The French reformers, after executing the king and queen, Louis XVI and his wife Marie Antoinette, by guillotine, unleashed the Reign of Terror, during which 25,000 "counter-revolutionaries" were executed in a similarly bloody manner.

The Reign of Terror, for all practical purposes, ended the Age of Reason. The bloody brutality of the masses shocked much of the world and severely tested the Enlightenment's belief that mankind could govern itself. A period of general unrest followed in France, marked by corruption, runaway inflation, and war with neighboring European states. All of it crashed when Napoleon Bonaparte came to power in a *coup d'etat* of 1804.

Napoleon and the Jews

Shortly after assuming power, Napoleon Bonaparte (1769–1821), a Corsican officer, had himself crowned Emperor of France. During his ten-year reign, he embarked on a series of conquests which were unprecedented in modern history in terms of his rapid advance through Europe. A military genius, he took France on the offensive against the Austrian Empire, against the Italians and against the Russians. And he almost beat all of them, becoming the master of the Continent and rearranging the whole map of Europe.

(What brought him down was the fury of the Russian winter, and once other European countries saw that he was vulnerable, they joined forces and defeated him, first at Leipzig in 1813 and finally at Waterloo in 1815. Exiled as a prisoner of war to the island of Saint Helena, he died there either of cancer or by poisoning in 1821.)

As Napoleon marched through Europe, he liberated all the Jews from their ghettos. The idea of liberating the Jews and granting them civil rights had preceded him, but he really advanced it.

Napoleon was fascinated with the Jews, although he did not understand them. He wanted them to be integrated into the rest of European society, and he assumed that they were not because they were different — he reasoned that if they became like others, they would be accepted. So, he set about helping the Jews rid themselves of the customs that set them apart. He advocated, for example, that one-third of all Jews must intermarry with non-Jews. His actions seemed more motivated by his desire to improve the position of the Jews of France rather than his desire, if any, to preserve Judaism. He is quoted as saying:

> I will never accept any proposals that will obligate the Jewish people to leave France, because to me the Jews are the same as any other citizen in our country. It takes weakness to chase them out of the country, but it takes strength to assimilate them.[425]

Twice, in 1806 and in 1807, Napoleon convened gatherings of prominent Jewish leaders to promote his platform for "saving" the Jews. Here are some excerpts from Napoleon's Instructions to the Assembly of Jewish Notables (July 29, 1806):

> The wish of His Majesty is that you should be Frenchmen; it remains with you to accept the proffered title.... You will hear the questions submitted to you, your duty is to answer the whole truth on every one of

> them.... Is divorce valid, when not pronounced by courts of justice, and by virtue of laws in contradiction with the French code? Can a Jewess marry a Christian, or a Jew a Christian woman?... In the eyes of Jews are Frenchmen considered as brethren or as strangers? Do the Jews born in France and treated by the law as French citizens consider France as their country?... What kind of police jurisdiction have the rabbis among the Jews?[426]

The focus of these questions is obvious. Napoleon was asking the Jews to answer the great question that came out of emancipation: What is your primary identity? Are you first and foremost Jews or Frenchmen?

Jewish religious leaders were astonished by these questions. On the one hand, they wanted to cooperate with Napoleon and make life easier for the Jews of Europe. On the other hand, they could not possibly acquiesce to some of Napoleon's ideas which would have meant the destruction of Judaism. They answered him as diplomatically as possible, while adhering to Jewish Law:

> The only marriages expressly forbidden by the [Jewish] law are those with the seven Canaanite nations, with Amon and Moab, and with Egyptians.... The prohibition in general applies only to nations in idolatry. The Talmud declares formally that modern nations are not to be considered as such, since they worship, like us, the God of heaven and earth. And, accordingly, there have been, at several periods, intermarriage between Jew and Christians in France, in Spain, and in Germany...but we cannot deny that the opinion of the rabbis is against these marriages.[427]

Although Napoleon lost his wars in the end and ended up in exile, what he put in motion had a huge ripple effect. By the end of the nineteenth century the notion of keeping Jews as non-citizens was no longer tenable in the more liberal environment in Europe.[428]

With time, Jews were granted citizenship in every country in Europe. Interestingly, the last two countries to grant Jews citizenship were Switzerland (1874) and Spain (1918).

By the late nineteenth century, Jews — who had been economically and physically marginalized, and who had been locked out of trades and professions — were allowed (if not exactly welcomed) into all phases of European society.

Does that mean that the Enlightenment put an end to anti-Semitism?

Hardly.

It merely intellectualized it.

The New Anti-Semitism

Once the gates of the ghettos were thrown open, the Jews rose to the top quickly, gaining prominence and wealth. Despite their achievements, however, they were not generally accepted into society. Times had changed, but not that much.

It is true that in Western Europe in the nineteenth century, there were no pogroms against the Jews. The post-Enlightenment society did not behave that way, at least not in Western Europe. (We will talk about Eastern Europe and particularly Russia soon.)

But just because there were no pogroms doesn't mean that the non-Jews suddenly began to love the Jews. Anti-Semitism persisted, though it was of the intellectual rather than the emotional/physical variety.

In practice it meant that people like Baron Lionel Rothschild — one of the most prominent and richest Jews in England — could not take a seat in the British Parliament after his election in 1847 because he refused to take an oath on the Christian Bible. It took eleven years and the passing of the "Jewish Disabilities Act" for him to have that right. (He became the first Jewish member of the British Parliament in 1858.)

In theory Jews had equal rights, but in practice the story was very different. Many Jews saw conversion as the best way to advancement in enlightened Europe. A classic example was Benjamin Disraeli, who was twice the Prime Minister of England during the reign of Queen Victoria, and was only able to achieve that position because his family had converted to the Church of England.

This attitude toward conversion was best summed up by the German Jewish writer Heinrich Heine, whose original name was Chayim and who was baptized as a Lutheran in 1825:

> From the nature of my thinking you can deduce that baptism is a matter of indifference to me, that I do not regard it as important even symbolically. The baptism certificate is the ticket of admission to European culture....[429]

So yes, Jews were accepted into society as long as they were not "too Jewish." If a Jew was willing to compromise himself by taking an oath on the Christian Bible, or better yet, by eschewing his religion, he was tolerated. If he insisted on being true to the Torah, he was excluded.

(In the next chapter, we will examine one attempt of the Jews of Germany to circumvent this problem when we look at the beginnings of the Reform Movement within Judaism.)

It is interesting to note that, during this time of unprecedented toleration, the term "anti-Semitism" was first coined. It was the product of one of German's most prominent thinkers of the nineteenth century — Wilhelm Marr — who wanted to distinguish hatred of the Jews as members of a religion (anti-Judaism) from hatred of the Jews as members of a race/nation (anti-Semitism). After Darwin, racial thinking was popular, and Marr wanted to underscore the racial characteristics of the Jews. In 1879, he wrote a runaway bestseller called *The Victory of Judaism over Germandom* that was reprinted twelve times in six years. (Later, Hitler took Marr's idea to its fatal and logical conclusion: conversion doesn't help because it can't alter Jewish blood.)

Another important thinker was Karl Eugen Duehring, who in 1881 wrote *The Question of the Jew is a Question of Race*, in which he summed up what this kind of anti-Semitism meant:

> The Jewish question would still exist even if every Jew were to turn his back on his religion and join one of our major churches. Yes, I maintain that in that case the struggle between us and the Jews would make itself felt even more urgent. It is precisely the baptized Jew who infiltrates furthermost, unhindered in all sectors of society and political life. I return, therefore, to the hypothesis that the Jews are to be defined solely on the basis of race and not on the basis of religion.[430]

Jews who were dropping their religion and rising to power, wealth, and prominence did not pay enough attention to these ideas. If they had, they would have realized that their joy-ride was going to be a short one. Even if Jews escaped anti-Judaism by becoming Christian or secular, or even if they refashioned themselves to blend in, anti-Semitism — which didn't care what they believed or how they behaved as long as they were Jews — would bring them down in the end.

53.
THE REFORM MOVEMENT

As we saw in the previous chapter, the Enlightenment gave Jews new rights — human rights and civil rights — which they never had before. After centuries of physical and economic marginalization, the intoxicating allure of emancipation proved overwhelming attractive to many Jews in Western Europe. Many were anxious to prove their loyalty to their host country, and the best way to do this was to join the army, which for centuries had been closed to Jews. In Prussia and later Germany, disproportionately large numbers of Jews volunteered for military service. To quote David Friedlander, a Jewish volunteer in the Prussian army during the Napoleonic wars:

> [It was] a heavenly feeling to possess a fatherland! What rapture to be able to call a spot, a place, a nook one's own upon this lovely earth.... Hand in hand with your fellow soldiers you will complete the great task; they will not deny you the title of brother, for you will have earned it.[431]

Thanks to the new broadmindedness, Jews were even accepted into "polite society" as long as they were not "too Jewish" — as long as they didn't dress too differently, behave too differently, eat a different diet, or insist on wearing their "old-fashioned" religion on their sleeve.

The reaction to this from some Jews was a staunch refusal to get with the plan — in any way, shape, or form. But there was also the opposite reaction from others. These Jews went along with the spirit of liberation and modernity and abandoned what made them different from other people — such as keeping kosher, keeping Shabbat, etc.

Of course, as soon as Jews drop their religion, they begin to assimilate. Intermarriage rates climbed dramatically. In Germany, for example, the rate rose from 8.4 percent in 1901 to 30 percent by 1915.[432] About a quarter of a million Jews converted to Christianity during this time and countless others assimilated into the European culture.

Interestingly, the assimilation rate was higher where there were fewer Jews. In Eastern Europe, where the Jewish population was almost 5 million, 90,000 (or not quite 2%) converted to Christianity in order to have an easier life and mingle with mainstream society. But in Western Europe, where there were fewer Jews, the proportion was much higher. The majority of the Jews of France assimilated, as did the majority of the Jews of Italy and Germany.

Why? Because in Western Europe, the governments were more liberal and open, Jews were granted citizenship and non-Jews were generally less hostile, so the attraction to assimilate and join the mainstream was much greater.

Some Jewish converts to Christianity were very famous. Earlier we mentioned Benjamin Disraeli, the British Prime Minister who became the great architect of Victorian imperialism. But we must also mention Karl Marx, "the Father of Communism."

Marx was converted by his father at age six; his father himself had converted a few years earlier in order to be able to practice law. Marx, who eventually became an atheist, is the author of *The Communist Manifesto* and *Das Kapital*, ironically called the "Bible of the Worker." He is also famous for calling religion "the opiate of the masses."

A terrible example of a self-hating Jew, Marx blamed the world's problems on the Jews in his rage-filled *A World Without Jews*. Virulent hatred of Judaism and of other Jews was not uncommon with such converts. It infected, among others, Heinrich Heine, one of the most prominent figures in nineteenth century German literature, who called Judaism one of the world's three greatest evils (along with poverty and pain).

German Reform

One of the more dramatic reactions to the changes of this time period came from a group of German Jews who formed what became known as the Reform Movement.

The German Jews who began the Reform Movement in the early 1800s wanted to maintain some kind of connection to Judaism, but at the same time, they wanted to take advantage of the newly won rights and freedoms, which were available only if one became a full-fledged member of European society. Traditional Jewish lifestyle and national identity were viewed as barriers to this acculturation. So, these German Jews decided to eliminate some key aspects of Judaism, the most dramatic of which was the belief that the Torah was given to Jews by God at Mount Sinai.

For 3,000 years Jews never questioned that the Torah came from God. The various sects that appeared — such as the Sadducees and the Karaites — questioned the Oral Law or rabbinic law, but never the divine origin of the Torah. This was an earth-shattering precedent.

The first crack in the dam came from Moses Mendelssohn (1729–1786), a brilliant intellect who was known as the "hunchback philosopher." Although an observant Jew in terms of his lifestyle, he advocated the "rational" approach to religion, as he wrote in his *Judaism as Revealed Legislation*:

> Religious doctrines and propositions...are not forced upon the faith of a nation under the threat of eternal or temporal punishment but in accordance with the nature and evidence of eternal truths recommended to rational acknowledgment. The Supreme Being has revealed them to all rational creatures.

In effect, Mendelssohn was following the pattern of the thinkers of the Enlightenment, the "Age of Reason." Religion should be rational. If the law of God seems irrational, then man must follow reason. (Mendelssohn's children were not observant and within a few generations they had either assimilated or converted. Mendelssohn's grandson, the famous German composer, Felix Mendelssohn-Bartholdy, was baptized as a child by his assimilated parents.)

By exposing Judaism to this kind of skepticism, Mendelssohn opened the door through which others rushed in.

This is not to suggest that before him Judaism was closed to inquiry. Indeed, asking questions was always a big part of Judaism, but this type of questioning was grounded in certain beliefs and assumptions, which in the Reform Movement came tumbling down.

The first Reform service was conducted in 1810 by Israel Jacobson in his school chapel in Seesen, Germany, and his model was adopted by the first Reform synagogue — the New Israelite Temple — which opened in Hamburg in 1818.

This Reform service — in imitation of a German Protestant service — had a choir, robes, and an organ; it was conducted in German with German songs and German prayers in a deliberate attempt to emphasize nationalistic loyalty and identity. Here are excerpts from the constitution of the Hamburg synagogue:

> The worship service shall be conducted on Sabbath and holy days... Specifically, there shall be introduced at such services a German sermon and choral singing to the accompaniment of an organ...as shall apply to all those religious customs...which are sanctified by the Church.[433]

For Jews, this was quite a departure. Until then, Jews prayed in Hebrew, reciting the prayers composed by the Men of the Great Assembly and the Sanhedrin some 2,000 years earlier. Jews never played musical instruments during services, and certainly not an organ which was an instrument common to Christian churches.

Not long after, the Reform Movement went even further, as many of its congregations switched Shabbat from Jewish Saturday to Christian Sunday. And they made a point of calling their synagogues "temples," to emphasize that Reform Jews no longer looked to the rebuilding of the Temple in Jerusalem. In fact, Reform leader Samuel Holdheim (1806–1860), who became the head of the Reform congregation in Berlin, argued against the mention of Jerusalem, Zion, or the Land of Israel during services. He opposed circumcision, wearing of skullcaps or prayer shawls, or the blowing of the ram's horn (shofar) — in short, just about anything traditionally Jewish.

Another Reform leader, Abraham Geiger (1810–1874), who led Reform groups in Breslau, Frankfurt and Berlin, called circumcision "a barbaric act of blood-letting" and advocated against "the automatic assumption of solidarity with Jews everywhere."

These were big breaks with tradition. Ever since Abraham, circumcision was the way Jews marked their covenant with God. And Jews helping each other in times of trouble — one for all and all for one — was seen as an integral part of Jewish nature as defined by God (as we saw in chapter 14).

And then, the Reform Jews of Germany declared that they were not members of the nation of Israel; they stopped calling themselves Jews and adopted the name "Germans of the Mosaic persuasion."

The philosophy of the German Reform Movement evolved at conferences held in Brunswick in 1844 and in Frankfurt in 1845. These excerpts from conference speeches vividly illustrate how much the Jews of Germany wanted to demonstrate allegiance to their country of residence, which meant disavowing any allegiance to the Land of Israel and their people:

From the Reform Rabbinic Conference in Brunswick, 1844:

> For Judaism, the principal of human dignity is cosmopolitan, but I would like to put proper emphasis on the love of the particular people [among

> whom we live] and its individual members. As men, we love all mankind, but as Germans, we love the Germans as the children of the fatherland. We are, and ought to be patriots, not merely cosmopolitan.[434]

From the Reform Rabbinic Conference in Frankfurt, 1845:

> By considering the Hebrew [language] as being of central importance to Judaism, moreover, one would define it as a national religion, because a separate language is a characteristic element of a separate nation. But no member of this conference, the speaker concluded, would wish to link Judaism to a particular nation....
>
> The hope for national restoration contradicts our feelings for the fatherland.... The wish to return to Palestine in order to create there a political empire is superfluous.... But Messianic hope, truly understood is religious.... This latter religious hope can be renounced only by those who have a more sublime conception of Judaism, and who believe that the fulfillment of Judaism's mission is not dependent on the establishment of a Jewish state, but rather by the merging of Jewry into the political constellation of the fatherland. Only an enlightened conception of religion can replace a dull one.... This is the difference between strict Orthodoxy and Reform — both approach Judaism from a religious standpoint, but while the former [Orthodox] aims at restoration of the old political order, the latter [Reform] aims at the closest possible union with the political and national union of our times....[435]

The Orthodox

Along the way, the members of Reform Movement coined a new term to describe those who adhered to traditional Judaism — they called them "the Orthodox," implying that observant Jews were a relic of the past, as opposed to "the Reform" who were forward-thinking, modern, and progressive.

In places where the Reform Movement succeeded in attracting the majority of Jews, it did its best to force its agenda on the minority. In Frankfurt, for example, the *mikveh* (the ritual pool) was closed, kosher slaughter was banned, the teaching of the Talmud was forbidden. The Orthodox Jews were basically run out of town. In Frankfurt am Main, one of the oldest Jewish communities in Europe, only about 100 observant families remained by the middle of the nineteenth century.

Why? Because the German Reformers hoped to assimilate into the larger German culture. But, as long as there continued to exist a group of Jews who chose to openly identify as Jews — that is, to be Jews who irked the Germans — they would all lumped together in the eyes of anti-Semites.[436]

Of course, the Jews who would not go along with the Reform Movement weren't about to take all this sitting down.

The leader of the Orthodox counterattack against the Reform Movement was a rabbi by the name of Samson Raphael Hirsch (1808–1888). Born in Hamburg, he attended the University of Bonn and served as the chief rabbi of Moravia, a community of 50,000 Jews. He published several well-known works, such as *Horeb*, in which he sought to demonstrate the viability of traditional Judaism in the modern world.

In 1851 he moved to Frankfurt am Main, to serve as rabbi of the shrinking community and to wage a philosophical counteroffensive to the Reform Movement. As part of his fight he succeeded in setting up his own Orthodox institution in Frankfurt, called the Kahal Adas Yeshurin, and he created his own religious school system.

Rabbi Hirsch's aim was to show those Jews who wanted to be "modern" that it was possible within the context of traditional Judaism. There was no need to drop Torah in order to live in an evolving world, as the Torah makes provisions for that. This is what he wrote in 1854 in an article entitled "Religion Allied to Progress":

> Now what is it that we want? Are the only alternatives either to abandon religion or to renounce all progress? We declare before heaven and earth that if our religion demanded that we should renounce what is called civilization and progress, we would obey unquestioningly because our religion is for us the word of God before which every other consideration has to give way. There is, however, no such dilemma. Judaism never remained aloof from true civilization and progress. In almost every area, its adherents were fully abreast of contemporary learning and very often excelled their contemporaries. An excellent thing is the study of Torah combined with the ways of the world.[437]

Rabbi Hirsch emphasized that the normal Jewish way is to be fully in the world, but also to be fully immersed in Torah. It is not a question of "either Torah or the world" rather, it's a question of priorities. He made it very clear that the first priority is Torah. In contrast to Mendelssohn, he said that even if you don't understand some part of the Torah, you have to follow it anyway because it is the word of God.[438]

Despite the efforts of Rabbi Hirsch and others, the Reform Movement spread, not just inside Germany but to other countries as well, though each group of Reformers had its own take on it. For example, the Reform Jews of England in the West London Synagogue adopted a quasi-Karaite position. They respected the Torah as the word of God, but rejected the teachings of the Talmud.

In America, the Reform Movement also took on its character after it was transplanted there from Germany by several hundred thousand German immigrants in the mid-nineteenth century. We will take a look at it as we take up the story of Jewish life in America.

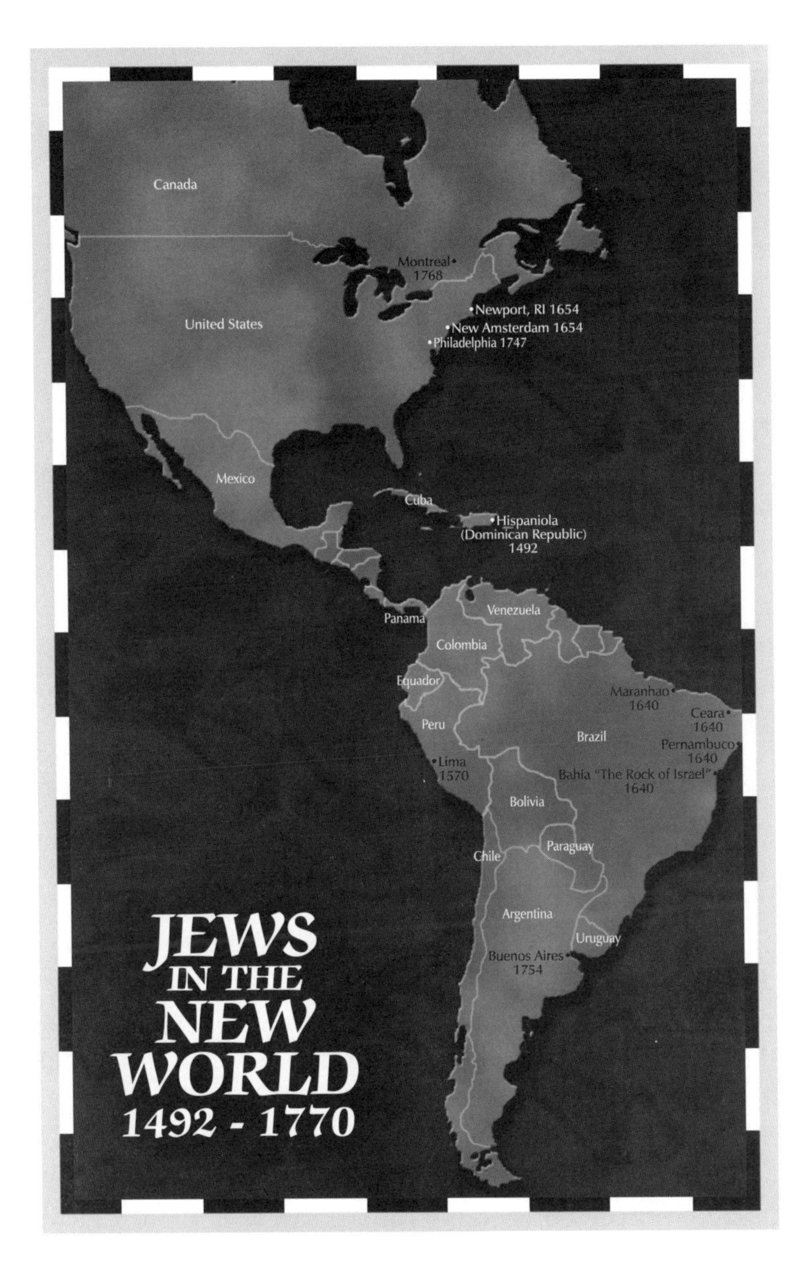

54.
JEWS AND THE FOUNDING OF AMERICA

The creation of the United States of America represented a unique event in world history. Founded as a modern republic, it was rooted in the Bible, and one of its earliest tenets was religious tolerance. Of course, this was because many of the earliest pilgrims who settled the "New England" of America in the early seventeenth century were Puritan refugees escaping religious persecutions in Europe.

These Puritans viewed their emigration from England as a virtual reenactment of the Exodus. To them, England was Egypt, the king was the Pharaoh, the Atlantic Ocean was the Red Sea, America was the Land of Israel, and the Indians were the ancient Canaanites. They were the new Israelites, entering into a new covenant with God in a new Promised Land.

Thanksgiving — first celebrated in 1621, a year after the *Mayflower* landed — was initially conceived as a day parallel to the Jewish Day of Atonement, Yom Kippur; it was to be a day of fasting, introspection, and prayer. Writes Gabriel Sivan in *The Bible and Civilization*:

> No Christian community in history identified more with the People of the Book than did the early settlers of the Massachusetts Bay Colony, who believed their own lives to be a literal reenactment of the biblical drama of the Hebrew nation...these émigré Puritans dramatized their own situation as the righteous remnant of the Church corrupted by the "Babylonian woe" and saw themselves as instruments of divine

> Providence, a people chosen to build their new commonwealth on the Covenant entered into at Mount Sinai.[439]

Previously, during the Puritan Revolution in England (which took place between 1642 and 1648), some Puritan extremists had even sought to replace English Common Law with biblical laws of the Old Testament, but they were prevented from doing so. In America, however, there was far more freedom to experiment with the use of biblical law in the legal codes of the colonies, and this was exactly what the pilgrims set out to do.

The earliest legislation of the colonies of New England was all determined by the Bible. For example, at the first assembly of New Haven in 1639, John Davenport clearly emphasized the primacy of the Bible as the legal and moral foundation of the colony:

> Scriptures do hold forth a perfect rule for the direction and government of all men in all duties which they are to perform to God and men as well as in the government of families and commonwealth as in matters of the Church...the Word of God shall be the only rule to be attended unto in organizing the affairs of government in this plantation.[440]

Subsequently, the New Haven legislators adopted a legal code — the Code of 1655 — which contained some seventy-nine statutes, half of which included biblical references, virtually all from the Hebrew Bible. The Plymouth Colony had a similar law code as did the Massachusetts assembly, which adopted in 1641 the so-called Capitall Laws of New England, based almost entirely on Mosaic law.

Of course, without a Jewish Oral Tradition, which helped the Jews understand the Bible, the Puritans were left to their own devices and tended toward a literal interpretation. This led in some instances to a stricter, more fundamentalist observance than Judaism had ever seen.

Jewish Symbolism in America

The Hebrew Bible also played a central role in the founding of various educational institutions, including Harvard, Yale, William and Mary, Rutgers, Princeton, Brown, King's College (later to be known as Columbia), Johns Hopkins, Dartmouth, etc. In virtually all of these colleges, Bible studies were required, and some even incorporated Hebrew words or phrases in their official emblem or seal. Beneath the banner containing the Latin *Lux et Veritas*, the Yale seal shows an open book with the Hebrew *Urim V'Tumim*, a part of the breastplate of the High Priest in the days of the Temple. The Columbia seal has the Hebrew name for God at the top center, with the Hebrew name for one of the angels on a banner toward the middle. Dartmouth uses the Hebrew words meaning "God Almighty" in a triangle in the upper center of its seal.

So popular was the Hebrew language in the late sixteenth and early seventeenth centuries that Harvard, Yale, Columbia, Brown, Princeton, Johns Hopkins, and the University of Pennsylvania taught courses in Hebrew — all the more remarkable because no university in England at the time offered such courses — and students had the option of delivering commencement speeches in Hebrew, Latin, or Greek.[441]

Many of the Founding Fathers of America were products of these universities — for example, Thomas Jefferson attended William and Mary, James Madison attended Princeton, and Alexander Hamilton attended King's College. Thus, we can be sure that most of these political leaders were not only well acquainted with the contents of the Bible, but also had a working knowledge of Hebrew. Notes Abraham Katsch in *The Biblical Heritage of American Democracy:*

> At the time of the American Revolution, the interest in the knowledge of Hebrew was so widespread as to allow the circulation of the story that "certain members of Congress proposed that the use of English be formally prohibited in the United States, and Hebrew substituted for it."[442]

Their biblical education colored the American founders' attitude toward not only religion and ethics, but most significantly, politics. We see them adopting the biblical motifs of the Puritans for political reasons. For example, the struggle of the ancient Hebrews against the wicked Pharaoh came to embody the struggle of the colonists against English tyranny. Numerous examples can be found which clearly illustrate to the extent to which political struggles of the colonies were identified with the ancient Hebrews:

- The first design for the official seal of the United States recommended by Benjamin Franklin, John Adams, and Thomas Jefferson in 1776 depicted the Jews crossing the Red Sea. The motto around the seal read: "Resistance to Tyrants is Obedience to God."
- The inscription on the Liberty Bell at Independence Hall in Philadelphia was a direct quote from the Book of Leviticus: "Proclaim liberty throughout the land unto all the inhabitants thereof."[443]
- Patriotic speeches and publications during the period of the struggle for independence were often infused with biblical quotations.

The basic framework of American governance clearly reflects the influence of the Bible and power of Jewish ideas in shaping the country's political development. Nowhere is this more evident than in the opening sentences of the Declaration of Independence:

> We hold these truths to be self-evident, that all men are created equal, that they are endowed by their Creator with certain unalienable rights, that among these are life, liberty and the pursuit of happiness.

Although these words echo the ideas of the Enlightenment, without a doubt, the concept that these rights come from God is of biblical origin.

This and the other documents of early America make it clear that the concept of a God-given standard of morality is a central pillar of American democracy. The motto IN GOD WE TRUST first appeared on U.S. currency in 1864 and a later Act of Congress made it the official motto of the United States.

Many more things can be said about the Jewish influence on the values of America, but this is, after all, a crash course. We next turn to the Jews themselves.

Early American Jews

The history of Jews in America begins before the United States was an independent country.

The first Jews arrived in America with Columbus in 1492, and we also know that Jews newly converted to Christianity were among the first Spaniards to arrive in Mexico with Conquistador Hernando Cortez in 1519. In fact, so many Jewish conversos came to Mexico that the Spanish made a rule precluding entry to anyone who could not prove Catholic ancestry going back four generations. Needless to say, the Inquisition soon followed, to make sure Jewish conversos were not really heretics, and burnings at the stake became a regular feature of life in Mexico City.

As for North America, recorded Jewish history there begins in 1654 with the arrival in New Amsterdam (later to be known as New York) of twenty-three Jewish refugees from Recife, Brazil (where the Dutch had just lost their possessions to the Portuguese). New Amsterdam was also a Dutch possession, but the governor, Peter Stuyvesant, did not want them there. Writes Arthur Hertzberg in *The Jews in America*:

> Two weeks after they landed, Stuyvesant heard the complaint from the

> local merchants and from the Church that "the Jews who had arrived would nearly all like to remain here." Stuyvesant decided to chase them out. Using the usual formulas of religious invective — he called the Jews "repugnant," "deceitful," and "enemies and blasphemers of Christ" — Stuyvesant recommended to his directors..."to require them in a friendly way to depart."[444]

The only reasons the Jews were not forced to leave was that the Dutch West Indian Company, which was heavily dependent on Jewish investments, intervened.

By 1776 and the War of Independence, there were an estimated 2,000 (mostly Sephardic) Jewish men, women, and children living in America. And, although their numbers were relatively small, their contribution to the cause was significant. For example, in Charleston, South Carolina, almost every adult Jewish male fought on the side of freedom. In Georgia, the first patriot to be killed was a Jew (Francis Salvador). Additionally, the Jews provided significant financing to the patriots.

The most important of the financiers was Haym Salomon, who loaned a great deal of money to the Continental Congress. In the last days of the war, Salomon advanced the American government $200,000. He was never paid back and died bankrupt.

President George Washington remembered the Jewish contribution when the first synagogue opened in Newport, Rhode Island, in 1790. (It was called the Touro Synagogue and it was Sephardic.) He sent this letter, dated August 17, 1790: "May the children of the stock of Abraham who dwell in the land continue to merit and enjoy the goodwill of the other inhabitants. While everyone shall sit safely under his own vine and fig tree and there shall be none to make him afraid."

Note the reference to the "vine and fig tree." That unique phrase is a reference to the words of prophet Micah, prophesying the Messianic utopia:

> But in the last days it shall come to pass that the mountain of the house of the Lord shall be established in the top of the mountains, and it shall be exalted above the hills; and people shall flow to it. And many nations shall come, and say, "Come, and let us go up to the mountain of the Lord, and to the house of the God of Jacob, and He will teach us of His ways, and we will walk in His paths, for Torah shall go forth from Zion, and the word of the Lord from Jerusalem." And He shall judge between many peoples and shall decide concerning far away strong nations; and

> they shall beat their swords into plowshares, and their spears into pruning hooks; nation shall not lift up sword against nation, nor shall they learn war any more. But they shall sit every man under his vine and under his fig tree; and none shall make them afraid; for the mouth of the Master of Legions has spoken it.[445]

This interesting choice of words by Washington is not surprising considering the enormous influence the Hebrew Bible had on the pilgrims as well as on the founding fathers of the new nation.

It should be noted, however, that some of the other founding fathers were a bit more ambivalent about the Jews than was Washington.

John Adams, who made some highly complimentary comments about the Jews,[446] also noted that "it is very hard work to love most of them." Furthermore, he looked forward to the day when "the asperities and peculiarities of their character" would be worn away, and they would become "liberal Unitarian Christians."

Thomas Jefferson thought Jews needed more secular learning so that "they will become equal object of respect and favor," implying that without such learning they could not expect to be respected. Writes Arthur Hertzberg in *The Jews in America*:

> Jefferson was thus expressing the view of the mainstream of the Enlightenment, that all men could attain equal place in society, but the "entrance fee" was that they should adopt the ways and the outlook of the "enlightened." Jefferson did not consider that a Yiddish-speaking Jew who knew the Talmud was equal in usefulness to society with a classically trained thinker like himself.[447]

This idea that there was freedom in America as long as you were not "too Jewish," kept most Jews away. Until 1820, the Jewish population of America was only about 6,000!

This changed in the 1830s, when Reform German Jews who had scrapped traditional Judaism and were not "too Jewish," began to arrive. The great migrations of poor, oppressed Jews from Eastern Europe would follow near the turn of the century. But before we take up that story, we must look to see what was happening to the Jews of Europe.

55.
PALE OF SETTLEMENT

The Enlightenment, which emancipated the Jews of Western Europe, did not quite reach Eastern Europe, where most Jews lived in the eighteenth and nineteenth centuries. The largest concentration of Jews was then located there — about 5 million, which represented 40 percent of the Jewish population worldwide.

From 1791 until 1915, the Jews living in Eastern Europe were largely confined by the Czars of Russia — starting with Catherine the Great — to an area known as the Pale of Settlement (meaning "borders of settlement").

The Pale consisted of twenty-five provinces that included Ukraine, Lithuania, Belorussia, Crimea, and the eastern side of Poland, which had been partitioned between Russia, Prussia, and Austria and ceased to exist as a country in 1772. The western side of what had formally been Poland was absorbed into the Austro-Hungarian Empire; it contained important Jewish communities (such as those located in Galicia) and not an insignificant number of Jews. The physical and economic situation of the Jews of the Austro-Hungarian Empire was generally much better than that of their fellow Jews living in Czarist Russia. The Jews of Russia were specifically expelled from Moscow and St. Petersburg and forced into the Pale. Later, they were also expelled from rural areas within the Pale and forced to live only in shtetls.

Despite the oppression, some amazing things happened in the Pale.

For one thing, charity — *tzedakah*, which in Hebrew means "justice" — thrived, as Jews helped each other. The historian Martin Gilbert writes in his *Atlas of Jewish History* that no province in the Pale had less than 14 percent of Jews on relief, and Lithuanian and Ukrainian Jews supported as much as 22 percent of their poor population:

> Among the charitable societies organized by Jews were those to supply poor students with clothes, soldiers with kosher food, the poor with free medical treatment, poor brides with dowries and orphans with technical education.[448]

This was an incredibly sophisticated social welfare system. In times of great hardship, no Jew was abandoned.

Such caring for each other did not escape the notice of non-Jews, and converts had to be turned away. In fact, as far back as the Middle Ages, rabbis had instituted *takanot* (rabbinic enactments) which forbade conversion to Judaism.[449] The primary fear was that there would be an anti-Semitic backlash against the Jews for "stealing" a Christian from his faith, but there was also another reason — concern about conversions motivated solely by the benefits of the Jewish welfare system. Why would a Christian want to convert to Judaism, which could possibly lead to arrest and execution? Because they realized that no Jew ever starved to death in the street, whereas if you were a Christian peasant you could easily starve to death in the street because no one was going to take care of you. The government wasn't going to do it, and the Church wasn't going to do it. So, the rabbis took measures to prevent a flood of such insincere conversions.

Torah Learning

Another amazing thing that happened in the Pale, despite the oppression, was the creation of the modern yeshiva.

Torah study (as we saw in chapter 51) had become a preserve of the elite in the eighteenth century; it was a "luxury" generally unavailable to the masses of Eastern European Jewry. But, in 1803, Rabbi Chaim ben Isaac of Volozhin (1749–1821), a student of the Vilna Gaon, set about to revolutionize the concept of the yeshiva and make it open to any Jew independent of his ability to pay.

Most yeshivas during this period were small institutions of learning, supported by individual towns in which they were based. Rabbi Chaim proposed the establishment of a large institution for top students supported by many communities. He sent letters to the chief rabbis of cities throughout Europe, asking them to send to him their best students to study at his yeshiva in Volozhin, Lithuania, where he promised to provide them with financial support, top teachers, and a high-level standardized curriculum. The response to his letter was very positive and many students were sent to the Volozhin Yeshiva.[450]

Unfortunately, the Volozhin Yeshiva didn't last too long, as the Czarist government of Russia saw what was going on and tried to force it to adopt a more secular curriculum as part of making it less Jewish. It was closed by the Czarist government in 1879 and reopened in 1881. While the Volozhin Yeshiva was able to yield to some of the demands of the Czarist government, the requirement that all faculty members have diplomas from recognized Russian educational institutions in order to teach "Russian language and culture" was not acceptable. And so, the yeshiva was closed again in 1892 by Russian inspectors, with its students exiled.

Although it had been in operation less than 100 years, it had become the model and inspiration for the modern yeshiva. By the time Volozhin Yeshiva closed for good, other yeshivas based on its model were already in operation, many started by students of Volozhin. A letter written in 1865 by Rabbi David Moses of Krynki, a former student of Volozhin, attests to the greatness of Rabbi Chaim and the yeshiva he founded:

> The yeshiva of Volozhin is the mother and source of all the yeshivas and Talmud Torahs in the world. The latter are as pipes which come from the source.... Before our holy rabbi [Rabbi Chaim] founded the "house of God," the world was empty, literally without form; it was void, for even the term yeshiva was unknown, let alone what activities took place in one.... Were it not for the fact that our holy rabbi founded his yeshiva, the Torah would have (God forbid) been forgotten to Israel.[450]

Another major educational innovation of the period was the founding of the Beis Yacov School for girls. The school was founded by Sarah Schenirer in Krakow, Poland in 1918 and later developed into a large education network that spread to both America and Israel.

The Mussar Movement

During the era that saw the rebirth of Torah studies, there arose in the Pale a new emphasis on what should be the primary focus of those studies. The impetus came from a very important development within Judaism called the "Mussar (Ethical) Movement." Its founder was a most unusual man, Rabbi Israel Lipkin of Salant (1810–1883), better known as Rabbi Israel Salanter.

Many stories are told about his goodness. Among the most famous is the story of his disappearance from his synagogue one Yom Kippur. As the congregation fretted for his safety, delaying services until he arrived, one young mother took the opportunity to rush back home to check on her baby, whom she had left alone. There, she found the rabbi, rocking the cradle. Hearing the baby crying, he had stopped to comfort it, putting the needs of another human being ahead of his personal spiritual fulfillment.

Rabbi Salanter, though the epitome of kindness, could also be confrontational when the question of ethics or morality was at stake. Such was his stance when he learned that a poor widow's two sons were drafted into the Russian Army, because a rich man had bribed the officials not to take his son. He confronted the entire community in the synagogue regarding the matter in order to win justice for the widow.

Rabbi Salanter was driven to establish the study of morality and ethics as a distinct subject within the larger curriculum of the yeshiva. He felt that the emphasis on Talmudic study had neglected the importance of developing one's relationship to God and becoming a better person in relationship to one's fellows. To rectify this omission, the eighteenth century work by Rabbi Moshe Chaim Luzatto — *The Path of the Just* — was adopted as the manual of the Mussar Movement.

When Rabbi Salanter initiated ethical studies, his system was controversial simply because it was new. Orthodox Jews were worried at first that this might be another type of "reform" and the time spent on ethics studies would detract from the time spent on other types of studies. But the Mussar Movement overcame their misgivings and its teachings are now central to the curricula of many yeshivas.

The most famous of the yeshivas specializing in ethical studies were two: the Navaradok Yeshiva, founded in 1896 by Rabbi Joseph of Navaradok, a disciple of Rabbi Salanter; and the Slobodka Yeshiva founded in 1863 by Rabbi Nosson Tzvi Finkel (which moved to Hebron, Israel, and, when destroyed by the Arabs, to Jerusalem and later to Bnei Brak).

Other yeshivas, many of which were founded by the graduates of the Volozhin Yeshiva and which incorporated the teachings of Rabbi Salanter and the Mussar Movement were:

- the Mir, founded in 1815 (the great yeshiva which relocated to Shanghai during the Holocaust and eventually moved to Jerusalem and Brooklyn);
- Telshe, founded in 1875 (now in Cleveland, Ohio);
- Slutzk, founded in 1896 (now in Lakewood, New Jersey);
- Pressburg, founded in 1807 by Rabbi Moses Sofer (the Chatam Sofer)

in the Austro-Hungarian Empire (today called Bratislava in Slovakia) which was the largest and most influential yeshiva in Central Europe.

Forced Secularization

While most of the students studying in the yeshivas accepted and embraced the Mussar Movement after an initial hesitation, the non-religious Jews continued to oppose it. Chief among those was a group called the *Maskilim* ("the Enlightened Ones"), whose members opposed traditional Judaism in any way, shape, or form.

This was the group that aided the Czarist government in the closing of the Volozhin Yeshiva. Why? Because the *Maskilim* wanted their fellow Jews to drop Judaism and join the Russian culture. They argued: "Let's study Russian culture...let's speak in Russian and write in Russian...let's be just like them, and they'll accept us, and we'll be able to integrate more effectively into society and end the horrible poverty so many live under."

An important figure among the *Maskilim* was Dr. Max Lilienthal (1813–1882), a German Jew who came to Russia as director of the "enlightened" Jewish School of Riga. He was eventually appointed by the Russian government (of Czar Nicholas I) as the Minister of Jewish Education, and he made it his mission to convince the Jews of the Pale of the Czar's "benign intent" in establishing a new educational system for them.

A glimpse at part of the "Plan for Russification" created by these *Maskilim* for the Jews of Eastern Europe in 1841 gives a clear sense of their plans for the Jews of Eastern Europe:

> The Russian government's objectives in the encouragement of enlightenment among the Jewish people [should]...pay special attention to the teaching of Russian history and language, for there is nothing which unites diverse ethnic groups...more than the dissemination of information concerning that nation's history and literature.... In order to thwart the harmful influence of the Talmud, without at this stage destroying the book... the rabbis should be empowered to prepare a short religious text...in accordance with the accepted principles regarding civil responsibilities to the Czar and the motherland...[Also] the Jews must be ordered to change their dress for the clothing commonly worn throughout the country....[451]

This was during the time when the Czar was attempting to "restructure" the Jewish society in Russia, with laws forbidding the wearing of traditional clothing, decrees against Talmud study, and division of Jews into "the useful" (farmers, artisans, skilled workers) and "the useless" (unskilled workers, rabbis, orphans, the sick, and the unemployed).

In this climate, in 1843, a conference was convened on the subject of Jewish education, which pitted Lilienthal against Rabbi Yitzchak of Volozhin and Rabbi Menachem Mendel Schneersohn, the Rebbe of Chabad Lubavitch, also known as the "Tzemach Tzedek." Lilienthal could not stand up to the arguments of these rabbis, who managed to win the right for Jews to retain their traditional school system in competition with Lilienthal's new school system.[452]

Within a decade, Lilienthal's schools closed for lack of faculty and students, though Lilienthal's defenders claimed that he left because he realized that the Czar's "benign intent" was to convert Jews to Christianity. He migrated to Cincinnati, Ohio, where he headed up a Reform congregation.

56.
THE CZARS AND THE JEWS

It is arguable which of the Russian Czars was the worst to the Jews. We'll start with Czar Nicholas I (who ruled from 1825–1855) as one of the prime contenders and work our way down.

In 1827, Czar Nicholas I introduced what became known as the Cantonist Decrees. (The name came from the word "canton," meaning "military camp.") These decrees called for the forced conscription of Jewish boys into the Russian Army. These boys were between the ages of twelve and eighteen, and they were forced to serve for twenty-five years! During their army service, every effort was made to convert them to Christianity.

Due to the horrendous conditions under which they were forced to serve, many of the boys who were conscripted didn't survive, and if they did, few continued to identify themselves as Jews. As far as the Jewish community was concerned, either way was a death sentence. Some Jewish parents were so desperate they would actually cut off their sons' right index finger, because without an index finger they couldn't fire a gun and were exempt from service. Other people would try and bribe their sons' way out.

The Cantonist Decrees raise the pressure on the Jewish community to new extremes. Each Jewish community had to produce a certain number of boys for the army, and the community leadership was held responsible for failure to meet this quota. It's not to hard to imagine the turmoil caused by forcing community leaders to decide which boys had to go and which boys could stay.

As if that wasn't bad enough, there was the government-sponsored anti-Semitism, which gave rise to the worst canard about Jews, which unfortunately is alive and kicking to this day.

In 1903, the Russian secret police began to circulate a forgery which became the most famous anti-Semitic "document" in history — *The Protocols of the Elders of Zion*. These Protocols purported to be the minutes of a secret meeting of world Jewish leaders, which supposedly took place once every hundred years for the purpose of plotting how to manipulate and control the world in the next century.

As ridiculous as this might sound, the Protocols were seized upon as "proof" that the world was dominated by Jews who were responsible for all of the world's problems.

Fans and proponents of the Protocols have included such notable anti-Semites as: Henry Ford, the founder of Ford Motor Company; Adolf Hitler, as might be expected; Egyptian President Gamal Abdel Nasser; and King Faisal of Saudi Arabia, among others.

Despite the fact that the Protocols are a proven forgery whose allegations are completely ridiculous, and that they are considered an expression of the worst kind of anti-Semitism, the Protocols continue to sell briskly today and are carried by such huge bookstore chains as Barnes and Noble and Amazon.com in the name of "freedom of speech."

Pogroms

In chapter 48, we spoke of pogroms, mob violence against Jews, when we discussed the murderous attacks of the Ukrainian Cossack Bogdan Chmielnicki in the seventeenth century.

In Czarist Russia, there were so many pogroms that it is simply impossible to even begin to list them all. (In one four-year period there were nearly 300 pogroms, for example.)

These pogroms were seldom spontaneous, though incitement by Christian clergy around the Christian holidays could drive the masses into a frenzy. However, in Czarist Russia, most of the pogroms were government organized. Why would the Czarist government organize mobs to target Jews? Because Jews were the classic scapegoats for the economic problems of Russia (and those of many other countries in history).

Of course, the problems of Russia had nothing to do with the Jews. They were caused by the totally backward, feudal, and highly corrupt regime. One of the ways of diverting attention from the corruption was to blame the Jews and encourage the masses to blow off steam by taking it out on the ready-made scapegoats.

The problems of Russia got worse after Czar Alexander II (who was one of the more competent czars and who was relatively benign to the Jews) was assassinated in 1881 by an anarchist who threw a bomb at his carriage. And when the problems of Russia got worse, the problems of the Jews got worse as well.

The government of the new Czar Alexander III (who ruled 1881–1894) organized one pogrom after another to keep the anger of the masses focused on the Jews. In addition to the pogroms, Alexander III promulgated a series of laws against the Jews called the May Laws; they included such prohibitions as:

> It is henceforth forbidden for Jews to settle outside the cities and townships.
>
> The registration of property and mortgages in the names of Jews is to be halted temporarily. Jews are also prohibited from administering such properties.
>
> It is forbidden for Jews to engage in commerce on Sundays and Christian holidays.[453]

Writes Rabbi Berel Wein in *Triumph of Survival*, describing the reign of Alexander III:

> Expulsions, deportations, arrests, and beatings became the daily lot of the Jews, not only of their lower class, but even of the middle class and the Jewish intelligentsia. The government of Alexander III waged a campaign of war against its Jewish inhabitants.... The Jews were driven and hounded, and emigration appeared to be the only escape from the terrible tyranny of the Romanovs.[454]

It did not help matters any that, during the reign of Alexander III, a terrible famine struck Russia in which 400,000 peasants died. Those who survived were bitter, and their resentments grew (which would erupt eventually in an aborted revolution of 1905 and, later, in the successful Russian Revolution of 1917 which ushered in communist rule).

The Last Romanov

When Alexander III died, he was succeeded by Nicholas II, the last of the Romanovs, whose incompetence and inflexibility helped bring about the Russian Revolution. The new czar had to cope with the mess left behind by his father, and he did so badly.

During his reign, one of the most famous pogroms took place — in Kishinev, on Easter, April 6–7, 1903. The Kishinev pogrom followed a surge of tension in Russia (two years before the first, unsuccessful revolution). Wanting to divert the mob, the Czarist government once again organized a pogrom against the Jews.

Strange as it may sound, the Kishinev pogrom received considerable international attention. This was because, by this time, pogroms were something that the "enlightened" Western world no longer found acceptable. (If only they knew what they themselves would do to the Jews forty years later!)

Here is an excerpt from a lengthy description of the pogrom printed in the *New York Times*:

> It is impossible to account the amounts of goods destroyed in a few hours, the hurrahs of the rioting, the pitiful cries of the victims filling the air. Wherever a Jew was met he was savagely beaten into insensibility. One Jew was dragged from a streetcar and beaten until the mob thought he was dead. The air was filled with feathers and torn bedding. Every Jewish household was broken into, and the unfortunate Jews in their terror endeavored to hide in cellars and under roofs. The mob entered the synagogue, desecrated the biggest house of worship and defiled the Scrolls of the Law.... The conduct of the intelligent Christians was disgraceful. They made no attempt to check the rioting. They simply walked around enjoying the frightful sport. On Tuesday, the third day, when it became known that the troops had received orders to shoot, the rioters ceased.[455]

After two days of mayhem, the Czar said, "Okay, enough — mission accomplished. Now it's time to stop it." He tried to pretend that he was trying to restore order the whole time, though there were 12,000 Russian soldiers stationed in the city who could have stopped the violence at the outset, but who did nothing for two days, while 118 Jewish men, women, and children were murdered; 1,200 were wounded; and 4,000 families were rendered homeless and destitute.[456] As soon as the Czar said stop, it stopped. Until the next time.

Between 1903 and 1907 there was a period of great internal unrest in Russia. Nicholas' incompetence, coupled with excessive taxation and the humiliating defeat of Russia in the Russo-Japanese War, led to the first Russian Revolution, which failed but which brought about a few short-lived reforms in the government. This period also proved disastrous for the Jewish community — there were 284 pogroms with over 50,000 casualties. The level of violence was unbelievable.

There was only so much of this kind of thing that people could take. The Jewish community was being devastated, and people were looking for a way out. Jews were joining all of the anarchist, Communist, Socialist, Bundist movements that they could find in the hopes that they would be able to change the situation in Russia. Jews have been history's great idealists, and during this time they were desperate to find some way of making things better. (We will cover their activism when we discuss the events surrounding World War I.)

Another thing that we see in this time period is mass emigration of Jews out of Russia. Between 1881 and 1914, some 50,000 Jews left every year to an estimated total of 2.5 million Jews. Despite these emigrations, the Jewish population of Russia stayed constant — at about 5 million Jews, due to the very high birthrate. Had these Jews not left Russia there would have been 7–8 million Jews there.

And it was America which absorbed most of the Jewish immigrants during this period of time.

We might recall from chapter 23 that when the Jews were exiled by the Babylonians, the exile had happened in two stages. First the Babylonians took away 10,000 of the best and the brightest. That turned out to be a blessing in disguise, because when the Jews arrived en masse in Babylon, there was a Jewish infrastructure in place. Jewish life could continue and, as a result, we saw hardly any assimilation during the Babylonian exile.

However, when the poor Jews of Russia arrived en masse in America at the end of the nineteenth century — passing through the famous Ellis Island — they found no Jewish infrastructure in place. Preceding them in the migration of the 1830s were German Jews (about 280,000 of them) who were either Reform (and did not believe that the Torah was God-given), or they were secular Jews who totally eschewed Jewish tradition.

Thus, the poor Russian Jews stepped into the Golden Land of Assimilation.

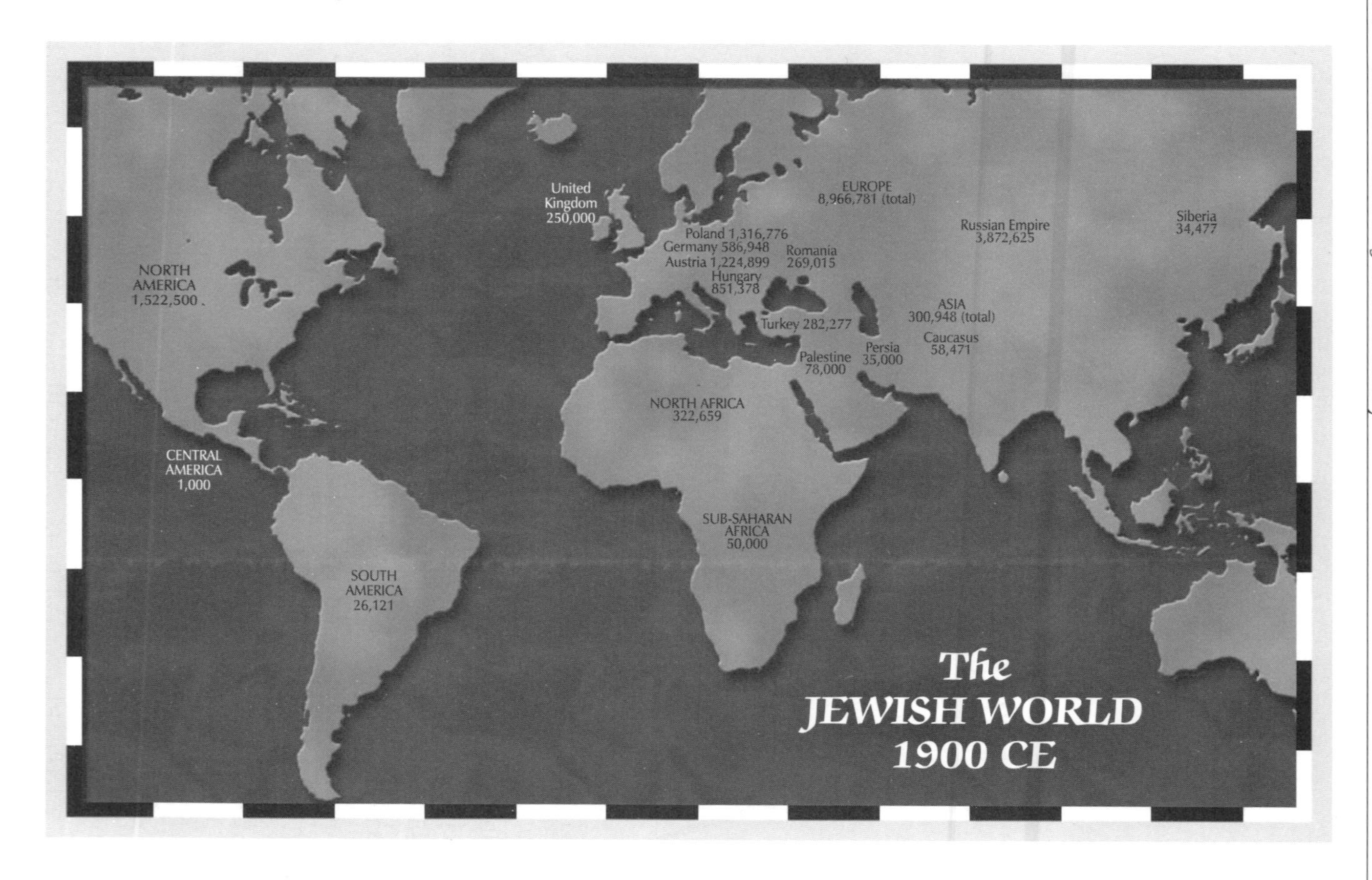
United
Kingdom
250,000
EUROPE
8,966,781 (total)
Russian Empire
3,872,625
Siberia
34,477
Poland 1,316,776
Germany 586,948
Austria 1,224,899
Hungary
851,378
Romania
269,015
NORTH
AMERICA
1,522,500
ASIA
300,948 (total)
Turkey 282,277
Caucasus
58,471
Persia
35,000
Palestine
78,000
NORTH AFRICA
322,659
CENTRAL
AMERICA
1,000
SUB-SAHARAN
AFRICA
50,000
SOUTH
AMERICA
26,121
The
JEWISH WORLD
1900 CE

57.
JEWISH LIFE IN AMERICA

When we last left off the story of the Jews of America — at the beginning of the nineteenth century — they numbered only about 6,000. The reality that there was freedom in America but only as long as you were not "too Jewish" kept most Jews away.

That changed in the 1820s, when the Jews of Germany began to arrive.

The German Jews were not "too Jewish." They were either Reform Jews who had dropped the basic tenets of traditional Judaism (see chapter 53 for details), or they were "enlightened" secular Jews who had dropped Judaism altogether. By 1850, there were some 17,000 Jews living in America. By 1880, their numbers had increased to about 270,000.

Most of these Jews moved to the New York area, which at that time had a Jewish population of 180,000. It would soon grow to 1.8 million.

In New York City, the Jewish area was the Lower East Side of Manhattan. Those who succeeded quickly moved up to the Upper East Side. And these Jews did remarkably well in the New World. Some of those who made it into the ranks of the rich and famous were:

- Marcus Goldman, founder of Goldman, Sachs & Co.;
- Charles Bloomingdale, founder of Bloomingdale's department store;
- Henry, Emanuel and Mayer Lehman, founders of Lehman Brothers;
- Abraham Kuhn and Solomon Loeb, founders of the banking firm Kuhn, Loeb and Co.;

- Jacob Schiff, Loeb's son-in-law and a major American financier;
- Joseph Seligman, who started out as a peddler and who became one of the most important bankers in America;

These are just a few famous names; there were many others.[457]

American Reform Movement

The German Jews of New York built the largest Reform synagogue in the world (Temple Emanuel on the Upper East Side), and many others. By 1880 there were about 200 synagogues in America, the majority (90 percent) of them Reform, because these were the Jews who were coming to America from Germany.

With this migration, the focus of the Reform Movement moved from Germany to the United States. In America, the Reform Movement continued in the tradition of its German origins, spelling out its ideology in the famous "Pittsburgh Platform," which was drawn up and adopted there in 1885 at a convention of its leadership:

> We recognize in the Mosaic legislation a system of training the Jewish people for its mission during its national life in Palestine, and today we accept as binding only its moral laws, and maintain only such ceremonies as elevate and sanctify our lives, but reject all such as are not adopted to the view and habits of modern civilization....
>
> We hold that all such Mosaic and rabbinical laws as regulate diet, priestly purity and dress originated in ages and under the influence of ideas entirely foreign to our present mental and spiritual state....
>
> We consider ourselves no longer a nation, but a religious community, and therefore expect neither a return to Palestine, nor a sacrificial worship under the sons of Aharon, nor the restoration of any of the laws concerning the Jewish state....[458]

This last statement — which detached the American Reform Movement from the 2,000-year-old Jewish longing to return to the Land of Israel (in imitation of the ideology espoused by the German Reform Movement) — is the reason why early American Reform Jews did not support the Zionist Movement, nor the founding of the State of Israel, as we shall see.

The father of the American Reform Movement was Isaac Meyer Wise (1819–1900). He was a German Jewish immigrant who was the founder and the first president of Hebrew Union College in Cincinnati, Ohio, which opened in 1875. It was the first American rabbinical seminary, and it had unusually liberal standards. Writes Joseph Telushkin in *Jewish Literacy*:

> One issue that sets the Reform rabbinate apart...is its refusal to impose any religious standards on its rabbis. In many ways, this is a continuation of Reform's historical commitment to free inquiry. Today, quite literally, there is no religious action a Reform rabbi can take for which he or she would be thrown out of the Central Conference of American Rabbis, the official body of Reform rabbis.[459]

When, in 1883, the first graduating class of Hebrew Union College in Cincinnati was ready to receive its diplomas, the seminary threw a lavish banquet. The more traditional attendees were horrified when course after course presented one *treif* [nonkosher] dish after another: clams, soft-shell crabs, shrimps, frogs' legs. Worse yet, the meat meal was followed by ice cream for desert [in violation of the prohibition against mixing meat and milk].[460]

The so-called "*treif* banquet" compelled the more traditional Jews — who thought that the Reform had gone too far but who did not want to be Orthodox — to find another alternative. The search for that alternative led to the founding of another movement within Judaism: the Conservative Movement.

The Conservative Movement

In 1886, more traditional Jews who were offended by the ideology of the Reform Movement founded an alternative to the Hebrew Union College. It was called the Jewish Theological Seminary, and it became the bastion of the new, purely American, Conservative Movement.

The head of the Jewish Theological Seminary, a respected Jewish scholar from Cambridge, England, named Solomon Schechter (1850–1915), helped shape the ideology of the new movement. He spelled it out in his work, *The Catholic Israel.* (He chose a poor title for his work — by "catholic" he did not mean the Roman Catholic Church, he meant "universal.") He wrote:

> It is not the mere revealed Bible that is the first importance to the Jew, but the Bible as it repeats itself in history. In other words, as it is interpreted by tradition. Another consequence of this conception of tradition is that neither scripture nor primitive Judaism but general custom which forms the real rule of practice. Liberty was always given to the great teachers of every generation to make modifications and innovations in harmony with the spirit of existing institutions. Hence a return to Mosaism [Orthodoxy] would be illegal, pernicious and indeed, impossible.[461]

In other words, the ideology of the Conservative Movement would be to uphold the Torah as the revealed word of God, but the interpretation of that word of God need not uphold the tradition as passed down from Moses.

This was a dramatic departure from the traditional attitude toward the interpretation and application of Jewish law. One of the pillars of traditional Jewish belief was (and is) that the Talmud is the source for all Jewish law and that those rabbis who lived closer to the revelation at Mount Sinai had a clearer understanding of Jewish law and its application. Therefore, their decisions could not be discarded. New rulings on modern issues must reflect established principles.

When the Conservative Movement discarded this pillar of traditional Judaism, it opened the door to countless problems, as was soon apparent. Although the founders of the Conservative Movement felt Reform had gone too far, the behavior of their followers proved virtually indistinguishable from that of Reform Jews. (We will discuss these repercussions further when we take up the subject of assimilation.)

The Great Migrations

This, then, was the spiritual state of the majority of American Jewry — defined chiefly by the German Jews who migrated in the 1830s — when the great migrations from Eastern Europe began around the turn of the century.

How many Jews came to America in this time period? As noted earlier (in chapter 56) between 1881 and 1914, some 50,000 Jews left Eastern Europe every year, for a total of 2.5 million Jews, most of whom came to America. The vast majority of these Jews were poor and arrived in New York with nothing. They had little to lose in coming to America (except perhaps their Judaism).

And, alas, this is what happened. The great rabbis did not come among them, and lacking teachers and religious leaders to counter the pressures from the Americanized German Jews, these poor Eastern European Jews assimilated quickly.

The pious, yeshiva-educated Jews did not join in the great migrations. For the most part, the rabbis preached against immigration, fearing that America was the Golden Land of Assimilation disguised as the Golden Land of Economic Opportunity. And in many ways their fears were well-founded. The greatest test for the vast majority of these new arrivals was the issue of keeping Shabbat. America in the late eighteenth and early nineteenth centuries had a six-day work week, with Sunday as the only day of rest. Many of the new arrivals found employment in the sweatshops of the garment industry. It was miserable work, for minimal wages, and often under appalling conditions. The Philadelphia-born social worker, Charles Bernheimer, described the conditions in a Philadelphia sweatshop in 1905:

> Before you have reached the shop, you have probably climbed one, two or three flights of stairs, littered with debris.... The room is likely to be ill-smelling and badly ventilated.... Consequently, an abnormally bad air is breathed which is difficult for the ordinary person to stand long. Thus result tubercular and other diseases which the immigrant acquires in his endeavor to work out his economic existence.... In the busy season, the employees are required to work long hours, sometimes as high as fifteen, perhaps eighteen, a day.[462]

Under these conditions, taking Saturday off for Shabbat observance was simply not an option if you wanted to keep your job. But if you lost your job, finding new employment wasn't so easy. Since those who tried to keep Shabbat by not coming to work were immediately fired, the result was that the overwhelming majority stopped observing Shabbat in order to eat. Once Shabbat observance was dropped, the rest of Jewish observance usually followed. This same story repeated itself countless times until virtually all those who arrived in America as observant Jews dropped their religious observance soon after their arrival.

This is not to say that things were better for those who stayed in Eastern Europe — far from it. Two hundred years of Czarist persecution and economic marginalization had taken a tremendous toll on the Jewish community. The anti-Semitism was constant, the hardships were many, and the poverty was great. Spiritually and ideologically the Jewish community was also under tremendous attack and beginning to crumble from the onslaught. The lure of secular enlightenment and other ideologies (such as Marxism and socialism) drew many Jews away from religious observance and even lured some of the brightest out of the yeshivas. Many of the *Maskilim* came from Torah-observant homes and even studied in the great yeshivas of Eastern Europe.[463]

There can be little doubt that, had the Nazis not snuffed out Jewish life in Eastern Europe during the Holocaust, the community would have gradually disintegrated under internal strain and external pressure. Still the rabbinic leadership of Eastern Europe felt that the spiritual abyss of America posed a far greater threat than life in Eastern Europe, because it lacked virtually any Orthodox infrastructure. Explains Arthur Hertzberg in *The Jews of America*:

> In 1893, the most distinguished moralist among the rabbis of Europe, Israel Meir Ha-Kohen [better known as the Chafetz Chaim]...went beyond exhortation; he ruled against mass migration to America. He knew that this emigration could no longer be stopped, but he pleaded with those who would heed the views of rabbis to prefer persecution in Russia to economic success in the United States.... [Such] opinions became so fixed that they would remain firm among the major leaders of European Orthodoxy even in the inter-war period, as the situation of European Jewry was radically worsening for all Jews, for all socio-economic classes.[464]

Despite the decision by most of the rabbinic leadership to remain in Europe, several important rabbis did arrive and began to lay the foundation for what would later become the thriving Orthodox community of the United States. Some of the more notable personalities included:

- Rabbi Yaacov Joseph from Vilna, who in 1887 became the first and only "chief rabbi" of New York.
- Rabbi Moshe Feinstein, who arrived in 1936 to lead the Mesivta Tiferet Yerushalayim Yeshiva in New York; he went on to become the foremost legal authority in the Jewish world.
- Rabbi Eliezer Silver, who became the leader of the Orthodox rabbinate in America, known as the Agudas HaRabbonim.
- Rabbi Shraga Feivel Mendlowitz, who founded the first Orthodox school system, Torah Umesorah, in 1944, and became the driving force behind the Jewish day-school system.
- Rabbi Aharon Kotler, who founded the Lakewood Yeshiva in 1943 and was the driving force behind the growth of Orthodox Judaism in America.
- Rabbi Moshe Soloveitchik and his son, Rabbi Joseph Soloveitchik, who were the rabbinic leadership of Yeshiva University in New York.

The Tired and the Poor

While the German Jews succeeded easily in America, life was much harder for the Eastern European Jews who came in the great migrations. We find, for example, at the beginning of the 1900s there were 64,000 families packed into 6,000 tenement houses of Manhattan's Lower East Side.

These poor, Yiddish-speaking, religious Jews reflected badly on the German Jews who came before them and who by this time had become quite Americanized. Therefore, the German Jews embarked on a program of rapid acculturation of their poor cousins, and they invested heavily in this cause.

Their underlying fear was anti-Semitism. This fear was real, because despite the religious tolerance of America, anti-Semitism was alive and doing well in the New World. There were no pogroms, but there was social isolation and other types of discrimination.

For example: In 1843, a dozen young men applied for membership to the Old Fellows Lodge, but were refused membership because they were Jews. (They organized a club of their own — called the Independent Order of B'nai B'rith.)

Another example: In 1869, Joseph Seligman, the well-known banker, was refused hotel accommodations in Saratoga Springs, New York, the summer resort for the well-to-do of his day because, no matter how rich and famous, he was a Jew.

If upper-class Jews not considered good enough to mingle with American non-Jews, one can just imagine how the immigrant masses were viewed.

In 1894, Henry Adams (a descendant of John Quincy Adams) organized the Immigration Restriction League to limit the admission to America of "unhealthy elements" — Jews being first among these. In his famous book, *The Education of Henry Adams*, he listed those he would not accept into America:

> Not a Polish Jew fresh from Warsaw or Cracow — not a furtive Jacoob or Ysaac still reeking of the Ghetto, snarling a weird Yiddish to the officers of the customs....[465]

He found many supporters for his cause, but he did not win. Indeed, one might say he lost when in 1906, President Theodore Roosevelt appointed Oscar Straus — the first Jew to serve in the United States cabinet — as the secretary of commerce and labor, whose purview of responsibility was immigration.

However, the anti-Semites did not give up easily, as we will see in the next chapter when we examine the factors which led to the baring of the evil face of anti-Semitism in the twentieth century.

58.

THE FACE OF ANTI-SEMITISM

In this chapter we will briefly examine the anti-Semitism that, with the coming of the Enlightenment in the eighteenth century, hid itself under the veneer of "civil" society, only to bare its face of evil in the Holocaust.

Of course, in Russia and in the Pale of Settlement of Eastern Europe, anti-Semitism never went underground (as we saw in chapters 55 and 56). But in the Western world the situation was different. Some of the worst cases of anti-Semitism before the rise of the Nazis in Germany were instigated by the French, whose country was the birthplace of the Enlightenment. It is shocking to learn, for example, that it was the French consul, Ratti Menton, who brought a blood libel against the Jews in 1840, when a Capuchin monk disappeared in Damascus, Syria. In response to his accusations, the Syrian authorities seized more than sixty Jewish children to coerce their parents into confessing. Several Jews were arrested and tortured. Two died under torture and several others were permanently disabled; only one "confessed."

Pressured by French authorities, the Syrians would have tried these Jews on false charges had not the Jewish world reacted. Jewish organizations instigated a protest by British and American leaders (including President Martin Van Buren) that caused the Syrians to drop the charges. (Notably, the Reform Jews of Germany, who had distanced themselves from identifying with other Jews, as we saw in chapter 53, did not participate in the protest.)

French anti-Semitism continued, however. In 1886, an anti-Semitic book, *La France Juive,* became the most widely read book in France. This was followed in 1892 by the founding of an anti-Semitic daily newspaper *La Libre Parole.* Writes Berel Wein in *Triumph of Survival*:

> Nowhere was [*La Libre Parole*] more popular than with the officer corps of the French army.... Stung by the anarchists and pacifists of the left, humiliated by its complete defeat in the Franco-Prussian War of 1870, the French army was frustrated, malevolent and paranoid. One of its main enemies was the "Jewish influence" in French life. This made the military the logical candidate for an anti-Semitic incident. It would not be long in coming.[466]

The Dreyfus Affair

That anti-Semitic incident — which became known in France as *L'Affaire* — was the famous case of Alfred Dreyfus, a captain in the French Army who in 1894 was falsely accused of spying.

The actual spy, Major Esterhazy, was not a Jew, but even though this fact was discovered in 1896, the French army ignored or suppressed the evidence against Esterhazy and would not back away from its accusations for anti-Semitic reasons.[467] "Secret" documents, parts of which were forgeries, were produced, and Dreyfus was tried and convicted of treason in a closed courtroom before a military tribunal. He was stripped of his rank and sentenced to life imprisonment on Devil's Island off the coast of French Guiana in South America. On January 3, 1895, he was paraded through the streets of Paris while a mob jeered: "Death to the Jews."

One of those covering this fiasco was a Hungarian-Jewish journalist from Austria, Theodor Herzl, who was shocked to the core that Jew-hatred was so ingrained in the "civilized" French. He later wrote in his diary: "Where? In France. In Republican, modern, civilized France, a hundred years after the Declaration of the Rights of Man."

Even though Herzl was secular and quite assimilated, the Dreyfus trial made a powerful impression on him and brought him closer to the realization that the only answer to anti-Semitism and the only safe place for the Jews was a land of their own — the Land of Israel.[468]

While Herzl was not the founder of Zionism, he quickly rose to the top of the movement and convened the First Zionist Congress in Basle, Switzerland, in 1897, at which the World Zionist Organization was established. (We will discuss Zionism in greater detail in future chapters.)

Meanwhile, the travesty of the Dreyfus trial created a controversy. France's greatest writer, Emile Zola, published a stunning newspaper article in 1898 entitled "*J'Accuse*" ("I Accuse"), charging the government with a miscarriage of justice. For this, Zola (who was not a Jew) was convicted of libel and had to flee to England.

Eventually, after another two trials in which Dreyfus was again convicted, he was pardoned and, after having spent five years on Devil's Island, he was restored to his former military rank. (But he was not fully exonerated until 1906!)

World War I

On June 28, 1914, Archduke Francis Ferdinand, heir apparent to the Austro-Hungarian throne, was assassinated in Sarajevo by a Serbian nationalist. One month later, after its humiliating demands were refused, Austria-Hungary declared war on Serbia. Other declarations of war followed quickly, and soon every major power in Europe was involved. On one side were the Allies — chiefly France, Britain, Russia, Italy, and later the U.S.; on the other were the Central Powers — Austro-Hungarian Empire, Germany, and Turkey (i.e., the Ottoman Empire).

World War I, which lasted four years, was an incredibly destructive conflict in which 10 million people died and another 20 million were wounded. This was largely because by the time World War I erupted, lethal weapons capable of killing huge numbers of people had been perfected. Soldiers no longer needed to stand in close proximity to kill each other. Machine guns and heavy artillery did the job for them. And the end result was quite devastating.[469]

As for the Jews, 1.5 million fought in World War I. Jews fought in the Austrian army, in the German army, in the Russian army, in the French army. Jews (aligned with their host nations) fought against other Jews in this conflict, and 140,000 of them died.

Interestingly, World War I — which unquestionably set the stage for the Holocaust — began on August 1, 1914 (when Germany declared war on Russia), a date corresponding to the ninth day of the Hebrew month of Av. This was the day in Jewish history on which the first and second Temples were destroyed, as well as many other terrible things that happened to the Jewish people, as we have already seen.

In fact, World War I triggered a chain reaction that proved catastrophic to the Jews. The two major links in the chain reaction were the Russian Revolution and the rise of the Nazi Party in Germany.

Hitler would never have come to power were it not for Germany's defeat in World War I. As a result of that defeat, the punishing Versailles Treaty which brought Germany economically to its knees, and the worldwide depression following the war, Germany was thrown into economic chaos. But who was blamed for that economic plight by the "enlightened" Germans?

The Jews, of course.

World War II, which followed World War I by only twenty-one years, was in many ways a continuation of the same conflict, as we will learn.

Russian Revolution

Initially, the Czarist government did well in World War I against the Austro-Hungarian Empire, but it was badly beaten by the German army. As the war continued, the death toll and military setbacks proved more than Russia could handle.

The many years of corruption by the Czarist government had previously led to one aborted revolution in 1905. In March 1917, the revolution was finally successful. Initially, the czar was deposed[470] and replaced by a socialist (Menshevik) government which kept Russia in the war (not a popular move among the masses, who were weary of it). But by November, that government was overthrown by a Marxist (Bolshevik) government, which took Russia out of the war.

This Bolshevik takeover triggered a civil war in Russia which was to last until 1921. The Bolshevik victory in 1921 led to the creation of the U.S.S.R. (i.e., the Soviet Union), which would remain in power until its collapse in 1990.

Not surprisingly, the Jews — who were among the most oppressed people in Russia, and who always gravitated to movements that professed to "change the world" — were heavily involved in the Russian Revolution. (We saw earlier that the founder of the Communist ideology was Karl Marx, a Jew who converted to Christianity and then abandoned all religion.)

The motto of the Communist Party — "from each according to his ability, to each according to his need" — was attractive to many liberal-minded Jews. Imbued with the strong sense of social justice which comes from Judaism, they felt that the socialist government would greatly benefit the masses and improve the conditions in Russia. Indeed, many of the key figures of the Bolshevik Revolution were Jews.

The Jews who joined the Communist Party were not religious Jews, but the drive toward *tikkun ha'olam* ("repairing of the world") inspired them. Indeed, in absence of religious expression, this drive (toward what is identified as a Messianic utopia in Judaism) dominated their Jewish souls. The American literary critic Edmund Wilson summed up the Jewish attraction to communism when he said:

> The Jew lends himself easily to communism because it enables him to devote himself to a high cause, involving all of humanity, characteristics which are natural to him as a Jew.[471]

The leader of the Russian Revolution, Vladimir Ilyich Lenin (1870–1924) did try to root out anti-Semitism. He made a strong stand against it, because it had been such an intrinsic policy of the Czarist government. Furthermore, Lenin was well aware that there might not have been a Russian Revolution without the Jews. Unfortunately, Jewish communists, following the Marxist dictum that "religion is the opiate of the masses," did their level best to eradicate Judaism in Russia; this is evident in a propaganda piece by Yevsektsiya (the special department of the Soviet government set up to deal with Jews) entitled "The Liquidation of Bourgeois Institutions" published in October 1918:

> The Jewish community has hitherto been dominated by members of the property class who want to keep the masses in the dark by superimposing a Hebrew culture upon them. While the upper classes have been sending their children to public schools, they have provided only dark primary schools and synagogues for the offspring of the proletariat, in which nothing but nonsense is taught.... In the struggle against the authorized Jewish community no compromise can be made with the bourgeoisie.[472]

So the communist government of Russia, like the Czarist government of Russia, embarked on a policy of forced secularization of the Jews. (To be fair, they also did it to the members of the Russian Orthodox Church.)

Thus, the Jews of Russia were deliberately starved of their heritage, resulting in a huge Jewish population that was incredibly ignorant of their heritage. This, by the way, is a unique event in human history — the deliberate secularization of a community to such a large extent and for such a long period of time. (It was later duplicated by other communist regimes, particularly in China.)

Stalin and Trotsky

When Lenin died in 1924, a power struggle ensued, and Joseph Stalin (1879–1953) eventually seized power. In 1935, he initiated a series of purges which devastated Russia. These purges made Stalin the second biggest mass murderer of the twentieth century (after Mao Tze-tung), if we consider the sheer number of people he ordered killed and others whom he consigned to death in a vast network of labor camps. It is estimated that Stalin was responsible for the deaths of an estimated 25 million people (twice as many as Hitler, though probably only half as many as Mao).

An anti-Semite of the first order, Stalin was planning to deport 2–3 million Jews who had survived the Holocaust to Siberia, where they would have been killed. Fortunately, he died under mysterious circumstances before he could put his plan into action.[473] But he did succeed in purging all the Jews from the Communist government of Russia, the most famous of whom was Leon Trotsky (1879–1940).

The most important Jew in the Russian Revolution, Trotsky — whose real name was Lev Davidovich Bronstein — was a leading organizer of the Red Army. Along with Lenin, he engineered the Bolshevik seizure of power in 1917, and when Lenin died, he was Stalin's rival for succession. Stalin won and first ousted Trotsky as commissar of war, then expelled him from the party, and finally, in 1929, deported him from Russia. Trotsky survived in exile for more than ten years; he was murdered in Mexico City in 1940 on Stalin's orders.[474]

American Anti-Semitism

Thus far, we have described the open murderous anti-Semitism of the Russians and the insidious "intellectual" anti-Semitism of the French. But what about the land of tolerance — America?

In 1913, in Atlanta, Georgia, a Jew named Leo Frank was falsely accused of the murder of a 13-year-old Christian girl. So strong was the anti-Semitism in the American South that the testimony of a black man — a unique event in this racist region — was permitted against a white man. But, of course, the white man was a Jew.

Ironically, the black "witness" was the murderer — a fact that he had confessed to his own attorney, but this was kept secret. There had also been a real witness, but he did not come forward until many years later.

Frank was convicted and sentenced to death, but the governor of Georgia, John Slaton, convinced that Frank was innocent, commuted his sentence.

Then a horrible thing happened.

A Georgia mob kidnapped Frank from prison and lynched him. The lynching was photographed and made into postcards which sold briskly.

Not until 1986 — seventy-three years later! — was Frank awarded a posthumous pardon by the state of Georgia.

The Frank case led to the founding of the Anti-Defamation League. It became the leading Jewish group fighting anti-Semitism in America, and it had a lot of work on its hands, especially after the end of World War I and the 1929 stock-market crash, when things heated up for the Jews in America.

As we mentioned in our discussion of the *Protocols of the Elders of Zion* (see chapter 56), one of the big promulgators of anti-Semitism in America was Henry Ford, who spent a lot of his own money to get the Protocols translated into English and distributed in America as widely as possible. The Protocols became the second best-selling book in the United States in the 1920s and 1930s (after the Bible).

The Ford Motor Company's plant in Dearborn, Michigan, had a sign posted in its parking lot:

> Jews are traitors to America and should not be trusted by gentiles. Jews teach communism, Jews teach atheism, Jews destroy Christianity, Jews control the press, Jews produce filthy movies, Jews control money.

Henry Ford was not the only one. There were others.[475]

There were several conservative Christian political parties which were strongly anti-Semitic. For example: William Pelley's "Silver Shirts." An anti-Semitic newspaper, Gerald B. Winrod's *The Defender,* had 110,000 subscribers.

These American anti-Semites were fledgling fascists. Under the guise of patriotism, they championed the idea that Jews were the underlying cause of the economic woes of America — such as the stock market crash of 1929 — because it was the Jews who controlled business and banking. This kind of anti-Semitism rivaled that of Europe in the same period, but unlike in Europe, it never took hold with the same fatal consequences.

But all this Jew hatred did set the stage for the appeasement of Hitler when he assumed power in Germany. It also was one of the primary reasons why America did not do more to save the Jews once they began to flee the Holocaust, as we shall see in the next chapter.

59.
THE HOLOCAUST

As we begin to discuss this most painful of topics for the Jewish people, please keep in mind that this is a vast subject. At the moment there are some 1,200 books in print examining why it happened, how it happened, and all the details in between.

Some of the classics that give insight into the Holocaust are:

- *The Holocaust* by Martin Gilbert
- *The War Against the Jews* by Lucy S. Dawidowicz
- *Night by the Nobel Prize* Winner Elie Wiesel
- *The Diary of A Young Girl* by Anne Frank
- *Hitler's Willing Executioners* by Daniel Jonah Goldhagen[476]

Alternatively, one can visit:

- Yad Vashem Museum in Jerusalem, Israel
- The Holocaust Museum in Washington, D.C.
- The Museum of Tolerance in Los Angeles

A crash course cannot possibly do justice to this devastating event in which a nation (Nazi Germany) targeted a people (the Jews) and systematically and with breathtaking cruelty killed six million of them. The word "genocide" was coined to describe it. This word did not previously exist in the English language.[477]

Not only did Nazi Germany set out to eliminate the Jews from the face of the earth, virtually no other country on earth lifted a finger to stop them.

Of course, there were isolated incidents of great heroism on the part of some non-Jews, but history stands in mute testimony that this was a paltry effort. Most did nothing as the Jews died.

The Holocaust thrusts a question into the face of humanity: How could civilized people let this happen?

We have a clue to the answer from Adolf Hitler himself:

> Yes, we are barbarians! We want to be barbarians! It is an honorable title.... Providence has ordained that I should be the greatest liberator of humanity. I am freeing men from...the dirty and degrading self-mortifications of a false vision (a Jewish invention) called "conscience" and "morality."[478]

Adolf Hitler

To begin with we have to destroy some major myths. Adolf Hitler, who was born in 1889 in Braunau, Austria, had nothing but positive interactions with Jews in his childhood and youth, contrary to popular belief that attributes his actions to some early vendetta. When he was a young struggling artist, many of the people who supported him were Jewish. And later, some important figures in his life were also Jewish — like his family doctor or his commander in World War I who nominated him for the Iron Cross.

And yet, despite these positive experiences, Hitler had a deep-seated hatred of the Jews. In terms of Jewish history, such pathological hatred belonged only to the nation of Amalek. (Amalek, as we might recall from chapter 16, was the ultimate enemy of the Jewish people in history. Amalek's major ambition was to rid the world of the Jews and its moral influence and return the planet to idolatry, paganism, and barbarism.)

Hitler's hatred of the Jews — like the Amalekite's hatred of the Jews — was not illogical. We can even call it rational, in that he had a reason for his hatred that was clear in his mind, as we shall see.

Hitler also was not insane. He had his neuroses, but he was not crazy. In fact, he was a brilliant political manipulator. We can certainly say a lot of horrible things about him, but Hitler was one of the greatest public speakers in human history. Those who understand German and listen to tapes of his speeches can appreciate why those blonde, blue-eyed Germans cheered so heartily a man whose very appearance contradicted everything he preached. There he was with his black hair and brown eyes, as far away as he could come in appearance from the Aryans, the master race with which he wanted to populate the earth. And yet they gave him their loyalty and gave up their lives for him.

Hitler's rise to power began after the 1932 German elections when his party received more than 35 percent of the vote. A year later President Paul von Hindenburg appointed him as Chancellor of Germany. Immediately after he came to power, he set up Dachau — not as a concentration camp for Jews (that would come later) but as a place to put his political opponents. Little by little, he took the very sophisticated democratic system of the Weimar German Republic and turned it into a totalitarian state. Democratic rights were suspended, political opposition was suppressed, and books were burned.[479]

Once his dictatorship was in place, Hitler bullied his way into taking over much of Europe.

Initially Europe, and certainly the United States, did nothing, while Hitler, together with his Austrian fascist allies, pressured Austria into unifying with Germany in March 1938 (in violation of the Treaty of Versailles, the treaty that officially ended World War I). Then he took over a region called the Sudetenland, without the consent of the Czechs but with the blessing of European powers — particularly England and France. The Prime Minister of England at that time, Neville Chamberlain, showed how little England cared about the problems of Europe in this speech: "How horrible, fantastic, incredible it is that we should be digging trenches and trying on gas masks here because of a quarrel in a far-away country between people of whom we know nothing."

England and France negotiated a pact with Hitler in Munich on September 30, 1938, in effect promising to look the other way as Hitler dismembered Czechoslovakia. Afterwards Chamberlain, satisfied Europe would be safe from Hitler, declared:

> The settlement of the Czechoslovakian problem, which has now been achieved is, in my view, only the prelude to a larger settlement in which all Europe may find peace. This morning I had another talk with the German Chancellor, Herr Hitler, and here is the paper which bears his name upon it as well as mine.... I believe it is peace in our time...peace with honor.

A year after this infamous statement, World War II broke out — a war in which fifty million people would die. Such was the naiveté of a leader who thought that peace could be won by placating evil.

Nuremberg Laws

Some three years before he made his move into Europe, Hitler was already putting into place his program to eliminate the Jews.

It began in 1935 with the Nuremberg Laws. These laws basically cancelled all the rights that Jews had won in post-Enlightenment Germany.

For so many years before the Enlightenment, Jews were hated because they were different and refused to assimilate. Now, in the very country where they had assimilated the most easily, Jews were hated because they were blending in too well. Hitler's ultimate nightmare was that Jews would intermarry with Germans and poison the gene pool of the master race.[480]

Hence laws were passed to preserve "the purity of German blood." For example:

> Marriages between Jews and subjects of German or kindred blood are forbidden.
>
> A Reich citizen can only be a state member who is a German of German blood and who shows through his conduct and is both desirous and fit to serve in the faith of the German people and the Reich. The Reich citizen is the only holder of political rights.
>
> A Jew cannot be a citizen of the Reich. He cannot exercise the right to vote. He cannot occupy public office.
>
> Jews are forbidden to display the Reich's national flag or to show the national colors.

Systematically, Jews lost their citizenship, their political rights, and their economic rights. Then the violence started.

The first explosion of major Nazi violence against the Jews was *Kristallnacht,* "the night of broken glass." It happened on November 9, 1938. That night, 191 synagogues were destroyed and 91 Jews were killed, many beaten to death. Afterwards, some 30,000 Jews were arrested and fined a billion marks (equal to about $400 million) for the damage that had been caused by the Germans.

This was really the writing on the wall for the Jews. At this time many tried to get out of Germany. Unfortunately, very few places in the world would accept them. For example, when the Foreign Minister of Canada was asked how many Jews Canada should take, his response was "None is too many."

America took in only 200,000 Jews, due to the anti-Semitism that we discussed in chapter 58.

Even when it was clear that the Germans were persecuting the Jews, the U.S. State Department clung to such strict criteria for allowing Jews into the country that 75 percent of the spaces that were technically allotted to Jews by American law were never used. Amazingly, so many Jews who desperately wanted to enter America were unable to meet the requirements. (Canada was by far the most restrictive of all the Western countries, allowing only 5,000 Jewish refugees to immigrate.)

All told, about 800,000 Jews actually found refuge in various places in the world, but the majority were trapped.[481]

World War II

World War II started on September 1, 1939, when Germany invaded Poland. That brought England and France into the war in opposition to Germany. On June 22, 1940, France surrendered to Germany, leaving England to fight on alone. Eventually, the U.S. would join in, although not until 1941, when Japan, Germany's ally, bombed the U.S. naval base at Pearl Harbor.

By that time, virtually all of Europe was in Hitler's control. It happened quickly because the Germans were so good at waging war (and because countries like France, while well equipped, had military leaders who lacked the will to fight). The Germans had perfected the art of using concentrated, fast-moving armor and infantry together with intense artillery and air support — they called it *blitzkrieg*, meaning "lightning war." They were unstoppable.

They were stopped, of course — first and foremost by the Russians and second by the British and Americans — but it took years and cost many lives.

In the beginning of the conflict, Hitler had signed a non-aggression pact with Stalin, but in June 1941, he violated it and invaded the Soviet Union anyway. Here, too, the Germans were initially very successful, primarily because Stalin, despite all the evidence, refused to believe that Hitler would break his non-aggression pact and attack Russia. Stalin had also purged his whole army of most of his competent officers — he had killed them all.

Basically, the Germans advanced into the Soviet Union as fast as they could move. As many Jews resided there, Hitler immediately began his campaign to eliminate them. Special German units, called the *Einsatzgruppen*, began systematically executing people, and some 1.5 million Jews were killed by them alone. They were rounded up, usually next to a big ravine or pit which they were often forced to dig themselves, and then they were machine gunned over it. Those who did not die immediately from their gunshot wounds were buried alive.

This is what happened at the Babi Yar forest near Kiev in the Ukraine. There, according to German "official" records, 33,782 men, women, and children were executed over a ravine in September of 1941. The watchman at the old Jewish cemetery, near Babi Yar, recalled how the Ukrainian policemen cooperated in the effort:

> [They] formed a corridor and drove the panic-stricken people towards the huge glade with sticks, swearing and dogs (who were tearing at people's bodies), forcing the people to undress, to form columns in hundreds, and then to go in the columns of twos towards the mouth of the ravine.

At the mouth of the ravine, the watchman recalled:

> They found themselves on the narrow ground above the precipice, twenty to twenty-five meters in height, and on the opposite side there were the Germans' machine guns. The killed, wounded and half-alive people fell down and were smashed there. Then the next hundred were brought and everything repeated again. The policemen took the children by the legs and threw them alive down into the Yar.[482]

But the worst was yet to come.

A member of *Einsatzgruppe* D prepares to murder the last Jew in Vinnitsa, Ukraine, seen kneeling before a filled mass grave, on the Jewish New Year in September, 1941. Picture from an *Einsatzgruppen* soldier's personal album, labelled "Last Jew of Vinnitsa." All 28,000 Jews from Vinnitsa and its surrounding areas were massacred.

60.
THE FINAL SOLUTION

By the beginning of 1942, the Germans had under their control close to nine million Jews (of the total eleven million Jews living in Europe and the Soviet Union). It was their plan to murder them all.

Already, the *Einsatzgruppen* killing squads had machine gunned 1.5 million Jews (as we saw in the previous chapter), but this was not an efficient way of killing the remaining millions — it was too messy, too slow, and it wasted too many bullets.

So the Germans embarked on a policy called the "Final Solution" which was decided upon at a conference held in Wannsee, near Berlin, on January 20, 1942:

> Instead of immigration there is now a further possible solution to which the Fuhrer has already signified his consent. Namely deportation to the East. Although this should be regarded merely as an interim measure, it will provide us with the practical experience which will be especially valuable in connection with the future final solution. In the course of the practical implementation of the final solution Europe will be combed from West to East.[483]

The Final Solution — the systematic gassing of millions of Jews — was implemented by the top Gestapo brass, namely Adolph Eichmann and Reinhardt Heidrich.

Of the twenty-four concentration camps (besides countless labor camps), six specific death camps were established. They were:

- Auschwitz-Birkenau — where 1,500,000 were murdered;
- Chelmno — where 320,000 were murdered;
- Treblinka — where 870,000 were murdered;
- Sobibor — where 250,000 were murdered;
- Maidenek — where 360,000 were murdered;
- Belzec — where 600,000 were murdered.[484]

Auschwitz is the most famous because there the killing machine was the most efficient. Between the end of 1941 and 1944, as many as 12,000 Jews a day were gassed to death there and then cremated. In addition to the Jews, hundreds of thousands of others who were deemed threats to the Nazi regime, or considered racially inferior or socially deviant were also murdered.

Jews arriving at the Auschwitz during World War II.
Most were immediately sent to the gas chambers.

DENMARK
SWEDEN
LATVIA
LITHUANIA
•Stutthof
Neuengamme•
Ravensbruck •
HOLLAND
Bergen-Belsen•
Sachsenhausen •
Treblinka
Chelmno
POLAND
BELGIUM
GERMANY
Sobibor
Majdanek
Buchenwald•
•Theresienstadt
Belzec
Auschwitz
Flossenburg •
CZECH REPUBLIC
FRANCE
•Plaszow
BELARUS
Natzweiler•
SLOVAKIA
Dachau •
•Mauthausen
AUSTRIA
SWITZERLAND
HUNGARY
SLOVENIA
•Jasenovac
UKRAINE
ITALY
CROATIA
•Gospic
BOSNIA &
HERZEGOVNIA
•Sajmiste
SERBIA
MONTENEGRO
MACEDONIA
ALBANIA
GREECE
NAZI LABOR CAMPS
AND DEATH CAMPS
• LABOR CAMPS
DEATH CAMPS

As if cold-blooded murder of millions of Jews was not enough, it was accomplished with extreme and perverse cruelty. To bring the victims to the death camps, the Nazis packed them into cattle trains, standing-room only, without food or water, without heat in the winter, and without toilet facilities. Many died en route. Those who reached their destination had their heads shaved, the hair to be used for stuffing mattresses. Stripped of all clothing, most were herded naked into the gas chambers.

Dr. Johann Kremer, a German SS surgeon, described the gassing of a group of French Jews, including 150 boys and girls under the age of fifteen:

> These mass murders took place in small cottages situated outside the Birkenau camp in the woods.... All the SS physicians on duty in the camp took turns to participate in the gassing, which were called *Sonderaction* ("Special Action").... When the transport with the people who were destined to be gassed arrived at the railway ramp, the SS officer selected, from among the new arrivals, persons fit to work, while the rest — old people, all children, women with babies in their arms and other persons not deemed fit to work — were loaded onto lorries and driven to the gas-chamber. There people were first driven into the barracks huts where the victims undressed and then went naked into the gas-chambers. Very often no incident occurred, as the SS men kept people quiet, maintaining that they were to bathe and be deloused. After driving all the victims into the gas-chamber, the door was closed and an SS man in a gas-mask threw contents of a Zyklon-B (cyanide gas) tin through an opening in the side wall. The shouting and screaming of the victims could be heard through the opening, and it was clear that they were fighting for their lives.[485]

Bizarre and sadistic "medical experiments" were done on many victims without the use of anesthetics. Some people were sewn together to make artificial Siamese twins. Others were submerged in freezing water to test the limits of human endurance.

Some of those deemed strong enough were used as slave labor for the Nazi war effort. On starvation rations, they were pushed to their physical limit and then killed or sent to the death camps.

The Jews were even debased in death. Gold fillings were torn from the mouths of the corpses. In some instances soap was made from their rendered bodies and lampshades from their skins.

Resistance Efforts

Any attempt at escape or resistance was met with brutal reprisals. For example, on March 14, 1942, a number of Jews escaped from a work detail in Ilja, Ukraine, and joined the partisans. In revenge, all old and sick Jews were shot in the street and 900 others were herded into a building and burned alive.

Sam Halpern, a survivor of the Kamionka labor camp, explained: "I would never consider escaping. I will not have others killed because of my decision."[486]

Nevertheless, in at least five camps and twenty ghettos, there were uprisings. The most famous attempt was the Warsaw Ghetto rebellion. On April 19, 1943, the Nazis began the liquidation of the ghetto — that is, shipping off Jews to Auschwitz — and were met with armed resistance.

Mordechai Anielewicz, who was twenty-three years old and one of the leaders of the Warsaw Ghetto Uprising, wrote in his last letter (dated April 23, 1943):

> What happened is beyond our wildest dreams. Twice the Germans fled from our ghetto. One of our companies held out for forty minutes and the other, for over six hours.... I have no words to describe to you the conditions in which Jews are living. Only a few chosen ones will hold out; all the rest will perish sooner or later. The die is cast. In the bunkers in which our comrades are hiding, no candle can be lit for lack of air.... The main thing is: My life's dream has come true; I have lived to see Jewish resistance in the ghetto in all its greatness and glory.[487]

But in the end, the Jews were no match for the artillery, machine guns, and troops of the Germans. (Compare 1,358 German rifles against 17 guns among the Jews.) It was only a matter of time before the entire ghetto was destroyed; those hiding in the bunkers were gassed, burned, or buried alive.

Unprecedented

The Nazi attempt to deliberately, systematically eliminate an entire people from the planet was unprecedented in human history.

Hitler targeted the Jews for a specific reason, which was not just racial. The elimination of the Jews had a unique "status" in Hitler's master plan. While he certainly killed millions of others (gypsies, communists, etc.), he made exceptions for all these groups. The only group for which no exception was made was the Jews — they all had to die. Writes Lucy Dawidowicz in *The War Against the Jews*:

> The final solution transcended the bounds of modern historical experience. Never before in modern history had one people made the killing of another the fulfillment of an ideology, in whose pursuit means were identical with ends. History has, to be sure, recorded terrible massacres and destructions that one people perpetrated against another. But all, however cruel and unjustifiable, were intended to achieve an instrumental ends, being means to ends and not ends in and of themselves.[488]

In other words, the elimination of the Jews was not the means to an end. It was an end in itself. What that end was Hitler explained himself in his writings and speeches.

Hitler believed that before monotheism and the Jewish ethical vision came along, the world operated according to the laws of nature and evolution: survival of the fittest. The strong survived and the weak perished. When the lion hunts, the young, the sick, and weak are always the first victims. Nature is brutal but nature is balanced. There is no mercy. So, too, in antiquity the great empires, the Babylonians, Greeks, and Romans conquered, subjugated, and destroyed other peoples; they respected no borders and showed no mercy. This Hitler viewed as natural and correct. But in a world operating according to a divinely dictated ethical system — where a God-given standard applies and not anyone's power and might — the weak did not need to fear the strong. As Hitler saw it, such a system emasculated the strong, and this was neither normal nor natural. In his eyes, the Jews were to blame.

His plan was to take over the world, set up a pagan master race and return the planet to what he viewed was its ideal natural state — "unpolluted" by Jewish ideas and Jewish offshoots such as Christianity. The words of the Hitler Youth song make this very clear:

> *We are the joyous Hitler Youth.*
> *We do not need any Christian virtue*
> *Our leader is our savior*
> *The pope and rabbi shall be gone*
> *We want to be pagans once again.*

But to implement his plan, he had to get rid of the Jews first. As he said:

> The Ten Commandments have lost their validity.... Conscience is a Jewish invention. It is a blemish like circumcision.... The struggle for world domination is fought entirely between us, between the Germans and the Jews.[489]

Everything in his war machine was set up for this purpose. At the very end, when the Allies were destroying the German army, he was not as much bothered by this as he was by the fact that there were Jews still alive.

One of the clearest examples of Hitler's single-minded (and seemingly suicidal) desire to rid the world of the Jews can be seen in the extermination of the Jews of Hungary. Until March of 1944, the Hungarian government had refused to allow the deportation of Hungarian Jews. Then, the Germans occupied Hungary, and by mid-May (two weeks before D-Day, when the Allied forces invaded France), the mass deportations to Auschwitz began. The Nazi leadership worked with particular intensity, as the Soviet army was rapidly approaching Hungary and the Germans knew that they were going to lose the war. But there was no way that Hitler could allow such a large Jewish community to survive. He diverted trains that were badly needed to transport supplies and more soldiers to the Russian front just to send more Jews to Auschwitz. To him, the greater enemy was the Jew.

Between May 15 and July 8, approximately 400,000 Hungarian Jews were sent to their deaths in Auschwitz, which was working at peak capacity.

Hitler's obsession with the Jews remained his primary focus even in the last moments of his life. Just before he committed suicide in his bunker on April 30, 1945, he urged on the fight against the enemy of all humanity — the Jews. His last dispatch read:

> Above all, I enjoin the leaders of the nation and those under them to uphold the racial laws to their full extent and to oppose mercilessly the universal poisoner of all peoples: International Jewry.[490]

Historical Context

It is important to note here that the anti-Semitism which drove the Nazis to undertake the unthinkable did not exist in isolation. It was not even Hitler's personal philosophy.

We might recall (from chapter 52) that it was one of Germany's biggest thinkers of the nineteenth century — Wilhelm Marr — who coined the term "anti-Semitism." In so doing he wanted to distinguish hatred of the Jews as members of a religion (anti-Judaism) from hatred of the Jews as members of a race/nation (anti-Semitism). In 1879, he wrote a book called *The Victory of Judaism over Germandom*, a runaway bestseller, in which he warned:

> There is no stopping them [the Jews]. Are there no clear signs that the

> twilight of the Jews is setting in? No. Jewry's control of society and politics as well as its domination of religious and ecclesiastical thought is still in the prime of its development. Yes, through the Jewish nation Germany will become a world power, a western new Palestine. And this will happen not through violent revolution but through the compliance of the people. We should not reproach the Jewish nation. It fought against the Western world for 1,800 years and finally conquered it. We were vanquished. The Jews were late in their assault on Germany but once started there was no stopping them.... I am marshalling my last remaining strength in order to die peacefully as one who will not surrender and who will not ask for forgiveness. The historical fact that Israel became the leading social political superpower in the nineteenth century lies before us. We have amongst us a flexible, tenacious, intelligent foreign tribe that knows how to bring abstract reality into play in many different ways. Not individual Jews but the Jewish spirit and Jewish consciousness have overpowered the world. All this is the consequence of a cultural history so unique in its way, so grand that everyday polemic can achieve nothing against it. With the entire force of its armies the proud Roman Empire did not achieve that which Semitism has achieved in the West and particularly in Germany.[491]

Keep in mind that when Marr wrote these words, the State of Israel did not exist, nor was there even a hint in the geo-political situation that it might come into being anytime soon. In speaking of the Jewish national threat, Marr was speaking about the great ideological struggle between the Jewish worldview and paganism, which had been playing out throughout history. We saw the same struggle between the Greeks and the Jews (chapter 27) and between the Romans and the Jews (chapter 33). Hitler saw it as continuing between the Germans and the Jews.

Hitler's understanding of the role of the Jews in the world was not warped. His was, in fact, the traditional Jewish understanding. When the Jews accepted the Torah at Mount Sinai, they became the chosen people, whose role and responsibility was to bring a God-given code of morality to the world. They were to be "the light unto the nations," in the words of prophet Isaiah.

And this is what Hitler wanted to bring to an end because, as long as there were even a few Jews left on earth, they were going to continue that God-given mission. As Robert Wistrich explained in *Hitler's Apocalypse*:

> If only one country, for whatever reason, tolerates a Jewish family in it,

> that family will become the germ center for fresh sedition. If one little Jewish boy survives without any Jewish education, with no synagogue and no Hebrew school, it [Judaism] is in his soul. Even if there had never been a synagogue or a Jewish school or an Old Testament, the Jewish spirit would still exist and exert its influence. It has been there from the beginning and there is no Jew, not a single one, who does not personify it.[492]

When we look at it from that perspective, we get a completely different view of what the Holocaust was about. Traditional Judaism says that it was part of the ultimate struggle between good and evil which had been going on since the beginning of time. Dennis Prager and Joseph Telushkin summed it up as follows:

> From its earliest days, the raison d'etre of Judaism has been to change the world for the better.... This attempt to change the world, to challenge the gods, religious or secular, of the societies around them, and to make moral demands upon others...has constantly been a source of tension between Jews and non Jews.... We now understand why so many non-Jews have regarded the mere existence of Jews — no matter how few — as terribly threatening. The mere existence of Jews, with their different values and allegiances, constituted a threat to the prevailing order.[493]

Liberation

In the end, Hitler did not succeed in his plan to completely eliminate the Jews. He managed to murder a significant portion of the world's Jewish population, thus teaching the world the meaning of evil.

When the Allied armies (Russians from the east and the Americans and British from the west) liberated the camps at the close of the war, they were met with scenes of unspeakable horror. The films made by the Allied forces upon entering the camps were so horrific that they were not publicly shown for many years.

The post-Holocaust death total in Europe was unimaginable. Intentionally using minimum figures and probable underestimates, Sir Martin Gilbert (in his work *The Holocaust*) finds that at least 5,950,000 Jews were murdered between 1939 and 1945. This figure represents 69 percent of the entire Jewish population of Europe. Hundreds of communities, some a thousand years old, were completely obliterated. Eastern-European Jewry had been virtually wiped out.

And they continued to die. The defeat of Nazi Germany did not end the deaths of Jews. In spite of Allied efforts to save them, many victims perished after liberation from weakness and illness. In Belse, 13,000 died after the British liberators arrived. Some who did survive met death at the hands of partisans or peasants when they left the camps. Some tried to reach their old homes, but either found nothing left or found that they now had new tenants who were very opposed to the return of the original owners.

The worst example occurred in the town of Kielce in Poland on July 4, 1946. When the 200 surviving Jews returned to their village, the local Poles, who were upset to see that any had survived, instigated a blood libel, accusing the Jews of the kidnap and ritual murder of a Polish child. In the ensuing violence, forty of the Jews, all Holocaust survivors, were murdered by the Polish townspeople.

Unable to return to their previous homes, Jews sat for years in refugee camps waiting for some country that would have them. Many sought to enter the Land of Israel — then in the hands of the British and called the Palestine Mandate — but the British barred them entry. They tried to enter illegally and many perished in the effort, as we shall see in chapter 64.

JEWISH POPULATIONS BEFORE & AFTER THE HOLOCAUST

COUNTRY	ESTIMATED PRE-WAR JEWISH POPULATION	NUMBER OF JEWS MURDERED	PERCENTAGE OF JEWS MURDERED
POLAND	3,300,000	3,000,000	90
UKRAINE	1,500,000	900,000	60
HUNGARY	650,000	450,000	70
ROMANIA	600,000	300,000	50
BELORUSSIA	375,000	245,000	65
BALTIC COUNTRIES	253,000	228,000	90
GERMANY & AUSTRIA	240,000	210,000	90
RUSSIA	975,000	107,000	11
THE NETHERLANDS	140,000	105,000	75
FRANCE	350,000	90,000	26
BOHEMIA & MORAVIA	90,000	80,000	89
SLOVAKIA	90,000	75,000	83
GREECE	70,000	54,000	77
BELGIUM	65,000	40,000	60
YUGOSLAVIA	43,000	26,000	60
BULGARIA	64,000	14,000	22
ITALY	40,000	8,000	20
LUXEMBOURG	5,000	1,000	20
NORWAY	1,800	900	50
DENMARK	8,000	?	?
FINLAND	2,000	?	?
TOTAL	8,861,800	5,933,900	67

61.
RETURN TO THE LAND OF ISRAEL

Yearning for the Land of Israel had never left the Jewish people.

We see it in the Psalms that Jews constantly recite: "If I forget you, O Jerusalem..." or, "When the Lord brings about our return to Zion, we will be like dreamers...."

We see it in the statements of the rabbis, such as this one by Rabbi Nachman of Breslav: "Wherever I go, I'm always going to Israel."

We see it in Jewish poetry, such as that of Judah HaLevi: "My heart is in the East but I am in the most far West."

We see it in holiday rituals: "Next year in Jerusalem."

And, of course, we see it in countless blessings recited daily: "Have mercy, Lord our God, on Israel Your people, on Jerusalem Your city, on Zion.... Rebuild Jerusalem, Your holy city, speedily in our days, and bring us there to rejoice in its rebuilding...."

The rebirth of Israel is an unprecedented phenomenon in human history. That a people should go into exile, be dispersed, and yet survive for 2,000 years, that they should be a nation without a national homeland and that they should re-establish that homeland is a miraculous, singular event. No other people has ever done such a thing.

A Look Back

Before we discuss the Jews' return to their homeland, let us look back at history and review briefly what had been happening in the Land of Israel from the time that the Temple was destroyed by the Romans in 70 C.E.

Shortly thereafter, Jerusalem was leveled, rebuilt on the Roman model, and renamed "Aelia Capitolina," but the name lasted only through the time of Roman occupation. The Land of Israel was renamed Palestine — after the extinct Philistines, some of the worst enemies of the Jews in ancient times — and this name survived forever after in Christian writings. Most Jews were forced to leave this Palestine due to economic hardship and persecution, and those few that remained were barred from Jerusalem (except on the ninth of Av). The Byzantine Empire — the Constantinople-based Christian version of the Roman Empire — continued the earlier policy, and Jews were not allowed into Jerusalem until the Muslims conquered the Byzantines in 638 C.E.

Once the Muslims took over the Land of Israel, they held onto it, with the brief exception of the period of the Crusades. The Turkish Ottoman Empire ruled there the longest: from 1518 to 1917. Yet, during all this time, the Muslims generally treated the Holy Land as a backwater province. There was no attempt to make Jerusalem an important capital city, and only a few Muslim dynasties attempted to improve its infrastructure (notably, the Umayyads in the seventh century, the Mameluks in the thirteenth century, and the Ottoman Sultan, Suleiman the Magnificent, who rebuilt the walls of the city in sixteenth century). Similarly, there was only limited development in the rest of the land, which was barren and populated by relatively few Arabs. The only major new city built was Ramle, which served as the Ottoman administrative center.

Mark Twain, who visited Israel in 1867, described it like this in *Innocents Abroad*:

> We traversed some miles of desolate country whose soil is rich enough but is given wholly to weeds — a silent, mournful expanse.... A desolation is here that not even imagination can grace with the pomp of life and action. We reached Tabor safely...[but] we never saw a human being on the whole route. We pressed on toward the goal of our crusade, renowned Jerusalem. The further we went the hotter the sun got and the more rocky and bare, repulsive and dreary the landscape became.... There was hardly a tree or a shrub anywhere. Even the olive and the cactus, those fast friends of a worthless soil, had almost deserted the country. No landscape exists that is more tiresome to the eye than that which bounds the approaches to Jerusalem.... Jerusalem is mournful, dreary and lifeless. I would not desire to live here. It is a hopeless, dreary, heartbroken land.... Palestine sits in sackcloth and ashes.

During the Muslim era, life for the Jews in Israel was for the most part easier than under the Christians. In 1210, following the demise of the Crusaders, several hundred rabbis, known as the "*Ba'alei HaTosafot*," resettled there, marking the emergence of the first Ashkenazi European community in Israel. In 1263, the great rabbi and scholar Nachmanides, also known as the Ramban, established a small Sephardic community on Mount Zion outside the Jerusalem city walls. (Later, in the 1400s, that community moved inside the walls, where they established the Ramban Synagogue which is going strong to this day.) When Nachmanides came to Jerusalem there was already a vibrant Jewish community in Hebron, though the Muslims did not permit them entry into Ma'arat HaMachpelah, where the Jewish patriarchs and matriarchs are buried. Indeed, this ban continued until the twentieth century.

More Sephardic Jews started to migrate to Israel following their expulsion from Spain in 1492. In the sixteenth century, large numbers of Jews migrated to the northern city of Tzfat (also known as Safed), and it became the largest Jewish population in Israel and the center of Jewish mysticism — the Kabbalah. In the eighteenth century, a student of the Ba'al Shem Tov named Gershon Kitover started the first Hassidic community in Israel. This community was part of what was called Old Yishuv. (Today you can visit the Old Yishuv Court Museum in the Old City of Jerusalem, and learn some fascinating facts about the community.)

Growth in the Nineteenth Century

Between 1808 and 1812, three groups (numbering about 500) of disciples of the Vilna Gaon, Rabbi Eliyahu Kramer, came to the Land of Israel. Initially they settled in Tzfat, but after several disasters including a devastating earthquake, they moved to Jerusalem, setting up numerous Torah study groups (called *kollels*). Their arrival revived Ashkenazic Jewry in Jerusalem and impacted on the customs and religious practices of the religious community in Israel.

Others followed and by 1880, there were about 40,000 Jews living in the Land of Israel, among some 400,000 Muslims.[494]

One of the major figures of this time period was Moses Montefiore (1784–1887) — the first Jew to be knighted in Britain. Montefiore had made his fortune with the Rothschilds, who amassed huge wealth in the Napoleonic Wars. According to one version of the story, they used carrier pigeons, and they knew about the victory at Waterloo before anyone else; this is how they made a killing on the London stock market. With his fortune made by age forty, Montefiore embarked on a career in philanthropy, becoming a tireless worker for the Jewish community of Israel. At that time, most Jews lived in what is now called the Old City of Jerusalem, specifically in the area now called the Muslim Quarter. The main entrance to the city for the Jews was through Damascus Gate, and of the many synagogues in Jerusalem, many of them were in the Muslim Quarter close to the site where the Temple stood on Mount Moriah.

The city was very overcrowded and sanitary conditions were terrible, but due to the lawlessness of that time, people were afraid to build homes and live outside. In 1858, Montefiore built the first settlement outside the walls of the Old City, now called Yemin Moshe. After he opened the door, more neighborhoods were built in the New City. One of the earliest ones, built in 1875, was Mea Shearim (which, contrary to popular lore, does not mean "Hundred Gates" but "Hundred Measures," as in Genesis 26:12).

Besides Montefiore, another extremely important personality in this period was Baron Edmond de Rothschild (1845–1934), a man who, more than anyone else, made the resettlement of Jews in the Land of Israel financially possible. During his lifetime he spent 70 million francs of his own money on various agricultural settlements (Rosh Pina, Zichron Yacov, Pardes Hannah, to name but a few) and business enterprises such as the Carmel Winery. So important and generous was Rothschild that he was nicknamed *HaNadiv HaYaduah*, "The Famous Contributor."

Although Rothschild was quite assimilated and disconnected from the Jewish yearning for the land, he was greatly influenced by Rabbi Shmuel Mohilever, who was one of the first religious Zionists from Poland. Mohilever converted Rothschild to his ideology and, from that point on, the rich banker began to look at Israel as an "investment." He made it possible for thousands of Jews to return to the land and survive there.

Early Political Zionism

Political Zionism did not appear until late in the nineteenth century, when it surfaced as a reaction to the intolerable persecution of the Jews of Russia. The early political Zionists, being largely secular, did not feel a special yearning for Israel rooted in tradition or religion. Rather, they felt that the Land of Israel was the only place where Jews could create a national identity, regain their pride and productivity, and hopefully escape the horrible anti-Semitism of Czarist Russia and other places.

One important organization involved in early political Zionism was called Hibbat Zion, "Love of Zion," founded in 1870, whose members were called *Hovevei Zion*, "Lovers of Zion." A major personality among the Hovevei Zion was Judah Leob Pinsker (1821–1891), a Polish doctor. Pinsker started out as one of the *Maskilim*, a group which wanted their fellow Jews to drop Judaism and merge with Russian culture, reasoning that if Jews were socially accepted, then Russian anti-Semitism would disappear. But after the pogroms that followed the assassination of Czar Alexander in 1881, he and many other of the *Maskilim* came to the conclusion that their efforts were futile. Like Theodor Herzl later, Pinsker was shocked at the depth of European anti-Semitism. The only solution, he came to believe, was for Jews to live in their own national homeland. Pinsker published his ideas in a pamphlet called *Auto-Emancipation*. In it, he penned these memorable words:

> We must reconcile ourselves to the idea that the other nations, by reason of their inherent natural antagonism, will forever reject us.[495]

In 1882, another important organization was formed in Russia. It was called "Bilu," an acronym of the opening words from a verse in the Book of Isaiah: "*Beit Yaacov lechu venelech* — House of Jacob, come, let us go...."[496] Bilu was very active in the early settlement movement, what came to be called the First Aliyah — the first large migration of Jews from Russia and Romania to the Land of Israel.

The word *aliyah* means "ascent." To migrate to Israel — to make aliyah — means to come from a low place and to "go up." (In antiquity, the term *aliyah* referred to a trip to Jerusalem, usually during one of the pilgrim festivals, Pesach, Shavuot, or Sukkot, and implied going up to the holiest place on earth — the Temple.)

The year 1882 marked the first such aliyah, when Jews began to arrive in the Land of Israel in droves. Some 30,000 Jews came in two waves between 1882–1891 and founded twenty-eight new settlements. Hundreds of thousands of acres were purchased by these early Zionists from absentee Arab landowners, who usually lived elsewhere in the Middle East. The majority of the lands purchased were in areas that were neglected and considered undevelopable — such as the sandy coastal plain or the malaria-infested swamps in the north. Amazingly, and with much effort, the settlers made the barren land bloom again.

What drove many of these early immigrants was an idealism that was captured by Zev Dubnov, a member of Bilu:

> My final purpose is to take possession of Palestine and to restore to the Jews the political independence which they have now been denied for two thousand years. Don't laugh. It is not a mirage. It does not matter if that splendid day will come in fifty years' time or more. A period of fifty years is no more than a moment of time for such an undertaking.[497]

In fact, it would take sixty-six years. Meanwhile, Jews would continue to come, reclaim the land and build a strong political movement, demanding the return of their ancient homeland.

62.
MODERN ZIONISM

We cannot study Zionism without studying Theodor Binyamin Ze'ev Herzl (1860–1904).

As a correspondent during the Alfred Dreyfus affair (which we covered in chapter 58), Herzl was shocked to hear the civilized French screaming, "Death to the Jews!" He determined then and there that the solution to anti-Semitism was the establishment of a Jewish national state.

Although Zionism was not his invention, Herzl became the driving force of the movement. There were several factors that made him a powerful leader:

- He was from Western Europe (and not Eastern Europe) — a part of the world considered to be more enlightened.
- He was very well-educated (he had a Ph.D. in law from the University of Vienna).
- He was a well-known journalist who could write and speak well.
- He was financially well-off and politically well connected (having married into a prominent Austrian-Jewish family).
- He had a charismatic presence and a striking appearance.

Even though he was raised as an assimilated Jew and was woefully ignorant of the religion of his forefathers, the anti-Semitism of Vienna and the Dreyfus affair had had a powerful impact on him. He became obsessed with Zionism and relentlessly traveled throughout Europe, meeting many heads of state, in his attempt to gain support for a Jewish state.

In 1896, he published a book titled *The Jewish State: An Attempt at a Modern*

Solution of the Jewish Question (*Der Judenstaat*), which gained him much notoriety and transformed him into a leading personality in the Zionist movement. In 1897, on August 29th, Herzl convened the First Zionist Conference in Basle, Switzerland. Present were 197 delegates from sixteen countries who formulated the initial Zionist policy. This gathering proved a major event in the establishment of the modern State of Israel. Afterward, Herzl wrote in his diary:

> Were I to sum up the Basle Congress in one word, which I shall guard against pronouncing publicly, it would be this: at Basle I founded the Jewish State. Perhaps in five years, but certainly in fifty, everyone will know it.[498]

On May 14, 1948, fifty years and nine months later, the State of Israel was founded.

Unfortunately, Herzl did not live to see it happen. He died at age forty-four of a heart attack, following the stormy controversy over the proposal that the Jewish people make their home in Uganda. Herzl, who had provisionally supported the idea, settled the controversy by convincing his detractors that he had remained faithful to Jewish settlement in the Land of Israel. Thus, he managed to preserve the unity of the Zionist Movement, but his weak heart gave out in the process.

Herzl's is a tragic story. Having given his life and fortune for the cause, he died bankrupt, leaving his family in turmoil. His estranged wife, Julia, died at age thirty-five. And his three children — Pauline, Hans, and Trude — all suffered untimely deaths. Pauline became a drug addict and died in France. Hans, after becoming a Catholic, shot himself on the day of Pauline's funeral. Trude, who was mentally ill, died at Theresienstadt at the hands of the Nazis. Herzl's only grandchild, Stephen Theodor (Trude's son), changed his name to Norman and committed suicide by jumping from a bridge in Washington D.C. in 1946.

Herzl was buried in Europe, but in 1949, after the State of Israel was founded, his body was disinterred and brought to Jerusalem. He is buried in a cemetery now known as Mount Herzl, where heads of state and military heroes are also buried.

Key Personalities

Of the many key personalities at this time, we must mention three:

- Chaim Weizmann (1874–1952)
- David Ben Gurion (1886–1973)

- Asher Hersh Ginsberg (1856–1927)

Weizmann was a Russian-born chemist, who early on in his youth became associated with the group Hovevei Zion ("Lovers of Zion"). After Herzl's death in 1904, he became the de facto leader of the Zionist Movement.

Interestingly, Weizmann invented artificial acetone — the chief ingredient in cordite, or smokeless gunpowder — in 1915 in the middle of World War I. His invention enabled the British to mass-produce gunpowder for the war effort.

Because of this, he became friendly with Arthur Balfour, the foreign secretary of England. Balfour, who in 1917 promised British support for a national homeland for Jews in Palestine, said that acetone converted him to Zionism. (We will discuss the Balfour Declaration in the next chapter.)

David Ben Gurion was born David Gruen in Plonsk, Poland. A very striking personality, he was small in stature but a real powerhouse. Although he came from a religious family which was fervently Zionistic, he, like most of the movement's leaders, abandoned his religious roots early on.[499]

Ben Gurion arrived in Israel in 1906 at age twenty, working in the orange groves and in the wine cellars of the early settlements. He was active in the Poalei Zion ("Workers of Zion"), but he took some controversial positions in his party — such as that immigrants and settlers have the right to manage their own affairs without interference from the Diaspora, that immigrating to Israel was the obligation of every party member, and that Hebrew should be the sole language of his party. At that time, Israel was still under the control of the Ottoman Empire and Ben Gurion, who had studied law in Constantinople, favored loyalty to Turkey and adoption of Ottoman citizenship for Jews. However, when World War I broke out and the Turks began to persecute Zionists, he ran into trouble with the authorities and was exiled. He went to New York, where he founded the Ahdut ha-Avodah ("United Labor") Party.

(The second part of Ben Gurion's story — when he returned to Israel from New York to become the head of the Jewish Agency in 1935 and then the first Prime Minister of Israel in 1948 — will be covered in the next chapter.)

The third key personality was Asher Hersh Ginsberg, whose pen name was Ahad HaAm. He was originally one of the *Maskilim* who became disillusioned with their plan to acculturate the Jews to Eastern-European society. He became the great intellectual leader of the early Zionist movement. He envisioned the Jewish state not as a refuge for the oppressed Jewry of the world, but rather a place where the modern Jew could create a new secular, progressive, "enlightened" state which would become the center of a new modern Jewish culture. In

1897, he wrote in *The Jewish State and the Jewish People*:

> This Jewish settlement...will become in course of time the center of the nation, wherein its spirit will find pure expression and develop in all its aspects to the highest degree of perfection of which it is capable. Then, from this center the spirit of Judaism will radiate to the great circumference, to all the communities of the Diaspora, to inspire them with new life and to preserve the overall unity of our people. When our national culture in Palestine has attained that level, we may be confident that it will produce men in the land of itself who will be able, at a favorable moment, to establish a state there — one which will be not merely a state of Jews but really a Jewish state.

Ginsberg personified the dominant element in the Zionist movement — "enlightened" Jews who wanted to solve the problem of anti-Semitism by helping Jews to assimilate. Only later, when they found their efforts were futile — in the face of terrible persecution which persisted no matter how much the Jews tried to blend in — did they turn to working for a Jewish homeland. Since many had been born into Torah-observant households and had consciously left religion behind in the quest to assimilate, most carried their negative attitudes toward Judaism into their new Zionist ideology.

The key factor which shaped their worldview was a brand of nationalism that was founded upon a desire to create a physical Jewish homeland and a new kind of Jew to build and maintain this homeland. Many of these early Zionist thinkers felt that centuries of ghettoization and persecution had robbed the Jews of their pride and strength. To build a homeland required a proud, self-sufficient Jew: a Jew who could farm, defend himself, and build the land. The pious, poor, ghettoized Jew — who presented a pathetic image of a man stooped-over and always at the mercy of his persecutors — had to go. To build a state required something altogether different — a "Hebrew."

The early Zionists called themselves Hebrews and not Jews, and deliberately changed their German, Russian, or Yiddish names to sound more Hebraic and nationalistic. (For example, David Gruen became David Ben Gurion, Shymon Perski became Shimon Peres, etc.) It was a deliberate attempt to create a totally new Jewish identity and eliminate any aspect of the old. They believed that this new Jewish state, populated by fighting, farming Hebrews, would revitalize the Jewish people, restore Jewish pride, and put an end to anti-Semitism once and for all.

While there is no doubt that the Jewish immigrants who created the modern Jewish state accomplished amazing feats against all odds, Zionism has not proven to be the solution to anti-Semitism and, ironically, today the number-one excuse for Jew-hatred in the world is Zionism and the State of Israel. These early Zionist leaders knew, of course, that religion had preserved Jewish identity in the ghettos and shtetls of Europe, but in the modern Jewish state, they felt there would be no need for it. Of course, the Bible would have to be used as a source of Jewish history and culture, but there was no room for religion or ritual in the modern Jewish state.

Reaction to Zionism

The strong anti-religious attitude of much of the early Zionist leadership put them at complete odds with vast majority of the rabbinic leadership of Europe, who maintained that Torah and its commandments were the essence of what Judaism was all about, and a Jewish nation without these key ingredients would be a like a body without a soul. More than that, the Torah explicitly states, over and over again, that the ability to live and prosper in the land is totally dependent on the Jewish people keeping its commandments.[500] How could a Zionist leadership that was largely anti-religious and bent on driving Jews away from Judaism possibly succeed in creating a Jewish presence in the Land of Israel?

The position of Rabbi Tzadok HaKohen Rabinowitz (1823–1900), who was known as the Tzadik of Lublin, typified this view:

> We surely know that if we were believers and truly trusted in the salvation of the Lord and were observers of the commandments of God, we would even today be dwelling in our Holy Land.... "Why did the land perish? Because they abandoned My laws which I put before them." It has already been made clear that the Zionists reject all the commandments and cleave to every manner of abomination.... It may be assumed that, if the Zionists gain domination, they will seek to remove from the hearts of Israel belief in God and in the truth of Torah.... They have thrown off their garments of assimilation and put on a cloak of zeal, so that they appear zealous on the behalf of Judaism. They are, in fact, digging a mine beneath our faith and seeking to lead Israel from beneath the wings of the Shechina, the divine Presence.[501]

The anti-religious sentiment within Zionism was not the only problem. As with the Reform Movement in Germany in the nineteenth century, the Zionist leadership often took an active role in trying to "help" new arrivals to the Land of Israel assimilate into their new identity by actively seeking to separate Jews from Judaism and Torah observance. This was often achieved by deliberately placing new immigrants, often Sephardic Jews, into secular environments such as anti-religious collective farms known as "kibbutzim." This led to the rapid secularization of a significant proportion of Jewish immigrants from Muslim countries who, having not experienced the European Enlightenment, had remained overwhelmingly observant, ironically, until their arrival in Israel.

The biggest irony in all of this is that 100 years later, secular Zionism has largely disappeared as an ideology, with the vast majority of secular Israelis no longer characterizing themselves as Zionist. Religion and observance, however, are rapidly rising among the general population. The most recent survey (conducted in 2007) indicates that 30 percent of Israelis describe themselves as religiously observant and another 40 percent say they are traditional. Totally secular Jews are now the minority, and truly anti-religious Jews are a very small percentage of the population. (The core of anti-religious sentiment in Israel today rests with a small but very powerful and influential Ashkenazi elite, who still largely control the courts, newspapers, television, radio, universities, and the army.)

Back at the turn of the twentieth century, when the majority of the rabbis of Europe took a decidedly anti-Zionist stance, not all Orthodox Jews agreed. There were numerous religious Zionists who were some of the fiercest advocates for returning to the land. As we saw in the previous chapter, it was Rabbi Shmuel Mohilever, one of the first religious Zionists from Poland, who heavily influenced Baron de Rothschild to support early settlements. Another key figure was Rabbi Abraham Isaac Kook (1865–1935), Torah scholar and Kabbalist, who arrived in Palestine in 1904 and was one of the leading Torah authorities in pre-state days. He saw God's hand in the foundations laid by the secular Zionists and endeavored to work with them. He wrote his famous *Orot* ("Lights") about the holiness of the newborn nationalism. In 1921, he became the first chief rabbi of Palestine.

A year after the Fifth Zionist Congress met in 1901, a group of religious Zionists, in an attempt to synthesize modern Jewish national identity with the traditional Jewish identity founded the Mizrachi Movement (an abbreviation of the words *merkaz ruchani,* meaning "spiritual center"). The Mizrachi manifesto stated:

> In the lands of the Diaspora the soul of our people — our Holy Torah — can no longer be preserved in its full strength, nor can the commandments, which comprise the entire spiritual life of the people, be kept in their original purity.... The people have found one remedy for this affliction — to direct their hearts to that one place which has always been

> the focus of our prayers.... Zion and Jerusalem.... It has, therefore, been agreed by all those who love the spirit of their people and are faithful to their God's Torah, that the reawakening of the hope of the return to Zion will provide a solid foundation as well as lend a special quality to our people. It will serve as a focus for the ingathering of our spiritual forces and as a secure fortress for our Torah and sanctity.[502]

Today, the Mizrachi Movement has evolved into the right-wing religious-nationalist camp in Israel. These Jews serve valiantly in the Israeli army (the IDF) and are the backbone of the settler movement. (So, while secular Zionism has for the most part disappeared, religious Zionism is alive and well.) Among other religious groups, such as the ultra-Orthodox haredi community, the attitude today toward the State of Israel varies from pragmatic acceptance (there are several ultra-Orthodox parties in the Israeli political system) to total rejection of the system. The haredim generally do not participate in many of the institutions of State of Israel such as service in the Israeli army or sending their children to the state religious school system. The reason for this harks back to the conflict between the secular Zionist leadership and the rabbinic leadership in Europe in the late 1800s and early 1900s.

Back then, oddly enough, their anti-Zionist stance had placed the ultra-Orthodox and the Reform Jews of America and Germany in the same camp, albeit for different reasons. German Reform Jews said: "The hope for national restoration [to Israel] contradicts our feelings for the fatherland [Germany]." And American Reform Jews said: "We consider ourselves no longer a nation, but a religious community, and therefore expect neither a return to Palestine... nor the restoration of any of the laws concerning the Jewish state...." (see chapters 54 and 58 for more on this subject).

Still, whatever the reaction of the Jewish world at large, Jews kept returning to Israel.

In the previous chapter we covered the first aliyah, which brought 30,000 Jews to Israel between 1882 and 1891. The second aliyah — following the Kishinev Pogrom of Easter 1903 and the first aborted Russian Revolution of 1905 — brought another 40,000 Jews to Israel between 1904 and 1914.

The third aliyah — following World War I and the Russian Revolution — brought another 35,000 (between 1919 and 1923).

By this time, the dream of a Jewish homeland was no longer just a dream. It was becoming a reality as the victorious Allied Forces conquered the Ottoman Empire (which had picked the losing side in World War I) and the British assumed control of the Middle East.

63. THE BRITISH MANDATE

World War I changed the map of the world. It was a huge conflict waged over four years (1914–1918) that pitted the Allies (chiefly France, Britain, Russia, and later, the U.S.) and the Central Powers (Germany, Austria-Hungary, and the Turkish Ottoman Empire) against each other. The end result was very dramatic:

Russia of the Czars disappeared. In the midst of the war, and partly because of it, the Russian Revolution succeeded, creating the communist state known as the Union of Soviet Socialist Republics (U.S.S.R.).

The domination of Eastern Europe by Germany and the Austrio-Hungarian Empire ended. Poland — which had not existed for more than a hundred years, having been divided between Russia, Prussia (Germany), and Austria-Hungary — was recreated.

The entire Middle East, which had been part of the Ottoman Empire, was split into two great swaths: half to be controlled by France (the French Mandate), the other half by England (the British Mandate).

Balfour Declaration

It is important to keep in mind that the Ottoman Empire ruled the Middle East from the sixteenth century to the early twentieth century — that is, for some 400 years. During this time, the countries of Syria, Lebanon, Jordan, Iraq, Saudi Arabia, etc., did not exist. The residents of these areas were predominately Arab subjects of the Ottoman Empire living in loosely organized tribal communities.

The British Mandate — which was called "the British Mandate for Palestine" and also known as the Palestine Mandate — included the land mass on the West Bank of the Jordan River all the way to the Mediterranean Sea, as well as the land mass on the East Bank of the Jordan River.

When the British took over the Land of Israel, suddenly, the dream of a homeland for the Jews became a real possibility rather than just a fervent hope.

By this time, there were between 85,000 to 100,000 Jews living in the Land of Israel, of a total population of 600,000.[503] Most of the Arabs living in the land had migrated there only in the previous thirty years, attracted by the jobs created by the Jews who were building and farming. (Note that when Jews began to immigrate to Palestine in large numbers in 1882, fewer than 250,000 Arabs lived there.[504])

A big boost for a Jewish homeland came from Earl Arthur Balfour (1848–1930), then-British foreign secretary, who in 1917 promised his country's support. As mentioned in the previous chapter, Balfour became a friend of the Jewish cause in some measure because Chaim Weizmann's invention of artificial acetone, had enabled the British to mass produce smokeless gunpowder for the war effort.

A fascinating conversation is recorded between Balfour and Weizmann in 1906. Balfour argued that the Jews should consider the offer made by the British some three years earlier to emigrate to Uganda instead of Israel (at that time the Ottomans still controlled the Middle East). In response, Weizmann said to Balfour, "Would you take Paris over London?" Balfour replied, "But we already have London." (He meant, of course, Jews should take whatever they can get since beggars can't be choosers.) At which point Weizmann retorted, "Mr. Balfour, the Jews had Jerusalem when London was a marsh." That response gave Balfour pause.

"Are there many Jews who think like you?" he asked.

"I believe I speak the mind of millions of Jews whom you will never see and who cannot speak for themselves, but with whom I could pave the streets of the country I come from," Weizmann replied.

"If this is so, you will one day be a force," Balfour concluded.

Balfour's support for a Jewish homeland became known in history as the Balfour Declaration, which was issued in the form a letter to Lord Rothschild on November 2, 1917. It stated: "His Majesty's government looks with favor upon the establishment in Palestine of a national homeland for the Jewish people."

One month later, in December of 1917, the Turks surrendered Jerusalem to the British.

But talk is cheap, and when it came to the reality of creating such a state, the British had many other considerations and interests to take into account, as we shall see.

Failed Promises

Despite the support of certain British political figures, the British Foreign Ministry and others were generally much more pro-Arab, and the British government began carving out Arab countries from the lands of the Ottoman Empire.

Through their efforts, the country of Iraq was created in 1921. It was a monarchy with Faisal ibn Hussein, the son of the sherif of Mecca, as king. Soon thereafter, Iraqi oil started to flow to the West. Iraq has the second-largest known oil reserves in the world (after Saudi Arabia), and it is no wonder the British were interested in close ties with this country, as well as other oil-rich Arab states.

Another country created by the British was Jordan. In 1922, the British installed Abdullah ibn Hussein, another son of the sherif of Mecca, as emir of the new country called Trans-Jordan, later Jordan. It encompassed 75 percent of the total area of the British Mandate, but was confined to the East Bank of the Jordan River and did not include any part of the West Bank.

Why were the sons of the sherif of Mecca made rulers of these countries?

The British wanted alliances with all the Arab kingdoms. They had supported Ibn Saud of the Arabian Peninsula, who had fought the Turks alongside them. Ibn Saud got Saudi Arabia. But when that happened, the British had to pay off the Hussein Sherif of Mecca, who was in charge of the Islamic holy sites and who had also sided with British against the Ottomans in World War I. (The Hussein family are Hashemites, the tribe of Mohammed, the founder of Islam, and have been traditionally the keepers of Holy City of Mecca.) They had to give him and his children some land, so they gave them Iraq and Trans-Jordan — the land on the East Bank of the Jordan River.

Abdullah ibn Hussein (who got Jordan) was not adverse to the creation of a Jewish state and even met secretly with members of the Jewish Agency. He paid for his moderation with his life when he was gunned down by an assassin on the Temple Mount in Jerusalem on July 20, 1951. His brother, Faisal II (who got Iraq), was also willing to live at peace with a Jewish state and even welcomed the return of the Jewish people to the Land of Israel.

Despite all this country making, and despite the Balfour Declaration, the British could not get around to creating a country called Israel.

Why not? There was a clear British bias against the Jews, as is readily apparent to anyone who has studied the series of White Papers issued by the British government in the 1920s and 1930s. The reasons for this bias were:

The British had to deal with the issue of an Arab majority living in what was left of Palestine. They came up with many partition plans, all of which were rejected by the Arabs.

Many members of the British government and military were clearly anti-Semitic and had a romantic/patronizing attitude toward the Arabs.

The Arabs had oil and England needed oil. In the final analysis, the British had to take into consideration what was in their best strategic interests. Placating tens of millions of Arabs was more important in their eyes than saving a few hundred thousand Jews, even though this violated the terms of the British mandate, granted by the League of Nations, in 1922.[505]

Meanwhile the poor Jews, not knowing that the British were going to renege on their promise, kept migrating to the land.

The third migration or aliyah (between 1919 and 1923) brought 35,000 Jews to the land. The fourth aliyah (between 1924 and 1928) brought 80,000 Jews to the land. The fifth aliyah (between 1933 and 1939 as Hitler rose to power in Germany) brought 250,000 Jews to the land.

Arab Riots

The Arabs made it clear that they were not going to sit still for a Jewish state. In August of 1929, at the instigation of the preachers in the mosques, a series of riots broke out in which many Jews were massacred.

The *New York Times* in its history of Israel, *Israel: From Ancient Times to the Modern Nation,* writes of this time:

> The riots of August 1929 were ignited in Jerusalem over a rumor spread by Arab leaders that Jews were going to destroy Al-Aqsa Mosque, Islam's third most holy shrine. Fighting soon spread throughout Palestine. The worst massacres were in Hebron, sacred to Jew and Muslim alike, where 67 Orthodox Jews — men, women, and children — were slaughtered by Arabs and 50 more wounded. Pierre van Paassen, a reporter, described the horror that he witnessed by lamplight in a Jewish seminary

> in Hebron: "The slain students in the yard, the dead men in the synagogue, slashed throats and mutilated bodies." By the time order was restored, 133 Jews had been killed, 399 wounded.[506]

The 1930s saw more rioting and more massacres, especially in Jaffa and again in Hebron. In response, the British convened the Peel Commission, which almost totally did away with the Balfour Declaration that had originally promised a Jewish homeland in Palestine. In July of 1937, the Peel Commission issued a report stating that the Jews should be confined to a tiny state that would include a sliver of land along the Mediterranean coast and a small piece in the north abutting the west side of the Kineret lake ("Sea of Galilee").

In Arab eyes that was too much. They greeted the Peel Commission recommendation with a revolt which lasted until 1939. This revolt was led by Haj Amin Husseini (1893–1974), who was originally appointed as the Mufti of Jerusalem by the British.

It is interesting to note that in addition to hundreds of Jews who were killed by Arabs, some 3,000 Arabs died in this revolt at the hands of other Arabs and at the hands of the British. For all the British criticism of Israel today, at that time the British were not shy in their efforts to quell the rioting. They introduced the policy of housing demolition and used artillery to shell rebellious towns.

The revolt was finally crushed and the Mufti fled first to Beirut and later to Europe, where he became an ally of Adolf Hitler, organizing a Bosnian S.S. unit to kill Jews in the Balkans. After the war he was captured but escaped. He was later involved in fomenting violence, including the assassination of King Abdullah of Jordan in 1951. He died in Beirut in 1974. (Faisal Husseini, who was the PLO's representative in Jerusalem and who died of a heart attack in 2001, was a relative of his.)

Death Sentence

The British did not keep the promise contained in the Balfour Declaration, and neither did they keep the promise contained in the Peel Commission report.

They did, however, enforce one aspect of the Peel Commission report — that which limited Jewish migration to the land to only 15,000 a year for the next five years (1939–1943). By doing so the British doomed the Jews under the control of Nazis by ensuring they would no longer be able to find refuge in their homeland.

The British did this, knowing full well what the Germans were doing to the Jews — this was after the Nuremberg Laws and *Kristallnacht*. And still the British closed an escape route that would have saved millions of Jewish lives.

The Jews were desperate and they tried to come "illegally." In response, the British set up a blockade to keep them out.

Many Jews managed to circumvent the blockade, and it is estimated that 115,000 Jews got through. But 115,000 is a very small number compared to the six million Jews who died in the Holocaust and who could not find refuge anywhere — including the Land of Israel — because the British prevented it.

Meanwhile, the mainstream of the Zionist movement in Israel coalesced into the Jewish Agency, an organization headed by David Ben Gurion. Officially recognized by the British as representing Jewish aspirations, the Jewish Agency tried not to antagonize the British openly. But the Jewish Agency did have an underground military organization called the Haganah ("The Defense"), which tried to protect the Jewish settlements from the Arabs (since the British were doing next to nothing in this regard and were actually preventing the Jews from arming themselves).

There were other Zionists, who felt that the Jewish Agency was too conciliatory to the British. As they saw it, the British had broken promise after promise to the Jews and had openly sided with the Arabs. Therefore, they felt that the Jews had to be much more proactive. One of those who had a more aggressive attitude was Vladimir Jabotinsky (1880–1940). Originally from Odessa, Jabotinsky broke away from the mainstream Zionist movement and in 1923 formed the World Union of Zionist Revisionists. From 1936 on, this organization urged the evacuation of Eastern European Jews to Palestine. Had their pleas been heeded by the British, many Jews could have been saved from the Holocaust. At this time, Jabotinsky also became the head of the Jewish underground movement called Irgun Tzevai Leumi B'Eretz Israel ("National Military Organization in the Land of Israel") — simply known as the Irgun.

In 1941, Menachem Begin (1913–1992), who would later become Prime Minister of Israel, arrived from Russia; he assumed the leadership of the Irgun, which took a radical approach towards confronting the British and attacking the Arabs who were responsible for the death of Jews.

Another, even more radical group, was the Lochamei Herut Israel (meaning "Fighters for the Freedom of Israel") — better known as "Lehi" and called by the British the "Stern Gang" after its founder Avraham Stern (1907–1942). The future Prime Minister of Israel, Yitzchak Shamir, was one of the key leaders of Lehi.

After the devastation of the Holocaust, Jewish patience with the British withered, and these more radical groups engaged in violent resistance. For example, the Irgun blew up one wing of the King David Hotel in Jerusalem in 1946, which was then the headquarters of the British authorities in Palestine. Their prior warning was apparently received and ignored. Menachem Begin quotes one British official who supposedly refused to evacuate the building, saying: "We don't take orders from the Jews." As a result, the casualty toll was high: ninety-one killed and forty-five injured. Among the casualties were fifteen Jews. The Irgun also hanged two British army officers in retribution for the hanging of Irgun members and staged a daring breakout of the Acre (Acco) prison where the British held many Jews active in the resistance.

A senior British officer summed up the effects of the Jewish resistance groups:

> The British Army suffered greater losses in traffic accidents than in all the [Jewish] underground operations put together. But the blows to the Empire's pride and prestige were something which could not be digested. The break-in at the Acre Prison and hanging of the two sergeants were blows to our pride. The break-in at the prison gained the symbolic significance of the fall of the Bastille.[507]

But the British still did not give in.

64.
THE STATE OF ISRAEL

The British broke their promise to the Jews while they created new Arab countries out of the land of the former Ottoman Empire. In addition, because of Arab revolts and pressure, the British even barred entry to the Land of Israel to Jews fleeing the Holocaust. Even when the war was over, with the scope of the Holocaust fully known, thousands of Holocaust survivors were stranded in refugee camps because the British refused to relent.

One of the most egregious of the British actions involved the refugee ship *Exodus*, which the Royal Navy intercepted in 1947 in the Mediterranean Sea with 4,500 Jews aboard. The ship was brought into Haifa port under British escort; there, the Holocaust survivors were forcibly transferred to another ship and returned back to Germany via France.

Abba Eban, who was then the Jewish liaison to a special UN committee (called Special Committee On Palestine or UNSCOP), persuaded four UN representatives to go to Haifa to witness the brutality of the British against the Jews. Historian Martin Gilbert includes Eban's account of what happened there in *Israel: A History*:

> [In Haifa] the four members watched a "gruesome operation." The Jewish refugees had decided "not to accept banishment with docility. If anyone had wanted to know what Churchill meant by a "squalid war," he would have found out by watching British soldier using rifle butts, hose pipes and tear gas against the survivors of the death camps. Men, women and children were forcibly taken off to prison ships, locked in cages below decks and set out of Palestine waters." When the four mem-

bers of UNSCOP came back to Jerusalem, Eban recalled, "they were pale with shock. I could see that they were pre-occupied with one point alone: if this was the only way that the British Mandate could continue, it would be better not to continue it at all.[508]

UN Partition of Palestine

The British also wanted out of the problem. They had 100,000 soldiers/police trying to maintain control over a total population of about 600,000 Jews and 1.2 million Arabs. (Interestingly, until its independence in 1947, they had the same size force controlling India's population of over 350 million!)

And so it came to pass that the British turned the matter over to the UN, which decided to end the British Mandate over what was left of the Palestine Mandate (after the creation of the country of Jordan) and to divide the remaining land among the Arabs and Jews, based on the demographic reality within the country. Areas with a Jewish majority would go to the Jews, areas with an Arab majority would go to the Arabs, and Jerusalem would be under international control. Specifically, the Jews were to get: a narrow strip of land along the Mediterranean coast, including Tel Aviv and Haifa; a piece of land surrounding the Kineret lake (Sea of Galilee); a large piece in the south, which was the uninhabitable Negev Desert. The Arabs were to get: the Gaza Strip; a chunk of the north, including the city of Tzfat (Safed) and western Galilee; the entire central mountain region of Judea and Samaria (today known as the West Bank) up to the River Jordan.

The Arab reaction to this plan can be summed up in the words of Azzam Pasha, the Secretary General of the Arab League:

> The Arab world is not in a compromising mood.... Nations never concede; they fight. You won't get anything by peaceful means or compromise. You can, perhaps, get something, but only by force of your arms.... It may be that we shall lose Palestine. But it's too late to talk of peaceful solutions.[509]

Despite such vocal Arab opposition, on November 29, 1947, the United Nations voted for this partition plan.[510] Of those voting, 33 nations voted yes, including USA and USSR; 13 mostly Arab nations voted no; and 11 nations abstained. Hard-hearted to the end, the British did not vote yes; they abstained. They also announced that they would not cooperate in the execution of the partition plan and that they would depart from Palestine by August 1, 1948, though later they moved the date up to May 15.

As disappointed as the Jews were with the portion allotted for the Jewish state, they felt that something was better than nothing after all the waiting and the pain. However, the Arabs, always maximalist in their demands, rejected the UN resolution. The next day, Arab rioting began, and two weeks later volunteers from surrounding Arab countries began arriving into Palestine to fight the Jews.[511]

The British, happy to be out of the situation, were packing up to leave, and they turned their backs on what was going on. Writes David Ben Gurion in his *Israel: A Personal History*:

> The British did not lift a finger to stop this military invasion. They also refused to cooperate with the UN committee charged with supervising implementation of the General Assembly resolution. At the same time, the Arabs living in the district destined to become part of the Jewish state began evacuating their homes and moving to the Arab states neighboring Palestine at the orders of the Arab High Committee.[512]

In the midst of the confusion, the rioting continued, and almost 1,000 Jews were murdered by Arabs in the ensuing four months. One of the worst incidents occurred on April 13, 1948. A convoy of doctors and nurses making their way to Hadassah Hospital on Mount Scopus was ambushed by Arabs only 200 yards from a British police station. After a seven-hour shoot-out, during which the British did almost nothing, virtually all the members of the convoy (seventy-seven people) were killed. Some of the bodies were so badly burned that twenty-four were never identified.[513]

While this was happening, the British quietly encouraged the King of Jordan, Abdullah, to invade and annex the Arab sections to his kingdom. For Abdullah this was not enough. He wanted Jerusalem too. As a result, Jerusalem came under siege.

The focus of the struggle during April and May 1948 was the road to Jerusalem which passes through the mountains. The vehicles on that road were completely exposed to gunmen up above. It was on this road that all supplies to the Jews of the city had to come. But they could not get through. So steel plates were welded onto trucks in an attempt to create primitive armored cars that could withstand the constant ambushes. The narrow, winding road made easy targets of the overweight vehicles. Many were destroyed, and the convoys of badly needed food and other supplies were unable to reach Jerusalem. The residents of the Jewish Quarter of the Old City were completely cut off and hunger reigned.

The most intense fighting for control of the road to Jerusalem took place at the Kastel in the mountains to the west of Jerusalem. The Kastel was the site of an ancient fortress, and the Arab forces used the position as the staging area for attacks on the convoys. On April 5, 1948, the Haganah forces launched an attack on the Arab positions above the Jerusalem-Tel Aviv highway and the Kastel. The fighting was fierce and the position changed hands several times. And then an amazing incident happened. A young Yemenite Jew, who was not known for his shooting skills, killed Abdul Khader el-Husseini, the leader of the Arab forces. Demoralized, the Arab forces called off their counter-attack and, by the next day, had abandoned their positions to attend his funeral. As a result, a huge convoy of 250 trucks of food was able to resupply the city and several more convoys soon followed. Writes Berel Wein in *Triumph of Survival*:

> [On Shabbat, April 17, 1948] Jews left their synagogues and, with their prayer shawls still draping their shoulders, helped unload the convoy. The siege of Jerusalem was broken for the moment. The Arabs, however, mounted a strong counter-attack, and by the end of April once again cut the Jerusalem road...for the next seven weeks Jewish Jerusalem was isolated.[514]

A New State is Born

The official date for the creation of the two new entities was May 15, 1948. Thus, May 14 was to be the last day of the British Mandate. At 4 p.m., the British lowered their flag and immediately the Jews raised their own.

It was a flag designed in 1897 by the First Zionist Congress. It was white (the color of newness and purity), and it had two blue stripes (the color of heaven) like the stripes of a tallit, the prayer shawl, which symbolized the transmission of Jewish tradition. In its center was the Star of David.

Thus, on May 14, 1948, at 4:00 p.m., the fifth of Iyar, despite immense international pressure not to declare independence, the State of Israel came into being. After 2,000 years, the Land of Israel was once more in the hands of the Jews.

David Ben-Gurion, the first prime minister of Israel, reads Israel's Declaration of Independence in Tel Aviv, May 14, 1948.

David Ben Gurion read the Declaration of Independence over the radio:

The Land of Israel was the birthplace of the Jewish people. Here the spiritual, religious and national identity was formed. Here they achieved independence and created a culture of national and universal significance.... Exiled from Palestine, the Jewish people remained faithful to it in all the countries of the dispersion, never ceasing to pray and hope for their return and restoration of their national freedom. Accordingly we, the members of the National Council, met together in solemn assembly today and by virtue of the natural and historic right of the Jewish people and with the support of the resolution of the General of the United Nations, hereby proclaim the establishment of the Jewish state in Palestine to be called Israel.... We offer peace and amity to all neighboring states and their peoples and invite them to cooperate with the independent Jewish nation for the common good of all.... With trust in the Rock of Israel, we set our hands to this declaration at this session of the Provisional State Council in the city of Tel Aviv on Sabbath Eve, fifth of Iyar 5708, fourteenth day of May 1948.

Note that the Declaration of Independence of Israel — unlike the American

Declaration of Independence — does not mention God. This is because the hard-line secularists who dominated the Jewish Agency opposed any such thing. "Rock of Israel," which could be understood either as God or the Israel Defense Forces, became a compromise.

Secretary of the Israeli Cabinet, Zeev Sharef, described the scene in his book, *Three Days*:

> Rabbi Y. L. Fishman delivered the benediction of "Who has kept and sustained and brought us to this day," which the aged rabbi did in a trembling voice choked with emotion.... Suddenly the full impact of what had been done came home — the significance of the creation of the state.... As the signing of the document ended, "*Hatikvah*" was struck up by the orchestra, and it seemed as if the heavens had opened and were pouring out a song of joy on the rebirth of a nation. The audience stood motionless, transfixed.... "The State of Israel is established! This meeting is ended!" It had taken thirty-two minutes in all to proclaim the independence of a people who, for 1,887 years, had been under the servitude of other nations.... People embraced...tears of rejoicing streamed; yet there was grief for sons who had fallen and sons whose fate was in the womb of the future — grief and dread locked the innermost recesses of the heart. Outside thousands had gathered....[515]

Outside, the crowds were dancing in the streets. But not for long.

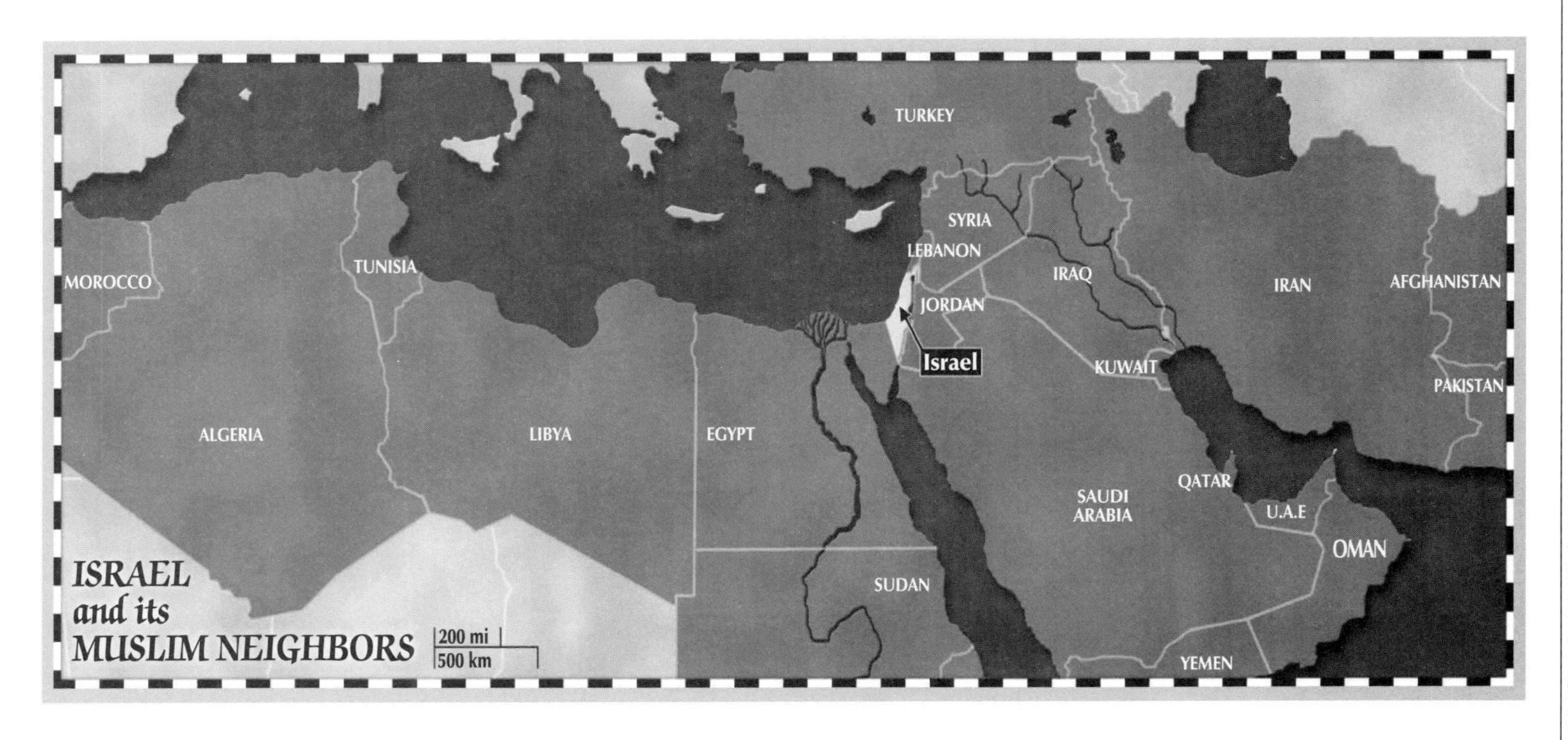
ISRAEL
and its
MUSLIM NEIGHBORS
200 mi
500 km
TURKEY
SYRIA
LEBANON
TUNISIA
MOROCCO
IRAQ
IRAN
AFGHANISTAN
JORDAN
Israel
KUWAIT
PAKISTAN
ALGERIA
LIBYA
EGYPT
QATAR
SAUDI ARABIA
U.A.E
OMAN
SUDAN
YEMEN

65.
WAR

No sooner had Israel become a state than it was plunged into war. Five of the neighboring Arab states attacked. These Arab states had previously voted against the UN partition of Palestine and now simply refused to recognize that historic and democratic vote.

Little Israel, which had virtually no heavy artillery, no tanks, no airplanes, had to defend itself against Egypt, Lebanon, Syria, Jordan, and Iraq! That's 600,000 Jews defending themselves against 45 million Arabs, while the United Nations did nothing.

And yet the Jews won. It was nothing short of a miracle.

But the victory was bittersweet. The Old City of Jerusalem — including the Jewish Quarter and access to the Kotel, the Western (Wailing) Wall — fell to the Jordanians. The Jews were driven out of the Old City, and their homes and synagogues looted and destroyed.

Even though the Jordanians signed an armistice agreement that would allow Jews access to the Western Wall and the cemetery on the Mount of Olives, they nevertheless barred Jewish access to these sites and desecrated thousands of tombs on the Mount of Olives. And, again, the world did not lift a finger to protest that the religious rights of a people were being violated.[516]

New Borders

The War of Independence lasted thirteen months. Some 6,000 Israelis died or a full 1 percent of the Jewish population at that time. (If that had happened in America, proportionally, 3 million people would have died. As upset as America was about the Vietnam War, it lost 52,000 soldiers in that conflict.)

Mount Herzl, the national cemetery, is full of graves without names. These are graves of Holocaust survivors who made it to Israel only to be handed a gun in order to fight for the survival of the Jewish nation. No one had time to get to know their names. They went down in history only as Yossi or Hershel or Moshe. It is tragic to see so many of these graves marked "Plony" (which is the Israeli version of "John Doe").

Already at the time of the UN partition vote, Arab residents of Palestine began fleeing in anticipation of war. The first to go were 30,000 of the wealthiest. By January 1948, the Palestine Arab Higher Committee asked other Arab countries to bar entry of refugees, because the Arab exodus from Palestine was so alarming. At the time of the declaration of the State of Israel, 500,000 Arabs fled as war broke out.[517]

At the same time, 820,000 Jews (out of a total estimated population of more than 870,000) were forced to flee Arab lands such as Syria, Iraq, Egypt, etc. Most of the property of these Jews, many of whom were wealthy, was confiscated, never to be returned. Of these Jewish refugees, about 580,000 settled in Israel.[518]

Once the war was over, Israel's Jewish population began to rise by leaps and bounds, with Jewish immigrants coming not only from Arab countries, but also from other states and more recently from Ethiopia and Russia. Israel's population statistics line up as follows:

1948: 600,000 Jews
1956: 1.2 million Jews
1973: 1.8 million Jews
1999: 4.7 million Jews
2007: 5.4 million Jews[519]
2009: 5.6 million Jews

Note that the population of Israel has increased by 930 percent (!) since the founding of the state. This increase has presented a special challenge, because of the huge economic burden of absorbing so many newcomers. However, while it has been a burden, the population growth has also been a big blessing. Immigration has had a tremendous impact on the country. The standard of living in Israel — which in 1948 was forced to ration food — has gone up enormously in the last two decades.

Was this a miracle? Clearly. But it certainly sounds like a step toward the fulfillment of the biblical prophecies:

> And the Lord your God shall return you from your captivity and have compassion upon you. He shall return and gather you from among all the nations. And the Lord your God will bring you back into the land your fathers inherited. He will make you even more prosperous and numerous than your fathers.[520]
>
> For thus says God, "Shout with joy for Jacob, exult at the head of the nations; proclaim your praise and say: 'O God, deliver Your people, the

remnant of Israel!' Behold, I will bring them back from northern lands, and gather them from the ends of the world...."[521]

But Israel has not only been able to absorb huge masses of people, it has not only survived living in a constant state of war, it has grown economically. And this despite various trade boycotts instigated by Arab nations. (For example, Pepsi Cola didn't do business in Israel for years because of the boycott. For many years, Subaru was the only Japanese car manufacturer to sell there.)

Keeping this in mind, it is absolutely miraculous what Israel has been able to accomplish. Not only did the "desert bloom," but in a relatively short time the once barren land was producing a surplus! This surplus was then exported to other, far more fertile countries like the United States. Another fulfillment of prophecy:

> But you, O mountains of Israel, shall yield your produce and bear your fruit for My people Israel, for their return is near. For I will care for you; I will turn to you, and you shall be filled and sown. I will settle a large population on you, the whole House of Israel; the towns will be resettled, and the ruined sites rebuilt.[522]

In 1997, the International Monetary Fund removed Israel from the list of developing countries, because it was by then fully developed, boasting the nineteenth highest standard of living in the world, just behind that of England.[523]

Six Day War

The Arab countries did not easily accept their defeat in 1948. All the while they were plotting a comeback.

On May 22, 1967, Egyptian President Gamal Abdel Nasser (1918–1970) declared that the Strait of Tiran — which is Israel's sea access to the Gulf of Aqaba and the Red Sea — was closed to all Israeli ships and any other ships bound for Israel. Blockading another country's port, according to international law, is considered an act of war, but initially Israel did not react, attempting to find a political solution.

Meanwhile, Nasser became more and more aggressive in his verbal attacks on Israel. On May 27, 1967, he declared: "Our basic objective will be the destruction of Israel." A few days later, on June 1, 1967, Iraq's president Abel Rahman Aref echoed Nasser's words: "Our goal is clear — to wipe Israel off the map."

Egypt and Syria already had an alliance combining their armies and now Egypt made a similar agreement with Jordan. It was clear that war was imminent. On June 5, 1967, Israel — realizing that the entire Arab world was about to attack — launched a preemptive strike.

It was one of the most brilliant preemptive strikes in history. In one fell swoop, Israeli planes destroyed the entire Egyptian Air Force as it sat on the ground, and a day later, they did the same thing to the entire Jordanian Air Force. Why didn't the Jordanians react after the Egyptians were bombed? Because the Egyptians were broadcasting that they had achieved a tremendous victory (when they had been completely crushed). Unaware of what was really happening, the Jordanians believed the propaganda and thus were unprepared.

In just six days, Israel captured large swaths of territory and won what is generally considered to be one of the greatest military victories in history:

- In the south, Israel seized the Sinai Peninsula (from Egypt).

- In the north, Israel seized the Golan Heights (from Syria); note that Syria, initially part of the French Mandate after World War I, became part of the United Arab Republic (together with Egypt and Yemen) in 1958; in 1961 Syria withdrew from the union, creating its own borders which included the Golan Heights.

- In the east, Israel captured Judea and Samaria, better known as the West Bank of the River Jordan, which Jordan annexed after 1948, though this land was never meant to be part of the country of Jordan when its borders were first drawn by the British in 1922.

- And most importantly, Israel reclaimed the Old City of Jerusalem, which was to have been "international" under the UN plan, but which Jordan unilaterally took over in 1948, barring all Jews from it.

Israeli paratroopers at the Western Wall after the capture of the Old City, June 1967.

For nineteen years, Jews had not been able to enter the Old City or pray at their most holy of sites, the Temple Mount or the Kotel (the Western Wall of the Temple Mount). Many of the soldiers fighting the Six Day War had not yet been born when this site was lost to the Jewish people. They had only seen it in photographs. Entering the Old City, they did not know where to go, and when they found it, they openly wept.

On the radio, the paratrooper who was leading the Old City forces, announced: "*Har HaBayit b'yadenu* — The Temple Mount is in our hands."

People were jubilant. They couldn't believe the miracle that had happened.

It must be stressed that the Jewish behavior in victory was in stark contrast to the Arab behavior after their victory over the Old City in 1948, when five dozen synagogues were looted and destroyed. Jewish soldiers did not dynamite the Dome of the Rock or any other mosque in the Old City, and access to these sites for Arabs has continued uninterrupted.

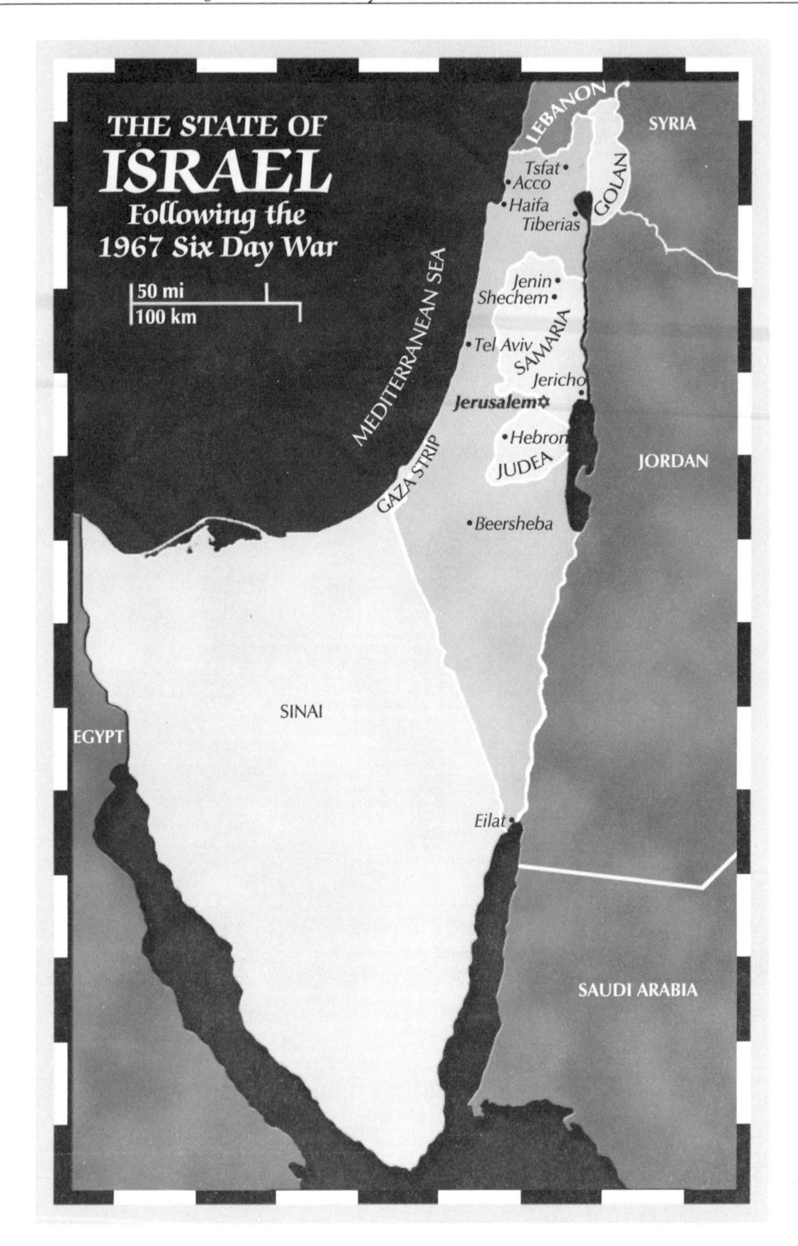

PLO

The Palestinian Liberation Organization (PLO) was founded in January 1964 by Ahmed Shukeiry as a representative organization of the Arab refugees of the 1948 war. It was never a peaceful organization, however. In fact, Shukeiry once predicted an Arab victory over Israel, saying: "Those [Jews] who survive will remain in Palestine. I estimate that none of them will survive." The first and consistent aim of the PLO was the elimination of the State of Israel and its replacement by the State of Palestine.

(It is important to note that a State of Palestine had never existed in history. The Arab people living in this land during the days of the Ottoman Empire were simply Arabs with no national identity. After the Ottoman Empire collapsed, in the days of the British Mandate, both Jews and Arabs were considered "Palestinians" by the British.)

Egyptian-born Yasser Arafat (1929–2004) was the head of Fatah, the PLO's terrorist group, and after the Six Day War he took control of the entire organization. One of the most infamous acts carried out under Arafat's direction in the early days was the kidnap and murder of eleven Israeli athletes at the 1972 Munich Olympics.

When this atrocity happened, the world again stood silent. The Olympic Games went on while the terrorists were holding the Jewish athletes. The Israelis wanted to intervene but the Germans refused their help. In the end, the Germans totally botched the rescue attempt, which led to the deaths of all the athlete hostages. Israel later hunted down and killed many of the terrorists responsible for Munich.

Since that time, the PLO and its various factions have carried out literally countless numbers of terrorist attacks against Israelis. To list them all would take a book in itself.

JEWISH/ARAB POPULATION OF ISRAEL AND THE TERRITORIES

YEAR	JEWS	ARABS*	TOTAL	% OF JEWS
1890	43,000	489,000	532,000	8%
1914	94,000	595,000	689,000	13.642%
1922	84,000	660,000	744,000	11.290%
1931	175,000	849,000	1,024,000	17.089%
1947	630,000	1,324,000	1,954,000	32.241%
1960	1,911,300	1,340,100	3,251,400	58.783%
1970	2,582,000	1,045,000	3,627,000	71.188%
1980	3,282,700	2,100,000	5,382,700	60.986%
1995	4,495,100	3,506,900	8,002,000	56.173%
2005	5,275,700	5,139,100	10,414,800	50.656%

*MUSLIM & CHRISTIAN

66. PEACE

Since the UN partition vote in November of 1947, Israel has consistently called on the surrounding Arab nations to live in peace with the Jewish state, but these offers have almost always been rejected. On May 14, 1948, the day the State of Israel was created, Prime Minister David Ben Gurion stated:

> In the midst of wanton aggression, we yet call upon the Arab inhabitants of the State of Israel to preserve the ways of peace and play their part in the development of the state, on the basis of full and equal citizenship and due representation in all its bodies and institutions.... We extend our hand in peace and neighborliness to all the neighboring states and their peoples, and invite them to cooperate with the independent Jewish nation for the common good of all.

The response — delivered the next day by Azzam Pasha, Secretary General of the Arab League — characterized the uncompromising Arab attitude toward the fledgling Jewish state:

> This will be a war of extermination and a momentous massacre which will be spoken of like the Mongolian massacre and the Crusades.[524]

Immediately following Israel's victory in the Six Day War, the Israeli government, led by Prime Minister Levi Eshkol, accepted the UN Resolution 242 and offered to return the captured territories to the surrounding Arab countries in return for peace treaties with its Arab neighbors. In August 1967, the Arab

League rejected the offer with three loud No's:

No peace with Israel.

No negotiations with Israel.

No recognition of Israel.

Yom Kippur War

Between March of 1969 and August 1970, Egypt initiated a war of attrition against Israel along the Suez Canal. The Egyptians shelled Israeli positions and Israel retaliated with counter-raids. This "low-level" conflict cost Israel the lives of 200 soldiers before a ceasefire was finally signed.

Three years later, on October 6, 1973 — on Yom Kippur, the holiest day of the Jewish year — the Egyptian and Syrian armies launched simultaneous mass attacks in the south (the Suez Canal) and the north (the Golan Heights). Israeli military leaders, while aware of the battle preparations by Egypt and Syria were, nonetheless, caught off guard by the surprise attack. The invading Arab armies breached Israel's poorly manned defenses and poured into the Sinai and the Golan.

Egypt and Syria had learned the lessons of the Six Day War and had invested heavily in training their troops and equipping their armies with a huge number of anti-aircraft and anti-tank missiles. Unlike in the Six Day War, when Israel achieved complete air supremacy within three hours, this time Israeli jet-fighters suffered heavy losses from surface-to-air missiles, while Israeli armor was similarly crippled by shoulder-fired anti-tank missiles.

Despite initial setbacks, Israel was able to mobilize its reserve troops and successfully counterattack,[525] not only beating back the invading armies, but also inflicting massive damage. The tide turned, and Israel invaded Egypt and Syria. Israeli armor was on the road to Cairo and Damascus, and only threats of Soviet military intervention brought an end to the fighting on October 24th.

Israel had won a great victory, but at a terrible cost. Some 2,378 Israelis died in the Yom Kippur War (compared to 766 in the Six Day War).[526] The nation's confidence was badly shaken, and the euphoria that followed the Six Day War vanished. Israel had survived, but had come within a hair's breadth of annihilation.[527]

Peace Accords

In 1979, Egyptian President Anwar Sadat — in a bold move that ultimately cost him his life (he was assassinated by radical Muslims in Cairo in 1981) — broke from the traditional Arab rejectionist position and signed a peace treaty with Israeli Prime Minister Menachem Begin. In exchange, Israel returned every square inch of the Sinai Peninsula it won in 1967.

For a time, Israel knew peace on its southern border, but not so in the north. Southern Lebanon had been largely taken over by the PLO and was used as a staging area for attacks against Israel. On June 6, 1982 — as a response to an assassination attempt against Israel's ambassador to the United Kingdom, Shlomo Argov — the government of Israel ordered an invasion into Lebanon. The invasion was called "Operation Peace for the Galilee" but came later to be known as the First Lebanon War. After battles with the PLO, and Syrian and Lebanese Muslim forces, Israel occupied southern Lebanon. Surrounded in West Beirut, the PLO negotiated safe passage out of the country with the aid of international overseers on August 21, 1982.

Grassroots frustration with the PLO to achieve results led to an uprising in Gaza and the West Bank called the *Intifada* (Arabic for "shaking off") which lasted from 1987 until 1993. Then, operating out of Tunisia, the PLO took credit. The First Intifada — there would soon be a second — was characterized by riots, violent attacks against Israelis, and suicide bombings.

During the Gulf War of 1991, when virtually all Arab states opposed Saddam Hussein's invasion of Kuwait, the PLO became the Iraqi dictator's most vocal supporter, while Palestinians in Gaza and West Bank cheered as Scud missiles rained down upon Israeli population centers.[528]

The Palestinian uprising came to a close when, on September 13, 1993, Israeli Prime Minister Yitzchak Rabin and PLO Chairman Yasser Arafat signed the Oslo Peace Agreement with the aim of ending the Arab-Israeli conflict and creating a Palestinian state. (This was followed by a peace treaty with King Hussein of Jordan on October 26, 1994.)

By virtue of the Oslo accords, the PLO — which was on the verge of collapse and which found its leadership challenged by an even more violent terrorist group called Hamas — was given a new lease on life. Now renamed the Palestinian Authority, the PLO leadership returned to the West Bank and Gaza, where, armed with the help of Israel, it took over oversight of various towns and lands transferred from Israeli to Palestinian control. But hopes that peaceful co-existence would result were soon crushed, as ongoing terror attacks caused Israel to lose confidence in the peace process.

Second Intifada

In the year 2000, Israeli Prime Minister Ehud Barak tried to bypass the interim steps prescribed by Oslo and jumpstart a final settlement. Meeting with Arafat and U.S. President Bill Clinton at Camp David, Barak made an unprecedented offer to completely withdraw from virtually all lands taken in 1967 in order to create a Palestinian state on this territory. Arafat turned his back on this offer and walked out of the meeting.[529]

Having closed the door on diplomacy, Arafat then initiated the Second Intifada, which lasted five years and which led to the deaths of more than 1,000 Israelis in various terrorist attacks, many of them suicide bus bombings.

In launching the Second Intifada, Arafat was emboldened by Israel's withdrawal from southern Lebanon earlier that year. That withdrawal was followed by the immediate collapse of the South Lebanese Army and Hezbollah's occupation and militarization of the Lebanese border with Israel.

In July of 2006, Hezbollah — backed by Syria and Iran — initiated an unprovoked attack on a patrol on Israel's side of the border. All the Israeli soldiers were killed or wounded and two were taken captive.[530] The attack triggered a thirty-three day Second Lebanon War in which Hezbollah fired thousands of missiles into cities and towns in northern Israel, and the Israeli forces re-invaded southern Lebanon.

Israeli Prime Minister Golda Meir once remarked that: "We will only have peace with the Arabs when they love their children more than they hate us."

Events of the past few years have unfortunately shown that the Arab world, for the most part, is not moving in the direction of peace. The Muslim world, especially Iran, continues to demonize, delegitimize, and threaten to destroy Israel. Palestinian children are taught to hate Jews and Israel and to aspire to be martyrs and suicide bombers.

Despite Israel's painful withdrawal from Gaza in the summer of 2005, the situation there has further deteriorated with the Hamas takeover in 2007. There is frequent (sometimes daily) firing of rockets and mortar rounds into southern Israel. It is clear that Hamas, the other violent Palestinian factions, as well as many other Islamic states, have still not abandoned their dream of destroying Israel.

Even a cursory overview of the events of the last sixty years make two points abundantly clear:

The conflict has never been about the creation of a Palestinian state — as the many rejected opportunities demonstrate — rather, the real issue is the inability of the Arab/Muslim world to accept a Jewish state of any size. The Arab goal remains the destruction of Israel. (Iran has now assumed the leading role in this campaign.)

If the Arabs were to lay down their arms there would be no more war, but if the Israelis were to lay down their arms, there would be no more Israel.

Yet, despite all these obstacles, Israel continues to hope for peace; its economy continues to expand; the high-tech industry is booming and the population continues to grow, as the Diaspora slowly diminishes and the Jewish people return home.

Perhaps the Israel Ministry of Tourism said it best when it coined the slogan — *Israel: The Miracle on the Mediterranean.*

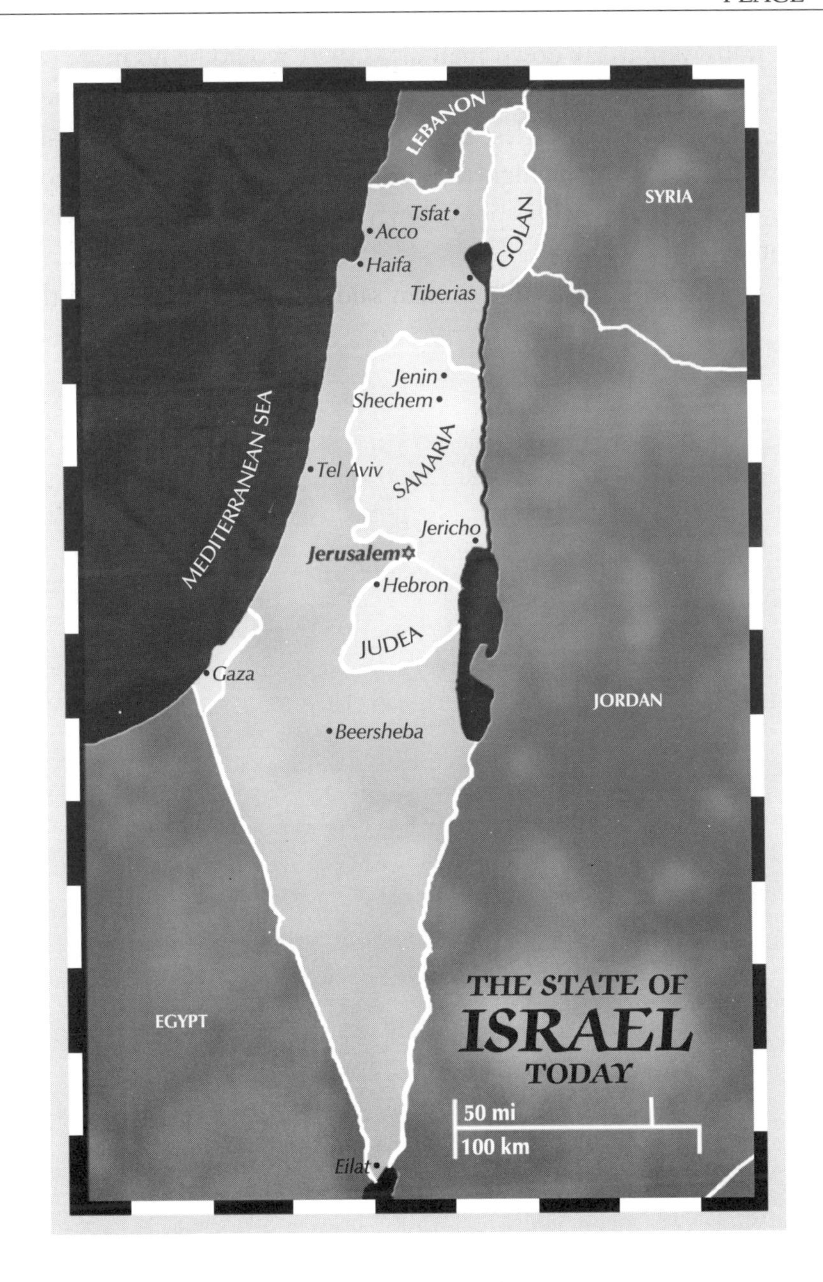
LEBANON
SYRIA
GOLAN
Tsfat
Acco
Haifa
Tiberias
Jenin
Shechem
MEDITERRANEAN SEA
SAMARIA
Tel Aviv
Jericho
Jerusalem
Hebron
JUDEA
Gaza
JORDAN
Beersheba
EGYPT
THE STATE OF
ISRAEL
TODAY
50 mi
100 km
Eilat

THE HISTORY OF THE MODERN STATE OF ISRAEL

YEAR	SIGNIFICANT EVENTS
1882–1903	First Aliyah, large-scale immigration since Roman exile, brings 30,000 Russian Jews to the Land of Israel
1896	Theodor Herzl publishes *The Jewish State*
1897	First Jewish Zionist Congress convened in Basle, Switzerland
1904–1914	Second Aliyah, mainly from Russia and Poland, brings 40,000 to the Land of Israel
1909	First kibbutz founded in Israel at Degania
1918	World War I ends and with it the 400-year rule of the Ottoman Empire over the Middle East
1917	Balfour Declaration promises a Jewish homeland in Palestine
1919–1923	Third Aliyah, mainly from Russia, brings 35,000 to the Land of Israel
1922	Britain granted the Mandate for Palestine
1921–1922	Kingdoms of Jordan and Iraq established
1924–1928	Fourth Aliyah, mainly from Poland, brings 80,000 to the Land of Israel
1929	Arab massacre of Jews in Hebron, Tzfat, Haifa, Jaffa, and Jerusalem
1933	Adolf Hitler becomes chancellor of Germany
1933–1939	Fifth Aliyah, mainly from Germany, brings 250,000 Jews to the Land of Israel
1937	Peel Commission rescinds Balfour Declaration but still envisions Jewish presence in the Land of Israel
1936–1939	Arab Revolt against British rule in Palestine — anti-Jewish riots
1939	British "White Paper" severely limits Jewish migrataion
1939–1945	World War II and Holocaust
1947	UN resolution calls for the partition of Palestine into Jewish and Arab states
May 14, 1948	End of British Mandate and Declaration of Independence by the new State of Israel
May 15, 1948	Israel invaded by five Arab states
1948–1949	Israel's War of Independence
1948	Jordan seizes west bank of the River Jordan. Egypt seizes Gaza Strip
1948	Mass migration to Israel of 580,000 Jews driven out of Arab states
1949	Israel signs armistice agreements with Egypt, Jordan, Syria, and Lebanon
1949–1967	Jerusalem divided, Jordan bars Jews from the Old City and the Western Wall (Wailing Wall)
1956	Sinai Campaign

THE HISTORY OF THE MODERN STATE OF ISRAEL

YEAR	SIGNIFICANT EVENTS
1963	Palestine Liberation Organization (PLO) is established
1967	Six Day War; Jerusalem reunited
1969–1970	Egypt's war of attrition against Israel
1972	Eleven Israeli athletes murdered at Munich Olympic Games
1973	Yom Kippur War
1976	Israel's dramatic rescue of hostages at Entebbe, Uganda
1979	Israel-Egypt peace treaty signed; Israel gives back Sinai
1981	Israel bombs Iraq's nuclear reactor
1982	Israel enters Lebanon to roust PLO
1984	"Operation Moses," airlift of 7,800 Ethiopian Jews to Israel
1987–1993	First Intifada — widespread Palestinian violence against Israelis
1988	US recognizes the PLO
1989	Start of mass migration of Jews from the former Soviet Union
1991	Persian Gulf War; Israel attacked by Iraqi Scud missiles
1991	"Operation Solomon," airlift of 14,500 Ethiopian Jews
1993	Oslo Accords signed establishing Palestianian autonomy and the Palestinian Authority
1994	Israel-Jordan peace treaty signed
1995	Prime Minister Yitzhak Rabin assassinated by Jewish student at peace rally
1996	Israel retaliates for Hezbollah attacks from Lebanon
2000	Israel withdraws from Lebanon
2000	Camp David meeting between U.S. President Bill Clinton, Israeli Prime Minister Ehud Barak and Palestinian Authority Chairman Yasser Arafat ends when Arafat walks out
2000-2005	Second Intifada — widespread Palestinian violence against Israelis
2005	Israel withdraws from Gaza
2006	Second Lebanon War launched by Hezbollah against Israel
2007	Terrorist organization Hamas takes over Gaza
2008	Israel celebrates sixtieth birthday
2009	Israel invades Gaza Strip to prevent rocket fire into Israel

67.
THE MIRACLE OF JEWISH HISTORY

On January 16, 1996, then-President of Israel, Ezer Weizmann, gave a speech to both Houses of Parliament of Germany. He spoke in Hebrew to the Germans, fifty years after the Holocaust, and in it he beautifully summed up Jewish history:

> It was fate that delivered me and my contemporaries into this great era when the Jews returned to re-establish their homeland...I am no longer a wandering Jew who migrates from country to country, from exile to exile. But all Jews in every generation must regard themselves as if they had been there in previous generations, places and events. Therefore, I am still a wandering Jew, but not along the far flung paths of the world. Now I migrate through the expanses of time from generation to generation down the paths of memory....
>
> I was a slave in Egypt. I received the Torah on Mount Sinai. Together with Joshua and Elijah, I crossed the Jordan River. I entered Jerusalem with David and was exiled with Zedekiah. And I did not forget it by the rivers of Babylon. When the Lord returned the captives of Zion I dreamed among the builders of its ramparts. I fought the Romans and was banished from Spain. I was bound to the stake in Mainz. I studied Torah in Yemen and lost my family in Kishinev. I was incinerated in Treblinka, rebelled in Warsaw and emigrated to the Land of Israel, the country from where I have been exiled and where I have been born and

from which I come and to which I return.

I am a wandering Jew who follows in the footsteps of my forebearers. And just as I escort them there, now and then so do my forebearers accompany me and stand with me here today. I am a wandering Jew with the cloak of memory around my shoulders and the staff of hope in my hand. I stand at the great crossroads in time, at the end of the twentieth century. I know whence I come and, with hope and apprehension, I attempt to find out where I am heading.

We are all people of memory and prayer. We are people of words and hope. We have neither established empires nor built castles and palaces. We have only placed words on top of each other. We have fashioned ideas. We have built memorials. We have dreamed towers of yearning, of Jerusalem rebuilt, of Jerusalem united, of a peace that will swiftly and speedily establish us in our days. Amen.

Supernatural

When we look back at the history of the Jewish people, which we have just examined at lightning speed in the pages of this book, we have to keep in mind that the very survival of the Jewish people through recorded time is nothing short of miraculous. The very fact that Jews exist as a nation today stands in testimony to the existence of God who acts in history. By any historical measure, the Jewish people should have disappeared long ago.

This was perhaps summed up best by David Ben Gurion, the first Prime Minister of the State of Israel. He said: "A Jew who does not believe in miracles is not a realist."

Why did he say that? Because miracles are the only possible explanation for the existence of the Jewish people.

More than 300 years ago, King Louis XIV of France asked Blaise Pascal, the great French philosopher, to give him proof of the supernatural. Pascal answered: "Why, the Jews, Your Majesty — the Jews."

An astonishing answer. The best proof of the supernatural that Pascal could think of was: "the Jews."

We don't have to speculate what Pascal meant when he gave this answer, because he took the trouble to spell it out in his 1670 work *Pensees*. Pascal said that the fact that the Jewish people survived until then was nothing short of a supernatural phenomenon. There simply was no logical explanation for it.

As we have seen from this book, Jewish history simply doesn't comply with the rest of history; it does not make sense. Many scholars, historians, and writers have noticed this and remarked about it.

Mark Twain (a.k.a. Samuel Clemens), the great American writer, who was an agnostic and a self-acknowledged skeptic, penned this in 1899 in *Harper's Magazine*:

> The Egyptian, the Babylonian, and the Persian rose, filled the planet with sound and splendor, then faded to dream-stuff and passed away. The Greek and Roman followed, made a vast noise and they are gone. Other peoples have sprung up and held their torch high for a time, but it burned out and they sit in twilight now or have vanished. The Jew saw them all, beat them all, and is now what he always was, exhibiting no decadence, no infirmities of age, no weakening of his parts, no slowing of his energies, no dulling of his alert and aggressive mind. All things are mortal, but the Jew. All other forces pass, but he remains. What is the secret of his immortality?

Leo Nikolaivitch Tolstoy, unlike Twain, was not an agnostic. He was a very religious Russian Orthodox Christian. He is also a very famous Russian author from the last century, perhaps best known for his *War and Peace*. He wrote this in 1908:

> The Jew is the emblem of eternity. He whom neither slaughter nor torture of thousands of years could destroy, he whom neither fire, nor sword, nor Inquisition was able to wipe off the face of the earth. He who was the first to produce the oracles of God. He who has been for so long the guardian of prophecy and has transmitted it to the rest of the world. Such a nation cannot be destroyed. The Jew is as everlasting as eternity itself.

In 1935, Nikolai Berdyaev, one of Russia's most famous philosophers of the twentieth century, wrote:

> The Jews have played an all-important role in history.... Their destiny is too imbued with the "metaphysical" to be explained either in material or positive historical terms.... Their survival is a mysterious and wonderful phenomenon demonstrating that the life of this people is governed by special predetermination, transcending the process of adaptation.... The survival of the Jews, their resistance to destruction, their endurance under absolute peculiar conditions and the fateful role played by them in history — all point to the particular and mysterious foundations of their destiny.

Keeping the Faith

There is another reason why the Jewish people survived as a nation through the millennia despite all the persecutions that we have barely touched on in this book — they have clung to their religion. The early Zionist writer Ahad Ha'Am (Asher Hirsch Ginsberg) is famous for saying: "More than Israel has kept Shabbat, Shabbat has kept Israel."

One of the most important lessons of Jewish history is that the more the Jews have been connected to Judaism — in lifestyle, in education, etc. — the more likely their children and grandchildren have remained Jewish instead of assimilating into oblivion.

Today, there are approximately thirteen million Jews in the world, when there should be five hundred million (according to natural population growth). The reasons why: (1) persecution, and (2) assimilation.

ESTIMATED WORLD JEWISH POPULATION

YEAR	TIME FRAME	POPULATION
11th c. B.C.E.	Jews settled in the Land of Israel (Time of Judges)	2,000,000
5th c. B.C.E.	Post-destruction of First Temple	300,000
2nd c. B.C.E.	Time of Greek occupation of Israel	500,000
1st c. C.E.	Time of Roman occupation of Israel	7,000,000
2nd c. C.E.	Post the Jewish revolts against Rome	2,000,000
5th c. C.E.	Byzantine (Christian) Empire dominates	900,000
11th c. C.E.	Islam dominates	1,300,000
15th c. C.E.	Time of Inquisition	1,900,000
18th c. C.E.	Time of Enlightenment	1,100,000
19th c. C.E.	Time of Emancipation of the Jews	3,500,000
1900	Time of rising Zionism	10,600,000
1940	Start of World War II	17,000,000
1945	Post-Holocaust	11,000,000
1960	Israel flourishes between wars	12,600,000
2000	2nd Millenium	13,000,000

The greatest strength of the Jewish people is also their greatest weakness. Jews are a "stiff-necked people." They have stubbornly clung to their beliefs and, as a result, outlasted all of the ancient empires of history while changing the way the entire world looks at morality and the concept of God. Jewish ideas — of one God, of a loving God, of a universal vision for humanity — have been at odds with the philosophies of all these empires, and to hold up that vision has required an unbelievable strength of character.

And yet, what is the greatest weakness of the Jewish people? Their stubborn individuality makes them unbendable.[531] Every Jew thinks he/she is right. The hardest job on earth must be to unify and lead the Jewish people.

Of course, this stubbornness, when focused in the right direction (through Jewish education and Jewish values) has enabled the Jewish people to accomplish great things. When unified, the Jewish people are an unbeatable force in human history. As the *Zohar* states:

> The Torah is like oil in a lamp, and Israel is its wick, causing the light of God to shine forth on all creation.[532]

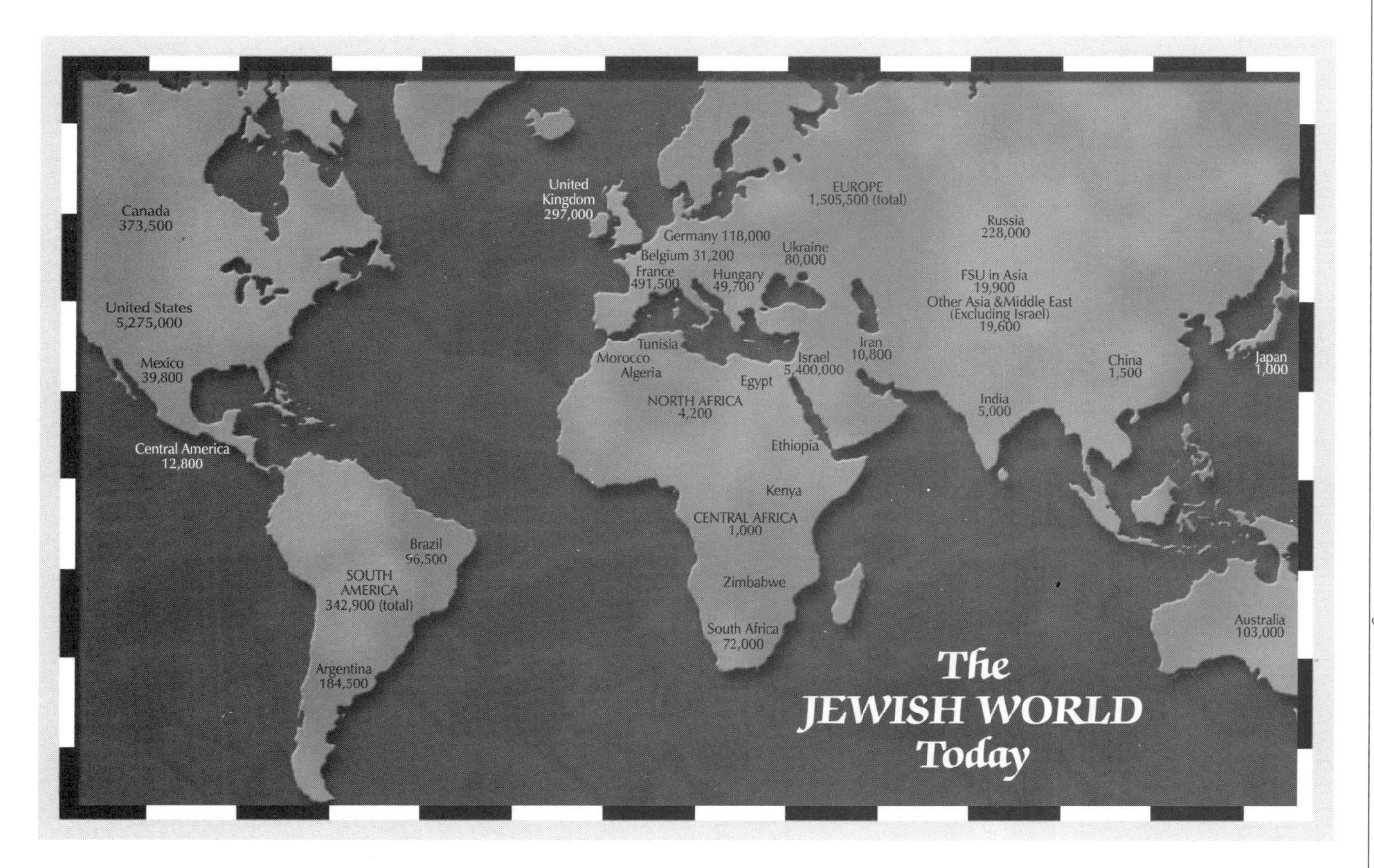
Canada 373,500
United States 5,275,000
Mexico 39,800
Central America 12,800
Brazil 96,500
SOUTH AMERICA 342,900 (total)
Argentina 184,500
United Kingdom 297,000
EUROPE 1,505,500 (total)
Germany 118,000
Belgium 31,200
France 491,500
Hungary 49,700
Ukraine 80,000
Russia 228,000
FSU in Asia 19,900
Other Asia &Middle East (Excluding Israel) 19,600
Tunisia
Morocco
Algeria
Egypt
Israel 5,400,000
Iran 10,800
NORTH AFRICA 4,200
Ethiopia
Kenya
CENTRAL AFRICA 1,000
Zimbabwe
South Africa 72,000
India 5,000
China 1,500
Japan 1,000
Australia 103,000
The JEWISH WORLD Today

68.
CONCLUSION

In this concluding chapter, we will examine what this all means from the metaphysical point of view. We will review the highlights of Jewish history we have learned thus far and ask: What does this all mean? Why are we going through all this? What is the point of human existence?

Many people believe that God created man to serve Him. However, this is not the Jewish perspective. If God is infinite, then He has no needs or wants. He lacks nothing, and there is absolutely nothing that human beings can do for Him. So why were we created?

One of the most fundamental ideas in Judaism is that God created us to forge a relationship with Him. Thus, connecting to God is what our soul yearns for. Every pleasure we experience and every meaningful relationship we form in this world is just a small taste of the ultimate relationship of our soul with our Creator.[533]

That is what the concept of the Garden of Eden was (and is) all about. The Garden of Eden is the ideal physical-spiritual reality, where we are freed from all the things that distract us (bills, shopping, carpools, etc.) and are totally focused on achieving the purpose of creation: elevating ourselves and the world around us to the highest possible relationship with God.

The plot line of human history should have been very straightforward — God placed us in a perfect environment (the Garden of Eden) where we were free to do that which we were created for, and we spent the rest of history hanging out in Paradise, perfecting creation and building a relationship with Him.

Unfortunately, something went wrong. When Adam and Eve ate from the

Tree of Knowledge of Good and Evil, things began to fall apart. For a while it seemed like the whole purpose of creation was lost — as the great disasters such as violence that preceded the Flood and rebellion against God that characterized the Tower of Babel attest. Then, along came Abraham, the Hebrew, who changed the course of history; his descendants, the Jewish people, are supposed to complete the mission he started — to bring humanity back to its relationship with God.

The Mission

The Jewish people are supposed to lead the way back to God using the Torah as a compass. This means that they are out in front like the point man in an infantry unit out on patrol. Just as the point man's job is to lead the unit, so too the Jewish people's special role in history is to lead humanity to its goal. Just as the point man faces extra danger because he's out in front with special, added responsibility, so too the Jewish people have always faced unique challenges and dangers. To understand this analogy is to understand what lies behind anti-Semitism and the outrageous double standard by which Israel and the Jewish people are always judged.[534]

Because Abraham and his descendants, the Jews, chose this special responsibility for themselves, they will never be allowed to be like anyone else. Balaam, the evil prophet who sought to curse the Jews without success, said it best: "It is a nation that dwells alone and is not reckoned among the nations."[535]

This, ultimately, is the explanation as to why, despite all the odds, the Jewish people have continued to survive and why their history is so supernatural. Beginning with Abraham, circa 1800 B.C.E., their unique role in the world has been critical to the plot of human history. They cannot be allowed to disappear, and God promised that it would never happen:

> And I will establish my covenant between Me and you and your descendants after you throughout their generations, an eternal covenant, to be your God and God of descendants after you.[536]

If we were to chart the historical progress of humanity's return to God with the Jewish people leading the way, we'd see some big ups and downs, but the overall picture would be one of steady and impressive growth. When Abraham came on the scene, he was virtually the only person who believed in one God.[537] Today, there are billions of people, Christians and Muslims, whose ancestors were pagans but who now believe in a worldview rooted in Judaism. And the very foundations of modern democracy are based on Torah values. While it still has a way to go, humanity has been radically changed by ideas introduced by Abraham almost 4,000 years ago and spelled out at Mount Sinai 3,300 years ago. As John Adams, the second president of the United States, summed it up:

> I will insist that the Hebrews have done more to civilize men than any other nation. If I were an atheist and believed in blind eternal fate, I should still believe that fate had ordained the Jews to be the most essential instrument for civilizing the nations. If I were an atheist of the other sect, who believe or pretend to believe that all is ordered by chance, I should believe that chance had ordered the Jews to preserve and propagate to all mankind the doctrine of a supreme, intelligent, wise, almighty sovereign of the universe, which I believe to be the great essential principle of all morality, and consequently of all civilization....
>
> They are the most glorious nation that ever inhabited this earth. The Romans and their empire were but a bauble in comparison to the Jews. They have given religion to three-quarters of the globe and have influenced the affairs of mankind more and more happily than any other nation, ancient or modern.[538]

The Flow of Time

According to the traditional Jewish understanding of this great drama, the plot of history unfolds within a finite time frame and is a clearly delineated into a beginning, a middle, and an end. In the broadest of strokes, the Talmud lays out the basic themes:

> This world will exist for 6,000 years. In the [first] 2,000 years, there was desolation; for [the next] 2,000 years the Torah has flourished; and [the final] 2,000 years will be the Messianic Era....[539]

These 6,000 years are calculated from the birth of Adam and mirror the weekly cycle. Just as the Jewish week begins on Sunday and runs for six days through Friday, so too is human history meant to be comprised of a maximum of six millennia.[540] At the end of the six days of the weekly cycle, we enter Shabbat, the seventh day of spirituality and rest, and so too, after a maximum of 6,000 years of history, humanity will enter the seventh millennium called "the World to Come" (*Olam HaBa*). The "World to Come" is synonymous with the Garden of Eden and represents the culmination of the process of returning to God and perfecting the world.[541]

We see from the Talmud that this 6,000 years is subdivided into three 2,000 years periods, each with its own theme. The first 2,000 years, from Adam to the Tower of Babel, is called "desolation," because during that time humanity was spiritually desolate and had no relationship with God. The second 2,000 year period, from Abraham to the compilation of the Mishnah, the basis of the Talmud, is called "Torah." The theme of this period is Jewish national history in the Land of Israel and the flourishing of Torah scholarship. The final 2,000 year period is called "Messiah." The theme of this final phase is humanity's return to God. At the end of this period, sometime before the year 6000, comes the Messianic Era, which is the final preparatory stage before humanity enters "the World to Come."[542]

So where do we, today, fit into this chronology? We are in the final 2,000 year period. Specifically, at the end of the sixth millennium. (Friday, late afternoon, close to the approach of Shabbat, so to speak.) From the Jewish perspective we are standing at the edge of history, rapidly approaching the climatic chapter that precedes the Final Redemption.

Last Part of the Puzzle

Jewish history is like a 6,000-piece puzzle. At the beginning, you dump the pieces on the table and it makes no sense. But as you assemble piece after piece, a picture emerges — a picture that records the action of God in history. There's no chance or randomness here, because everything happens for a reason. By Jewish reckoning we have assembled almost all of these pieces and have only a few hundred left to go. History is moving toward a conclusion, its final destination. That final destination is just around the corner and what it will look like has been described by the prophet Isaiah in this famous passage:

> In the days to come, the mountain of God's house shall stand firm above the mountains and tower above the hills. And all the nations shall stream to it. And the many peoples shall go and say: "Come, let us go up to the Mount of God, to the House of the God of Jacob — that He may instruct us in His ways, that we may walk in His paths." And they shall beat their swords into plowshares and their spears into pruning hooks; nation shall not lift up sword against nation. Neither shall they learn war anymore.... At that time, the wolf shall dwell with the lamb, the leopard lie down with the kid, the calf and the beast of prey shall feed together with a little child to herd them.[543]

May that time come speedily and in our days!

CHRONOLOGY OF ALL MAJOR EVENTS OF JEWISH HISTORY

HEBREW YEAR	BEFORE COMMON ERA (B.C.E.)	
Day 6	3761	Creation of Adam
930	2830	Death of Adam
1056	2704	Birth of Noah
1656	2104	The Flood
1948	1812	Birth of Abraham
1996	1764	Tower of Babel; dispersion of mankind
2018	1742	Covenant between God and Abraham
2048	1712	Birth of Isaac
2108	1652	Birth of Esau and Jacob
2216	1544	Joseph sold into slavery by his brothers
2238	1522	Jacob and his family move to Egypt
2332	1428	Beginning of Egyptian slavery
2368	1392	Birth of Moses
2448	1312	Exodus from Egypt Jews receive the Torah at Mount Sinai
2488	1272	Joshua leads the Jews into the Promised Land
2488	1272	Time of Shoftim (Judges) begins
2636	1124	Deborah judges Israel
2813	947	Samson judges Israel
2881	879	Prophet Samuel anoints Saul as king of Israel
2883	877	Prophet Samuel anoints David as king of Israel
2924	836	King Solomon begins his rule
2928	832	Construction of First Temple begins
2935	825	First Temple inaugurated by King Solomon
2964	796	The Kingdom of Israel splits
3143	617	Time of Prophet Isaiah begins
3205	555	Exile of the Ten Tribes by the Assyrian Empire
3213	547	Sennacharib at gates of Jerusalem
3298	462	Time of Prophet Jeremiah begins
3338	422	First Temple destroyed by the Babylonians

CHRONOLOGY OF ALL MAJOR EVENTS OF JEWISH HISTORY

3390	370	Persian ruler Cyrus permits the return of Jews to Israel
3405	355	Purim victory
3408	352	Construction of Second Temple
3413	410-312	Time of the Men of the Great Assembly
3429	331	Alexander the Great reaches Jerusalem
3448	312	Era of prophets ends with death of Simon HaTzaddik
3500	260	Period of *Zugot* (Pairs) begins
3515	245	Torah (Septuagint) translated into Greek
3622	138	Maccabee Revolt begins
3625	135	Miracle of Hanukah. Hasmonean rule begins.
3697	63	Roman general Pompeii enters Jerusalem
3728	32	Time of Hillel and Shammai
3742	18	Herod the Great renovates the Second Temple
HEBREW YEAR	**COMMON ERA (C.E.)**	
3790	30	Death of Jesus Beginnings of Christianity
3826	66	Great Revolt of the Jews begins
3830	70	Second Temple destroyed by the Romans
3833	73	Fall of Masada
3892	132	Bar Kohba revolt begins
3895	135	Romans crush last Jewish revolt
3896	136	Rabbi Akiva martyred
3950	190	Rabbi Judah HaNasi records the Oral Tradition Time of *Tanaim* (Teachers)
4066	306	Roman Emperor Constantine converts to Christianity
4128	368	Jerusalem Talmud compiled
4236	476	Fall of Rome and beginning of Byzantine rule of Israel
4260	500	Babylonian Talmud compiled Time of *Amoraim* (Explainers)
4382	622	Beginnings of Islam
4398	638	Islamic conquest of Jerusalem
4500	740	Time of Khazar conversion

CHRONOLOGY OF ALL MAJOR EVENTS OF JEWISH HISTORY

4527	767	Karaite sect founded
4687	927	Time of Sa'adiah Gaon Time of *Gaonim* (Geniuses)
4800	1040	Birth of Rashi Time of *Rishonim* (First Ones)
4856	1096	First Crusade
4891	1131	Birth of Maimonides
4900	1140	Judah HaLevi writes *The Kuzari*
4904	1144	First Blood Libel against Jews in England
5002	1242	Burning of Talmud in Paris
5027	1267	Nachmanides arrives in Israel
5050	1290	Expulsion of Jews from England
5108	1348	The Black Plague
5155	1394	Expulsion of Jews from France
5200	1440	Time of *Achronim* (Last Ones)
5240	1480	The Inquisition begins in Spain
5252	1492	Expulsion of Jews from Spain Columbus discovers America
5276	1516	Ottoman Turks conquer the Land of Israel
5277	1517	Protestant Reformation; time of Martin Luther
5324	1564	*Shulchan Aruch* published by Rabbi Joseph Karo
5408	1648	Chmielnicki Pogroms in Eastern Europe
5414	1654	First Jewish settlement in New Amsterdam (New York)
5436	1676	Death of Shabbatai Tzvi, false messiah
5460	1700	Birth of Ba'al Shem Tov, founder of Hassidism
5532	1772	Time of *Mitnagim* and Vilna Gaon
5536	1776	American Revolution
5549	1789	French Revolution
5551	1791	Time of the Enlightenment France gives civil rights to Jews Russia confines Jews to the Pale of Settlement
5563	1803	Yeshiva of Volozhin established
5570	1810	Reform Movement founded in Germany
5621	1861	American Civil War

CHRONOLOGY OF ALL MAJOR EVENTS OF JEWISH HISTORY		
5641	1881	Russian Czar Alexander II assassinated; pogroms against Jews
5642	1882	Mass immigration of Russian Jews to America
5647	1887	Conservative Movement founded in America
5654	1894	Dreyfus trial in France
5657	1897	First Zionist Congress in Basle, Switzerland
5674	1914	World War I begins
5677	1917	Balfour Declaration
5678	1918	End of World War I, Ottoman Empire dissembled; British conquer Jerusalem
5680	1920	British Mandate for Palestine begins
5682	1922	Country of Jordan created by the British
5693	1933	Hitler comes to power
5693	1938	*Kristallnacht* riots against Jews in Germany
5698	1939	World War II and Holocaust begins
5708	1948	State of Israel declared and War of Independence
5717	1956	Suez Campaign
5727	1967	Six Day War and Reunification of Jerusalem
5734	1973	Yom Kippur War
5739	1979	Israel-Egypt peace treaty
5742	1982	First Lebanon War
5750	1990	Mass Russian immigration to Israel begins
5751	1991	Persian Gulf War
5753	1993	Oslo Accords
5766	2006	Second Lebanon War
5768	2008	Israel celebrates sixtieth birthday

ACKNOWLEDGMENTS

This *Crash Course in Jewish History* has had many incarnations. It started out in 1999 as a series of classes given to students at the Aish HaTorah Yeshiva in Jerusalem. In 2002, these classes were transcribed and edited into an online series for Aish.com. In 2007, in response to popular demand, an updated and expanded version was again featured on Aish.com. A decade after it all began, finally, we have the book.

There are so many books already written on Jewish history that one might well ask, "Do we really need another one?" While there are a lot of books on the topic, there are remarkably few that are written from the traditional Jewish perspective, which holds that all of human history — not just Jewish history — is a controlled process leading to a predetermined destination. There are also very few Jewish history books that are readable as books, having been written as textbooks or reference works. My goal in both teaching and writing has always been to take the student or reader on a fascinating and meaningful journey through time, and to try and create material that is traditionally Jewish yet scholarly and academic. This book represents the culmination of these efforts, and I hope that the reader will find it both enlightening and enjoyable.

Without the effort, input and support of many people this *Crash Course in Jewish History* would never have made it into print. I am especially grateful to the following for making it all possible:

Uriela Sagiv, who also edited my first book, *WorldPerfect*, and who not only edited the first online series, but also put a tremendous amount of time and effort into the final editing of this book.

Nechemia Coopersmith and Shraga Simmons, the directors of Aish.com, who put the history series online and published this book.

Rabbi Yacov Blackman and Rabbi Arnie Wittenstein, who had invested many hours in reading the manuscript, and who were enormously helpful.

My father, Dr. Ronald Spiro, and my wife, Ruth Spiro, for taking the time to painstakingly proofread the manuscript and offer their suggestions.

My graphic artist, Moshe Handel, whose skills have contributed much to the quality and clarity of this book.

Rabbi Noah Weinberg, *zt"l*, Rosh Yeshiva of Yeshiva Aish HaTorah in Jerusalem, for his clarity and spiritual guidance over the years. Rabbi Weinberg had a profound impact on my life and the lives of tens of thousands of Jews. He was not only the visionary behind Aish HaTorah but also the great driving force behind the creation of the modern *ba'al teshuvah* movement (movement of return to Judaism). His passing is an enormous loss for the Jewish people. Although he is sadly no longer with us, his impact will be felt for generations to come.

Rabbi Yitzchak Berkovitz for giving me much food for thought and direction in the initial stages of this project.

There are numerous other people who have provided critical support over the years and thus enabled me to complete the project. I would especially like to mention:

- Dennis Berman
- David and Rochelle Bromfman
- Aba and Pamela Claman
- David Efron
- Dr Robin Ely
- Michael and Diana Epstein
- Rene Feinstein
- Barnet and Callander Goldberg
- Marc Goldman
- Mitch and Joleen Julis
- Mitch and Karen Kuflik
- Richard and Phylise Sands
- Dr. Ronald and Nina Spiro

My wife Ruth and my children, Tzvi, Daniel, Chava, Sarah, and Adina, for their love and support.

Most of all, I would like to thank God, who makes all things possible.

APPENDIX

CHRONOLOGY OF EXPULSIONS OF JEWS & MAJOR ANTI-SEMITIC INCIDENTS

DATE	PLACE	EVENT
250	Canhage	Expulsion
224	Italy	Forced conversion
325	Jerusalem	Expulsion
351	Persia	Book burning
357	Italy	Property confiscation
379	Milan	Synagogue burning
415	Alexandria	Expulsion
418	Minorca	Forced conversion
469	Ispahan	Massacre
489	Antioch	Synagogue burning
506	Daphne	Synagogue burning
519	Ravenna	Synagogue burning
554	Diocese of Clement (France)	Expulsion
561	Diocese of Uzes (France)	Expulsion
582	Merovingia	Forced conversion
612	Visigoth Spain	Expulsion
628	Byzantium	Forced conversion
629	Merovingia	Forced conversion
633	Toledo	Forced conversion
638	Toledo	Stake burnings
642	Visigothic Empire	Expulsion
653	Toledo	Expulsion
681	Spain	Forced conversion
693	Toledo	Jews enslaved
722	Byzantium	Judaism outlawed
855	Italy	Expulsion
876	Sens	Expulsion
1009	Orleans	Massacre
1012	Rouen, Limoges, and Rome	Massacre
1012	Mayence	Expulsion
1021	Rome	Jews burned alive
1063	Spain	Massacre

CHRONOLOGY OF EXPULSIONS OF JEWS & MAJOR ANTI-SEMITIC INCIDENTS

DATE	PLACE	EVENT
1095	Lorraine	Massacre
1096	Northern France and Germany	Third of Jewish population massacred
1096	Hungary	Massacre
1096	Ralisbon	Massacre
1099	Jerusalem	Jews burned alive
1100	Kiev	Pogrom
1140	Germany	Massacres
1144	England	First blood libel
1146	Rhine Valley	Massacre
1147	Wurzburg	Massacre
1147	Belitz (Germany)	Jews burned alive
1147	Carenton, Ramenu, and Sully (France)	Massacres
1171	Blois	Stake burnings
1181	France	Expulsion
1181	England	Property confiscation
1188	London and York	Mob attacks
1190	Norfolk	Jews burned alive
1191	Bray (France)	Jews burned alive
1209	Beziers	Massacre
1231	Rome	Inquisition established
1236	France	Forced conversion/massacre
1239	London	Massacre and property confiscation
1240	Spain	Forced Conversion
1244	Oxford	Mob attacks
1255	England	Public hangings
1261	Canterbury	Mob attacks
1262	London	Mob attacks
1264	London	Mob attacks
1270	Weissenberg, Magdeburg, Armstadt, Coblenz, Singzig, and Erfurt	Jews burned alive
1278	Genoa (Spain)	Mob attacks

CHRONOLOGY OF EXPULSIONS OF JEWS & MAJOR ANTI-SEMITIC INCIDENTS

DATE	PLACE	EVENT
1283	Mayence and Bacharach	Mob attacks
1285	Munich	Jews burned alive
1290	England	Expulsion
1298	Franconia, Bavaria, and Austria	100,000 Jews slaughtered
1306	France	Expulsion
1308	Strasbourg	Jews burned alive
1321	Teruel	Public executions
1328	Estella	5,000 Jews slaughtered
1348	France and Spain	Jews burned alive
1348	Switzerland	Expulsion
1349	Worms, Strasbourg, Oppenheim, Mayence, Erfurt, Bavaria, and Swabia	Jews burned alive
1349	Heilbronn (Germany)	Expulsion
1349	Hungary	Expulsion
1354	Castile (Spain)	12,000 Jews slaughtered
1368	Toledo	8,000 Jews slaughtered
1370	Majorca, Penignon, and Barcelona	Mob attack
1377	Huesca (Spain)	Jews burned alive
1380	Paris	Mob attack
1384	Nordlingen	Mass murder
1388	Strasbourg	Expulsion
1389	Prague	Mass slaughter and book burning
1391	Castille, Toledo, Madrid, Seville, Cordova, Cuenca, and Barcelona	Forced conversions and mass murder
1394	Germany	Expulsion
1394	France	Expulsion
1399	Posen (Poland)	Jews burned alive
1400	Prague	Stake burnings
1422	Austria	Jews burned alive
1422	Austria	Expulsion
1424	Fribourg and Zurich	Expulsion

CHRONOLOGY OF EXPULSIONS OF JEWS & MAJOR ANTI-SEMITIC INCIDENTS

DATE	PLACE	EVENT
1426	Cologne	Expulsion
1431	Southern Germany	Jews burned alive
1432	Savory	Expulsion
1438	Mainz	Expulsion
1439	Augsburg	Expulsion
1449	Toledo	Public torture and burnings
1456	Bavaria	Expulsion
1453	Franconia	Expulsion
1453	Breslau	Expulsion
1454	Wurzburg	Expulsion
1463	Cracow	Mob attack
1473	Andalusia	Mob attack
1480	Venice	Jews burned alive
1481	Seville	Stake burnings
1484	Cuidad Real, Guadalupe, Saragossa, and Teruel	Jews burned alive
1485	Vincenza (Italy)	Expulsion
1486	Toledo	Jews burned alive
1488	Toledo	Stake burnings
1490	Toledo	Public executions
1491	Astorga	Public torture and execution
1492	Spain	Expulsion
1495	Lithuania	Expulsion
1497	Portugal	Expulsion
1499	Germany	Expulsion
1506	Lisbon	Mob attack
1510	Berlin	Public torture and execution
1514	Strasbourg	Expulsion
1519	Regensburg	Expulsion
1539	Cracow and Portugal	Stake burnings
1540	Naples	Expulsion
1542	Bohemia	Expulsion
1550	Genoa	Expulsion

CHRONOLOGY OF EXPULSIONS OF JEWS & MAJOR ANTI-SEMITIC INCIDENTS

DATE	PLACE	EVENT
1551	Bavaria	Expulsion
1555	Pesaro	Expulsion
1556	Sokhachev (Poland)	Public torture and execution
1559	Austria	Expulsion
1561	Prague	Expulsion
1567	Wurzburg	Expulsion
1569	Papal States	Expulsion
1571	Brandenburg	Expulsion
1582	Netherlands	Expulsion
1593	Brunswick	Expulsion
1597	Cremona, Pavia, and Lodi	Expulsion
1614	Frankfort	Expulsion
1615	Worms	Expulsion
1619	Kiev	Expulsion
1635	Vilna	Mob attack
1637	Cracow	Public torture and execution
1647	Lisbon	Jews burned alive
1648	Poland	Third of Jewry slaughtered
1649	Ukraine	Expulsion
1649	Hamburg	Expulsion
1652	Lisbon	Stake burnings
1654	Little Russia	Expulsion
1656	Lithuania	Expulsion
1660	Seville	Jews burned alive
1663 C.E	Cracow	Public torture and execution
1664	Lemberg	Mob attack
1669	Oran (North Africa)	Expulsion
1670	Vienna	Expulsion
1671	Minsk	Mob attacks
1681	Vilna	Mob attacks
1682	Cracow	Mob attacks
1687	Posen	Mob attacks

CHRONOLOGY OF EXPULSIONS OF JEWS & MAJOR ANTI-SEMITIC INCIDENTS

DATE	PLACE	EVENT
1712	Sandomir	Expulsion
1727	Russia	Expulsion
1738	Wurttemburg	Expulsion
1740	Little Russia	Expulsion
1744	Bohemia	Expulsion
1744	Livonia	Expulsion
1745	Moravia	Expulsion
1753	Kovad (Lithuania)	Expulsion
1761	Bordeaux	Expulsion
1768	Kiev	3,000 Jews slaughtered
1772	Russia	Expulsion
1775	Warsaw	Expulsion
1789	Alsace	Expulsion
1801	Bucharest	Mob attack
1804	Russian villages	Expulsion
1808	Russian countryside	Expulsion
1815	Lubeck and Bremen	Expulsion
1820	Bremes	Expulsion
1843	Austria and Prussia	Expulsion
1862	Area under General Grant's jurisdiction in the United States	Expulsion
1866	Galatz (Romania)	Expulsion
1871	Odena	Mob attack
1887	Slovakia	Mob attacks
1897	Kantakuzenka (Russia)	Mob attacks
1898	Rennes (France)	Mob attack
1899	Nicholayev	Mob attack
1900	Konitz (Prussia)	Mob attack
1902	Poland	Widespread pogroms
1904	Manchuria, Kiev, and Volhynia	Widespread pogroms
1905	Zhitomir (Yolhynia)	Mob attacks
1915	Atlanta, Georgia (U.S.A.)	Leo Frank lynched

CHRONOLOGY OF EXPULSIONS OF JEWS & MAJOR ANTI-SEMITIC INCIDENTS

DATE	PLACE	EVENT
1919	Bavaria	Expulsion
1919	Prague	Widespread pogroms
1920	Munich and Breslau	Mob attacks
1926	Uzbekistan	Pogrom
1929	Lemberg (Poland)	Mob attacks
1930	Berlin	Mob attack
1933	Bucharest	Mob attacks
1935	Germany	Nuremberg Laws
1938	Germany	*Kristallnacht* 191 synagogues destroyed
1939-45	Europe	Holocaust
1952	USSR	"Doctors' Plot"— Jewish doctors accused of poisoning Soviet leaders. Hundreds of Jews imprisoned or killed.
1972	Germany	Massacre of Israeli Olympic athletes
1976	Entebbe, Uganda	Hijack and rescue of Air France plane
1994	Argentina	Bombing of Jewish Community Center. 85 people killed.
2003	Turkey-Istanbul	2 synagogues bombed. 23 killed, 260 wounded.

NOTES

1. The classic example is the date given for the destruction of the First Temple by the Babylonians. Traditional Jewish chronology gives the date as Jewish year 3338 equal to 422 B.C.E., while secular histories give the date as 586 B.C.E., a difference of 164 years. The source of this discrepancy is the based on conflicting opinions as to the number of kings who reigned during the Babylonian-Persian period. For a much more detailed discussion of this topic see: First, Mitchell, *Jewish History in Conflict: A Study of the Major Discrepancy Between Rabbinic and Conventional Chronology*, Northvale, NJ: Jason Aronson, 1997.
2. Today there are a number of renowned scholars also challenging the modern chronology and even attempting to reconcile it with the Jewish chronology. Among them is British scholar Peter James who writes: "By re-dating the beginning of the Iron Age in Palestine from the early twelfth century B.C.E. to the late tenth, a completely new interpretation of the archaeology of Israel can be offered — one which is in perfect harmony with the biblical record" (James, Peter, *Centuries in Darkness*, Piscataway, NJ: Rutgers University Press, 1993, p. 318).
3. Deuteronomy 32:7.

Part 1

4. Yerushalmi, Joseph, *Zakhor: Jewish History and Jewish Memory*, Seattle: University of Washington Press, 1982, p. 8.
5. We do get details of Abraham's life as a young man in another Jewish text known as the Midrash.
6. It is a quest steeped in vociferous debate, and politics have now also entered the fray. Archaeological support for the traditional view point would clearly strengthen the Jewish people's ancient historical claim to the Land of Israel while the opposite evidence would clearly weaken their case.
7. That is, there are no documents that specifically mention Abraham, for example, or manu-

scripts that describe the events recorded in the Book of Genesis, though there is quite a bit of evidence when we get to the time of the divided monarchy in the First Temple period.

8. Speaking of camels, for years skeptics have confidently asserted that the Bible's origins could not be as Judaism has maintained, because the Bible relates that Abraham owned camels, while camels were not domesticated until much later. However, it has since been archeologically proven — through finds of drawings, figurines and even camelhair rope — that camels were clearly domesticated long before Abraham. See Younker, Randall W., "Late Bronze Age Camel Petroglyphs in the Wadi Nasib, Sinai," *Middle East Archaeological Society Bulletin,* 42:47–54, 1997; Free, Joseph P., "Abraham's Camels," *Journal of Middle Eastern Studies*, 3:187–193, July 1944; and www.apologeticspress.org/articles/1781
9. For further reading see: Mazar, Amihai, *Archaeology of the Land of the Bible*, New York: Doubleday, 1992; Lesko, Leonard, and Frerichs, Ernest (editors), *Exodus: The Egyptian Evidence*, Winona Lake: Eisenbrauns Pulishing, 1997 (including the essay by Abraham Malamat, "The Exodus: Egyptian Analogies" and the essay by Frank Yurco, "Merneptah's Cananite Campaigns and Israel's Origins"). Also see the following articles in the journal *Biblical Archeology Review*: "The House of David and the House of the Deconstructionists" by Anson Rainey, Nov/Dec, 1994; "Exodus Itinerary Confirmed by Egyptian Evidence" by Charles Krahmalkov, Sept/Oct, 1994; "Save us from Postmodern Malarky" by William Dever, March/April 2000.
10. *Biblical Archeology Review*, September/October 1991.
11. Genesis 1:26.
12. For more information on the subject of the Bible and science, creation, and the age of the universe see: Aviezer, Nathan, *Fossils and Faith: Understanding Torah and Science*, Hoboken, N.J.: Ktav, 2002; Aviezer, Nathan, *In the Beginning: Biblical Creation and Science*, Hoboken, N.J.: Ktav, 1990; Schroeder, Gerald, *Genesis and the Big Bang Theory*, New York: Bantam, 1990; Schroeder, Gerald, *The Hidden Face of God: Science Reveals the Ultimate Truth,* New York.: Touchstone, 2002; Schroeder, Gerald, *The Science of God: The Convergence of Science and Biblical Wisdom*, New York: Free Press, 1997.
13. Genesis 2:7. Also see *Targum Okelos*.
14. In the 3,000 year history of ancient Egypt, it was conquered only three times: by the Hyksos, the Assyrians and finally the Greeks. Compare that to the Land of Israel, which has been conquered and destroyed dozens of times.
15. Talmud, Tractate *Sanhedrin* 109a.
16. Twain, Mark, *The Complete Essays of Mark Twain*, New York: Doubleday: 1963, p. 249. See also "Concerning the Jews," an essay by Mark Twain in Harper's magazine, September 1897.
17. The Talmud (in Tractate *Shabbat* 97a) discusses this concept and uses the phrase *Hem maminim b'nei maminim*, "They (the Jews) are believers, the sons of believers." The first believer was, of course, Abraham. He passed on to his children a kind of spiritual genetics — a drive and intensity that has always characterized the Jewish people.
18. Genesis 12:1.
19. Talmud, Tractate *Nedarim* 32a.
20. Numbers 23:9.
21. For the complete comparison of the ancient world and Jewish values see Spiro, Ken, *WorldPerfect: The Jewish Impact on Civilization*, Deerfield, Florida: HCI, 2003.

22. "Disproportionate" is really an understatement. Take virtually any cause in modern history (communism, socialism, civil rights, anti–apartheid, labor unionization, anti-globalization, SDS, feminism etc.) and if it wasn't founded by Jews (who make up just one-quarter of one percent of the world's population) it is disproportionately run by Jews. The explanation of this phenomenon is that nothing comes as close to Abraham's original mission to perfect the world as a cause. This explains why so many Jews today, the vast majority of whom are disconnected from their Jewish heritage, nonetheless still have that high-powered Jewish soul pushing them to make an impact.
23. Van Den Haag, Ernest, *The Jewish Mystique*, New York: Stein and Day, 1969, p. 13.
24. Ibid., pp. 38–44.
25. Ibid., p. 38.
26. Genesis 12:1.
27. Numbers 23:9.
28. Genesis 12:2.
29. Berdyaev, Nikolai, *The Meaning of History*, London: World, 1935, pp. 86–87.
30. For a more detailed explanation of this impact see *WorldPerfect: The Jewish Impact on Civilization.*
31. From his letter to F.A. Van der Kemp, 1806.
32. Genesis 12:3.
33. Gould, Allan ed., *What Did They Think of the Jews?* Northvale, NJ: Jason Aronson, 1997, pp. 92–93.
34. Genesis 15:18–21.
35. Genesis 17:8.
36. Deuteronomy 11:10–12.
37. Deuteronomy 11:13–17.
38. See Midrash, *Bereishit Rabbah* 1:2; *Rashi* on Genesis 1:1.
39. Genesis 16:11–12, 21:18.
40. Genesis 17:19–21.
41. Jewish tradition notes that after Sarah's death, Abraham took Hagar back as wife and that he fathered more children with her. See *Rashi* on Genesis 25:1, "Ketura is Hagar...."
42. Following the *Koran*, the Muslim tradition substitutes Ishmael for Isaac in the Bible story. (See *Koran*, Sura II, Verses 110–140.). Muslims celebrate a holiday called *Id al Adchah* ("The Feast of the Sacrifice"), which commemorates Abraham's attempt to sacrifice Ishmael instead of Isaac, having replaced Isaac with Ishmael in the story as told in Genesis, Chapter 22.
43. Genesis 22:14.
44. Genesis, Chapters 20 and 21.
45. Genesis, Chapter 16.
46. The Biblical commentators allude to the deeper meaning behind the well story. Wells and water are a symbol for Torah and spirituality. Stuffing them up is symbolic of the historic gentile rejection of the spiritual-moral mission of the Jews.
47. See God's blessing to Abraham in Genesis 12:2–3.
48. The Talmud (in Tractate *Niddah* 45b) says that women have *binah yeserah*, an added intuitive intelligence.
49. For a deeper understanding of this story, as well as Isaac's perception of his two sons, see

Rabbi Samson Raphael Hirsch's commentary on Genesis, Chapter 27.

50. Genesis 25:29–34.
51. Genesis 27:22.
52. Genesis 32:29.
53. It's interesting to note that the human hand is also unique. Other primates do not have their thumb opposite their index finger and, therefore, do not possess the same level of manual dexterity.
54. Genesis 36:1–15.
55. See Rashi on Genesis 33:4.
56. This, of course, helps us understand why the "enlightened" Europe of the mid–twentieth century could explode into such deep and violent anti-Semitism as the Holocaust. This doesn't mean that everyone who comes from a Western country is an anti-Semite. Clearly, this is not the case. Most people today are a mish–mash of many ancient races. Indeed, Amalek is no longer identifiable as a nation, but its spirit lives on.
57. Genesis 28:13–15.
58. *Pirkei Rabbi Eliezer* 35, *Midrash Tehillim* 91:7, *Zohar* 1:131a and 1:72a. Also see: Kaplan, Aryeh, *Jerusalem: The Eye of the Universe*, New York: NCSY, 1979, pp. 50–51.
59. According to Rashi, the mysterious stranger was the guardian angel of Esau, and the struggle between them was symbolic of the struggle between Esau and Jacob throughout history.
60. Genesis 32:29.
61. The name "Jews" came later, after the first exile from the Land of Israel and is derived from the ruling tribe of Judah.
62. There is reason to believe that Esau still hated Jacob. See *Rashi* on Genesis 33:4.
63. See *Rashi* on Genesis 33:14. Rashi asks: "When will Jacob go to Esau?" In answer, he quotes the prophet Ovadiah: "A redeemer will go forth from Zion to judge the mountain of Esau." This is a clear allusion to the Messianic Era, when even Esau's descendants will return to God and recognize the Jewish people's unique role in history. Also see Talmud, Tractate *Avodah Zarah* 8b.
64. See *Sforno* on Genesis 37:18.
65. The fact that these ancient, sophisticated nations were so into idolatry is proof that there was really some kind of power in it. Yet one of the most fundamental principles of Judaism is that there is no other power besides God — that idolatry is an illusion. So where did idolatry get its power from? The answer is God, Himself. The essence of being human is to use free will to make choices, and the ultimate choice a person makes is to live with the reality of God. To make this choice meaningful there have to be other "real" options. God put real power into idolatry to enable humanity to exercise its free will in this most–meaningful of decisions.
66. See *Rashi* on Numbers 18:3.
67. See *Ibn Ezra* and *Ramban* on Genesis 39:19–20.
68. Planted around Israel's national Holocaust memorial — Yad VaShem — are approximately six thousand trees. These trees are known as "The Forest of the Righteous Gentiles." The trees were planted in recognition of non-Jews who helped Jews during the Holocaust, often at great personal risk. To date Yad VaShem has a compiled a list of approximately 21,000 people listed as "Righteous Among the Nations." As beautiful as this is, it is also sad. Hundreds of millions of people lived in Europe during the Holocaust, yet only a fraction

lifted a finger to offer assistance.

69. See *Sforno* on Genesis 41:18. Examples of very dramatic changes for the worse can be seen in the expulsion edict of the Jews from Spain in 1492 and the Nuremberg Laws in Germany in 1935.
70. It is precisely for this reason that I am a huge advocate for all Jews, religious, secular or anywhere in between, to learn the laws of *lashon hara* — correct speech. The pen is mightier than the sword and the damage wrought by slander is incalculable. Correct speech is not just for Jews — it lies at the foundation of all civil society.
71. Genesis, Chapter 38.
72. In Jewish Law, this is called *yibum*. This custom has many details that we won't go into, and it is not practiced in the modern Jewish world.
73. See the Midrash, *Breishit Rabbah* 85:5.
74. Sivan, Gabriel, *The Bible and Civilization*, Jerusalem: Keter, 1973, p.10.
75. It's interesting to note that, according to the Midrash, the brothers suspected that Benjamin was the thief. It seems that by the time we reach the climax of the story, the brothers had not totally worked out their hatred and mistrust, but Joseph could not hold himself back any longer. Maybe if Joseph had pushed them just a little harder, this hatred would have been purged forever and Jewish history could have taken a very different, and less painful, path. See Midrash, *Bereishit Rabbah* 92:8.
76. Genesis 45:5–8.
77. Talmud, Tractate *Megillah* 13:b.
78. See the Chumash with commentary by Rabbi Nosson Scherman, Brooklyn: Artscroll, 1994, p. 369.
79. Exodus 1:11.
80. For more on the Pharaoh of the Exodus see: Finegan, Jack, *Light from the Past: The Archeological Background of the Hebrew-Christian Religion*, Princeton, NJ: Princeton University Press, 1946, Volume 1, pp. 117–121.
81. A great example of this subjectivity can be seen is the Lachish Relief in the British Museum in London. Taken from the palace of the Assyrian Emperor, Sennacherib, this relief depicts the siege and capture of the city of Lachish in Israel about 2,700 years ago. The fall of the city is depicted along with the slaughter or capture and exile of the survivors yet nowhere in the inscription can one find a single dead Assyrian soldier. This is typical of all such ancient inscriptions.
82. Exodus 2:7–10. See *Rashi* on Exodus 2:7, and Midrash, *Shemot Rabbah* 1:30.
83. For a definition and description of prophecy see *Derech HaShem* (The Way of God), Part III, 3:4 and 4:6.
84. Exodus 3:6, 13–16, and 4:5.
85. "Whatever God does is for the good." (Talmud, Tractate *Brachot* 60b)
86. Exodus 7:8–12.
87. Talmud, Tractate *Eduyot* 2:10.
88. Newton, Isaac, *Portsmouth Papers* (unpublished).
89. Talmud, Tractate *Megillah* 14:a
90. Maharal, *Gevurot HaShem*, Chapter 51.
91. Deuteronomy 4:33.
92. Maimonides, *Mishneh Torah*, *Hilchot Yesodei HaTorah* 8:1; also see his *Moreh Nevuchim*

(Guide to the Perplexed) 2:33. And Judah HaLevi, *The Kuzari* 1:6, 1:81, 1:87.

93. Talmud, Tractate *Shabbat* 88a (see in particular *Tosafot* commentary), also see Talmud, Tractates *Shavuot* 29a, *Nedarim* 25a, and Midrash, *Breishit Rabbah* 87:9.
94. Talmud, Tractates *Brachot* 5a, *Sotah* 37b, *Chagigah* 6a, *Zevachim* 115a; also see *Sefer HaMitzvot, Shoresh* 1, and *Mishneh Torah, Hilchot Yesodei HaTorah,* Introduction.
95. There's a lot of material in the Bible that explains what happens later on in their wanderings, so obviously this wasn't given in advance at Mount Sinai. *Mishneh Torah, Hilchot Yesodei HaTorah,* Introduction; *Sefer Chasidim* 1016; Midrash, *Shemot Rabbah* 5:18; Midrash, BaMidbar Rabbah 14:35; Talmud, Tractates *Bava Batra* 15a, *Gittin* 60a, *Menachot* 30a.
96. Deuteronomy 34:10.
97. Numbers 12:6–8.
98. *Mishneh Torah, Hilchot Yesodei HaTorah* 7:1–6.
99. Exodus 32:28. Most of the idolaters were from the "mixed multitude" of individuals who left Egypt with the Jews because they were so impressed by what went on with the Ten Plagues. See *Rashi* on Exodus 32:4; Nachmanides on Exodus 32:7 and 32:28.
100. Deuteronomy 29:28; Talmud, Tractate *Sanhedrin* 43b.
101. This is epitomized by the expression "Follow in His ways." (Deuteronomy 28:9). An excellent example of this is the obligation to give 10% of one's income to charity. See also *Sefer HaChinuch* 611, and *WorldPerfect: The Jewish Impact on Civilization*, chapter 14.
102. Exodus 25:8. This commandment actually is related in the Book of Exodus prior to the sin of the Golden Calf and is considered by the biblical commentators a classic example of how God prepares the cure even before the disease — i.e., the elements for reconciliation are already in place before the Jews had violated their covenant with God.
103. Talmud, Tractate *Yoma* 54a/b. Also see: Kitov, Eliyahu, *The Book of Our Heritage*, Jerusalem: Feldheim, 1978, Vol. 3, pp. 257–258.
104. For more information on this fascinating subject see Kleiman, Yaakov, *DNA & Tradition: The Genetic Link to the Ancient Hebrews*, Jerusalem: Devora, 2004.
105. For example, the first person called up during the Torah reading is a *kohen*.
106. For an explanation of the discrepancy between the Christian/Western dating and Jewish chronology, see Author's Note at the beginning of this book.
107. Numbers 13:27–33.
108. The obvious question arises: The Jewish people had just seen God destroy the most powerful civilization in the ancient world, so why should they be afraid of the Canaanites? The answer is that while they were in the desert, they lived a supernatural existence (manna from heaven, water from a rock, clouds of glory and pillars of fire). They recognized that upon entering the land all that would end, and they would have to resort to a normal (and much more difficult) way of life. Their reluctance to enter was, therefore, primarily fueled by a desire to prolong their supernatural existence. Their mistake was in not trusting in God enough to see that He would help them through natural means to conquer, settle and prosper in the land.
109. A number of years ago I was sitting in lecture given by one of Israel's foremost military historians, Meir Pe'il. And he beautifully illustrated this point. He said that he has taught in numerous war colleges around the world (West Point, Sandhurst, etc.) and viewed many of the world's armies in action. "On one point every army in the world is the same. In every army in the world the officers give orders, but in the Israeli army the officers have to explain things."

110. Numbers 20:12.
111. See: Maharal's commentary on Numbers 20:12, and Maimonides' *Shemonah Perakim* 7.
112. *Machshavot Magazine*, Volume 46, p. 4.
113. *Mishneh Torah*, Introduction; Midrash, *Dvarim Rabbah* 9:4; Midrash, *Tehillim* 90:3; Talmud, Tractate *Bava Batra 14a* (see commentary of the *Tosafot*). The accuracy of the transmission process of both the Written and Oral Torah has always been a crucial factor in the preservation of both the Torah and the Jewish people. The laws regarding the accuracy of a Torah scroll are very strict. During the weekly reading of the Torah portion, even the smallest mistake on the part of the reader is corrected by the entire congregation. A Torah scroll (which is always copied by hand) that has even the smallest error (one missing or wrong letter of the 304,805) cannot be used and must be fixed within thirty days or buried. A brief quote from the Talmud illustrates this point: Rebbe Meir said, "When I came to study with Rebbe Yishmael, he said to me, 'My son, what is your line of work?' I told him I was a scribe. He said to me, 'My son, be careful with your work, for it is the work of heaven. Should you perhaps omit one letter or add one letter, you could destroy the entire world.'" (Talmud, Tractate *Eruvin* 13a.)
114. Deuteronomy 1:17; Deuteronomy 16:18; Exodus 23:2. The best detailed description of the *Sanhedrin* can be found in *Mishneh Torah, Hilchot Sanhedrin*. Also see chapter 11 of *WorldPerfect: The Jewish Impact on Civilization.*

PART II

115. Joshua 1:1–7.
116. Talmud, Tractate *Bava Batra* 75a; *Rashi* on Numbers 27:20.
117. *Seder Olam Rabbah*, Chapter 12.
118. Only the Gergashites made for Africa. See Jerusalem Talmud, Tractate *Sheviit* 16b.
119. Judges 2:8–14.
120. Talmud, Tractate *Avoda Zara* 25a.
121. Judges 21:25.
122. Judges 1:33–35.
123. Judges 2:12.
124. Judges 2:16.
125. Judges, Chapters 4–5.
126. Judges 4:1–3.
127. Judges, Chapters 6–8.
128. Judges 6:1–6.
129. Judges 7:2.
130. Judges 8:34.
131. Judges 13:1.
132. Judges, Chapters 13–16.
133. Judges 16:28–30.
134. 1 Samuel, Chapters 1–16.
135. 1 Samuel 8:5–7.
136. 1 Samuel 8:7.

137. Deuteronomy 17:14–15.
138. 1 Samuel 8:6.
139. Talmud, Tractate *Kiddushin* 22a.
140. For a more detailed description of the rights and responsibilities of a Jewish king and his relationship with the judiciary (*Sanhedrin*) see *Mishneh Torah, Hilchot Sanhedrin* and *Hilchot Melachim.*
141. Deuteronomy 17:16–20.
142. Talmud, Tractate *Megillah* 14a.
143. 1 Samuel 9:9.
144. Exodus 30:22–28. This oil was called *shemen mishchat kodesh*, sacred anointing oil. The Hebrew word for Messiah — *Mashiach* — comes from this word *mashach*, meaning "anointed."
145. For more on Saul's greatness and the reason for his downfall see Talmud, Tractate *Yoma* 22b.
146. So evil is this nation that its name is to be erased from history books — it is to be totally wiped out to the point where even its livestock is to be destroyed, so no one will see one of Amalek's cattle and say, "That was Amalek's cow." Despite the seeming extreme harshness of this commandment an Amalekite is not doomed by birth. While the innate tendency of the Amalekite nation is toward total war with the Jewish people, every human being, including Amalek, has free will. Even an Amalekite can say, "The ideology of my nation is evil, and I choose to do otherwise." An Amalekite can opt out of his national ideology and even convert to Judaism. Talmud, Tractate *Gittin* 57b, *Sanhedrin* 96b.
147. Exodus 17:14–16.
148. Rauschning, Hermann, *Voice of Destruction (Hitler Speaks),* New York: Putnam, 1940, pp. 87, 220–222.
149. 1 Samuel 15:18–19.
150. 1 Samuel 15:26–28.
151. 1 Samuel 16:7.
152. The siege of Troy is dated to the thirteenth century B.C.E. which roughly corresponds to the time that Joshua led the Jews into the Promised Land.
153. 1 Samuel 17:8–9.
154. 1 Samuel 17:37.
155. 1 Samuel 17:47.
156. Zechariah 4:6.
157. 1 Samuel 18:7–9.
158. 2 Samuel 7:11–16 and 1 Chronicles 17:10–13. "The royal scepter will not depart from Judah nor the law from his descendants." (Genesis 49:10)
159. Many peoples around the world have taken this idea one step further and actually have claimed that their royal family and even they, themselves, are actual descendants of the ancient Hebrews. One fascinating example are the Makuya sect in Japan who claim that there is an ancient connection between the Japanese and the Jews and that the Royal family of Japan is actually descended from King David. Another example are the British. For 700 years, every king and queen of England was crowned king while sitting on a throne mounted on a large block of limestone. The stone is called the "Stone of Scone." The thirteenth century king, Edward I stole the stone from the Scots. (It was returned to Scotland

in 1997.) Scottish tradition held that the stone was the "pillow" that Jacob rested his head on when he had his dream, and that it was used as a coronation stone by the early Hebrew kings and was kept in Solomon's Temple in Jerusalem. After the destruction of the First Temple in 422 B.C.E., the stone found its way first to Ireland and later to Scotland. As outrageous as this idea may sound, it shows us the centrality and importance of the Davidic line in history.

160. Initially, after Shaul's death, David was crowned king of the tribe of Judah and made his capital in Hebron, while Shaul's younger son, Ishboshet, ruled in his father's place. However, after two years Ishboshet was murdered; David had the murderers executed for the crime.
161. See 2 Samuel 24:24 and 1 Chronicles 21:25.
162. Cline, Eric H., *Jerusalem Besieged*, Ann Arbor: University of Michigan Press, 2004, p. 2.
163. It is often mentioned that the Western Wall is the holiest spot in the world for the Jews. This is simply not true. The Western Wall is merely a retaining wall built around Mount Moriah by Herod the Great more than 2,000 years ago. The holiest spot is atop Mount Moriah itself, where the Holy of Holies once stood. Today, this holiest of places is hidden behind the Western Wall and under the Muslim shrine called the Dome of the Rock.
164. 2 Samuel 6:16–23.
165. Recounted in 2 Samuel, Chapters 11 and 12.
166. Talmud, Tractate *Shabbat* 56b.
167. Talmud, Tractate *Sanhedrin* 107b. As a prophet, David saw that Bathsheba was destined for him. (Solomon's birth and kingship are proof of this point.) The issue was not that Bathsheba was meant to be his wife, but rather how and when he acquired her.
168. 1 Kings 2:2–3.
169. 1 Kings 3:7–13.
170. Talmud, Tractate *Eruvin* 21b.
171. 1 Kings 5:11–14.
172. Today's Ethiopian Jews have a tradition that they are the descendants of the union of King Solomon and the Queen of Sheba.
173. *Yalkot Shimoni Divrei Hayamim*, 1085.
174. The Bible — in 1 Kings 10:3 — relates that Solomon "had answers to all her questions; there was nothing that the king did not know."
175. 1 Kings, Chapters 5–8.
176. 1 Kings 8:27–29.
177. Isaiah 42:6.
178. Deuteronomy 17:17.
179. Talmud, Tractates *Shabbat* 56b and *Sanhedrin* 21b.
180. Midrash, *Shir HaShirim Rabbah* I, 1:10.
181. The Talmud states: "We will not accept converts in the Messianic Era, similarly, they did not accept converts, neither during the time of David nor during the time of Solomon." (Talmud, Tractate *Avodah Zarah* 3b)
182. 1 Kings 11:4–6.
183. For a detailed discussion of Solomon's wives see Talmud, Tractate *Shabbat* 56b and *Sanhedrin* 21b. The Talmud especially criticizes Solomon's marriage to the daughter of Pharaoh Necho of Egypt. While this marriage was a major political coup for Solomon, the princess's secret idolatrous activities sewed seeds for many problems in the future.

184. 1 Kings 11:9–13.
185. 1 Kings 12:7.
186. 1 Kings 11:26–40.
187. 1 Kings 12:28.
188. 1 Kings 16:30.
189. 1 Kings 18:27.
190. 1 Kings 18:36–37.
191. The dates that you will find inscribed in the British Museum (and in other history books and other museums housing Middle Eastern artifacts) do not agree with Jewish dating that we are following in this series. This is because this book relies on the traditional Jewish dating system for ancient history — that is, for the dates "before the common era," B.C.E. as explained in the introductory Author's Note.
192. 2 Kings 17:6–18.
193. Parfitt, Tudor, *The Thirteenth Gate: Travels Among the Lost Tribes of Israel.* London: Weidenfeld and Nicolson, 1987. Also see: Shachan, Avigdor, *In the Footsteps of the Lost Ten Tribes*, Jerusalem: Devora, 2007.
194. Midrash Rabba, Genesis 11:5.
195. 2 Kings 18:3–5.
196. 2 Kings, Chapter 19.
197. 2 Kings 21:2–6.
198. 2 Kings 21:11–14.
199. See Talmud, Tractate *Yoma* 52b for a description of Josiah hiding the Ark; also see *Yoma* 53b and 54a. And Kaplan, Aryeh, *Jerusalem: The Eye of the Universe*, p. 22.
200. Jeremiah, 36:23. Recent excavations in David's City have also unearthed a clay seal with the name "Jehucal son of Shelemiah." Jehucal was a court officer during the reign of King Hezekiah as noted in Jeremiah 37:3.
201. 2 Kings 25:9.
202. Jeremiah 36:10.
203. Lamentations 4:4–5, 8–10.
204. Quoted by *Rashi* and *Radak* in commentary on 2 Kings 25:4.
205. 2 Kings 7–9.
206. See Talmud, Tractate *Yoma* 9b.

PART III

207. Psalms 137.
208. Talmud, Tractates *Gittin* 88a and *Sanhedrin* 38a.
209. Leviticus 26:44.
210. Nor only is the concept of multiple exiles and dispersion unique in history, the very survival of the Jews is a singular event. No other nation has ever survived without a homeland, yet from the destruction of the Second Temple in 70 C.E. until the rebirth of the modern State of Israel in the twentieth century, the Jewish people survived in Diaspora without a state.
211. Talmud, Tracate *Pesachim* 87b–88a: "Ulla said: '[They were exiled to Babylon] so that they should be able to eat an abundance of dates and engross themselves in Torah study.' "

212. For description of the honors bestowed by the Babylonians on King Jehoiachin see 2 Kings 25:27. For more about the *Reish Galusa* see Talmud, Tractate *Sanhedrin* 5a.
213. 1 Chronicles, Chapter 3; also see *Seder Olam Zuta*. Later, in Israel there was a similar, but even more prestigious position — the *Nasi* — the president of the Jewish supreme court, the Sanhedrin. This position can be traced back to the sages who led the Jewish people after Moses, but the title is specifically associated with the leaders of the Sanhedrin during the Second Temple period and after its destruction. From the time of the Second Temple onward (similar to the *Reish Galusa* in Babylon) the position was hereditary and held by the descendants of Hillel until 429 C.E., when it was finally abolished by the Byzantines. (Talmud, Tractate *Pesachim* 66a; *Mishneh Torah, Hilchot Sanhedrin* 1:3.)
214. Jeremiah 25:11–12.
215. For a detailed discussion of the different kings of Babylon and Belshazzar's error see Talmud, Tractate *Megillah* 11b–12a; also see *Otzer HaIggeres*, p. 149.
216. Jeremiah 29:10.
217. Daniel 5:1–5.
218. Daniel 5:25–28.
219. Ezra 1:3.
220. Ezra 2:64.
221. For detailed explanation see Talmud, Tractate *Megillah* 11b, and *Otzer HaIggeres* p.149.
222. The Book of Esther is best read with the commentary from the Talmud's Tractate *Megillah*, because there are a lot of fascinating details to the story that are left out from the simple telling. However, these details are beyond the scope of this book. In particular see *Megillah* 11a–13b.
223. Deuteronomy 31:18.
224. Talmud, Tractate *Megillah* 13b.
225. Talmud, Tractate *Yoma* 52b–53b.
226. Talmud, Tractate *Yoma* 53b.
227. Talmud, Tractate *Sanhedrin* 21b.
228. Ezra 10:18–44.
229. Nechemiah 10:30–31.
230. Nechemiah 2:17.
231. Talmud, Tractate *Yoma* 9a.
232. See Talmud, Tractate *Yoma* 19b, for an account of a Sadducee High Priest who died due to his improper actions while in the Holy of Holies.
233. See *Rashi* on Shir HaShirim 6:5.
234. Talmud, Tractate *Yoma* 9b.
235. *Derech HaShem* (The Way of God), Part III, 3:4 and 4:6. See also Talmud, Tractate *Nedarim* 38a.
236. Talmud, Tractate *Sanhedrin* 11a.
237. Talmud, Tractates *Nedarim* 37b and *Kiddushin* 30a.
238. *Avot* 1:1.
239. Talmud, Tractate *Megillah* 17b. The process was completed after the destruction of the Second Temple by the *Sanhedrin* sitting in Yavneh. In addition to prayer, the Men of the Great Assembly also instituted the blessings said before and after food as well as Kiddush and Havdalah, the blessings before and after Shabbat.

240. Exodus 15:26.
241. *Nefesh HaChaim* 2:13.
242. In his *Contra Apion* (1:197), Josephus numbers the male population alone at 120,000. (Josephus, *The New Complete Works of Josephus*, Grand Rapids, MI: Kregel Publications, 1999, p. 949)
243. The modern marathon race of twenty–six miles commemorates the tradition that a messenger ran that distance from Marathon to Athens with news of the victory and then dropped dead.
244. Aristotle, *Politics* VII.16.
245. For a more detailed explanation of the brutality of the ancient world see *WorldPerfect: The Jewish Impact on Civilization.*
246. For an excellent overview of Greek warfare see: Connolly, Peter, *Greece and Rome at War,* London: Greenhill Books, 1998.
247. Plato, *Symposium* 178c.
248. Talmud, Tractate *Yoma* 69a; Josephus, *Jewish Antiquities* 11:326–347. (*The New Complete Works of Josephus*, pp. 384–386)
249. Talmud, Tractate *Yoma* 69a.
250. Grant, Michael, *From Alexander to Cleopatra: The Hellenistic World,* New York: Charles Scribner & Sons, 1982, p. 75.
251. Schiffman, Lawrence H., *Text and Tradition: A Source Reader for the Study of the Second Temple and Rabbinic Judaism*, Hoboken, N.J.: Ktav, 1998, p. 42.
252. The Greek historian Hecateus lived circa 360–290 B.C.E. He is quoted by Josephus in his *Contra Apion* 1:198–199 (*The New Complete Works of Josephus*, p. 949).
253. See Talmud, Tractate *Megillah* 9a: "Rabbi Simon ben Gamliel said: 'Even books of scripture the sages did not permit to be written in any foreign language other than Greek.'" It is important to mention that the Talmud here refers to the original, pure ancient Greek, not the common Greek dialect, *koine*, of the Hellenistic world nor the modern Greek of today.
254. Talmud, Tractate *Megillah* 9b.
255. Deliberate mistranslations were perpetrated by Christians scholars in order to "bend" the text to prove Christian theology. The classic example is Isaiah 7:14 where the Hebrew word almah meaning "young woman/maiden" is deliberately mistranslated into "virgin" (*betulah* in Hebrew) to support the Christian concept of virgin birth.
256. Incidentally, this denial of the Oral Law will recur later in Jewish history with the Karaite schism, as we will see in Chapter 42.
257. Wein, Berel, *Echoes of Glory*, Brooklyn, NY: Shaar Press, 1995, p. 38.
258. Josephus, *Jewish War*, 2:166, (*The New Complete Works of Josephus,* p. 739).
259. 2 *Maccabees* 6:1.
260. 1 *Maccabees* 1:41–64.
261. Wein, Berel, *Echoes of Glory*, p. 63.
262. Jewish dates and Christian dates (adopted by the Western World) show a discrepancy of approximately thirty years for this time period.
263. 1 *Maccabees* 2:19–22.
264. 1 *Maccabees* 2:27.
265. Talmud, Tractate *Shabbat* 21b.
266. 1 *Maccabees* 4:52–56.

267. In 133 B.C.E., Elazar fell in battle while thrusting a spear into the belly of war elephant on which he thought the king was riding; the elephant fell on him, crushing him death. Judah was killed at the battle of Elasa in 132 B.C.E., and Jonathan fell in another battle in 113 B.C.E.
268. 1 *Maccabees* 13:41–42.
269. Wein, Berel, *Echoes of Glory*, p. 89.
270. Perhaps the greatest irony of the legacy of the Maccabees is what is named after them today: the Maccabiah Games (the Jewish Olympic Games, started in 1932 and held every four years in Israel). There is virtually no cultural institution that more typifies ancient Greek culture than their athletic competitions. That the Maccabees, who gave their lives to save Judaism from Greek influence, should have Greek–style sporting events named after them is the saddest of endings to this tragic story.
271. The relationship between the Jews and the Romans actually began during the Maccabean Revolt when Judah Maccabee made an alliance with Rome.
272. Genesis 36:1.
273. Herod's first leadership role was as governor of the Gallilee — a position granted to him by his father — Antipater. Early on in his career he demonstrated his brutality by ruthlessly crushing a revolt in his region.
274. At the battle with Anthony at Actium.
275. Talmud, Tractate *Megillah* 6a.
276. The Talmud relates the following story:

     Herod went and killed [most of] rabbis. However, he left Bava ben Buta alive in order to use him as an advisor. Herod put a crown of sharpened porcupine skin around his eyes, [and the sharp spines] blinded him. One day Herod, [pretending to be an ordinary citizen], sat down before Bava ben Buta and said, "Rabbi, do realize the terrible things this no–good slave Herod is doing?" Replied Bavas ben Buta, "What should I do to him?" Said Herod [trying to trap him], "I want you to curse him." Replied Bava ben Buta, "[How can I curse him?] It says, 'Even in your thoughts do not curse a king.'" [Ecclesiastes 12:20] Retorted Herod, "But he is no king; [he does not meet the criteria of a Jewish king.]" Replied Bava ben Buta, "He certainly is no less than a rich man and the same verse continues, 'and in your bedchamber do not curse the rich.' He certainly is no different than a leader, and it says, 'Do not curse the leader of your people.' [Exodus 22:27] ... Herod then confessed, "I am Herod. If I had know that the rabbis were so careful [with their words], I would not have killed them. Now please tell what I can do to rectify what I have done?" Replied Bava ben Buta, "Since you snuffed out the light of the world, [that is what the rabbis are called]...you should involve yourself in [increasing] the light of the world [i.e. the Temple]...Someone who has not seen the new Temple that Herod built has never seen a magnificent building." (Talmud, Tractate *Bava Batra* 3b–4a)
277. Talmud, Tractate *Bava Batra* 4a.
278. Josephus, *The Jewish War*, 5:222–223 (*The New Complete Works of Josephus*, pp. 856–857).
279. Josephus, *The Jewish War*, 1:443–444 (*The New Complete Works of Josephus*, p. 706).
280. Talmud, Tractate *Yoma* 35b.
281. Talmud, Tractate *Ketubot* 16b–17a.
282. Talmud, Tractate *Eruvin* 13b.
283. Talmud, Tractates *Eruvin* 53a, *Shabbat* 112b, *Sanhedrin* 11a, and *Brachot* 20a.

284. See Rashi on Talmud, Tractate *Ketubot* 57a, and also Talmud, Tractate *Chagiga* 3b.
285. Talmud, Tractate *Sanhedrin* 88b.
286. Montanelli, Indro, *Romans Without Laurels*, New York: Pantheon Books, 1959, p. 67.
287. Talmud, Tractate *Megillah* 6a.
288. Josephus, *The Jewish War*, 2:169–185 (*The New Complete Works of Josephus*, pp. 740–741).
289. Johnson, Paul, *History of the Jews*, New York: Harper Perennial, 1987, p. 136.
290. Josephus, *The Jewish War*, 2:305–306 (*The New Complete Works of Josephus*, p. 750).
291. Wein, Berel, *Echoes of Glory*, p. 155.
292. Talmud, Tractate *Gittin* 56a.
293. Josephus, The Jewish War, 5:451 (*The New Complete Works of Josephus*, p. 874).
294. See Talmud, Tractate *Gittin* 56a for the exact account of this story.
295. Talmud, Tractate *Taanit* 26a–b and Josephus, *The Jewish War* 6:93–110 (*The New Complete Works of Josephus*, pp.886–887). The Talmud describes the seventeenth day of Tammuz as the day the wall of the city was breached while Josephus describes it as the day the Antonia Fortress that stood to the north of the Temple Mount was demolished by the Romans.
296. Schiffman, Lawrence H., *Texts and Traditions: A Source Reader for the Study of the Second Temple,* Hoboken, NJ: Ktav, 1998, pp. 463–464.
297. Josephus, *The Jewish War* 6:271–272 (*The New Complete Works of Josephus*, p. 897). Josephus would have us believe that Titus tried to prevent the destruction of the Temple, but the accuracy of such a claim is greatly in doubt. Josephus, who was working for the Romans at this point and became an adopted member of the family of Vespasian and Titus, certainly tried to paint them in the best light possible.
298. Talmud, Tractate *Yoma* 9b.
299. If you visit the Forum (the ancient capitol of the Roman Empire) in the center of Rome, you can still see the Arch of Titus which stands along side the most famous landmark in Rome — the Coliseum. The correct name for this giant arena, which seated 50,000 people, was the Flaviun Amphitheater. It was completed in the year 80 C.E. and its primary function was blood sport such as gladiatorial combat. There is probably no other building in the Roman Empire that was more antithetical to Jewish values (i.e. respect for life) than the Coliseum. It is sadly ironic that the building was probably built by Jewish slave–laborers from the Jewish revolt, and the money for the construction probably came from the booty taken from the destruction of Jerusalem.
300. Masada remains the best preserved Roman siege-site in the world. Exactly as the Romans besieged and breached the walls is exactly how you see the site today.
301. Josephus, *The Jewish War* 7:323–336 (*The New Complete Works of Josephus*, pp. 929–930). The most obvious question about this dramatic speech is how did Josephus get the text. Josephus writes that rather than join in the mass suicide, two women and a few children hid and so the speech was preserved. The veracity of such a claim is much in doubt. Dramatic speeches were a common literary device created by many ancient historians to spice up the narrative, although there is little reason to doubt the accuracy of the story or the fact that the speech, even if it was contrived, was a fairly accurate representation of Zealot sentiments.
302. See Talmud, Tractate *Brachot* 28b.
303. The War of Kittos is barely mentioned in Jewish sources. The most extensive reference can be found in the Talmud, Tractate *Taanit* 18b.

304. Midrash, *Breishit Rabbah* 64:10.
305. In Tractate *Sanhedrin* 97b.
306. Numbers 24:17.
307. Schiffman, Lawrence H., *Texts and Traditions: A Source Reader for the Study of the Second Temple*, pp. 487–488.
308. Deuteronomy 8:17.
309. Talmud, Tractate *Taanit* 4:5.
310. Talmud, Tractate *Gittin* 57a.

PART IV

311. Wein, Berel, *Echoes of Glory*, p. 217.
312. See: *Avot D'Rebbi Natan*, Chapter 6.
313. Talmud, Tractates *Ketubot* 62b–63a, *Nedarim* 50a, *Chagigah* 15b–16a.
314. The amphitheater facing the Mediterranean at Ceasarea has been excavated and visiting it one cannot but remember Rabbi Akiva's ordeal there.
315. Talmud, Tractate *Brachot* 61b. Many of the great sages and martyrs of that generation have been memorialized in the story of the Ten Martyrs that is read every year as part of the Yom Kippur service. There are several different versions of the story and although what we read today seems to indicate that they were all executed on the same day they were, in fact, killed over a period of several years as part of Hadrian's strategy to eradicate Judaism.
316. Wein, Berel, *Echoes of Glory*, p. 224. Also see: Talmud, Tractate *Avodah Zara* 10a–b; Midrash, *Breishit Rabbah* 67:6; 75:5
317. Midrash, *Tanchumah Ki Tisa* 34; Talmud, Tractate *Gittin* 60a.
318. For a detailed explanation of actions of Rabbi Judah HaNasi see Maimonides, *Mishneh Torah*, Introduction. See also *Iggerot D'Rabbi Sheriram Gaon* 1:1.
319. HaRif on Talmud, Tractate *Eruvin* 35b.
320. The Thirteen Principles of Faith are based on the teachings of Maimonides and encompass the basic philosophy of Judaism. The twelfth principle states: "I believe with complete faith in the coming of the Messiah, and even though he may delay, nevertheless I anticipate every day that he will come."
321. A description of the anointing oil is found in the Book of Exodus (30:22–30): "God spoke to Moses saying: 'Now, take for yourself choice spices...pure myrrh, fragrant cinnamon... fragrant cane...cassia...and a hin of olive oil. Of it you shall make oil of sacred anointment. With it you shall anoint the Tent of Meeting and the Ark of the Covenant...You shall anoint Aharon and his sons and sanctify them to minister to Me."
322. 1 Samuel 16:13.
323. Maimonides, *Mishneh Torah, Laws of Kings*, Chapter 12. For sources for these points in the order listed here see: Genesis 49:10; Deuteronomy 17:15; Numbers 24:17; Genesis 49:10; 1 Chronicles 17:11; Psalms 89:29–38; Jeremiah 33:17; 2 Samuel 7:12–16; Isaiah 2:4; Isaiah 11:1–12; Isaiah 27:12–13; Isaiah 40:5; Micah 4:1; Micah 4:3; Zephaniah 3:9; Ezekiel 37:24–28.
324. Isaiah 2:3–4, 11:6.
325. Ezekiel 38:1–16 and Zechariah 12:1–3.

326. Although Yeshu sounds close to Yoshua and Notzri is the modern Hebrew word for Christian, connecting this Yeshu to Jesus is very problematic especially since some authorities consider the name Yeshu to be nickname and not the name of a real person. (References to the name Yeshu can be found in Talmud, Tractates *Brachot* 17b and *Sanhedrin* 43a, 103a; see also Rashi on *Brachot* 12b, on *Rosh HaShanah* 17a, and on *Yoma* 40b.)
327. It is important to mention that these references (see Talmud, Tractates *Sanhedrin* 43a, 67a, and *Sotah* 47a) are not found in most modern editions of the Talmud. In medieval Europe and during the Renaissance, the Talmud was subject to censorship and on several occasions it was publicly burned. When the printing press was invented (in 1453) the Christian printers, who printed the Talmud, printed only the censored versions. Anything perceived as anti-Christian or anti-Gentile was left out. Today, even though no such censorship exists, these passages have, in most editions, not been reinserted back into the text of the Talmud. There is a small book entitled *Chesronot HaShas* ("That Which is Missing from the Talmud") which contains all the missing parts of the Talmud.
328. Josephus, *Jewish Antiquities*, 18:63–64 (*The New Complete Works of Josephus*, p. 590).
329. The most likely author of this reference is Eusebius, the fourth century Bishop of Caesarea. The reason for such an insertion into the text is obvious. The lack of any mention in Josephus (who misses nothing in this time period) was very problematic for Christianity. Eusebius inserted a short reference to Jesus in the text of Josephus's Jewish Antiquities to cover up his glaring absence.
330. Matthew 22:37–40.
331. Deuteronomy 6:5.
332. Leviticus 19:18.
333. The negative attitude of the rabbis toward these splinter sects is reflected in a section of the Talmud that discusses the additional blessing added into the eighteen blessings of the Amidah, the silent prayers recited three times daily by observant Jews: "These eighteen [benedictions] are [really] nineteen. Rabbi Levi said: 'The blessing against the heretics was added at Yavneh.' Rabban Gamliel said to the sages: 'Is there nobody who knows how to create a blessing against the heretics?' Shmuel HaKatan arose and created it [circa 80 C.E.]. (Talmud, Tractate *Brachot* 28b)
334. Montanelli, Indro, *Romans Without Laurels*, New York: Pantheon Books, 1959, p.128.
335. Grant, Michael, *The World of Rome*, London: Weidenfeld & Nicolson, 1962, p. 129.
336. Grant, Michael, *The Jews in the Roman World*, London: Weidenfeld & Nicolson, 1973, p. xi.
337. Josephus, *Jewish Antiquities* 20:195 (*The New Complete Works of Josephus*, p. 655).
338. Sachar, Howard, *A History of Israel*, New York: Knopf, 1979, p. 111.
339. Gager, John C., *Kingdom and Community: The Social World of Early Christianity*, Englewood Cliffs, NJ: Prentice-Hall, 1977, p. 140.
340. Johnson, Paul, *A History of Christianity*, New York: Simon & Schuster, 1976, p. 68.
341. Ibid., p. 76.
342. Nicholls, William, *Christian Anti-Semitism: A History of Hate*, Northvale, NJ: Jason Aronson, 1995, p. 90.
343. Goldberg, M. Hirsch, *Jewish Connection,* Landham, MD: Scarborough House, 1993, p. 33.
344. Koran, Sura 5:71–73.

345. Goiten, S.D., *Jews and Arabs: Their Contacts Through the Ages*, New York: Schocken, 1964, pp. 58–59.
346. Johnson, Paul, *A History of the Jews*, New York: Harper & Row, 1987, p. 167.
347. Koran, Sura 53:19–23.
348. Smith, Huston, *The Religions of Man*, New York: Harper & Row, 1958, p. 219.
349. Koran, Sura 2:61, Sura 5:85, Sura 4:48–49.
350. Koran, Sura 59.
351. The early centuries after the founding of Islam were marked by not only rapid conquest but by a great deal of cultural and intellectual creativity in the fields of mathematics, astronomy, medicine etc. During these early years of Islam, Jews generally fared better than in Christians lands. There were even extended periods of considerable tolerance such as the "Golden Age of Spain" (eighth to eleventh centuries C.E.) during the Ummayed Dynasty, where many Jews rose to prominent positions and prospered. It would be wrong, however, to assume that Jews and other non-Muslims were ever treated as equals under Muslim rule. Under Islamic domination pagans had the choice of conversion to Islam or death. Non-Muslim monotheist (Jews, Christians, Zoroastrians, etc.) were given the status of *ahl al-dhimma* or *dhimmi* ("the protected people."). As monotheists they were allowed to live and practice their religion, but were subject to special taxes and much discriminatory and humiliating legislation. While some Muslim dynasties were more tolerant and open and some more cruel and fanatical, all adhered to this concept of *dhimmi* which until today is part of mainstream Islamic law. For more on this topic see: Yeor, Bat, *The Dhimmi: Jews and Christians under Islam*. Rutherford, NJ: Fairleigh Dickenson University Press, 1985.
352. For a good explanation of the concept of *Jihad* see Lewis, Bernard, *The Middle East: A Brief History of the Last 2,000 Years*, New York: Scribner, 1997, pp. 233–8.
353. Wein, Berel, *Echoes of Glory*, p. 299.
354. Another great rabbinic scholar in Babylon was Rav Ashi, the editor-in-chief of the Babylonian Talmud in the early fifth century.
355. Wein, Berel, *Echoes of Glory*, p. 267.
356. There was a brief, transitional period (475 C.E.–590 C.E.) between the Tannaim and the Amoraim called the Savoraim. They put the "finishing touches" on the Babylonian Talmud by completing the final editing of the text. The Amoraim were followed by the Gaonim, the "great ones" or "geniuses." The Gaonim were the heads of the yeshivas in Babylon.
357. Wein, Berel, *Echoes of Glory*, p. 277.
358. *Sura* 17:1–3 reads: "Glory be to Him [Allah] who carried his servant [Mohammed] by night from the sacred place [masjid or mosque] of Mecca to the sacred place that is more remote [Al–Aksa] whose precinct we have blessed..."
359. For an excellent short explanation of the early Islamic connection to Jerusalem see Lewis, Bernard, *The Middle East: A Brief History of the Last 2,000 Years*, New York: Scribner, 1997. pp. 68–71. Lewis points out that one of the earliest Islamic names for Jerusalem was *Bayt al Maqdis*, clearly derived from the Hebrew phrase for the Jewish Temple, Beit HaMikdash. He also mentions that an equally early Islamic tradition mentions that Al-Aksa means "heaven."
360. It is interesting to contrast the Christian and Muslim treatment of the Temple Mount. Part of the early Christian theology was that God had destroyed the Temple and exiled the Jews because the Jews had rejected Jesus. Leaving the Temple Mount in ruins and filled with

garbage was the Christian way of proving this theological point. The Byzantines then built the Church of the Holy Sepulcher (the traditional site of crucifixion and burial of Jesus) to the west of Temple Mount, its domes rising higher than the remaining Temple Mount platform, as a physical demonstration of the victory of Christianity over the Judaism. The Muslims, on the other hand, chose to clean off the Temple Mount and build their structure (the Dome of the Rock) over the site where the Jewish Temple stood. Building over Judaism's holiest site was their way of proving that Islam had supplanted Judaism. In addition, the dome of the Dome of the Rock is slightly larger than the domes of the Church of the Holy Sepulcher and Arabic inscription on the inside of the Dome of the Rock is taken from the Koran (Sura 112) which reads: "Say: He is God alone. God the eternal! He has no children, and He was not born..." an obvious attack against the Christian concept of Jesus as the son of God. (Islam teaches that Jesus was a prophet and that the notion that God has children is a pagan idea.) The Dome of the Rock is, therefore, an architectural demonstration of Islamic theology: Islam is the one true faith.

361. Karaism reached the peak of its popularity in Israel the tenth and eleventh centuries. After the Crusader conquest of the land in 1099, the center of the movement shifted to Constantinople and later to the Crimea and Lithuania.
362. While the term Sephardi is often used to categorize all Jews who came from the Middle East/Muslim world, the term is not really accurate. Many of these communities have little or no connection historically with the Jews of Spain. The more accurate term would be *Edot HaMizrach* or "Communities of the East" which would cover all Jewish communities that are not Ashkenazi. Of course, the Ashkenazi Jews are not necessarily of German origin, they could have come anywhere from Central or Eastern Europe.
363. Genesis 12:2–3.
364. See his essay in *The Hebrew Impact on Civilization* (Runes, Dagobert D., editor), New York: Philosophical Library, 1951, pp. 349–356.
365. For translations of key excerpts from Maimonides' seminal works see: Finkel, Avraham Yaakov, *The Essential Maimonides*, Northvale, NJ: Jason Aronson, 1996.
366. The story is assumed to be a legend and the actual creator of the first yeshiva in France was probably Rabbi Gershom Me'or HaGeolah (965–1040). However, the story does reflect the grim reality of kidnap and ransom which was an unfortunate feature of Jewish life during this period.
367. Phelps-Brown, Henry, *Egalitarianism and the Generation of Inequality*, Oxford: Oxford University Press, 1988, p. 33.
368. No European kings participated in the First Crusade, but it did attract the cream of the nobility of Western Europe — France, Germany, and Italy — most of whom were of Norman extraction.
369. However it would be a mistake to view contemporary Muslim hostility to the West as a by-product of the Crusades and Christian Europe's invasion of the Middle East. It is important to remember that the Muslim world initiated the conflict with its invasion of Spain in 711, its attempt to conquer France in 732 (at the Battle of Tours) and its numerous attempts to conquer Constantinople. These Islamic military campaigns drew their legitimacy from the Islamic concept of *Jihad* — the Islamic imperative to place the whole world under Muslim sovereignty (as noted in chapter 41). For a good overview of a history of the spread of Islam see: Karsh, Efraim, *Islamic Imperialism*, New Haven, CT: Yale University Press, 2006.

370. For anyone interested in knowing more about specific Crusades, the authoritative source is a book by Hans Eberhard Mayer and John Gillingham, called *The Crusades*, Oxford: Oxford University Press, 1988.
371. From the contemporaneous accounts of Robert the Monk and Fulcher of Chartres as quoted in *The First Crusade: A New History* by Thomas Asbridge, Oxford: Oxford University Press, 2004, pp. 33–36.
372. Quoted by Krey, August in *The First Crusade*, Princeton, NJ: Princeton University Press, 1921.
373. Elon, Amos, *The Pity of It All*, New York: Picador, 2002, p. 101.
374. Quoted by Asbridge, Thomas in *The First Crusade: A New History*, p. 316.
375. Shanks, Hershel, *Jerusalem: An Archeological Biography*, New York: Random House, 1995, pp. 238–239.
376. Kroyanker, David, *Jerusalem Architecture*, New York: Vendome Press, 1994, pp. 37–43.
377. Gilbert, Martin, *Jerusalem: An Illustrated Atlas*, Jerusalem: Steimatzky, 1994, p. 21.
378. It's interesting to note that, following the Crusades, successive Muslim dynasties left much of the coastal plain of Israel (between Jaffa and Haifa) desolate out of a lingering fear that the Crusaders might one day return. This turned out to be a blessing for the early Zionist movement in the late nineteenth and twentieth centuries, as they were able to purchase large tracts of land and settle the coastal plain. Today, this coastal plain is home to the cities of Tel Aviv, Petach Tikva, Herzliya, Kfar Saba, Raanana, Netanya, Hadera, Pardes Hanna and Zikron Yaacov.
379. Gould, Allan (editor), *What Did They Think of the Jews?* Northvale, NJ: Jason Aronson, 1991, pp. 24–25.
380. Despite the Church's prohibition against Christian involvement in usury, Christians and even members of the clergy continued the practice throughout Europe. For a more detailed description of money lending see: Baron, Salo, and Kahan, Arcadius, *Economic History of the Jews*, Jerusalem: Keter, 1975, pp. 43–47.
381. Dundes, Alan, *The Blood Libel: A Case in Anti-Semitic Folklore*, Madison, WI: The University of Wisconsin Press, 1991, p.41.
382. "Body and blood [of Christ] are truly contained in the sacrament of the altar under the species of bread and wine, transubstantiated by the divine power — the bread into his body and the wine into his blood." Text from the decision of the Fourth Lateran Council of 1215 as cited by Lohse, Bernard in *A Short History of Christian Doctrine: From the First Century to the Present*, Philadelphia: Fortress Press, 1966, p.153.
383. To read more about this subject see: Prager, Dennis, and Telushkin, Joseph, *Why the Jews?* New York: Simon & Schuster, 1983. See also Trachtenburg, Joshua, *The Devil and the Jews*, Philadelphia: JPS, 2002.
384. Edict of Expulsion of King Edward I as quoted by Rubin, Alexis, P. (editor) in *Scattered Among the Nations: Documents Affecting Jewish History 49 to 1975*, Northvale, NJ: Jason Aronson, 1995, pp. 76–77.
385. Ibid., p. 118.
386. Tuchman, Barbara, *The Distant Mirror: The Calamitous Fourteenth Century*, New York: Knopf, 1978, pp. 112–114.
387. From a speech by Professor Michael Curtis, author of *Antisemitism in the Contemporary World*, Boulder: Westview Press, 1986.

388. Rubin, Alexis P. (editor), *Scattered Among the Nations: Documents Affecting Jewish History 49 to 1975*, pp. 57–58.
389. Nachmanides himself recorded the entire debate in a work entitled *The Disputation at Barcelona*. See also: Sachar, Howard M., Farewell Espana: *The World of the Sephardim Remembered*, New York: Knopf, 1994, pp 39–40.
390. Netanyahu, Benzion, *The Origins of the Inquisition*, New York: Random House, 1995, p. 159.
391. Ibid., p. 1095.
392. We should note, however, that the very first Inquisition actually took place in 1233 under orders from Pope Gregory IX to combat a group of French–Christian heretics called Albigenses. This first Inquisition was relatively mild and did not as a rule sentence people to death. Not so the Spanish Inquisition which was directed against Jewish heretics.
393. Netanyahu, Benzion, *The Origins of the Inquisition*, p. 3.
394. For a more detailed description of the Jewish ancestry of these personalities see: Reston, James Jr., *The Dogs of God: Columbus, the Inquisition, and the Defeat of the Moors*, New York: Doubleday, 2005, pp. 17 and 30; and Amler, Jane Frances, *Christopher Columbus' Jewish Roots*, Northvale, NJ: Jason Aronson, 1993, pp. 78–83. (So many Jews lived in Spain for so long and so many were conversos that it is most probable that virtually everyone in Spain today — who can trace their ancestry back to Spain of 500 years ago or more — has some Jewish skeletons in the genetic closet.)
395. Rubin, Alexis P. (editor), *Scattered Among the Nations: Documents Affecting Jewish History 49 to 1975,* pp. 86–90.
396. For those interested, there are a lot of fascinating tidbits collected by Jane Frances Amler in *Christopher Columbus' Jewish Roots*, Northvale, NJ: Jason Aronson, 1993. See also Goldberg, M. Hirsh, *The Jewish Connection*, pp. 110–113.
397. Sachar, Howard M., *Farewell Espana: The World of the Sephardim Remembered*, p. 76.
398. Genesis 12:3.
399. Rubin, Alexis P. (editor) *Scattered Among the Nations: Documents Affecting Jewish History 49 to 1975*, pp. 87–8.
400. Ibid., pp. 89–90.
401. Prager, Dennis, and Telushkin, Joseph, *Why the Jews?* pp. 19–20.
402. Kobler, Franz (editor), *A Treasury of Jewish Letters*, Volume 2, Philadelphia: JPS, 1953, pp. 497–502.
403. In a letter dated April 3, 1887 to Bishop Mandell Creighton.
404. Johnson, Paul, *History of Christianity*, pp. 280 and 363.
405. Mercer, Derrik (editor), *Chronicle of the World*, London: DK Publishing, 1996, p. 391.
406. Boccaccio, Giovanni, Decameron, Harmondsworth, Middlesex: Penguin, 1978, pp. 85–86.
407. Phelps-Brown, Henry, *Egalitarianism and the Generation of Inequality*, p. 68.
408. Subsequently, Luther went into hiding in Wartburg Castle where he translated the Bible from Greek to German. His translation appeared in 1522 and had a tremendous political impact on the church and on German culture and language.
409. Although it was ostensibly a religious conflict between Protestant and Catholics, the rivalry between the Austrian Habsburg dynasty and other powers was a more central motive, as shown by the fact that Catholic France supported the Protestant side in order to weaken the

Habsburgs, thereby furthering France's position as the pre–eminent European power. This increased the France–Habsburg rivalry which led later to war between France and Spain.

410. Luther actually lived in a part of Germany from where the Jews had long–since been expelled. It may well be that he, like William Shakespeare, never actually met a Jew.

411. Rubin, Alexis P. (editor), *Scattered Among the Nations: Documents Affecting Jewish History 49 to 1975*, pp. 94–96.

412. Ibid., pp. 89–90. (For more on Luther's plan see: *A History of the Jews* by Paul Johnson, p. 242, and also *Why the Jews?* by Dennis Prager and Joseph Telushkin, p. 107.)

PART V

413. Rabbi Joseph Karo was Sephardi, and Rabbi Moses Isserles (known as Rema), a Polish rabbi from Krakow, wrote an Ashkenazi commentary to the *Shulchan Aruch*. (See Chapter 48.) To this day, the *Shulchan Aruch* by Joseph Karo, as amended by Moses Isserles and with its later commentaries, dictates Jewish law.

414. No popular account (including this book) can provide a complete, precise and accurate explanation of the Kabbalah. Because of the great difficulty involved in truly mastering Kabbalistic text, study of Kabbalah has traditionally been limited to older scholars who had already mastered the Written and Oral Law. But, because Kabbalah is associated with Jewish mysticism, it has always been an alluring subject to the masses as we see today. The problem is that, to truly begin to understand Kabbalah, one must have significant knowledge of the entire corpus of Jewish learning — the entire Hebrew Bible as well as the Talmud, etc. — and be fluent in ancient Hebrew and Aramaic. Modern attempts to spread the study of Kabbalah among the masses of Jews poorly educated in their religion and even to non-Jews have often been ill-conceived, ineffectual, and misleading. Trying to seriously study Kabbalah without having first mastered the rest of the Torah would be equivalent to trying to study advanced astrophysics before mastering basic addition and subtraction.

415. *The Memoirs of Gluckel of Hameln*, New York: Schocken Books, 1977, pp. 46–47.

416. Jospe, Raphael (editor), *Great Schisms in Jewish History*, Hoboken, NJ: Ktav, 1981, p. 129.

417. Jung, Carl G., *C.G. Jung Speaking*, Princeton, NJ: Princeton University Press, 1977, pp. 271–272.

418. For those interested in reading more about them, see Kaplan, Aryeh, *Chassidic Masters: History, Biography and Thought*, Brooklyn: Moznaim, 1991.

419. Ibid., p. 4.

420. Pantheism is the doctrine identifying the deity with the various forces and workings of nature.

421. Mendes-Flohr, Paul, and Reinharz, Jehuda (editors) *The Jew in the Modern World: A Documentary History*, Oxford: Oxford University Press, 1995, p. 390. (For more on this subject see Wein, Berel, *Triumph of Survival*, Brooklyn, NY: Shaar Press, 1990, pp. 86–119.)

422. Ibid., p. 118.

423. Johnson, Paul, *The Intellectuals*, New York: Harper Perennial, 1988, pp. 21–22.

424. Levy, Richard S., *Anti-Semitism in the Modern World*, Lexington, MA: D.C. Heath & Co., 1990.

425. As quoted by Ben Weider in Napoleon and the Jews. http://www.napoleonicsociety.com/
426. Mendes-Flohr, Paul, and Reinharz, Jehuda (editors), *The Jew in the Modern World: A Documentary History*, pp. 125–126.
427. Ibid., p. 129.
428. Ibid., pp. 12–132; see also Wein, Berel, *Triumph of Survival*, pp. 69–77. It's interesting to note that many of the rabbis of Eastern Europe, such as Rabbi Shneur Zalman of Liadi, thought it better to back the anti-Semitic czar than Napoleon when he invaded Russia. While this might seem strange, clearly the logic was "better the devil you know than the one you don't know." In hindsight this proved to be largely correct as the mass assimilation brought on by emancipation proved to be far more devastating than the unceasing hostility of the anti-Semites. This illustrates one of the great truisms of Jewish history: it is more difficult to stay Jewish not in times of poverty or persecution but rather in times of wealth and freedom.
429. Mendes-Flohr, Paul, and Reinharz, Jehuda (editors), *The Jew in the Modern World: A Documentary History*, pp. 258–259.
430. Ibid., p. 333.
431. Elon, Amos, *The Pity of It All*, p. 95. World War I is a great example: 120,000 Jews served in the German army and 12,000 died in the war. Hitler even received his Iron Cross from a Jewish commanding officer.
432. Ibid., p. 225.
433. Mendes-Flohr, Paul, and Reinharz, Jehuda (editors), *The Jew in the Modern World: A Documentary History*, p. 161.
434. Ibid., pp. 183–185. From a speech by Samuel Holdheim (1806–1860), a German Reform rabbi and author, and one of the more extreme leaders of the early Reform Movement.
435. Ibid., pp.178–185. (For more on this subject, see *History of the Jews* by Paul Johnson, pp. 333–335, and *Triumph of Survival* by Berel Wein pp. 52–53.)
436. One could also make a psychological argument that on a subconscious level the continued presence of observant Jews in the community would serve as a constant painful reminder that these non–observant Jews had rejected their heritage and strayed from the path.
437. Mendes-Flohr, Paul, and Reinharz, Jehuda (editors), *The Jew in the Modern World: A Documentary History*, pp. 197–202. See also *Collected Writings of Samson Raphael Hirsch*, Jerusalem: Feldheim, 1996.
438. For more on this subject see: Klugman, Eliyahu Meir, *Rabbi Samson Raphael Hirsch: Architect of Torah Judaism for the Modern World*, Brooklyn: Mesorah Publications, 1996.
439. Sivan, Gabriel, *The Bible and Civilization*, Jerusalem: Keter, 1973, p. 236.
440. Katsh, Abraham, *The Biblical Heritage of American Democracy*, New York: Ktav, 1977, p.97.
441. Ibid., pp. 51–72.
442. Ibid., p. 70.
443. Leviticus 25:10.
444. Hertzberg, Arthur, *The Jews in America*, New York: Simon & Schuster, 1989, p. 21.
445. Micah 4:1–4. (Note that the Prophet Isaiah uses virtually the same words in Isaiah 2:2–4.)
446. John Adams in a letter to F. A. Van Der Kemp, 16 February 1809: "I will insist that the Hebrews have done more to civilize men than any other nation. If I were an atheist and believed in blind eternal fate, I should still believe that fate had ordained the Jews to be the most

essential instrument for civilizing the nations. If I were an atheist of another sect...I should still believe that chance had ordered the Jews to preserve and propagate for all mankind the doctrine of a supreme, intelligent, wise almighty sovereign of the universe, which I believe to be the great essential principle of all morality, and consequently of all civilization... They are the most glorious nation that ever inhabited this earth. The Romans and their Empire were but a bauble in comparison to the Jews. They have given religion to three quarters of the globe and have influenced the affairs of mankind more, and more happily than any other nation, ancient or modern." As quoted by Gould, Allan, in *What Did They Think of the Jews?* pp.71–72.

447. Herzberg, Arthur, *The Jews in America*, p. 87.
448. Gilbert, Martin, *Atlas of Jewish History*, New York: Morrow, 1969, p. 73.
449. Abrahams, Israel, *Jewish Life in the Middle Ages*, New York: Atheneum, 1969, p 59.
450. Mendes-Flohr, Paul, and Reinharz, Jehuda (editors), *The Jew in the Modern World: A Documentary History*, pp. 394–395.
451. Ibid., p. 385.
452. Wein, Berel, *Triumph of Survival*, p. 157.
453. Rubin, Alexis P. (editor), *Scattered Among the Nations*, pp. 193–196.
454. Ibid., p. 173.
455. *New York Times*, May 11, 1903, p. 3.
456. Mendes-Flohr, Paul, and Reinharz, Jehuda (editors), *The Jew in the Modern World: A Documentary History*, p. 409.
457. For a fascinating look at Jewish life in America in the nineteenth and early twentieth centuries see Stephen Birmingham's books: *Our Crowd: The Great Jewish Families of New York and the Rest of Us: The Rise of America's Eastern European Jews.*
458. Isaacs, Ronald H., and Olitzky, Kerry M. (editors), *Critical Documents of Jewish History*, Northvale, NJ: Jason Aronson, 1995, pp. 58–59.
459. Telushkin, Joseph, *Jewish Literacy*, New York: Morrow, 1991, p. 393.
460. Isaacs, Ronald H., and Olitzky, Kerry M. (editors), *Critical Documents of Jewish History*, pp. 60–61.
461. Mendes-Flohr, Paul, and Reinharz, Jehuda (editors), *The Jew in the Modern World: A Documentary History*, pp. 497–498.
462. Ibid., pp 481–82. Given these terrible conditions and the strong sense of social justice that has always been a part of the Jewish people, it is no wonder that Jews played such a crucial role in creating labor unions and fighting for workers' rights and against child labor.
463. One of the best examples was Chaim Nachman Bialik (1873–1934) who is considered the poet laureate of modern Hebrew and one of the leading Jewish intellectuals of his age. Born in southern Russia, he attended the famous Volozhin Yeshiva, but broke with traditional Judaism at age 18.
464. Hertzberg, Arthur, *The Jews of America*, p. 157.
465. Ibid., p. 189.
466. Wein, Berel, *Triumph of Survival*, p. 233.
467. The one member of the French army who was truly interested in the truth — and who discovered that Esterhazy was the spy — was Lieutenant General George Picquart. He was consistently ignored and hounded by the French army. When Esterhazy was finally brought to trial, he was acquitted, and sadly it was Picquart who sent to prison for sixty days.
468. Ironically, today the number one excuse for hating Jews in the world is Zionism and the

State of Israel. Even though it is merely an excuse, accusations against Israel and the supposed occupation of Palestinian lands are the fuel used to keep anti-Semitism alive and have lead to attacks against both Jews and Jewish targets around the world.

469. The war also proved to be very damaging to both the spiritual and economic well-being of the Jewish communities especially in Eastern Europe. Poverty and hardship increased greatly. The chaos left in the wake of the war — combined with the spread of Marxist, socialist and other revolutionary ideas greatly — weakened the spiritual cohesion of Eastern European Jewry.
470. The Czar and his family were murdered by the Bolsheviks in 1918.
471. Gould, Allan (editor), *What Did They Think of the Jews?* p. 337.
472. Mendes-Flohr, Paul, and Reinharz, Jehuda (editors), *The Jew in the Modern World: A Documentary History*, pp. 431–432.
473. This event, known as the "The Doctors' Plot," was an alleged conspiracy to eliminate the leadership of the Soviet Union by means of Jewish doctors poisoning top leadership. After the death of Stalin in March 1953, the new Soviet leaders declared that the case was fabricated. It was just a modern variation on the ancient blood libels common in medieval Europe.
474. Initially Stalin was meant to share power with two other men — Lev Kamenev and Grigori Zinovev, both Jews — but Stalin had them both arrested and executed after show trials in 1936.
475. See: Black, Edwin, *IBM and the Holocaust: The Strategic Alliance Between Nazi Germany and America's Most Powerful Corporation*, New York: Crown, 2001; and Black, Edwin, Nazi Nexus: *America's Corporate Connections to Hitler's Holocaust*, Washington, DC: Dialog Press, 2009.
476. On the Internet, see http://www.aish.com/holocaust
477. Raphael Lemkin (1900–1959), who coined the word "genocide" in 1944, was a lawyer of Polish-Jewish descent. He first used the word in print in his Axis Rule in Occupied Europe, Washington, DC: Carnegie, 1944.
478. Raushning, Hermann, *Voice of Destruction* (*Hitler Speaks*).
479. The great German-Jewish writer Heinrich Heine commented after watching a book burning in Germany in 1920: "Where they burn books, they will also, in the end, burn human beings." See also, Elon, Amos, *The Pity of It All: A Portrait of the German–Jewish Epoch* 1743–1933, p. 119.
480. It is interesting to note that throughout history non-Jews were happy to have Jews leave the fold of Judaism, convert to Christianity and marry out of their faith. During the vast majority of Jewish history in Europe, Jews stubbornly clung to their identity and usually refused to convert to Christianity even under duress. It is only when we get to nineteenth and twentieth centuries do we find significant numbers of Jews abandoning their faith and consciously attempting to assimilate. Precisely at this point in history the reason for anti-Semitism takes a dramatic course change. In medieval Europe the Jews were hated for being different, now the Jews were hated for trying to be the same as the non-Jews. While neither of these two reasons is the true cause of anti-Semitism, history shows that assimilation is never the solution. Perhaps the most ironic aspect of anti-Semitism is that the greatest explosions of Jew-hatred have usually taken place in places where Jews are most comfortable among the non-Jews. Germany is arguably the best example of this phenomena. For more on this topic see: Dennis Prager and Joseph Telushkin, *Why the Jews?*
481. For more on this subject read *While Six Million Died: A Chronicle of American Apathy* by

Arthur D. Morse. New York: Random House, 1968. It is a stinging indictment.

482. Gilbert, Martin, *The Holocaust: A History of the Jews of Europe During the Second World War,* New York: Henry Holt, 1985, pp. 202–203.
483. Mendes-Flohr, Paul, and Reinharz, Jehuda (editors), *The Jew in the Modern World: A Documentary History*, p. 663.
484. Estimated number of victims killed in these concentration camps taken from Yad Vashem's website: www.yadvashem.org.
485. Quoted by Martin Gilbert in *The Holocaust: A History of the Jews of Europe During the Second World War*, p. 438.
486. Sam, Halpern, *Darkness and Hope*, New York: Shengold, 1996.
487. Mendes-Flohr, Paul, and Reinharz, Jehuda (editors) *The Jew in the Modern World: A Documentary History*, p. 675.
488. Dawidowicz, Lucy S., *The War Against the Jews 1933–1945*, New York: Bantam Books, 1975. p. xxiii.
489. Rauschning, Hermann, *Voice of Destruction (Hitler Speaks),* pp. 220, 242.
490. Mendes-Flohr, Paul, and Reinharz, Yehuda, (editors), *The Jew in the Modern World: A Documentary History*, p. 699.
491. Ibid., pp. 331–332.
492. Wistrich, Robert, *Hitler's Apocalypse*, Philadelphia: St. Martin's Press, 1986, p. 122.
493. Prager, Dennis, and Telushkin, Joseph, *Why the Jews?* p. 23.
494. For detailed information on the demographics of Palestine during the Ottoman period and the British Mandate period see: Peters, Joan, *From Time Immemorial: The Origins of the Arab-Jewish Conflict Over Palestine*, New York: Harper & Row, 1984.
495. Cruise-O'Brien, Connor, *The Siege: The Story of Israel and Zionism*, London: Paladin Grafton Books, 1988, p. 46.
496. Isaiah 2:5.
497. Cruise-O'Brien, Connor, *The Siege: The Story of Israel and Zionism*, p. 42–43.
498. Ibid., p.80.
499. Ben Gurion's attitude toward religion and its place in the Jewish state could be categorized as hostile or at best ambivalent, and many of his policies regarding dealing with new immigrants and army service were designed to push observant Jews towards dropping their observance. He could also take a harsh and event violently confrontational attitude toward political rivals such as toward Menachem Begin and the Irgun (the military wing of the break-away Revisionist Zionism Movement founded by Zev Jabotinsky in 1923) which culminated with Ben Gurion's order to sink the Altalena, an Irgun arms ship, off the coast of Tel Aviv on June 21, 1948. Sixteen Irgun members were killed in the incident which could have led to civil war.
500. Deuteronomy 7:6–11; 8:11–19; 10:12–13; 11:8–25.
501. Mendes-Flohr, Paul, and Reinharz, Jehuda (editors), *The Jew in the Modern World: A Documentary History*, pp. 544–545.
502. Mendes-Flohr, Paul, and Reinharz, Jehuda (editors), *The Jew in the Modern World: A Documentary History*, p. 546.
503. Johnson, Paul, *The History of the Jews*, p. 430.
504. Peters, Joan, *From Time Immemorial*, p. 244.
505. For an excellent summary of the period see: Cruise-O'Brien, Connor, *The Siege: The Story of Israel and Zionism.*

506. Correspondents of the New York Times, *Israel: from Ancient Times to the Modern Nation*, New York: Macmillan, 1997, pp. 38–39.
507. Dan, Uri, *To the Promised Land*, New York: Doubleday, 1988, p. 120.
508. Quoted by Gilbert, Martin, *Israel: A History*, New York: Doubleday, 1998, p. 145.
509. From a speech delivered on September 16, 1947, see: Bard, Mitchell, *Myths and Facts: A Guide to the Arab-Israeli Conflict*, Chevy Chase, MD: AICE, 2006, p. 359.
510. There can be little doubt that one of the primary reasons for UN support for a Jewish state came out of European guilt for the Holocaust. The death of millions of Jews "bought" enough sympathy to allow for the creation of a Jewish state. Sadly, since the partition vote of 1947, the UN voting record on Israel has gotten progressively worse: In 1975 the UN voted to declare Zionism as a racist ideology (Resolution #3379) and since 1990 fully two-thirds of all UN resolutions have condemned Israel. For more on this topic see: Gold, Dore, *Tower of Babble: How the United Nations Has Fueled Global Chaos*, New York: Crown Forum, 2004, and Shawn, Eric, *The UN Exposed: How the United Nations Sabotages America's Security*, New York: Sentinel, 2006.
511. While armies from surrounding Arab countries had to wait until the British departed to officially invade, the actual fighting began immediately after the UN partition vote and the British did little or nothing to stop it.
512. Ben Gurion, David, *Israel: A Personal History*, New York: Funk & Wagnalls, 1971, p. 65.
513. Collins, Larry, and Lapierre, Dominique, *O Jerusalem*, New York: Pocket Books, 1972, p. 327.
514. Wein, Berel, *Triumph of Survival*, p. 397. In May 1948, once the War of Independence had officially begun, Arab forces were able to close the road off once again by firing from the British police station at Latrun. The Haganah tried several times to take Latrun but failed. Just as Jerusalem was about to fall, an alternative road (nicknamed the "Burma Road") was quickly cut through the rocky hills allowing badly needed supplies to arrive and prevent the fall of Jerusalem to the Arabs.
515. Sharef, Zeev, *Three Days*, New York: Doubleday, 1962. See also: Blech, Benjamin, *Eyewitness to Jewish History*, New York: John Wiley & Sons, Inc., 2004, p. 267.
516. For fascinating details about Israel's War of Independence see: Slater, Leonard, *The Pledge*, New York, Simon & Schuster, 1970.
517. Gilbert, Martin, *The Arab-Israeli Conflict: Its History in Maps,* Jerusalem: Steimatzky, 1984. There is much debate about the exact number of refugees, both Jewish and Arab and the causes of the refugee problem. The vast majority of Jewish refugees from Arab lands were either expelled from these countries or chose to leave due to rising anti-Semitism caused by the Arab-Israeli conflict. The Arab refugees from Israel (both in 1948 and 1967) also left for a variety of reasons: many heeded the "advice" of Arab leaders to get out of the war zone and to return after Israel was destroyed; others chose to flee from the fighting; and some were also driven out by Israeli forces. Whatever the causes, two points are clear: (1) Had the Arabs not attacked Israel there would have been no cause to flee and therefore no refugees; (2) While Israel absorbed hundreds of thousands of Jewish refugees, the Arab world deliberately refrained from doing the same with Arab refugees out of recognition that even sixty years later, these refugees remain a powerful tool in the propaganda war against Israel.
518. Gilbert, Martin, *The Arab-Israeli Conflict: Its History in Maps*, p. 48.
519. As of 2007 Israel is now considered to the largest Jewish population in the world, surpassing

that of the United States. More Jews now live in Israel than at any time since the destruction of the first Temple and the Babylonian Exile 2,500 years ago. Given current demographic trends it is now estimated that within a few decades, the majority of the Jewish people will be back in the Land of Israel.

520. Deuteronomy 30:3–5.
521. Jeremiah 31:6–7.
522. Ezekiel 36:8–11.
523. All of this development was accomplished in less than forty years, in a constant state of war, terrorism and economic boycotts and in a country with no natural resources which had to absorb millions of immigrants, many of them destitute.
524. *New York Times*, May 16, 1948. See also Morris, Benny, *Righteous Victims: A History of the Zionist–Arab Conflict 1881–2001*, New York: Vintage, 2001.
525. Ironically, the Arab armies had chosen Yom Kippur as the day to attack, believing that the front lines would be largely empty and the country totally off guard. This proved to be a major miscalculation. The Israel army has always depended on its reserves (civilians who have to be mobilized) to fight its wars. If the need arises, these men must be mobilized, equipped and then moved in mass to the front. Yom Kippur is the only day of the year when virtually the entire population is in synagogue and, therefore, easy to locate (remember there were no cell phones in 1973) and mobilize. It is also the only day where all the roads in the country are empty, and it is, therefore, the easiest day to transport the reservists to the front.
526. The number of Arab dead has never been released.
527. The tremendous victory of the Six Day War not only caused euphoria, it also created a feeling of invincibility and arrogance in the collective conscious of the general population and its political and military leadership. Even prior to the Six Day War General Ariel Sharon bragged: "A generation will pass before Egypt threatens us again." (See Oren, Michael, *Six Days of War*, Oxford: Oxford University Press, 2002, p. 151.) Less than seven years later the Yom Kippur War put an end to those sentiments and also forced Israelis to re–evaluate their attitude towards the victims of the Holocaust. Prior to the war the victims of the Holocaust were generally viewed as "sheep to the slaughter" — powerless victims who went passively to their deaths. Israel was viewed as the answer to the Holocaust. The modern proud, fighting Israeli would ensure that another Holocaust could never happen again. Yet, in 1973, despite its army and its attitude, Israel was almost destroyed.
528. Israel did not participate in the Gulf War, as the U.S. feared its involvement would jeopardize the Arab coalition which was mobilized to fight Saddam Hussein. Instead, Israel had to stand idly by while 39 Iraqi scud missiles descended on Tel Aviv and Haifa causing vast damage but miraculously causing almost no casualties.
529. If one studies the history of the Arab-Israeli conflict, or more specifically the Israeli–Palestinian conflict, it becomes clear that the issue has never really been about creating a Palestinian state (such a state could have been created numerous times in the past sixty years), but rather it has really been about the Arab world's inability to accept a Jewish state of any kind, no matter what the borders.
530. Only after their bodies were returned after a lopsided prisoner exchange in 2008 did it become clear that they were also killed in the ambush.
531. The Talmud in Tractate *Beitzah* 25b states: "Why was the Torah given to Israel? Because they are aggressive and stubborn.... If the Torah had not been given to Israel, no nation

or tongue could withstand them." Rashi comments: "The Torah serves to moderate their energy and subdue their heart."

532. *Tikunei Zohar* 21:60a.
533. Luzzatto, Rabbi Moshe Chaim. *Derech HaShem* (The Way of God), 1:2:1.
534. The *Washington Post* columnist, Charles Krauthammer, summed it up: "Jews is news. Whatever a Jew or better yet the Jewish State, Israel, does, it always grabs the headlines. The double standard to which the world holds Israel is nothing short of supernatural. The fact that two–thirds of all UN resolutions passed since 1990 have condemned Israel is classic illustration of this point. No one seems to care that Israel, the only democracy in the Middle East, is surrounded by twenty-two nondemocratic, totalitarian Arab states with little or no human rights or free speech. Syria occupies Lebanon for decades, but the world ignores it. Pol Pot kills 1.5 million Cambodians in the 1970's yet the UN never passed one resolution condemning him, yet when Israel starts building a fence to keep out suicide bombers the world goes mad. A 2003 European Union survey listed Israel as the number one country in the world threatening world peace beating out such peaceloving nations as North Korea, Iran, Syria and Libya."
535. Numbers 23:9.
536. Genesis 17:7.
537. Although unbeknown to Abraham, far away from where he lived, Shem and Ever, the descendants of Noah were quietly keeping up his monotheistic tradition. (See Talmud, Tractate *Megillah* 12a; Rashi's commentary on Genesis 28:9.)
538. From his letter to F. A. Van der Kemp, 1806.
539. Talmud, Tractate *Sanhedrin* 97a.
540. Just as it is a Jewish custom to bring in Shabbat early (before sunset on Friday) so too, we may usher in this final phase of history before the 6,000–year deadline.
541. Rabbi Moshe Chaim Luzzatto, *Derech HaShem* (The Way of God), 1:3:4.
542. The concept of Messiah is central to Christianity but actually originates in Jewish sources. (The word Messiah comes from the Hebrew word mashach meaning "anointed," i.e. chosen by God.) The Messiah's job is to prepare humanity to return to the ideal state that existed prior to humanity's fall related in the Book of Genesis. This future, ideal state is called Olam HaBa, "the World to Come." The Messianic Era which proceeds this period is to be ushered in by the Messiah, a descendent of King David. The entire period is characterized by the Jewish people's collective return to Judaism and Israel and culminates in the whole world returning to a relationship with God. The great twelfth century philosopher Maimonides summarizes the concept of Messiah (in his *Mishneh Torah, Laws of Kings,* Chapter 12) as follows: "The King Messiah will arise and restore the kingship of David to its former state and original sovereignty. He will rebuild the Temple and gather the dispersed of Israel. If there arise a king from the House of David who meditates in Torah, occupies himself with the commandments...prevails upon Israel to walk in the ways of Torah...fights the battles of God, it may be assumed that he is the Messiah. If he does these things and succeeds, rebuilds the Temple on its site, and gathers the dispersed of Israel, he is beyond all doubt the Messiah. He will prepare the whole world to serve God together."
543. Isaiah 2:2–4; also Micah 4:1–4.

BIBLIOGRAPHY

Abrahams, Israel. *Jewish Life in the Middle Ages*. New York: Atheneum, 1969.

Amler, Jane Frances. *Christopher Columbus' Jewish Roots*. Northvale, NJ: Jason Aronson, 1993.

Asbridge, Thomas. *The First Crusade: A New History*. Oxford: Oxford University Press, 2004.

Aviezer, Nathan. *Fossils and Faith: Understanding Torah and Science*. Hoboken, NJ: Ktav, 2002.

Aviezer, Nathan. *In the Beginning: Biblical Creation and Science*. Hoboken, NJ: Ktav, 1990

Bard, Mitchell. *Myths and Facts: A Guide to the Arab-Israeli Conflict*. Chevy Chase, MD: AICE, 2006.

Barnavi, Eli (editor). *A Historical Atlas of the Jewish People: From the Time of the Patriarchs to the Present*. London: Kuperard, 1998.

Baron, Salo, and Kahan, Arcadius. *Economic History of the Jews*. Jerusalem: Keter, 1975.

Bayme, Steven. *Understanding Jewish History: Text and Commentaries*. Ktav, 1997.

Ben Gurion, David. *Israel: A Personal History*. New York: Funk & Wagnalls, 1971.

Ben-Sasson, H. H. (editor). *A History of the Jewish People*. Cambridge, MA: Harvard University Press, 1976.

Berdyaev, Nikolai. *The Meaning of History*. London: World, 1935.

Birmingham, Stephen. *Our Crowd: The Great Jewish Families of New York*. New York: Dell, 1967.

Birmingham, Stephen. *The Rest of Us: The Rise of America's Eastern European Jews.* New York: Berkeley, 1967.

Black, Edwin. *IBM and the Holocaust: The Strategic Alliance Between Nazi Germany and America's Most Powerful Corporation.* New York: Crown, 2001.

Black, Edwin. *Nazi Nexus: America's Corporate Connections to Hitler's Holocaust.* Washington, DC: Dialog Press, 2009.

Blech, Benjamin. *Eyewitness to Jewish History.* New York: John Wiley & Sons, 2004.

Boccaccio, Giovanni. *Decameron.* Harmondsworth, Middlesex: Penguin, 1978.

Cahill, Thomas. *The Gift of the Jews: How a Tribe of Desert Nomads Changed the Way Everyone Thinks and Feels.* New York: Doubleday, 1998.

Cantor, Norman. *The Civilization of the Middle Ages.* New York: HarperCollins, 1993.

Cantor, Norman. *The Sacred Chain: A History of the Jews.* New York: Harper Collins, 1994.

Carroll, James. *Constantine's Sword: The Church and the Jews.* New York: Houghton Mifflin, 2001.

Cline, Eric H. *Jerusalem Besieged.* Ann Arbor: University of Michigan Press, 2004.

Christ, Karl. *The Romans: An Introduction to Their History and Civilization.* Berkeley: University of California Press, 1984.

Collins, Larry, and Lapierre, Dominique. *O Jerusalem.* New York: Pocket Books, 1972.

Connolly, Peter. *Greece and Rome at War.* London: Greenhill Books, 1998.

Comay, Joan. *Who's Who in Jewish History After the Period of the Old Testament.* New York: Oxford University Press, 1995.

Correspondents of the *New York Times. Israel: from Ancient Times to the Modern Nation.* New York: Macmillan, 1997.

Critchley, J. S. *Feudalism.* London: George, Allen & Unwin, 1978.

Cruise-O'Brien, Connor. *The Siege: The Story of Israel and Zionism.* London: Paladin Grafton Books, 1988.

Dan, Uri. *To the Promised Land.* New York: Doubleday, 1988.

Dashti, Ali. *Twenty Three Years: A Study of the Prophetic Career of Mohammad.* Costa Messa, CA: Mazda, 1994.

Dawidowicz, Lucy S. *The War Against the Jews 1933–1945.* New York: Bantam, 1975.

Dillenberger, John, and Welch, Claude. *Protestant Christianity: Interpreted Through Its Development.* New York: Charles Scribner and Sons, 1954.

Donin, Hayim Halevy. *To Be A Jew*. New York: Basic Books, 1972.

Dundes, Alan. *The Blood Libel: A Case in Anti-Semitic Folklore*. Madison, WI: The University of Wisconsin Press, 1991.

Eisen, Yosef. *The Miraculous Journey: A Comprehensive History of the Jewish People from Creation to the Present*. Jerusalem: Targum Press, 2004.

Elon, Amos. *The Pity of It All: A Portrait of the German-Jewish Epoch 1743–1933*. New York: Picador, 2003.

Ethics of the Fathers (Pirkei Avot). Brooklyn, NY: Artscroll Mesorah, 1995.

Fendel, Zechariah. *Legacy of Sinai*. New York: Rabbi Jacob Joseph School Press, 1981.

Finegan, Jack. *Light from the Past: The Archeological Background of the Hebrew-Christian Religion*. Princeton, NJ: Princeton University Press, 1946.

Finkel, Avraham Yaakov. *The Essential Maimonides*. Northvale, NJ: Jason Aronson, 1996.

Finkelstein, Louis, (editor). *The Jews: Their Religion and Culture*. New York: Schocken, 1973.

First, Mitchell. *Jewish History in Conflict: A Study of the Major Discrepancy Between Rabbinic and Conventional Chronology*. Northvale, NJ: Jason Aronson, 1997.

Frank, Anne. *The Diary of a Young Girl*. New York: Doubleday, 1952.

Gager, John C. *Kingdom and Community: The Social World of Early Christianity*. Englewood Cliffs, NJ: Prentice-Hall, 1977.

Gilbert, Martin. *Atlas of Jewish History*. Eighth edition. London and New York: Routledge, 2010.

Gilbert, Martin. *Israel: A History*. New York: Harper Perennial, 2008.

Gilbert, Martin. *Jerusalem: An Illustrated Atlas*. Fourth edition. London and New York: Routledge, 2008.

Gilbert, Martin. *The Arab-Israeli Conflict: Its History in Maps*. Ninth edition. London and New York: Routledge, 2008.

Gilbert, Martin. *The Holocaust: A History of the Jews of Europe During the Second World War*. New York: Henry Holt, 1985.

Glover, T. R. *The Ancient World: A Beginning*. London: Penguin, 1944.

Gluckel of Hamelin. *The Memoirs of Gluckel of Hamelin*. New York: Schocken, 1977.

Goiten, S.D. *Jews and Arabs: Their Contacts Through the Ages*. New York: Schocken, 1964.

Gold, Dore. *Tower of Babble: How the United Nations Has Fueled Global Chaos*. New York: Crown Forum, 2004.

Goldberg, M. Hirsch. *Jewish Connection*. Landham, MD: Scarborough House, 1993.

Goldhagen, Daniel Jonah. *Hitler's Willing Executioners*. New York: Knopf, 1996.

Gould, Allan ed. *What Did They Think of the Jews?* Northvale, NJ: Jason Aronson, 1997.

Grant, Michael. *From Alexander to Cleopatra: The Hellenistic World*. New York: Charles Scribner & Sons, 1982.

Grant, Michael. *The Jews in the Roman World*. London: Weidenfeld & Nicolson, 1973.

Grant, Michael. *The World of Rome*. London: Weidenfeld & Nicolson, 1962.

HaLevi, Judah. *The Kuzari* (translated by Korobkin, N. Daniel). Northvale, NJ: Jason Aronson, 1998.

Sam, Halpern. *Darkness and Hope*. New York: Shengold, 1996.

Hertzberg, Arthur. *The Jews in America*. New York: Simon & Schuster, 1989.

Herzog, Chaim. *The Arab-Israeli Wars: War and Peace in the Middle East from the War of Independence through Lebanon*. New York: Random House, 1984.

Hirsch, Samson Raphael. *Collected Writings of Samson Raphael Hirsch*. Jerusalem: Feldheim, 1996.

Hopkins, Keith. *A World Full of Gods: The Strange Triumph of Christianity*. New York: Free Press, 1999.

Isaacs, Ronald H., and Olitzky, Kerry M. (editors). *Critical Documents of Jewish History*. Northvale, NJ: Jason Aronson, 1995.

James, Peter. *Centuries in Darkness*. Piscataway, NJ: Rutgers University Press, 1993.

Johnson, Paul. *A History of Christianity*. New York: Simon & Schuster, 1976.

Johnson, Paul. *A History of the Jews*. New York: Harper & Row, 1987.

Johnson, Paul. *The Intellectuals*. New York: Harper Perennial, 1988.

Josephus. *The New Complete Works of Josephus*. Grand Rapids, MI: Kregel Publications, 1999.

Jospe, Raphael (editor). *Great Schisms in Jewish History*. Hoboken, NJ: Ktav, 1981.

Jung, Carl G. *C.G. Jung Speaking*. Princeton, NJ: Princeton University Press, 1977.

Kaplan, Aryeh. *Chassidic Masters: History, Biography and Thought*. Brooklyn: Moznaim, 1991.

Kaplan, Aryeh. *Jerusalem: The Eye of the Universe*. New York: NCSY, 1979.

Kaplan, Aryeh. *The Living Torah*. New York: Moznaim, 1981.

Kaplan, Aryeh. *Handbook of Jewish Thought*. New York: Moznaim, 1979.

Karsh, Efraim. *Islamic Imperialism*. New Haven, CT: Yale University Press, 2006.

Katsh, Abraham. *The Biblical Heritage of American Democracy.* New York: Ktav, 1977.

Kitov, Eliyahu. *The Book of Our Heritage.* Jerusalem: Feldheim, 1978.

Kleiman, Yaakov. *DNA & Tradition: The Genetic Link to the Ancient Hebrews.* Jerusalem: Devora, 2004.

Klugman, Eliyahu Meir. *Rabbi Samson Raphael Hirsch: Architect of Torah Judaism for the Modern World.* Brooklyn: Artscroll Mesorah, 1996.

Kobler, Franz (editor). *A Treasury of Jewish Letters.* Philadelphia: Jewish Publication Society of America, 1953.

Krey, August. *The First Crusade.* Princeton, NJ: Princeton University Press, 1921.

Kroyanker, David. *Jerusalem Architecture.* New York: Vendome Press, 1994.

Koran (translated by J.M. Rodwell). New York: Dutton, 1978.

Kurinsky, Samuel. *The Eighth Day: The Hidden History of the Jewish Contribution to Civilization.* 1994.

Lesko, Leonard and Frerichs, Ernest (editors). *Exodus: The Egyptian Evidence.* Winona Lake: Eisenbrauns Pulishing, 1997.

Lemkin, Raphael. *Axis Rule in Occupied Europe.* Washington DC: Carnegie, 1944.

Levy, Richard S. *Anti-Semitism in the Modern World.* Lexington, MA: D.C. Heath & Co., 1990.

Lewis, Bernard. *Islam* (Volumes I & II). New York: Harper and Row, 1974.

Lewis, Bernard. *The Middle East: A Brief History of the Last 2,000 Years.* New York: Scribner, 1997.

Lewis, Bernard. *The Middle East and the West.* New York: Harper & Row, 1964.

Lewis, Bernard. *Semites and Anti-Semites.* New York: W.W. Norton & Company, 1999.

Lohse, Bernard. *A Short History of Christian Doctrine: From the First Century to the Present.* Philadelphia: Fortress Press, 1978.

Luzzatto, Rabbi Moshe Chaim. *The Way of God.* Jerusalem: Feldheim, 1977.

Maimonides. *Guide to the Perplexed.* New York: Dover, 1956.

Maimonides. *Mishneh Torah.* Jerusalem: Mossad HaRav Kook, 1982.

Mayer, Hans Eberhard and Gillingham, John. *The Crusades.* Oxford: Oxford University Press, 1988.

Mazar, Amihai. *Archaeology of the Land of the Bible.* New York: Doubleday, 1992.

Mendes-Flohr, Paul, and Reinharz, Jehudah, (editors). *The Jew in the Modern World: A Documentary History.* Oxford: Oxford University Press, 1995

Mercer, Derrik (editor). *Chronicle of the World*. London: DK Publishing, 1996.

Midrash Rabba. Jerusalem: Mercaz HaSefer, 1986.

Montanelli, Indro. *Romans Without Laurels*. New York: Pantheon Books, 1959.

Morris, Benny. *Righteous Victims: A History of the Zionist-Arab Conflict 1881–2001*. New York: Vintage, 2001.

Morse, Arthur, D. *While Six Million Died: A Chronicle of American Apathy*. New York: Random House, 1968.

Morton, Frederic. *The Rothschilds: A Family Portrait*. Greewich, CT: Crest Books, 1963.

Nachmanides. *The Disputation at Barcelona*. New York: Shilo, 1983.

Netanyahu, Benzion. *The Origins of the Inquisition*. New York: Random House, 1995.

Newton, Isaac. *Portsmouth Papers* (unpublished).

Nicholls, William. *Christian Anti-Semitism: A History of Hate*. Northvale, NJ: Jason Aronson, 1995.

Oren, Michael. *Six Days of War: June 1967 and the Making of the Modern Middle East*. Oxford: Oxford University Press, 2002.

Pagels, Elaine. *The Gnostic Gospel*. New York: Random House, 1989.

Pagels, Elaine. *The Origin of Satan*. New York: Random House, 1995.

Parfitt, Tudor. *The Thirteenth Gate: Travels Among the Lost Tribes of Israel*. London: Weidenfeld and Nicolson, 1987.

Peters, Joan. *From Time Immemorial: The Origins of the Arab-Jewish Conflict Over Palestine*. New York: Harper & Row.

Phelps-Brown, Henry. *Egalitarianism and the Generation of Inequality*. Oxford: Oxford University Press, 1988.

Prager, Dennis, and Telushkin, Joseph. *Why the Jews?* New York: Simon & Schuster, 1983.

Pryce-Jones, David. *The Closed Circle: An Interpretation of the Arabs*. London: Paladin, 1989.

Rauschning, Hermann. *Voice of Destruction (Hitler Speaks)*. New York: Putnam, 1940.

Reston, James Jr. *The Dogs of God: Columbus, the Inquisition, and the Defeat of the Moors*. New York: Doubleday, 2005.

Robello, Alfredo Mordechai. *The Legal Condition of the Jews in Roman Empire*. Jerusalem: Hebrew University Press, 1980.

Roth, Cecil. *A History of the Jews: From the Earliest Times Through the Six Day War.* New York: Schocken, 1971.

Roth, Cecil. *The Jewish Contribution to Civilization.* London:The East and West Library, 1956

Roth, Cecil. *A Short History of the Jewish People.* London: East and West Library, 1948.

Rubin, Alexis, P. (editor), *Scattered Among the Nations: Documents Affecting Jewish History* 49 to 1975. Northvale, NJ: Jason Aronson, 1995.

Runes, Dagobert, D. (editor). *The Hebrew Impact on Civilization.* New York: Philosophical Library, 1951.

Sachar, Howard. *A History of Israel.* New York: Knopf, 1979.

Sachar, Howard M. *Farewell Espana: The World of the Sephardim Remembered.* New York: Knopf, 1994.

Schafer, Peter. *Judeophobia: The Attitudes toward the Jews in the Ancient World.* Cambridge, MA: Harvard University Press, 1997.

Scherman, Nosson (editor). *The Chumash.* Brooklyn: Artscroll, 1994.

Schiffman, Lawrence H. *Texts and Traditions: A Source Reader for the Study of the Second Temple.* Hoboken, N.J.: Ktav, 1998.

Schroeder, Gerald. *Genesis and the Big Bang Theory.* New York: Bantam, 1990.

Schroeder, Gerald. *The Hidden Face of God: Science Reveals the Ultimate Truth.* New York: Touchstone, 2002.

Schroeder, Gerald. *The Science of God: The Convergence of Science and Biblical Wisdom.* New York: Free Press, 1997.

Shachan, Avigdor. *In the Footsteps of the Lost Ten Tribes.* Jerusalem: Devora, 2007.

Shanks, Hershel. *Jerusalem: An Archeological Biography.* New York: Random House, 1995.

Sharef, Zeev. *Three Days.* New York: Doubleday, 1962.

Shawn, Eric. *The UN Exposed: How the United Nations Sabotages America's Security.* New York: Sentinel, 2006.

Simms, Marion P. *The Bible in America.* New York: Wilson-Ericson, 1936.

Sivan, Gabriel. *The Bible and Civilization.* Jerusalem: Keter, 1973.

Slater, Leonard. *The Pledge.* New York: Simon & Schuster, 1970.

Smith, Huston. *The Religions of Man.* New York: Harper & Row, 1958.

Spiro, Ken. *WorldPerfect: The Jewish Impact on Civilization.* Deerfield, FL: HCI, 2003.

Tanach. Brooklyn, NY: Artscroll/Mesorah, 1996.

Talmud (Babylonian). Jerusalem: Tal-Min, 1981.

Telushkin, Joseph, *Jewish Literacy*. New York: Morrow, 1991.

Tcherikover, Victor. *Hellenistic Civilization and the Jews*. New York: Antheum, 1970.

Trachtenburg, Joshua. *The Devil and the Jews*. Philadelphia: JPS, 2002.

Trevor-Roper, Hugh. *Hitler's Table Talk*. Oxford: Oxford University Press, 1953.

Tuchman, Barbara. *The Bible and the Sword*. New York: New York University Press, 1956.

Tuchman, Barbara. *The Distant Mirror: The Calamitous 14th Century*. New York: Knopf, 1978.

Twain, Mark. *The Complete Essays of Mark Twain*. New York: Doubleday: 1963.

Van Den Haag, Ernest. *The Jewish Mystique*. New York: Stein and Day, 1969.

Wein, Berel. *Echoes of Glory*. Brooklyn, NY: Shaar Press, 1995.

Wein, Berel. *Triumph of Survival*. Brooklyn, NY: Shaar Press, 1990.

Wiesel, Elie. *Night*. New York: Bantam, 1982.

Wilson, A.N. *Jesus: A Life*. New York: Norton, 1992.

Winton, Thomas, (editor). *Documents from Old Testament Times*. New York: Harper & Row, 1958.

Williamson, Ronald. *The Jews in the Hellenistic World*. Philo, Cambridge: Cambridge University Press, 1989.

Wise, Michael, Abegg, Martin and Cook, Edward. *The Dead Sea Scrolls: A New Translation*. San Francisco: HarperCollins, 1996.

Wistrich, Robert. *Anti-Semitism: The Longest Hatred*. London: Thames Methuen, 1991.

Wistrich, Robert. *Hitler's Apocalypse*. Philadelphia: St. Martin's Press, 1986.

Yeor, Bat. *The Dhimmi: Jews and Christians under Islam*. Rutherford, NJ: Fairleigh Dickenson University Press, 1985.

Yerushalmi, Joseph. *Zakhor: Jewish History and Jewish Memory*. Seattle: University of Washington Press, 1982.

INDEX

A

B

C

F

I

J

N

O

P

R

T

U

V

W

Y

Z

Aish.Com

Since its launch in February 2000, Aish.com has become the world's largest Jewish content website of its kind, logging millions of monthly user sessions and 390,000 unique e-mail subscribers.

Aish.com is the lifeline for hundreds of thousands of people across the globe seeking Jewish answers to life's most perplexing issues. Our goal is to give every Jew the opportunity to discover their heritage in an atmosphere of open inquiry and mutual respect, offering Torah's wisdom for living for the modern world.

Aish.com features include:

- Rabbi Ken Spiro's Crash Course in Jewish History
- Over 10,000 articles on personal growth, parenting, dating, spirituality, Israel, Jewish holidays, and the weekly Torah portion
- 24-hour live webcam from the Western Wall
- Cutting-edge blogs in audio, video, and text formats
- Innovative short movies that have become viral sensations around the world
- Sites in Hebrew, Spanish, and French
- Ask-the-Rabbi service which has answered 25,000 readers' questions
- AishAudio, sister site featuring thousands of MP3 lectures on every subject in Judaism

Aish.com is not just information, but inspiration. A recent survey found that 86% of readers said that Aish.com has inspired them to do more Torah learning, and 75% said that Aish.com has led them to increased affiliation with Jewish organizations or increased attendance at synagogue.

Headquartered in Jerusalem near the Western Wall, Aish.com is a division of Aish HaTorah, an apolitical network of Jewish educational centers in thirty-five branches on five continents.